AMERICA'S
QUARTERBACK

ALSO BY KEITH DUNNAVANT

AMERICA'S QUARTERBACK

BART STARR AND THE RISE OF THE
NATIONAL FOOTBALL LEAGUE

Keith Dunnavant

Thomas Dunne Books ⚘ New York
St. Martin's Press

THOMAS DUNNE BOOKS.
An imprint of St. Martin's Press.

AMERICA'S QUARTERBACK. Copyright © 2011 by Keith Dunnavant. All rights reserved. Printed in the United States of America. For information, address St. Martin's Press, 175 Fifth Avenue, New York, N.Y. 10010.

www.stmartins.com
www.thomasdunnebooks.com

Library of Congress Cataloging-in-Publication Data

Dunnavant, Keith.
   America's quarterback : Bart Starr and the rise of the National Football League / Keith Dunnavant.
        p. cm.
   ISBN 978-0-312-36349-9
  1. Starr, Bart.   2. Football players—United States—Biography.
3. Quarterbacks (Football)—United States—Biography.   4. Green Bay Backers (Football team)—History.   I. Title.
   GV939.S73D86 2011
   796.332092—dc23
   [B]

                                                                          2011019928

ISBN 978-0-312-36349-9

First Edition: September 2011

10 9 8 7 6 5 4 3 2 1

For two of the heroes of my life: my mother and father, Marjorie and Bob Dunnavant, of Athens, Alabama.

Thanks for the power of your example and for a lifetime of inspiration, encouragement, and faith.

CONTENTS

INTRODUCTION

In 2010, the NFL Network anointed Jerry Rice, the acrobatic and elusive wide receiver for the San Francisco 49ers, as the greatest player in National Football League history—edging Cleveland Browns fullback Jim Brown and New York Giants linebacker Lawrence Taylor.

The same blue-ribbon panel of experts selected Joe Montana No. 4, making the immortal Joe Cool, hero of Super Bowls XVI, XIX, XXIII and XXIV, the highest-ranking quarterback *in The Top 100.*

But one legendary quarterback's name was hard to find—one man who long ago learned to accept being overlooked and underrated.

The eternal struggle for respect looms large in the epic saga of former Green Bay Packers quarterback Bart Starr.

Even as the cable channel rated Starr as the 51st greatest player in NFL history, placing him in the elite pantheon of football heroes, sandwiched between Terry Bradshaw and Eric Dickerson, a closer examination of the list revealed a predictable but troubling subset: Among quarterbacks, he ranked a head-scratching 13th, trailing a long list of talented, celebrated and accomplished offensive leaders . . . with impressive but still inferior résumés.

Perhaps the voters missed the Ice Bowl.

Perhaps they lost count while adding up his championship rings.

Or, perhaps, they simply bought one of professional football's most enduring myths.

Four decades after he ended a remarkable career, Starr remains a largely misunderstood figure, discounted by many football historians as a robotic extension of the iconic Vince Lombardi.

Beyond the various subjective measures of greatness that caused all those other quarterbacks to jump past Lombardi's field general, the familiar argument against the Most Valuable Player of the first two Super Bowls can be reduced to a counterintuitive notion for a zero-sum world: Sometimes winning is *not* the only thing.

While leading the Green Bay dynasty during the days of The Beatles and the space race, as the NFL stormed out of the shadows to become an American obsession, Starr rarely attracted the respect he deserved. Frequently overshadowed by Lombardi's dominant aura, it was easy and convenient to diminish his role in the Packers' unparalleled success.

He was not gifted with an especially powerful arm, so he was never confused with bomb-throwers like Sammy Baugh, Joe Namath, Dan Marino, or John Elway.

He was not very fast on his feet, so he was never able to elude defenders like Fran Tarkenton.

He was not a force of nature like Johnny Unitas.

But he was a clutch player who delivered time after time, lifting the Packers with the power of his mighty will while setting a new standard for offensive leadership.

The cerebral, poised, and efficient Starr, who methodically piloted the Packers through the most dominant seven-year run in professional football history, remains the only quarterback to win five NFL championships.

The bottom line for quarterbacks has always been the bottom line, so until Peyton Manning, Tom Brady, Drew Brees, or some future quarterback puts five trophies in the case, Starr will occupy a unique position in NFL history.

Like many football historians, Kerry Byrne once bought the company line: Starr, who led the league in passing efficiency three times, was just the guy who handed off to Paul Hornung and Jim Taylor. But then the editor of the Cold Hard Football Facts Web site began to look deeper—into the numbers—and soon reevaluated Starr's place in the history books.

"If you believe in numbers, in substance over style, there's really only one conclusion to draw," Byrne said, "Bart Starr was the best quarterback ever."

Determining with any authority the greatest quarterback who ever played the game is a difficult, if not impossible, task. It is an answer that ultimately depends on the framework of the question. But when all the style points are stripped away, football is a game of achievement, empirically demonstrated by first downs, victories and championships. In this realm, Bart Starr has no peer.

Even though he ranks just 73rd, through the 2010 season, in all-time touchdown passes (152) and 61st in passing yards (24,718), Starr finished his career with what was, at the time of his retirement, the highest completion percentage (57.4) in league history. While his more celebrated rival, Baltimore Colts phenom Johnny Unitas, attempted 2,037 more passes and amassed 15,516 more yards across his career, the two men averaged an identical 7.8 yards per attempt—attesting to both quarterbacks' potency, but also to Starr's undeniable efficiency.

For anyone who truly appreciates the critical link between turnovers and victories, his astounding 1.2 interception percentage during his MVP season of 1966—the lowest in NFL history until the advent of modern passing offenses—is impossible to ignore. At the peak of his career, he was the most mistake-free passer of the age. This undeniable truth played a central role in Green Bay's stampede through the sixties, especially after the once vaunted running attack lost its stride.

No quarterback has ever approached his high level of performance in the postseason, leading *Wall Street Journal* columnist Allen Barra to call him "the greatest big-game quarterback in NFL history."

While guiding the Packers to a best-ever 9-1 mark in the playoffs, Starr completed 130 of 213 passes for 1,753 yards, 15 touchdowns, and just 3 interceptions. (This includes a 1965 playoff game against the Colts, when he went down with an injury early in the first quarter, and backup Zeke Bratkowski took over, piloting the victory.) His postseason passer rating of 104.8 blows away all competitors, including Joe Montana, Terry Bradshaw, Roger Staubach, and John Elway.

"No quarterback has ever performed so well, so consistently in pressure situations," said NFL Films president Steve Sabol, who has been chronicling the league's progression for a half century. "Bart was the master of the calculated risk, converting all those crucial third downs on the way to one big victory after another."

Unlike modern-day quarterbacks, Starr called nearly all the plays for the Packers, skillfully applying knowledge gained from intense film study and Lombardi's careful instruction to become the foremost audible master of his age. Quarterbacks before him invented the play-action pass, but he perfected it, raising it to an art form while learning how to use his intelligence as a powerful weapon in Green Bay's historic run.

Forever redefining what it meant to be a successful quarterback at a time of mounting sophistication, Starr became a critical progenitor in the offensive lineage of the NFL, launching the progression toward Roger Staubach, Terry Bradshaw, Joe Montana, and Tom Brady.

Even now, his DNA flows through the sport, especially when a tenacious and brainy quarterback like Peyton Manning steps behind center, looks across the line, and checks off, exploiting the accumulation of his acquired wisdom.

Even as Starr became the most successful quarterback in the history of football, he somehow transcended the game.

Equal parts ordinary and exceptional, Starr's unlikely journey from 17th round draft pick to the Pro Football Hall of Fame—punctuated by rejection, redemption, humiliation, and heartbreak—reflected the American Century in ways large and small. His overachieving life, spent chasing success and validation, offered powerful clues about who we are as a society, confirming something fundamental in the American character. While he emerged as a clean-cut and gentlemanly icon of a sport predicated on controlled violence, his life turned on difficult relationships with two paternal figures, each a metaphor for a generation of fathers and sons. The two family tragedies that deeply affected his life reflected both the excesses and limitations of twentieth-century America.

America's Quarterback is the story of a man who was propelled by a force far more universal, and ultimately, far more powerful, than his athletic talent.

Even as he dodged menacing defenders and rallied his teammates en route to one title after another, the unassuming Starr was engaged in a different sort of struggle: for his contextual place in the dramatic sweep of professional football history.

Sometimes, an entrenched myth can only be busted with a mountain of truth.

ONE

BUBBA'S GHOST

Suddenly, someone screamed.

The sound of pain rang out from the house next door like an alarm, shattering the peace of an ordinary Sunday afternoon in 1947.

Then a kind of darkness descended upon Bart Starr's world.

Long before this turning point, his story began with a very different sort of scream, a life-affirming wail, in the bleak year of 1934, when the context for most everything was the widespread economic hardship of the Great Depression. Despite the hope embodied by President Franklin Delano Roosevelt and his New Deal, unemployment still hovered near 24 percent and vast numbers of Americans struggled just to provide food, clothing, and shelter for their families. Beyond the widespread despair, the world kept turning. Going to the movies remained a unifying thread of American culture, as audiences flocked to see Clark Gable and Claudette Colbert in the comedy *It Happened One Night*, director Frank Capra's first big hit. Donald Duck made his first appearance in a Walt Disney cartoon, a pivotal early step in the building of an entertainment collosus. Newspapers contained numerous stories about notorious bank robber John Dillinger, whose bloody rampage ended in a hail of bullets outside a Chicago theater, betrayed by the infamous lady in red. More than half a century after Thomas Edison perfected the electric lightbulb, the Tennessee Valley Authority began supplying power to previously unwired parts of the rural South. The sports pages focused on colorful and lethal boxer Max Baer, who utilized his devastating right to knock out Primo Carnera to become Heavyweight Champion of the World. In the year when radio penetration of American homes reached 50 percent and millions routinely sought comfort in FDR's fireside chats, the World Series broadcasts contained commercial advertisements for the first time, with Ford Motor Company paying the staggering sum of $100,000 to be the sole sponsor as the St. Louis Cardinals bested the Detroit Tigers in seven games. Few Americans cared so much about the still-struggling National Football League. In the far north outpost of Green Bay, Wisconsin, a group of local businessmen raised $15,000 to prevent the NFL's Packers from folding.

Another milestone in the history of the Green Bay Packers failed to make the papers. On January 9, 1934, Ben and Lulu Starr of Montgomery, Alabama, welcomed Bryan Bartlett Starr into the world. Happy and proud, they named their first born after the father (Bryan was Ben's middle name) and the doctor who delivered him (Haywood Bartlett).

Ben, the great-grandson of a full-blooded Cherokee Indian, had been born in the small southeastern Alabama town of Dadeville. When both of his parents died shortly after World War I, he was raised by his grandfather in Anniston, about one hundred miles north of Dadeville. Forced to drop out of high school to help support the family, Ben worked as a mechanic and welder. He was a large man with dark hair, a square jaw, and a commanding aura.

On a fateful night in 1932, he met Lulu Inez Tucker, a pretty, petite brunette, at the home of a mutual friend. Lulu, the daughter of railroad engineer, grew up in the capital city of Montgomery. The connection was immediate, and they were married less than four months later. Romance moved fast in those days.

The newlyweds set up housekeeping in Montgomery, where Ben landed a job as a blacksmith. Two years after Bart's arrival, Lulu gave birth to a second son, Hilton. They often called him Bubba.

Better jobs took the Starrs to Columbia, Tennessee, and back to Montgomery, before the march to World War II prompted the father's Army National Guard unit to be mobilized. Two years at Fort Blanding, near Gainesville, Florida, were followed by an extended assignment at Northern California's Fort Ord, where the family stayed behind when Ben was shipped off to the Pacific.

The frequent moves proved to be a kind of education for young Bart. "I will always be grateful for the things I learned from having to adapt to different circumstances and environments," he said.

Free to roam the area adjacent to the military housing neighborhood of Ord Village, Bart and Hilton sometimes sat for hours, watching the waves crash into the picturesque Pacific shoreline, often wondering about their father, who existed for four years only in the form of letters. Like many young boys of the time, they closely followed the progress of the war through reading newspapers and watching newsreels. The epic struggle against Hitler and the Japanese was a constant fact of life—manifested by rationed staples and movie stars hawking war bonds—but at times, it could seem distant, especially as they rode the school bus through the fertile agricultural fields and along the towering cliffs each morning and afternoon. Bart often was distracted by the natural beauty of the landscape just outside the window.

The Starr household was managed like an extension of the military, even after Ben was shipped overseas. Lulu was a wonderful cook and a very loving mother, but was also a strict disciplinarian who made sure Bart and Hilton attended church, creating a wholesome environment in keeping with their Methodist faith. The boys were taught to understand their responsibilities to live an orderly and obedient life consistent with the military way—and the consequences for exceeding her boundaries.

Like all boys, they tested the limits.

After learning that the army conducted training exercises in a forest near their home, Bart and Hilton began scavenging the area for discarded equipment. Fearing for their safety, Lulu forbade further maneuvers but they kept sneaking off, looking for canteens and other prized loot. Somehow, she found out and administered a paddling neither boy would ever forget.

"If I catch you in there again, you'll really get one," she warned.

Bart knew she meant business.

"We couldn't figure out how she knew we were back in there," he recalled.

She could *smell* their disobedience.

The boys didn't realize that the area was covered with numerous eucalyptus plants, producing a pungent order that betrayed their activities.

The lure of the forest was difficult to resist, but the boys knew their mother meant business.

"We got the message and stopped going in there," Bart said.

During a Saturday outing to the movies—as they settled in to watch *Cowboy Serenade*, starring matinee idol Gene Autry—Bart and Bubba stumbled upon a different sort of treasure.

Bart's ten-year-old heart raced as he pointed toward the movie screen. "Look! There he is!"

Hilton stared at the flickering black-and-white film with a skeptical eye. Could it be?

The newsreel of General Douglas MacArthur's dramatic return to the Philippines in October 1944 moved fast, so the Starr boys sat through the feature presentation three times just to get two more looks at the stern-looking, unidentified man in the background. Each time, they carefully studied the soldier's face, comparing it to their prized memories. Desperate, like millions of American children, for any sort of connection with a father who had been away fighting in World War II for nearly three years, the brothers eventually walked out of the darkened theater convinced that the anonymous GI was their very own daddy.

"We were so pumped up," Bart said. "We came out of that place two feet off the ground."

The bond between the boys was unshakable, but their personalities contrasted sharply. Hilton, who wore glasses from an early age, was aggressive, tough, and known to have a mean streak. Bart was introverted and timid, and tended to keep his feelings to himself. The sibling rivalry that developed between them was probably inevitable, but it was eventually enabled and exacerbated by their very demanding father.

Lulu and the boys were back living in Montgomery when the war ended, and after Master Sergeant Starr decided to make a career of the military—switching over to the newly independent U.S. Air Force—he planted the family flag firmly in Alabama's Capital City. Understanding that he would have to spend other tours overseas, Ben wanted his boys to have a stable home environment, so he and Lulu bought a small, white frame house on a middle-class street for $3,500, a figure roughly equivalent to the median American income at the start of the great postwar boom, when the deprivations of the Great Depression were being swept away by a new wave of optimism and consumerism. Southerners had not yet learned that they could not live without the wonder of air-conditioning, so during the stifling summer nights, the brothers—spoiled by the mild summers in Northern California—often struggled to sleep in their sweat-drenched sheets. When Ben finally broke down and bought an attic fan to pump a little air through the house, the boys suddenly felt rich. Like many children during the age of dramatic radio and Saturday matinees, when the power of imagination filled the air, they learned to make their own fun. The tight contours of the adjacent garage provided a kind of entertainment for Bart and Hilton, who frequently wagered pennies over their father's ability to back out without scraping his Chevy.

The war hardened Ben, accentuating his gruff, overbearing demeanor. Like Bull Meecham, the antagonist in Pat Conroy's novel *The Great Santini*, he was a domineering figure who drew precious little distinction between his troops and his family, demanding that his boys live within his exacting rules and meet his high standards, just like the men in his squadron. Forbidden from expressing their own views, they never considered challenging his authority.

"My dad was the toughest man I've ever known in my life," Bart said. "He intimidated me. He was my Master Sergeant."

Despite such feelings, Bart loved his father and relished every opportunity to spend time with him, especially when Ben worked part-time during several summers as a ticket-taker for Montgomery's minor league baseball team. He arranged for Bart to be a ball boy, which heightened the boy's interest in professional baseball.

"My dad was a fabulous role model," Starr said. "I wanted to be just like him."

A shared love of sports strengthened the connection between Bart and Hilton, who spent much of their free time competing with other neighborhood boys in sandlot baseball and football games. On the diamond, Bart imagined he was Joltin' Joe DiMaggio, the Yankee Clipper, master of the 56-game hitting streak, longest in baseball history, who existed to Bart primarily through radio broadcasts and newspaper pictures carefully studied. He once saved nickels and dimes for months just so he could ride the bus to visit his aunt Myrtle in Detroit, where the payoff pitch was a chance to see DiMaggio and the Yankees play the Tigers from a distant bleacher seat. It didn't matter that his hero, past his prime, failed to reach base.

His favorite football player was University of Alabama halfback Harry Gilmer, the passer in the Crimson Tide's version of the Notre Dame Box offense. Grantland Rice, the famed sportswriter most responsible for the breathless mythology of Notre Dame's Four Horsemen, once called Gilmer "the greatest college passer I've ever seen." Decades before Florida's Tim Tebow introduced the jump pass to twenty-first-century audiences, Gilmer gained national acclaim for his ability to leap into the air and fire a bullet into the distance. In photos of the day, he appeared to be taking flight. Like many other youngsters of the day—including future Florida State head coach Bobby Bowden, who grew up near the legendary passer in Birmingham—Bart spent many hours trying to emulate Gilmer's airborne fling, especially after seeing him up close during one of the Crimson Tide's annual games at Montgomery's Cramton Bowl.

"I was fascinated by Harry Gilmer and wanted to learn to throw the ball just like him," Starr said.

Starr eventually moved beyond the jump pass, convinced, like so many others, that he could never equal the master, but in working hard to incorporate some elements of Gilmer's fundamentals into his own style, the cerebral young man took the first tentative steps down the path of learning the passing game as a mechanical process.

The Starr boys' tackle football games—often contested on the lawn in front of Hurt Military Academy, without pads or headgear—could be intense, all-afternoon grudge matches where scrapes, bruises, and bloody appendages became badges of courage. Their mother tried to understand when her boys walked through the front door at dusk looking like war casualties, battered but wearing a warrior's glow.

Sports exposed the differences between Bart and Hilton. Their friendly rivalry took on a new dimension when the older brother began to believe he was competing for his father's approval.

Because he had not enjoyed the luxury of playing team sports as a child, Ben lived vicariously through his sons' exploits, which eventually graduated from sandlots to a youth team sponsored by the local Veterans of Foreign Wars post. Convinced that the tougher, faster, more competitive Hilton—who reminded Ben of himself—was the real athlete in the family, he showered him with attention and took every opportunity to criticize Bart while encouraging him to strive to be more like his little brother. Bart, the ever-dutiful son, endeavored to take his father's suggestions to heart.

But he could not help feeling jealous and resentful as his father routinely favored Bubba.

Unable to express his feelings, Bart suppressed the complicated mesh of psychological drama rattling around in his head, even as he loved and admired his brother.

The first window-rattling boom caught everyone by surprise.

It happened more than two thousand miles west of Montgomery on October 14, 1947, when Col. Chuck Yeager, piloting a Bell X-1 aircraft despite broken ribs, hurdled through the stratosphere high above the California desert on a top-secret mission and became the first man to surpass the sound barrier, producing what would come to be known as a sonic boom.

Like the birth of the atomic age two years earlier, the first Mach 1 flight symbolized man's unmistakable progress in the triumphant glow of American technological and industrial might, revealing that the sound barrier was just a number wrapped in a blanket of air, proving that nature could be tamed and harnessed.

But in many other areas of American life, danger still lurked in the invisible air.

Despite a steady procession of medical advances, many diseases—eventually to be conquered in the blur of twentieth-century achievement—continued to wreak havoc, including the mysterious scourge of polio, which crippled an average of 20,000 Americans every year, roiling the culture with hysteria and helplessness as epidemics swept across dozens of cities and towns.

Just months before Yeager's historic flight, Dr. Jonas Salk became the new head of the Virus Research Lab at the University of Pittsburgh School of Medicine. He soon began work on the polio vaccine that would one day make him famous. When, after years of trial and error, the inoculation was introduced to the public in 1955, eliminating polio almost overnight, Salk was hailed as a savior by a generation of once-fearful parents.

Like polio vaccines, tetanus shots would one day be commonplace, but in an era before the public health system worked closely with educators to require childhood vaccinations, the disease, which enters the body through an open wound and attacks the central nervous system, proved to be an elusive, and deadly, enemy.

In 1947, anything seemed possible and yet so many real-life barriers remained unshattered.

It was an age of transcendent achievement. And unspeakable tragedy.

When the Starr family returned from church on a warm Sunday afternoon in 1947, Bart and Hilton wound up next door, playing with the neighbor kids. They always seemed to be outside. Sometimes it was baseball; sometimes they rode bikes until their legs ached, sometimes they pursued fireflies in the gathering dusk. But they always seemed to be outside and on the move.

This time it was tag. Their barefoot, breathless, adrenaline-pumping chase was not just one of the simplest forms of athletic competition ever devised by man—it was a celebration of youthful exuberance. It was all about being young and full of life.

But in the blink of an eye, it became an object lesson about the fragility of life.

Racing around the house, Hilton pricked his foot on an old dog bone protruding out of the dirt.

His mother heard his scream and came running.

Lulu cleaned the wound the best she could, secure in the belief that her son would not require the still relatively new tetanus shot. She wanted to spare him the pain.

But his foot became infected, and he died of tetanus poisoning three days later.

Gloom enveloped the family like a fog.

"We were all heartbroken," Bart said. "It was so tragic. It nearly ripped our family apart."

The heaviest load landed on Lulu, who blamed herself.

"My mother was just devastated by guilt," Bart said.

The woman who would later marry Bart saw how the event reverberated throughout the rest of her mother-in-law's life.

"She carried a terrible burden," Cherry Starr said. "It affected their marriage. [Ben] held her responsible, and he shouldn't have because it was an accident . . . I don't think she ever got over it."

For Bart, the enormous pain of losing a brother was complicated by a different sort of burden.

"I felt guilty about resenting the attention that Bubba had received from Dad," he said.

Without anyone to confide in, he internalized the pain, spending many lonely hours in his room.

When Ben returned from a tour of duty in occupied Japan, he seemed distant. His relationship with Bart deteriorated as he mourned in his own way, acting at times like he had lost the wrong son. In addition to dealing with Hilton's death, Bart was forced to confront his little brother's ghost on a daily basis. The Master Sergeant pushed Bart even harder to excel as an athlete, to adopt his departed brother's toughness, aggressiveness, and fire. Bart bristled whenever his father punctuated many harsh rebukes with the phrase, "Your brother would have . . ."

The line cut like a knife through Bart's tender heart.

Every time.

The implication was clear: Bart would never be as good as Hilton.

Some children, confronted with such paternal badgering, surrender to the swirling doubts, accepting the father's verdict in a haze of pity, turning it into a self-fulfilling prophecy.

Others rebel, thumbing their nose at the authority figure, changing the subject, and rendering it moot.

But instead of feeling sorry for himself or resisting the pressure, instead of disrespecting his father or channeling his efforts elsewhere, Bart resolved to prove his old man wrong.

"I was determined to show him that I could be a good athlete," Bart said.

The connectivity between this youthful resolve, framed by tragedy, and all those years of Green Bay glory yet to come is impossible to overstate.

Even as it erected an emotional wall between the two men— demonstrating the fine line between cruelty and love—the Master Sergeant's psychological warfare motivated his son to fight, setting the tone for the rest of his life. In the years ahead, Bart would learn to appreciate the way his father toughened him; taught him the value of a strong work ethic; instilled in him a fierce tenacity; imbued him with a glowing ambition; and showed him how to harness such intangibles to reach beyond his physical limitations.

The wounds of youth would heal but the lessons produced by the pain would last a lifetime.

"That's one of the reasons I'll always love him," Bart, full of introspection, said from the distance of the twenty-first century. "I didn't really understand what he was doing at the time . . . but without the way he challenged me, I would have been a different person. He challenged me when I needed to be."

Ben Starr may have been incapable of adequately showing love to his oldest son, but he knew how to prepare him for Vince Lombardi.

The training continued when Bart returned home from football practice one afternoon during his sophomore year of high school, confronting another turning point.

After playing wingback in the Notre Dame Box at Montgomery's Baldwin Junior High School, Starr graduated to Sidney Lanier High, where the Poets ran the T formation, and was immediately moved to quarterback. He was overjoyed at the new position, which would allow him to showcase the passing skills he had honed on the sandlot, but he quickly became disenchanted when he was relegated to the junior varsity, considered too green for the powerful Lanier varsity. When he told his father that he planned to quit the team, Ben resisted the impulse to challenge his son.

"All right, it's your decision," he said calmly. "I'm glad you'll be home in the afternoons. I want you to weed the garden and cut the cornstalks. I want the garden cleaned up for fall."

Ben understood how much Bart hated working in the garden. Quickly reconsidering his decision, the boy showed up early for practice the next day and never again considered quitting.

The Master Sergeant knew how to get in his son's head.

Bart tried to be patient, determined to make his mark at Lanier, the only white high school in the city of roughly 100,000. In the late 1940s and early 1950s, Lanier football united Montgomery with a singularity of city-wide civic pride that future generations, accustomed to five public high schools, would be unable to fully understand.

Located along the Alabama River in the southern part of the state, Montgomery served as the first capital of the Confederacy at the start of the Civil War, before the seat of government moved to Richmond. It became the fifth capital of Alabama in 1846, when cotton was king and the plantation culture built on slavery dominated the state's economy. During Starr's childhood, the city flourished not only as the center of state government but as the home of Maxwell Air Force Base, whose origins could be traced to an early-twentieth-century joint venture between the federal government and the Wright Brothers. Montgomery produced two of the era's most influential and iconic musicians: country crooner Hank Williams, a tortured soul who was destined to flame out young; and jazz/pop master Nat King Cole, who moved to Chicago with his family as a child to flee the limitations and indignities of the segregated South.

The divide between black and white was especially stark in Montgomery, and Bart was not immune to the prejudice deeply ingrained in the culture. On a trip to Detroit to visit Aunt Myrtle with his father, Bart wandered off to find a neighborhood baseball game, anxious to see how his skills matched up against the boys in the big city. With him he carried the prized glove his father had bought him on his fourteenth birthday. When Ben stopped by to watch and learned that the pickup game included both blacks and whites—the kind of race-mixing forbidden in the segregated South—he embarrassed Bart by yanking him off the field and dragging him back to his aunt's house. Steaming mad, Ben punished his son by making him wash and rewash the family car in the blistering sun. Bart learned a lesson, but not the one his father intended.

"My father would become much more open-minded in later years," Bart said.

Two years after Jackie Robinson shattered the color barrier in Major League Baseball and five years before the Supreme Court's landmark *Brown v. Board of Education* ruling, Bart began his career as a quarterback at Sidney Lanier High. Size alone made the program a competitive test for Starr, as the Poets, strengthened by a sophisticated junior high school feeder system, routinely dressed nearly one hundred players.

A disciple of Paul "Bear" Bryant, then in the process of turning the

University of Kentucky into a national power, Lanier head coach Bill Moseley promoted Starr to the varsity heading into his junior season. As the backup to starter Don Shannon, Bart was still unpolished as a passer, but his focused, businesslike attitude made an impression on his coach, who noticed how well he took instruction. Determined to learn, to get a little bit better every day, Bart paid particular attention to Shannon's mechanics, trying to soak up the game like a sponge.

"He absorbed coaching so well," Moseley recalled. "We could put in a new wrinkle or a new play and I knew when he got home, he would be out in the yard [working on it]. He had the desire to do the job right."

In private moments, Bart dreamed a young boy's dream, imagining how it would feel to take control of the huddle at Cramton Bowl, Lanier's 25,000-seat home stadium, site of the annual Blue–Gray all-star game, and hit one perfect pass after another, leading the Poets to victory as the big crowd roared.

Determined to be ready, whenever his chance arrived, Starr studied assiduously and worked to perfect his mechanics, remembering the way Harry Gilmer cocked the ball, noticing the way Don Shannon pulled away from center.

During the first three weeks of the season, Starr called three or four plays total, just enough to chase the butterflies. Then, on an electric night at Cramton Bowl in October 1950, with Sidney Lanier locked in a scoreless game with powerful Tuscaloosa, riding a 17-game winning streak, someone clobbered Shannon, who tumbled to the ground in excruciating pain.

As Shannon was carried off the field with a broken leg, Moseley called for his backup quarterback.

"It was a sad situation, the kid going down like that," he said. "But I told Bart, 'This is your chance.'"

A hush fell over the crowd as sixteen-year-old Starr, a skinny 150 pounds, wearing a number 21 jersey, jogged onto the field. Like everyone else in the stadium, Moseley wondered how Bart would react in such a pressure-packed situation.

When he reached the huddle, several of his teammates began offering play-calling advice, but he quickly took control.

"Now, all you guys stop that jabbering," he said forcefully. "I'm the guy in charge in the huddle. I'll call the plays. When I want your advice, I'll ask."

Silence.

To the players accustomed to Starr's mild-mannered persona, it was like watching Clark Kent disappear into a phone booth.

On the first play, he faded into the pocket and hit halfback Bobby Barnes with a bullet near the sideline, and Barnes ran for a first down.

"He just came in and took over, like he was supposed to be there," Barnes recalled.

With Starr methodically driving the Poets for two touchdowns in the second half, Lanier upset Tuscaloosa, 13–0.

"It was like something out of a Hollywood movie," said receiver Nick Germanos. "One guy goes down and another guy gets his chance. You could tell Bart had been preparing for that opportunity for a long time."

Those Lanier players would always remember how it felt to be in the huddle the night when a Starr was born.

Like Wally Pipp, unlucky Don Shannon became the answer to a trivia question.

Without Shannon's unfortunate accident, the stars might never have aligned so perfectly for the man who replaced him.

Demonstrating a good command of the offense, developing into a solid passer, and rarely making mistakes, Starr led Lanier to an undefeated season.

During the final game of the year, he watched the opposing quarterback from Macon find repeated success with a bootleg play in which he adroitly hid the ball from the defense. Starr was so impressed, he decided to try to maneuver himself, saving it for a crucial situation near the goal line in the third quarter. Just like the other quarterback, he tucked the ball against his leg, causing the defense to bite on the fake, but instead of running up field, he suddenly fired a strike into the distance for a touchdown.

Now every football fan in Montgomery knew his name, but one accolade eluded him: His father's approval.

Ben never missed a game and attended many practices, watching intently from the distance, beyond a bunch of pine trees.

He was always there to point out what Bart did wrong.

Vito "Babe" Parilli was a natural.

The son of Italian immigrants, he was saved from a life in the steel mills of western Pennsylvania by his rare athletic ability. Parilli was fast, tough, and a leader. Anyone with working eyes could see his gift, and by his senior year of high school, dozens of colleges were hot for his signature. He might have been a great running back, lowering his shoulder, darting into the daylight, but Paul "Bear" Bryant took one look at him on the field and came to a different conclusion.

Quarterback.

Maturing into a deadly accurate passer with a smooth release, Parilli led Kentucky to the 1950 SEC championship and an upset of national champion Oklahoma in the Sugar Bowl, becoming one of the most celebrated quarterbacks in the land.

The newspapers called him Sweet Kentucky Babe.

Heading into his senior year of high school, in the summer of 1951, Starr was shocked when Bill Moseley arranged for him to be tutored by Parilli. It helped that Moseley was a former Kentucky assistant coach, and that his brother was Parilli's center. The Lanier coaching staff also included future head coaches Charlie Bradshaw and Matt Lair, who had played for the Wildcats under Bryant and believed most fervently in the Bear Bryant philosophy of football and life. Bryant was happy to help his protégés, especially when Moseley started telling him why he thought Starr could be his next great quarterback.

"It was a selfish move on my part, because I wanted Bart to be the best quarterback he could be for us that fall," Moseley said.

Early one morning, the Lanier coach and his quarterback started off from Montgomery in his 1950 Mercury. After driving all day through the two-lane roads of Alabama, Tennessee, and Kentucky, they spent the night with Moseley's wife's family in Somerset. The next morning, they got up and drove the rest of the way to Lexington. For the next two weeks, Bart lived in a dorm and spent several hours per day learning the quarterback position from one of the best who ever played the game.

On the first day, Starr was so nervous he dropped his food tray while moving through the cafeteria line, causing a clatter that reverberated throughout the large room, turning his face beet red. Eventually though, his butterflies subsided when he hit it off with Parilli, who quickly put him at ease.

"Bart was a great pupil and very respectful," Parilli said. "He called me sir. I wasn't much older than him, but he called me sir."

Starr would lie in bed at night, away from his family for the first time in his life, unable to believe his good fortune.

"I'd never worked with someone who had played the position, so it was really an eye-opening experience for me," Starr said. "A lot of the basic fundamentals and mechanics, I got from him. He was just such a fabulous player and I learned so much from him."

Even after becoming one of the leading quarterbacks in professional football, Starr would rank Parilli as one of the greatest faking quarterbacks he ever saw—a skill he analyzed step by step during those two weeks, slowly mastering a technique that would become fundamental to his game.

"Babe had extremely fast hands," Starr recalled. "He possessed the ability to keep his elbows tucked in fairly tight to the body so as not to show the defense the ball at any time. He would assume a position with his knees slightly bent, looking just like a master card dealer. . . ."

Parilli was impressed with Starr's soft passing touch and his intense desire to learn the position.

"He was very detailed in his approach," Parilli said. "He wanted to learn all he could. He wanted to learn what every player's assignment was [in every conceivable situation], and that showed a level of thinking that was beyond most high school quarterbacks."

When Starr returned to Montgomery, he covered the walls of his bedroom with photos of his tutor. "I just idolized him," he said.

As their coach-player relationship developed, Moseley noticed something different about the way Starr related to him: "When you tried to give him a little instruction, he always looked you in the eye."

This small bit of body language reflected the military training passed down from his father. It was a sign of respect—as Parilli and many others discovered, Starr was unfailingly polite and well mannered—and also suggested a surging confidence in his athletic abilities, which would become one of his most formidable assets as a quarterback.

But even as he became a big football hero at a school where nothing mattered more than football, he was still struggling to overcome his timid nature off the field, especially with the opposite sex. Throwing into an oncoming rush was easy, but trying to work up the courage to talk to a pretty young woman in the third row was torture.

But then he saw *her*.

Her name was Cherry Morton, and she was the most beautiful girl he had ever seen.

"Cherry was so hot you wouldn't believe it," recalled classmate Gary Waller.

Starr spotted the stunning brunette across a crowded hallway, and was immediately smitten. He wanted to ask her out but was afraid to, especially after he learned she had been dating a guy from a wealthy family, fearing he would be disqualified by his family's relatively modest means.

"I really had a mental challenge about asking her out," he said. "But I wanted to ask her out real bad."

Trapped between fear and desperation, Starr convinced his best friend and teammate, Nick Germanos, to approach her at school on his behalf. Cherry politely listened to the sales pitch before telling Germanos, "If he wants a date, he will have to ask me himself."

The message, relayed by his amused friend, landed with an embarrassing thud, but finally, Starr worked up his courage, approached Cherry, and asked her for a date with his own trembling lips. Still, the big football hero could not bring himself to look the object of his affection in the eye.

"The entire time, he was looking down at the floor," Cherry recalled many years later. "I promise you, he never looked at me. He was so painfully shy, it was really quite sweet."

On one of their first dates, Bart was crushed when he returned from the concession stand at the drive-in, popcorn in hand, to see Cherry sound asleep in the car. He was sure he had blown it, but to his astonishment, Cherry's dozing did not reflect boredom.

"I was just that comfortable with him," she said. "He was the nicest person . . . very pleasant, very soothing."

At some point, Bart actually worked up the courage to look her in the eye.

Dating the lovely Cherry Morton gave Starr a whole new level of confidence. But he could not yet conceive how profoundly she would affect his life.

In the fall of 1951, the Korean War raged without General Douglas MacArthur, who had been fired by President Harry Truman; Bobby Thomson's "shot heard 'round the world" lifted the New York Giants past the Brooklyn Dodgers for the National League pennant, before they lost the

World Series in six games to the Yankees; and a federal court sentenced Ethel and Julius Rosenberg to death for espionage. Montgomery, like much of the country, remained blissfully unaffected by a mounting cultural phenomenon. While millions of people in the metropolitan centers of the East—and a small but growing audience in the nearby cities of Birmingham and Atlanta—began altering their plans to stay home and watch *I Love Lucy*, Alabama's capital city was still outside the footprint of television.

"I remember in high school learning the word television," recalled Gary Waller, Lanier class of 1952. "I knew television was a word. But I didn't know a soul who had a television. I mean, not one."

Like his classmates, Starr came of age on the front side of a cultural fault line, just before television, rock 'n' roll, and the civil rights movement.

These three developments were destined to impact American society in unimagined ways, shaping a new era embroidered by the cultural connectivity of television, the rebellion at the heart of rock 'n' roll, and the barrier shattering personified by the civil rights movement, but in 1951, as the tidal wave slowly gathered, just over the horizon, Starr was focused on school, football, and Cherry Morton—not necessarily in that order.

Energized by his time with Babe Parilli, which improved his mechanics and bolstered his confidence, Starr entered his senior season at Lanier as the unquestioned leader of a very good team. The Poets' bid for a second consecutive undefeated season ended in week four, with a crushing 26–6 defeat to Birmingham power Ramsey. But the All-America quarterback was impressive throughout the 9-1 season, highlighted by a road victory over Kentucky powerhouse DuPont Manual. After playing in a prestigious all-star game in Memphis, he was pursued by a long list of colleges who recognized his potential as a big-time quarterback.

All of his friends expected him to go to Kentucky, believing the tutorial with Sweet Kentucky Babe had sealed the deal.

"I was very impressed by Coach Bryant and the Kentucky program, and I fully intended to go to Kentucky," Starr said.

His mind was made up.

But love intervened, proving more powerful than even than the charismatic Bryant.

When the romance turned serious and Bart discovered Cherry was planning to attend Auburn University to study interior design, he started reconsidering his desire to play for the Wildcats—because it was a long drive from Lexington, Kentucky, to Auburn, Alabama, especially in the days before interstate highways.

"I was afraid I would lose her," he said.

Convinced he could maintain the relationship if he could stay within reasonable driving distance, Starr reversed field and accepted a scholarship to tradition-rich Alabama, Harry Gilmer's old school, joining Lanier teammates Bobby Barnes and Nick Germanos.

It was probably the only time Auburn ever assisted archrival Alabama in landing a hot prospect.

"Best audible I ever called," Starr surmised many years later, despite the burden of knowing what happened next.

TWO

TIDE PRIDE

On the train ride back from a recruiting visit to Kentucky, the Master Sergeant remarked several times about how far the land of bluegrass and thoroughbreds seemed to be from Montgomery, so when Bart decided to attend the University of Alabama, located about a two-hour drive from their house, his father was understandably happy because he would be able to see his boy play football.

"I felt really good about the choice, because I was going to play at a school with such a great tradition," Bart said.

The decision was destined to roil his life in ways he could not possibly imagine.

The Alabama program rocketed to national prominence under Wallace Wade, a taciturn Tennessean who led the Crimson Tide to a landmark victory over Washington in the 1926 Rose Bowl, launching the Tuscaloosa school into the college football stratosphere alongside Notre Dame, Michigan, and Southern Cal. The long list of Bama stars included Green Bay Packers end Don Hutson, one of the greatest players in the history of professional football.

Starr's frame of reference began with Frank Thomas's powerful Alabama teams of the forties, especially the so-called "war babies" led by his boyhood hero, Harry Gilmer. After an undefeated season in 1945—which included a 34–14 thumping of Southern Cal in the Rose Bowl and a No. 2 final ranking behind Red Blaik's Army powerhouse—Thomas became ill and coached much of the 1946 season from a trailer parked on the practice field. When the future College Football Hall of Famer retired after a disappointing 7-4 campaign—the worst of his tenure—the administration lured one of his former assistants, Harold "Red" Drew, back to Tuscaloosa after one losing season as the head coach at the University of Mississippi.

A native of Maine who was known for smoking cigars and peppering the practice field with sarcastic one-liners ("Hey, Bewildered," he once yelled out to a butterfingered receiver, "I hope your wife never lets you hold that baby, 'cause you'll drop it right on its head!"), Drew was not an inspirational figure or a strategic innovator. In the storied history of Alabama football, he was destined to be remembered in a lukewarm haze, if he was remembered at all. His first four teams finished 8-3, 6-4-1, 6-3-1, and 9-2. After the 1951 Crimson Tide, humiliated at home by Villanova, posted a 5-6 mark—the school's first losing season since 1903—some alumni started making noise about getting rid of him, but the players signed a petition on his behalf and many others rallied to his defense. Dr. Albert Huey Green, president of the A-Club letterman's association, voiced support for Drew: "We are more interested in having the right type of coaching staff for shaping good character. We do not feel it is necessary to win every game."

An editorial backing a renewal of Drew's contract in *The Crimson White*, the student newspaper, reflected how lower expectations were seeping into the program: "In these days of modern football, our team cannot even hope to have an undefeated year."

Even as the Crimson Tide's glorious past appeared to be at war with an era of creeping mediocrity, Starr packed his bags and entered a world where the projection of raw athletic skill could take a player just so far.

"There were plenty of good high school athletes on that team," said quarterback Clell Hobson, the Alabama starter in 1951–52. "On top of talent, you had to be a pretty competitive individual to make it and play in those days."

Line coach Hank Crisp, the last link to the Wade era, was a walking monument to what it took to make the grade at Alabama. A grizzled figure with a leathery face and a stub for a right hand, Crisp could still get down in a three-point stance and whip any player on the team, wielding his wits, his strength, and his deformed hand like lethal weapons. He served, at various times, as Alabama's basketball, baseball, and track coach as well as athletic director. He was feared and beloved. Bear Bryant once rode Crisp's rumble seat out of Arkansas—and looked upon the crusty old cuss like a father.

"He appeared to be an old man, but he was agile, quick, and mean," said linebacker Harry Lee, who played for Alabama in the early 1950s and, like many others, credited Crisp with making him a football player.

Arthur "Tarzan" White, a big, tough, mean All-America lineman in the mid-1930s, once became so fed up with the coach's incessant badgering that he picked him up, like a sack of potatoes, and threw him over the practice field fence.

When Crisp walked back through the gate with a determined look, White knew he was in trouble and resigned to pay the price for his disrespect.

"All right, let's get it over with . . ."

Crisp clocked him a few times and they got back to work.

"Coach Hank was the toughest man any of us had ever known," recalled halfback Young Boozer, who played during the same period. "We were scared to death of him but we loved him."

Center Ralph Carrigan thought of himself as the baddest hombre on the Alabama teams of the early '50s. After one especially humbling "bull-in-the-ring" session, when he was repeatedly blocked to his knees by the much older, smaller, and unpadded coach, Carrigan, dripping blood, demanded the chance to go again.

"Nah, Ralph," Crisp said with a sneer. "I don't want to have to kill you."

Long before the advent of modern equipment tempered a certain amount of the game's inherent violence, football in the 1950s required a significant level of toughness and immunity to pain. Unless a foul was especially flagrant, the officials tended to let the athletes play the game in those days, leaving a certain amount of enforcement to the players themselves. When Harry Lee watched a Tennessee player shove a teammate's head into the dirt as he was climbing off the field—way after the whistle—he pushed his way up to the much larger Volunteer's face.

"Look, you big ole sonofabitch, if you ever do anything like that again, I'm gonna whip your ass!"

Towering over Lee, the Tennessee player scowled, shoved a finger into his opponent's chest and took notice of his jersey number. "You see that goalpost down there?" he said, pointing to the opposite end of the field. "After the ballgame, you meet me there and we'll settle this!"

When the game was over, Lee made sure he was a long way from the goalpost.

"I was cocky but I wasn't stupid," he said.

The plastic helmets used by Alabama and other college teams in the era were promoted as instruments of significant progress over the old leather headgear—which could be squeezed, like Charmin bath tissue—but without bars or mouthpieces, they provided limited protection from many routine collisions. While returning a kickoff against Tennessee in 1951, Bama's Bimbo Melton was clotheslined. The violent crash broke his jaw.

Eight-year-old Edgar Welden, who grew up next door to the Melton family in Wetumpka, was tossing a football in the backyard of his grandparents' house in Montgomery, listening to the game on the radio with his grandfather.

"When they started talking about Bimbo being hurt, I was really concerned because he was my idol," Welden said.

Two or three days later, when the family brought Melton home to recuperate, Welden rushed next door to see him.

"I never will forget how helpless he looked, lying in bed with his jaw wired shut . . . unable to eat or drink except through a straw," Welden said. "Pretty dramatic stuff for an eight-year-old. It taught me how rough football could be."

The equipment manager fashioned a crude face mask for Bimbo—the first ever for a Tide player—and he quickly returned to action, broken jaw and all.

"You were expected to play," Lee said. "Unless you couldn't walk."

In at least one instance, the upgrading of equipment made walking difficult. Prior to the 1951 season opener against Delta State at Montgomery's Cramton Bowl, the Alabama players pulled on new uniforms that included thigh pads sewn directly into the pants. Soon, the athletes learned that the pads were so out of position that they slammed painfully against their genitals.

"You'd mash your balls like crazy just running onto the field," Lee recalled. "It was unreal."

The next week they switched back to the old pants.

The modern age of athletic grant-in-aid scholarships was dawning, but the recruiting process remained unsophisticated and many athletes never visited campus before showing up for their first practice. Coaches enforced a rigid sense of discipline governing behavior, and most players—motivated by the dictates of the prevailing culture and the fear of risking their scholarship—never thought of challenging their authority figures.

Some athletes went to great lengths to hold on to the lifeline of a free education.

When Alabama freshman basketball player Sid Youngelman was kicked off the team for missing practice in 1951, he shoved head coach Floyd Burdette up against a wall and threatened him. Burdette, fearing for his safety, took the matter to Hank Crisp, who was then doubling as the athletic director, and demanded that Youngelman, a six-foot-four, 230-pound forward from Brooklyn, New York, be sent home.

It was well after the first of the year, and Alabama had already invested a significant amount in Youngelman's tuition, housing, and meals, so Crisp, who was responsible for balancing the books, devised another idea for how to deal with the big, strong, tough kid who liked to hit people. He called the basketball player into his office and laid it on the line.

"You can either stay here and play football and do what we tell you," Crisp said. "Or, you can go home."

Youngelman knew very little about football, but he didn't want to go back to Brooklyn. When spring practice opened a few weeks later, Crisp started the process of turning him into a ferocious tackle who would win three varsity letters and play eight seasons in the NFL.

With the Korean War death toll mounting, fear of the draft provided additional incentive for athletes to hold on to their scholarships. Several players were drafted, never to return to the field; many others avoided this fate by serving in ROTC. In the summer of 1951, Clell Hobson's National Guard unit was mobilized and he appeared to be on his way to the war zone.

"I didn't want to go. Nobody wanted to go," said Hobson, a native of Tuscaloosa. "But I was going. I was about to get on that train."

He packed his bags, but at the last moment, the unit was demobilized and he never went to war.

In the fifties, the University of Alabama, with an undergraduate enrollment of about six thousand students, exuded the intimate feel of a small college. For all the tradition of the mighty Crimson Tide, the athletic program remained a small, thrifty operation. Denny Stadium, consisting of two separate permanent grandstands, seated 31,000 and often was not filled to capacity. It would be a long time before a vastly expanded stadium and various other revenue streams transformed Alabama athletics into a multimillion-dollar enterprise. Like most universities its size, the state's so-called capstone of higher learning sponsored only about a half dozen sports for men, none for women. The entire athletic payroll consisted of about a dozen people, and the head coach of every minor sport doubled as an assistant for the football team.

The football players lived in Friedman Hall, which some students affectionately referred to as "The Ape Dorm," poking fun at the prevailing image of the dumb jock. The chow hall was across the street. Joe Kilgore, who played for Frank Thomas in the 1930s, managed the dorm and lived in a small apartment with his wife and their three little girls. Some of the more responsible players often babysat the Kilgore children.

The student body, faculty, and athletic program remained all white, reflecting the pervasive—and largely unquestioned—segregationist tradition blanketing the South in the years just before *Brown v. Board of Education* and the Montgomery bus boycott. The only African-American face around the Crimson Tide family was "Hoochman" Collins, the beloved athletic department custodian and gofer who derived his name from his appreciation for cheap whiskey. Often accompanying the team on road trips, he would drift off to sleep in the corner of someone's room, cradling a bottle of booze. When he died, many years later, long after the program had been integrated, the letterman's association paid for his funeral and his gravestone.

The manpower shortages caused by the war prompted the National Collegiate Athletic Association to once again make freshmen eligible for varsity competition, so like his hero Harry Gilmer, Bart Starr arrived in Tuscaloosa at a fortuitous time.

With returning starter Clell Hobson firmly established as the quarterback on Alabama's Split T offense and Bobby Wilson backing him up, Starr found himself competing during preseason drills with fellow freshman Albert Elmore for the remaining quarterback slot on the varsity roster.

"You could tell right off that Bart was a great passer," said Elmore, who was known more for his running ability. "He was well suited to drop back, stay in the pocket and pick a receiver, which is what he had done in high school. That was his strong suit."

Even at Lanier, Starr was not much of a threat to run. "Not what you would call a speed merchant," said Bill Moseley, his old high school coach. At Alabama, his lack of running skills emerged as more of a liability. "He couldn't run a hundred yards in two weeks," recalled Tide defensive back Bobby Luna. But the combination of Starr's arm strength and his ability to learn and implement the system allowed him to win the coveted third quarterback slot. He proved impressive off the bench in several games, winning Freshman All-SEC honors.

"Bart was such a great competitor," Hobson said. "Watching him, I could see I better work hard to stay ahead of him, 'cause he was good and he was right there, ready to go."

Early in the season, junior fullback Tommy Lewis walked to the huddle and insisted that the freshman substitute call a specific running play.

"Shut up, Tommy!" he said forcefully, glaring at the upperclassman. "I'm calling the plays."

Laughing many years later at the scene—which echoed the exchange with a Lanier teammates on the night he replaced Don Shannon—Starr recalled that one of the many characteristics he tried to absorb from Babe Parilli during his 1951 summer camp was his huddle demeanor. "He taught me how important it was to be the boss in the huddle and to communicate absolute confidence and focus to the your teammates, because they will feed off that."

With All-American Bobby Marlow, one of the greatest runners in Crimson Tide history, rushing for a school-record 950 yards, Alabama finished 9-2 and ranked ninth in the final AP poll, earning a bid to face fourteenth-ranked Syracuse in the Orange Bowl.

Soon after his peers voted him SEC Coach of the Year, Drew was rewarded with a two-year contract extension and a raise.

Air travel was still a novelty and a luxury, experienced only by a lucky few, and the chartered flight to Miami was the first ever taken by many of the Alabama players. Several minutes into the air, the athletes began taking turns visiting the cockpit. When Tommy Lewis's time came, he bounded up the aisle like a child on Christmas morning, anxious to see all the controls and look out at the approaching vista.

His thrill quickly turned to fright as he watched the captain furiously checking his instruments and conversing with air traffic control.

"I've lost the oil pressure in my number one engine!

"Now I've lost the oil pressure in my number three engine!"

Lewis could count, and three minus two left one fully functioning engine. Miami was still at least two hours away.

As the pilot plotted a course back to Atlanta under emergency conditions and Lewis started turning white, the man with his hand on the yoke looked him in the eyes and said, "Boy, go back to your seat, sit down, and don't you say a damn word!"

When Lewis emerged from the closed cabin and returned to his seat, staring straight ahead, the other passengers were cutting up and having a big time, completely unaware of the developing situation. He didn't say a damn word, and in a few minutes the captain calmly announced that the plane would be returning to Atlanta to deal with a little mechanical problem. No big deal.

The team soon boarded a second plane with three good engines and arrived safely in Miami.

Like air travel, television was still new and exciting. As the rapidly expanding American television universe surpassed 20 million homes, January 1, 1953, marked an important milestone in college football history. For the first time, viewers from coast to coast could see all four major bowl games: the Rose Bowl, Sugar Bowl, Cotton Bowl, and Orange Bowl. At least those with access to a set: Only a few thousand black-and-white receivers existed in the entire state of Alabama, and most of those were centered in and around Birmingham, home to the state's only two stations, which had been broadcasting since the late 1940s. New stations in Mobile, Montgomery, Decatur, and Dothan would hit the airwaves over the next two years, and soon most everyone would have a TV. But in order to see the Big Four on New Year's Day 1953, many dedicated football fans across the state were forced to try to tune in faint signals from distant stations in Birmingham, Atlanta, and Nashville.

Having an expensive set and a pair of rabbit ears was not enough. You needed a powerful antenna pointed just right.

Possessing neither of these crucial elements, University of Alabama student Joe Adams gravitated to the next best thing: a prosperous friend with his finger on the technological pulse.

One of the roughly three television sets in Adams's southeastern Alabama hometown of Ozark was owned by Dr. Major Mills, a dentist and an Alabama grad with a passion for Crimson Tide football. When Mills learned that Bama's first bowl game since 1947 would be televised, he invited dozens of friends to his house for the historic event. Carefully manipulating his 175-foot antenna, Mills tuned in a distant station from Atlanta or Birmingham. It was just the third Alabama game ever televised—the 1951 Tennessee contest remembered for Bimbo Melton's injury put the Crimson Tide in the TV business—and many of the sixty-plus men and boys who crowded around the small set in his living room had never seen so much as a test pattern, so watching a major sporting event from a distant city still seemed like a technological marvel.

"The picture was very fuzzy," said Adams, home for the Christmas break. "It would fade in and out. And the place was so crowded, it was a struggle for everybody to be able to see the screen. But we thought it was the greatest thing."

Those fans would always remember where they saw the most lopsided game in bowl history.

Alabama's 61–6 victory over Syracuse shattered fifteen Orange Bowl records, including the winning team's total offensive yards (586). The Orangemen, champions of the East, could not stop the Crimson Tide, evidenced by several long scoring plays, including Cecil "Hootie" Ingram's 80-yard punt return, Hobson's 50-yard pass to Corky Tharp, and Marvin "Buster" Hill's 60-yard interception return. The rout went on for so long that the head of the Orange Bowl committee tried to persuade the timekeeper to speed things up, fearing CBS would be forced to suspend its coverage before the game ended.

Even some players lost track of time. When the clock ran down to zero with Alabama leading 41–6, the Crimson Tide's defense began walking off the field and toward the dressing room as an incredulous Red Drew called out to them.

"Christ! Where the hell are you going?"

The players thought the game was over . . . but it was just the end of the third quarter.

Drew began emptying his bench in the third quarter and all forty-six Alabama players saw action. Many fans left early so they could go watch the other televised games.

"One of the most incredible games I've ever been involved with," Starr said. "So many things went right for us that day."

Starr, who played much of the second half, tossed a 22-yard touch-down pass to Joe Cummings and then played a direct role in the assault on the record book. When informed that receiver Joe Curtis owned seven receptions on the day and needed one more to break the Orange Bowl mark, Starr threw to him once . . . and again . . . and again . . . and again.

Time after time, Starr hit him with perfect passes.

But Curtis kept dropping the ball as his teammates battered him with grief.

Finally, Starr threw to him a fifth time, put it right on the numbers, and Curtis pulled the ball in, securing his place in Orange Bowl history.

Back in Ozark, the crowd cheered the fuzzy picture and spoke hopefully about the bright future of the mighty Crimson Tide—and the promising young quarterback with the powerful arm.

Even before his first football season ended, Starr toyed with the idea of playing baseball. He believed he could make the Alabama team but he also wanted to be able to spend time with Cherry before football consumed him again. He was falling hard, and love eventually conquered baseball.

"He would actually drive all the way to Auburn, spend one hour with me, and drive all the way back to get back [to Tuscaloosa] by curfew," Cherry said.

His uncle Hilton, a big baseball fan, teased him about the decision. *How dare you turn down the chance to play college baseball so you can spend time with some girl!*

Starr also enjoyed basketball, and while he knew he didn't possess the skills to play for the hardwood Crimson Tide, he closely followed the program led by dynamic new head coach Johnny Dee.

Dee, a former Notre Dame quarterback under Frank Leahy, also became an assistant coach for the Alabama football team. He took a liking to Starr, recognizing his intelligence and his work habits.

After being offered the Alabama job while he was still on the Notre Dame basketball staff, Dee quickly rounded up five recent high school graduates who had tried out for the Fighting Irish team but failed to receive scholarship offers. None of the five—Jerry Harper of Kentucky; George Linn, Dennis O'Shea, and Dick Gunder of Ohio; and Leon Marlaire of Illinois—had ever visited Alabama or the Deep South, but they were destined to leave an indelible mark on Crimson Tide sports history. In time, the starting five would form the nucleus of a basketball team forever known as the Rocket 8, winning the school's first Southeastern Conference championship in more than twenty years, giving the football school a powerful taste of hoopsmania.

Starr spent many hours watching the newly invigorated basketball team practice and play at tiny Foster Auditorium, carefully studying the way Dee coached, unaware of how their budding friendship would one day change his life.

Heading into his sophomore year, Starr captured the starting quarterback job on a veteran team expected to contend for the conference championship.

The Orange Bowl victory made a statement, but Alabama was still chasing Tennessee and Georgia Tech, the dominant Southeastern Conference teams of the early 1950s. Tennessee, led by the venerable General Robert Neyland, an austere figure who personified the traditional image of the gruff football coach, won the 1951 national championship by relying on a hard-nosed defense and a conservative offense that rarely beat itself. Neyland owned Drew: His 4-1-1 mark against archrival Alabama since 1947 gave grumbling Tide alums significant ammunition. Georgia Tech's Bobby Dodd was more of a strategist who coached football like a chess master and took pride in not pushing his players as relentlessly as men like Bear Bryant and Robert Neyland, but his Yellow Jackets—who captured a share of the 1952 national championship—played an equally potent brand of football.

The game was about to change dramatically.

Several months before the 1953 season, the NCAA rules committee voted to end the decade-long era of free substitution, forcing coaches to once again play one-platoon football. A player could enter the game just once per quarter. The switch tipped the scales toward versatility and endurance, providing an advantage to teams with eleven superior athletes. Neyland, who retired in 1953, campaigned for the change, but Dodd resisted, saying it "takes the coaching out of football."

"It was a defensive, ground-oriented type of football," recalled Albert Elmore, who played behind Starr. "Our ends were designed to play defense. If they could catch the ball, great, but that wasn't their primary responsibility. If you couldn't play defense, you couldn't play."

The change handicapped a veteran Alabama team, forcing several offensive stars to the bench.

Suddenly charged with playing defensive back while also mastering the Split T and punting for a sterling 41.4-yard average—second in the nation behind Georgia's Zeke Bratkowski—Starr took the change it stride. His lack of speed proved to be a hindrance on defense, but he was a sure tackler.

In an age when fans and the newsmen who catered to them still tended to see athletic stars through a romantic lens, the narrative of Bart Starr's life began to play out in Alabama newspapers. One of the first instances occurred in the *Birmingham News* on September 13, 1953, under the byline of longtime scribe Alf Van Hoose:

TUSCALOOSA—A person extremely close to the University of Alabama football picture paid Bart Starr a high, high compliment last week. Pointing to the determined 19-year-old Montgomery sophomore preparing diligently for a busy autumn weekend schedule, the observer remarked:

"Starr is the kind of boy I hope my son grows up to be like."

While praising Starr's athletic abilities, Van Hoose also took significant note of his "wholesome" character.

In a later, more cynical age, such a lead might have drawn snickers from skeptical editors and readers, branding the writer as sentimental, gullible, trite.

But in this case, it happened to be true.

Invariably, and without prompting, Starr's former teammates talk about his solid character.

"Bart is one of the finest Christian gentlemen I've ever known in my life," said former Alabama quarterback Clell Hobson.

"They don't make 'em any better than Bart Starr," said former Alabama defensive back and receiver Hootie Ingram.

Through the years, Starr's squeaky-clean, All-American image became a large part of his identity, no doubt causing many to wonder whether any successful athlete, steeled in the firmament of competition, could actually be such a nice guy. A life splattered with tales of womanizing, drunken escapades, and felony rampages certainly would make a biographer's job more colorful, but Starr was who he was: a little dull perhaps, compared to many of his contemporaries, but always authentic. Most never stopped to consider the connective tissue between his character and his athletic career, but the link between the two could be seen during his Alabama years.

Many young men who had grown up under the thumb of such a domineering father would have rebelled, especially after going off to college and gaining a measure of independence. But the unique circumstances of Starr's childhood pushed him the other way. In the gathering age of antiheroes personified by Marlon Brando, he rebelled by *not* rebelling. Desperately seeking his father's approval, he matured into a very disciplined, ethical, moral, polite, earnest young man who seemed to be driven by a sense of obligation to prove himself as an athlete and as a man—to embrace the transformative power of a strong work ethic as the ultimate weapon against the pathos of his life. The wholesome traits noticed by so many reflected something deeper than most realized. His humility off the field and his tenacity on the field were part of the same pounding life force.

"I just had a flaming, burning desire . . . and so much of that came back to my dad," he said.

And the memory of Bubba.

Surely, the introspective Starr must have considered how his life might have been different if his brother had lived, if the tragedy had not launched such a powerful chain reaction. But he rarely talked about Bubba. Most of his college teammates remained unaware of the situation until years later. The guilt attached to the event still lingered in the family, victimizing his parents, but somewhere along the way, Bart found a sense of peace.

Often, his Alabama teammates drew a distinction between the two Bart Starrs, but the waters were drawn from the same well.

"Bart was the nicest guy in the world off the field, but once he stepped between those white lines, look out," said halfback Tommy Lewis. "He took charge. He had tremendous mental toughness. There was a fierceness about him once he strapped that helmet on and went to war, and that made him an extremely good leader."

Starr improved significantly in his first year as the starter to have a solid sophomore season, but he was still young, still maturing as a quarterback, still prone to the kind of mistakes that would not characterize his later years. He moved the ball but often failed to score touchdowns. "He was basically a pocket passer [who] wasn't very good at improvising, which you had to do a lot with the passing game in those days," said receiver/defensive back Bobby Luna.

With Starr completing 49 percent of his passes for 870 yards—breaking Harry Gilmer's school record and ranking second in the SEC, behind Georgia's Bratkowski—Alabama won the Southeastern Conference championship in 1953, one of the strangest years in Crimson Tide history. The season began with an upset loss to lowly regarded Mississippi Southern in Montgomery and included an upset victory over fifth-ranked Georgia Tech, a loss to eventual national champion Maryland, and ties against LSU, Tennessee, and Mississippi State. The return to one-platoon reduced offensive output all across the country, and Alabama was not immune. The uneven 6-2-3 season secured a bid to play Southwest Conference champion Rice in the Cotton Bowl, when Starr and his teammates became witnesses to one of the most bizarre moments in college football history.

In the second quarter, with Rice leading 7–6, quarterback LeRoy Fenstemaker stepped behind center on first down from his own 5-yard line. Alabama's scouting report said that Rice never ran outside the tackles inside its own 20, so the Crimson Tide lined up with eight men in the box, determined to stuff the run. Just as halfback Dicky Maegle took the handoff, he saw a seam open up around right end, as Alabama's Tommy "Tarbucket" Tillman tumbled to the ground, so he lunged right and sprinted upfield near the Bama sideline.

Speeding toward midfield but being pursued by the entire Alabama team, Maegle moved into the open field. It appeared that only two players— Bill Oliver and Vincent DeLaurentis—still had a realistic chance to catch him, and the odds were not good. Maegle was fast. Starr, in the game at defensive back, would pick off Fenstemaker later in the game, but on this play, he was blocked. By the time he climbed off the turf and started giving chase with all he had, Maegle was far ahead and extending his lead.

After Alabama's first mass substitution of the game, teammates Tommy Lewis and Harry Lee were taking a breather on the sideline.

"Leaper, looks like he's going all the way," Lewis, holding his helmet, said to his buddy.

"Damn sure does," said Lee, who turned away to follow the pursuit.

Just then Lee felt something heavy fall on his sore foot, which some Rice player had crashed into a few minutes earlier, leaving him hobbling. His foot hurt like hell. When he looked down and saw Lewis's helmet at his feet, Lee turned to say something nasty to his teammate. But he was already gone.

Something in Lewis snapped and he raced onto the field.

Starr, still pumping his legs as fast as he could, watched in amazement at the drama unfolding perhaps five yards in front of him.

"I'm running down the field, near the sideline . . . and I see this figure come off the sideline and make this blind-side tackle," Starr recalled. "He just knocked the crap out of the guy."

As a stunned Maegle tumbled to the ground, Lewis, suddenly realizing what he had done, retreated to a sideline bench, slumping next to an old man wearing a cap who had apparently fallen asleep.

An eerie silence fell across the capacity crowd of 75,504. Then the Rice fans started booing.

As the officials awarded Maegle a 95-yard touchdown, Lewis buried his head in his hands and several teammates crowded around him, shielding him from the fast-approaching mob of photographers.

In the press box, NBC announcers Lindsey Nelson and Red Grange tried to explain the situation, which struck the two men as particularly spooky because they had discussed such a possibility the night before.

"In all my years as a sports announcer, I never experienced a more shocking moment," Nelson said many years later.

It was not the first time a player had been so mentally involved in a game that he temporary allowed his instincts to overwhelm his senses, but it was the first time such an event had ever happened on live national television.

Like millions of viewers, Starr struggled to deal with what he had just witnessed.

"I was so startled," he said. "You hardly knew what to think. It was the strangest thing I have ever seen on a football field."

The frustrating day continued as Starr struggled on offense, tossing two interceptions.

After Rice's decisive 28–6 victory, Lewis apologized to the Owls personally and became an unwitting national celebrity, appearing on *The Ed Sullivan Show*, *What's My Line?*, and several other network television programs. He wanted to go back in time and stop himself. He wanted to make it all go away. But even as he fretted over his infamous act, his competitiveness and sense of remorse touched sports fans all across the country when he explained, "I'm too emotional . . . too full of Bama." Newspapers praised his heart.

Lewis would carry the burden of guilt for a lifetime, but the fighting spirit that propelled him off the sideline endeared him to his teammates, who understood that the same impulse could have overpowered any one of them.

"Tommy was such a competitor, and I always admired that about him," Starr said. "In his mind he was still in the ballgame. He was out of it by being in it."

The first time, she said no.

In fact, Bart Starr threw two incomplete passes before Cherry Morton, the love of his life, agreed to run away with him, to be his wife, forever and ever.

"The third time," she said, "I finally caved in."

Nearly three years after she first turned his head, Starr had grown to love Cherry's vibrant personality, her strong values, and the way she made him feel. She was full of life but also very grounded and sensible. He imagined her as the mother of his children. He was just scratching the surface of her inner strength.

"I just knew I loved her very much and I wanted to get married," he said.

Cherry felt the same way. She kept putting him off only because they were still so young—both had turned twenty by then—and she wanted to make sure he was able to focus on school as well as football. "He wasn't concentrating as much on his studies as he was concentrating on me, going back and forth," said Cherry, who was finished with school for the summer and living with her parents, who had moved to Jackson, Mississippi.

She thought she was saying yes to a future military officer. The Korean War had ended in an armistice the previous year, but the draft remained a fact of life for all able-bodied young men. Bart, pursuing a major in education and a minor in history, was enrolled in the Air Force ROTC program, had a commitment to satisfy, and planned to make a career of the military.

The decision to elope on May 8, 1954, was made on the spur of the moment. His roommate Bobby Barnes owned a sporty new Mercury, thanks to his father, who ran a dealership in Montgomery. Bart, who typically puttered around Tuscaloosa in an undependable 1939 Ford, knew better than to try to take the old jalopy out of town, so he arranged to borrow Barnes's car.

"I've told Bart many times that he never would have had her if it wasn't for me," Barnes said.

Then he ran down the corridor of Friedman Hall and asked Nick Germanos to be his best man. Feeling the need to keep the event secret, the three of them plotted a course for Columbus, Mississippi, the first town across the state line. They stopped at a dingy service station along the way to change into nicer clothes and then found the home of the local justice of the peace, who performed the ceremony in his living room while his wife witnessed.

"Bart was so excited he didn't know what to do," Germanos said. "You should have seen the grin on his face."

In a situation mirroring Bear Bryant's life two decades earlier, Starr initially hid the union from his coaches, fearful of losing his scholarship. Because marriage caused complications that divided their focus, many coaches—including Red Drew—made it clear that the institution was something that should be delayed until after college. The risk was significant: if the coaches reacted badly and Starr lost his scholarship, he could kiss his football career and his college education good-bye.

"I was really worried about it, so that's why we decided to keep the whole thing a secret," Starr said.

He was also concerned about what their parents would say.

"Basically we were hiding it from Bart's parents—especially his mother," Cherry said. "My parents absolutely adored Bart. Sometimes I thought they liked Bart better than they liked me."

But as Bart drove Cherry back to Jackson and then returned to campus, they still felt compelled to maintain the complete circle of secrecy.

About three months later, Cherry's mother walked into the house with the mail and noticed a letter addressed to "Mrs. Bart Starr."

"Isn't this somewhat presumptuous?" she said to her daughter. "You'd think the boy was married to you."

Then Cherry broke down. Her eyes welled up with tears.

"Well, he is."

After the initial shock, Cherry's parents took the news just fine. Ben Starr understood, but Lulu reacted badly, initially threatening to have the marriage annulled "if I have to take it all the way to the Supreme Court."

"I don't think she would have been happy with anyone Bart married," said Cherry, who worked hard to cultivate a good relationship with Lulu through the years but never felt as close as she would have liked.

To placate Bart's mother, Bart and Cherry agreed to exchange vows during a formal ceremony at the First United Methodist Church in Montgomery.

Realizing they could no longer keep the union under wraps, Bart consulted his father, as he did on most important decisions. The Starrs were living temporarily in Tuscaloosa, where Ben was assigned to the same ROTC unit as his son. "Go tell your coaches now," the Master Sergeant advised. "It's the proper thing to do."

Baseball coach Tilden "Happy" Campbell also coached the football backfield, but like many players, Starr felt closest to Hank Crisp. In spite of his tough exterior, Coach Hank could be very compassionate toward his boys, and so he was with Starr, helping him smooth the situation over with Coach Drew.

"If I had lost my scholarship I really don't know how we would have made it," Starr said.

Forced to move out of the athletic dorm and provided with a small housing stipend, Starr brought Cherry to Tuscaloosa and they moved into a tiny apartment just south of campus. She landed a job working for the school photographer, and they got by. When they first moved in, the floor was so rotten that a large weed was sprouting through a crack. The cramped bedroom—furnished with a bedroom suite purchased for fifteen dollars—abutted the sidewalk, providing precious little space or privacy.

"We were in love and we were together," Cherry said. "That's all that mattered."

"Uh!"

Starr grunted as he extended his leg and felt a sharp pain in his lower back.

"You all right?" teammate Harry Lee asked as the punted ball flew into the distance.

"Think I might have pulled something . . ."

Trying to stay in shape on a summer day in 1954, Starr and three other players were out on the Alabama practice field, running through a punting and passing drill.

Instead of walking off the field and seeking treatment, Starr continued to kick through the pain.

"A very foolish decision on my part," he said.

When he woke up the following morning, the pain was excruciating and he could not raise his right leg above his waist. Diagnosed with a severe back sprain, he would spend the rest of the year battling the debilitating injury.

Prior to a game against LSU in Baton Rouge, Starr sprawled his body across a taping table in the locker room, unable to move anything but his head without pain.

"We had to pick him up like he was on a board and stand him up so he could walk out on the field," recalled Harry Lee.

Somehow, Starr dug deep before the hostile crowd at Tiger Stadium and played one of the greatest games of his career, completing 8 of 9 passes for 105 yards and a touchdown while leading Alabama to a 12–0 victory.

The gutsy performance opened a window into the competitive nature that would define his life. Despite the intense pain, he was determined to play because winning was so important to him. "Lotta boys, they'd want to be sitting down somewhere if they had the sort of back he has," trainer Fred Posey told a reporter as Starr unwrapped his tape. "But not Bart. He wants to win too much."

Watching Starr's steady progression, admiring his guts, Drew called him "the best passer the University of Alabama ever had," an enormous compliment, considering the enduring legend of flying wizard Harry Gilmer.

But his determination to play was hindering his recovery. Facing the very real possibility that he might never play again, the doctors placed him in traction at Tuscaloosa's Druid City Hospital, where he was unable to climb out of bed for more than a week. "It was awful," Cherry recalled. "He was so miserable. Football was the love of his life—outside of me— and he thought his career was over."

In his absence, Albert Elmore tossed three touchdown passes to lead the Crimson Tide to an impressive 27–0 victory over Tennessee in Knoxville. Alabama's first victory over the Volunteers since 1947 was cause for celebration, so when the coaches walked through the door, they found the players whooping and hollering, feeling good about themselves. Then Coach Hank flashed an irritated look and opened his mouth.

"Shut up, you nitshits! You ain't beat nobody yet!"

The room fell silent, like a morgue.

"That threw a bucket of cold water on everything," Harry Lee said. "I don't know if there was any connection, but we didn't play well in any game after that."

With Starr sidelined for most of the season, the Crimson Tide scored just two touchdowns in its remaining six games, finishing a disappointing 4-5-2 season.

"It was so frustrating," Starr recalled. "I remember feeling so helpless at times, wanting to perform but not being able to."

After Georgia Tech crushed Alabama 20–0 in November, student Joe Adams, who had moved from the stands to the press box, saw something that struck him as symbolic of a program in meltdown: When the game ended, Red Drew and Hank Crisp walked straight from the bench to the bus, bypassing the dressing room. "I was a rather obscure figure but I sensed that things were coming apart," said Adams, the sports editor of *The Crimson White.*

Six weeks after the noise in Knoxville, the full measure of Alabama's collapse could be heard at Birmingham's Legion Field after a crushing 28–0 defeat at the hands of Auburn, a team it once routinely dominated.

This time, no one had to tell the Bama players to be quiet.

"The Alabama dressing room was a bedlam of silence," observed the *Montgomery Advertiser*'s Walter J. Moseley.

Not long after Adams wrote a column suggesting that communication had broken down between the players and coaches—that the team had lost pride and focus—Drew was fired, ending his eight-year run with a 55-29-7 mark.

Starr felt bad for his coach, but he had his own problems. He was about to face an obstacle even more vexing than his battered body.

"Shoot! Shoot!"

The cheers began an instant after George Linn's sneakers hit the floor.

With time running out in the first half of a basketball game against North Carolina on January 4, 1955, Alabama's Linn jumped toward the backboard, gathered a rebound, landed cleanly, and glanced at the old-fashioned scoreboard clock, winding toward the buzzer, at the opposite end of tiny Foster Auditorium. It showed about three seconds.

"Shoot! Shoot!"

Like several of his football teammates, Starr was seated in the balcony above the Alabama basket as the six-foot-four Linn, aware of the time, convinced a pass was futile, took aim and flung the ball into the distance.

"I knew there was no time to dribble," Linn later explained. "I just threw the ball."

The buzzer sounded with the ball still in flight, and when it went it, hitting the net with a dramatic swoosh, the little gym fell momentarily silent.

"None of us could believe what we had seen," Starr said.

After flinging the ball, Linn started walking off the court, but he watched it all the way. "When the thing went in, I was too astonished to change my walk or expression," he explained. "I just didn't know how to react."

The disbelief quickly turned to pandemonium as the capacity crowd of about 3,500 began cheering wildly at the longest shot any of them had ever seen.

Frank McGuire, the venerable North Carolina head coach, walked onto the floor, stood where Linn had stood, gazed into the distance with a sense of wonder, and marked the spot for posterity with the heel of his shoe. The hurl measured 84 feet 11 inches, and was hailed as the longest in college basketball history.

After wrapping up a 77–55 victory over the Tar Heels, Alabama head coach Johnny Dee told a reporter, "How could there possibly be a longer one?"

Fortunately for Bart Starr, Johnny Dee was a man who believed in long shots.

Hired with great fanfare after a short, unsuccessful tenure at Oklahoma A&M—soon to rebrand itself Oklahoma State—former Alabama tackle and kicker J. B. "Ears" Whitworth vowed to recapture the Crimson Tide's winning tradition.

"These boys have got some fire," Whitworth surmised after his first spring practice. "They want to play."

Prior to the 1955 season, the depth of Alabama's rich heritage was reflected in a ranking of the most successful college football programs of the previous quarter-century, which appeared in newspapers across the country:

1. Notre Dame 184-38-15 (.829)
2. Tennessee 185-50-12 (.787)
3. Alabama 178-52-14 (.774)

Furman Bisher, a noted sportswriter who would later cause a great national stir by accusing Paul "Bear" Bryant of teaching "brutal" football, visited campus before the season. Placing the new regime in context, Bisher talked about the numerous photographs of great Crimson Tide teams of the past lining the hallway leading into the athletic offices. "You walk down that hallway . . . and you get the feeling some of the old guys are scowling," Bisher wrote in *The Atlanta Journal*. "It is no longer fashionable to fear Alabama."

Under Whitworth, once-dominant Alabama negotiated the leap from mediocre to hapless at warp speed.

In 1955, the year Elvis Presley teamed up with Colonel Tom Parker and Americans began buying Scrabble boards, Bud Wilkinson's powerful Oklahoma Sooners cast a large shadow across the college football landscape. Riding a winning streak that would eventually reach a record forty-seven games, Oklahoma completely dominated the Big Seven conference while capturing three national championships in seven years. Whitworth's basic philosophy of football could best be described as Sooner envy. "That's the way they do it at Oklahoma," he said over and over until the players wanted to puke, unaware of how ridiculous he sounded as the Crimson Tide kept losing.

The seeds of Whitworth's failure had been planted even before he coached his first game: University officials prevented him from hiring a full staff of his own coaches. Like Red Drew before him, the new head coach had been saddled with the impossible situation of having his boss, athletic director Hank Crisp, pulling double duty as the football team's line coach. Crisp was a well-respected assistant, a molder of men all the way back to the Rose Bowl teams produced by Wallace Wade, but his presence promoted dissension—especially when he openly argued with Whitworth on the field.

"They would fight on the field, argue and fuss, in front of everybody," said end Baxter Booth. "It was unbelievable. How in the world can you have discipline like that?"

Whitworth was indecisive, disorganized, and in way over his head.

Largely recovered from his debilitating back injury, Starr worked hard during the off-season to regain his momentum, eager to bounce back from a frustrating 1954 and lead the Crimson Tide to a big season in 1955. But instead, he mostly watched as a dark cloud descended across the once-proud Alabama football program.

Determined to emphasize the run and go with a youth movement to build for the future, Whitworth left passing specialist Starr—future member of the Pro Football Hall of Fame, hero of the Ice Bowl—to ride the bench as the Crimson Tide finished 0-10.

The history of football is littered with great pros who never developed fully in college, but it would be difficult to find a future pro of such prominence who was so fully wasted as Bart Starr during his senior year in Tuscaloosa. With Albert Elmore and Clay Walls taking most of the snaps, Starr played only sparingly on the only winless team in Alabama history.

The situation dented Starr's confidence. When Whitworth played him, usually after the game had already been lost, he felt less sure of himself, and he often performed poorly.

During a late-season loss to powerful Georgia Tech at Birmingham's Legion Field, when the issue was already decided, Starr methodically drove the Crimson Tide deep into enemy territory. His pass to Don Coyle in the end zone was right on the money. But Coyle dropped it.

One year after Drew called him "the best passer the University of Alabama ever had," Starr felt completely demoralized, believing his football career was over.

"That season was a very, very difficult time for Bart," Cherry recalled. "He worked so hard and then watched it all slip away."

One year after the back injury caused him so much physical pain and filled him with such frustration, Starr severely sprained his ankle, which prevented him from punting even as he struggled to deal with a different sort of torture.

Rejection.

The dark days of Ears Whitworth would grow darker still in the months and years ahead. Battered by a complete breakdown of discipline—manifested, most tellingly, in a player strike over restrictive dorm rules—as well as meddling alumni and his own ineptitude, Whitworth produced a three-year record of 4-24-2, the worst such run in Crimson Tide history. Soon, Alabama hired a man named Bryant, and in no time at all, it was morning again in Tuscaloosa.

When the most painful football season in Alabama history ended, running out the clock on his college career, Starr stopped by Johnny Dee's office and told him about his ambition, deep simmering, to play professional football. Like many others, Dee had been frustrated by the way Whitworth's staff had overlooked Starr.

"Coach Dee was a very savvy guy and a good judge of people," recalled Rocket 8 star Jack Kubiszyn. "He apparently saw something in Bart that Whitworth and his people didn't."

Eager to help, Dee told him, "The first thing we must do is get you in the Blue–Gray game."

The Blue–Gray Football Classic, contested on Christmas Day at Montgomery's Cramton Bowl, where Starr played his high school football, featured many of the nation's outstanding college seniors, making it a magnet for NFL scouts. In a less sophisticated era of professional football—when there were only five major college bowl games, leaving the majority of players available for all-star contests—the event and others like it served a vital function in the scouting process. After Dee wrangled an invitation for Starr, the quarterback traveled to his hometown, excited about the possibility of getting a chance to play for the South team and show what he could do.

Under the circumstances, he did not expect to start, but was crushed when he barely got into the game at all. He took a few snaps near the end and then it was over. The old friends who showed up to cheer him didn't know what to think. His father was confused and hurt.

Humiliated and bitter, Starr returned to campus after the Christmas break and once again sought Dee's counsel.

"I'm going to call someone in the NFL for you," Dee finally said. "I think you can play."

"I know I can . . . if I can get the opportunity."

Around this time, Starr first confided his professional football ambition to his wife. "I had no idea he aspired to play pro football," Cherry said. "It was just not something that had entered into my thinking about our future."

At a time when college football tended to be an end in itself rather than a launching pad for the NFL . . . when the vast majority of players at schools like Alabama moved directly into fields related to their majors . . . when the salaries in pro football remained modest . . . when the entire league consisted of just twelve teams and therefore produced fewer than five hundred playing positions at any given time—Starr's dream was complicated by an even more daunting fact.

In his senior year, he had essentially vanished, discarded by a winless team.

Bart who?

As Starr wondered if he was walking the fine line between dream and delusion, one man believed in him—one man who had the power to help him.

For some unknown reason, Johnny Dee had a feeling about Starr, so he called his friend Jack Vainisi, the director of player personnel for the Green Bay Packers.

"You need to look at this kid," he insisted.

Sometimes a phone call can change a man's life.

THREE

THE TENTH QUARTERBACK

The workout lasted less than an hour.

On his excursion across the South in preparation for the National Football League draft in January 1956, Lou Rymkus, an assistant coach with the Green Bay Packers, stopped in Tuscaloosa to meet the quarterback Jack Vainisi wanted him to see. How much Rymkus knew about Johnny Dee's intervention is unclear, but Vainisi was a sharp young man with a keen eye for talent who was so serious about his work that he once took a detour from his honeymoon—with his new wife in tow—to scout players.

Acting on Vainisi's gut feeling—or simply his thoroughness in following up on every possible lead—Rymkus put Starr through a light workout on the Alabama practice field: watching him pass, run, and punt. The man from Green Bay took notes about what he saw, asked him some questions, and eventually moved on to the next town and the next prospect.

He made no promises.

"I don't recall having much of a feeling afterward," Starr said. "He just thanked me and wished me well."

Clinging to a slim thread of hope that his football career was not over—that it had not evaporated during the frustrating, humiliating, demoralizing autumn of 1955—Starr returned his attention to his last semester of college and waited for the telephone to ring.

Long before Starr was born, a future he could not have envisioned began taking shape during a casual encounter on a street corner.

After making Knute Rockne's football team at the University of Notre Dame, Earl "Curly" Lambeau contracted a severe case of tonsillitis and was sent home to Green Bay, Wisconsin, a small city along the Fox River in the northeastern part of the state, where the winters could be brutally cold. He never returned to South Bend. Instead, he landed a job as a shipping clerk with a local meat-packing firm—earning $250 per month.

After encountering local newspaperman George W. Calhoun on the street during the summer of 1919, Lambeau and the scribe—who had covered his athletic exploits at Green Bay East High School—tossed around the idea of starting a football team of their own. (Details of the exchange have been lost to the fog of time, but one can only wonder how the history of football might have evolved differently if one of the men had simply arrived on the sidewalk a few moments earlier or later, thereby missing the other.) This spark led them to call a meeting on August 11, 1919, in the newsroom of the *Green Bay Press-Gazette*, where Calhoun worked as the sports editor. Attracted by the stature of both men, more than twenty young athletes showed up to express interest in such an enterprise, known in those days as a "town" team. The first order of business was convincing Lambeau's employer—Indian Packing Company—to donate five hundred dollars for the purchase of the team's uniforms and equipment and to authorize the use of the company's athletic field for their practices. The firm's involvement with the team would fade rather quickly, but the name stuck. Thus began the remarkable saga of the Green Bay Packers, the most unique franchise in American sports.

Scheduling games against similarly organized town or company teams in the surrounding region of Wisconsin, Illinois, and the Upper Peninsula of Michigan—from the big cities of Chicago and Milwaukee as well as smaller towns like Menominee and Sheboygan—the Packers played on an open field adjacent to Hagemeister Brewery without fences or bleachers. Someone associated with the club always passed a hat. At the end of a 10-1 season in the team's debut year of 1919, each player received sixteen dollars in compensation, which made them, in the narrowest possible terms, professionals. With Lambeau as their leader, the Packers developed a reputation for fighting hard and representing Green Bay well. After finishing 9-1 in 1920, the player-coach-founder enlisted the financial backing of two other employees of the renamed Acme Packing Company to obtain a franchise in the new American Professional Football Association.

Organized in the showroom of Ralph Hay's Humpmobile automotive dealership in Canton, Ohio, in 1920, the APFA—soon renamed the National Football League—featured teams scattered across the industrial Midwest such as the Massillon Tigers, the Muncie Flyers, the Racine Cardinals, the Decatur Staleys, the Columbus Panhandles, and the Canton Bulldogs. Their president, former Olympian Jim Thorpe, was mostly a figurehead. He spent the vast majority of his time on the field, running into the distance for the Canton Bulldogs. But the man who would one day be acclaimed as the greatest athlete of the twentieth century gave the league a measure of much-needed credibility. The Packers joined the league in 1921, the second year of competition; disbanded briefly because of a dispute over the illicit use of active college players; and returned in time for the 1922 season after Lambeau apologized for the infraction, promised to never let it happen again, and raised $250 to buy back the franchise. The transaction was made possible with the help of his friend, Don Murphy, who sold his car—a Marmon Roadster—to raise most of the cash. As part of the bargain, Lambeau allowed Murphy to play in one game the next season.

By 1926, the NFL consisted of twenty-two franchises operating rather haphazardly, including long-forgotten names like the Rock Island Independents, the Duluth Eskimos, the Frankford Yellow Jackets, the Rochester Jeffersons, and the Dayton Triangles. Chronic failure marked the early days of professional football. The league's membership fluctuated erratically in its first fifteen years, especially as the Great Depression deepened, reaching a low of ten teams in 1931, as franchises launched and folded with regularity, many of them unable to attract enough paying customers in an age when baseball's hold as the national pastime was unquestioned and the NFL was overshadowed by college football, not to mention boxing and horse racing. The first of several competitors, the original American Football League, arrived on the scene in 1936 but died quickly. Several teams started in small towns eventually migrated to more economically viable major cities, most notably George Halas's Decatur Staleys, who became the dominant Chicago Bears, setting a standard of excellence challenged only by their bitter rivals, the Green Bay Packers.

Rescued from likely extinction by a group of local businessmen who reformed the team as a corporation in 1923, known collectively in Green Bay lore as The Hungry Five, the Packers quickly emerged as one of the NFL's most powerful teams, relying on a potent passing attack—Lambeau himself was an early aerial phenom—and the elusive running of Johnny Blood to capture league championships in 1929, 1930, and 1931.

Like many athletes of the day, Johnny McNally felt the need to play under an alias; with a year of eligibility remaining when he first began playing professionally with the Milwaukee Badgers in 1925, he wanted to protect his college options. After walking past a movie theater and spotting the title for the Rudolph Valentino silent film *Blood and Sand* on the marquee, he decided to recast himself as "Johnny Blood." In those days, a little showmanship went a long way. The name fit perfectly in an age before most players wore any sort of protective pads or headgear, when flying elbows and closed fists often proved more important than speedy legs and powerful arms. Blood was a mean, tough, hard-charging player who lived up to his colorful name, taking the fight to the foes of Green Bay week after week, building a legend that everyone wanted to witness with their own two eyes.

Athletes often came and went like hobos, infusing the competition for the difference-makers with urgency and intrigue. In the days leading up to the 1935 Rose Bowl against Stanford, Alabama head coach Frank Thomas closed his practices to prying eyes, but Lambeau climbed a wall—tearing his trousers in the process—to catch a glimpse of Don Hutson, the Crimson Tide's All-America end. After several days of pursuit, Lambeau finally signed him to a contract reported to pay three hundred dollars per game, an enormous sum for the period and a tremendous coup, because every team in the league wanted Hutson. Like his peers, Curly was certain that his signature equated to a prosperous future of victories and ticket sales. Later, however, Lambeau discovered that John "Shipwreck" Kelly, the owner of the NFL's Brooklyn Dodgers, had inked Hutson to a deal on the very same day. When the thorny matter landed on the desk of commissioner Joe Carr, he ruled in a manner that made perfect sense: the team whose contract was postmarked earlier would be entitled to the big prize. Hutson, destined to go down as one of the greatest players in the history of the NFL, became a Packer because Green

Bay's paperwork was canceled seventeen minutes before Brooklyn's. His impact was immediate: In his first professional game, the blazing, sure-handed Hutson scored on an 83-yard touchdown pass. It was a preview of coming attractions.

During his rookie season, the Packers were forced to split his $300 weekly salary into twin $150 checks drawn on the town's only two banks, because neither institution—constrained by the Great Depression—could cash the full amount. At a time when less gifted players earned a fraction of Hutson's deal and many considered professional football little more than a bloody hobby, the so-called Alabama Antelope became an enormous draw who was worth every nickel. Hutson was something to see, a bullet flying down a field of grass, snagging passes with a ballet dancer's grace. A two-time league Most Valuable Player, he was the master of the well-timed fake. "Hutson is the only man I ever saw who could feint in three different directions at the same time," said an admiring Greasy Neale, the longtime Philadelphia Eagles head coach. In 1939, when most teams passed only out of desperation, usually on third-and-long, Hutson averaged 24.9 yards per catch, a record that would stand for nearly two decades. Credited with inventing many of the basic patterns around which the modern passing game evolved, he revolutionized offensive football to a degree few, if any, players ever equaled, forcing opposing coaches to devise ways to mitigate his skill, which caused a corresponding elevation of defensive strategy. Some teams blanketed him with triple coverage, but that only left them more vulnerable to Green Bay's powerful running game. "Papa Bear" George Halas studied him intently and tried every trick to stop him, but Hutson—whose statistical legacy once occupied an entire page of the NFL record book—set marks that receivers would still be chasing in the twenty-first century.

"We were still inventing the game in those days," Hutson told a journalist toward the end of his life. "And I was always trying to get open and head toward the end zone."

Hutson also played a significant role in saving the franchise.

When he arrived, the Packers had been forced into receivership after a fan tumbled out of the stands, was seriously injured, and won a $5,000 judgment against the club. Team president Lee Joannes canvassed the city, selling stock in small denominations to firefighters, policemen, businessmen, high school students, and housewives in a bid to "Save the Packers." The subsequent attendance gain attributed to Hutson allowed the team to survive, pay off its debts, and emerge from receivership while continuing to win big, capturing NFL championships in 1936, 1939, and 1944. But without a well-heeled owner or a large ticket base, the Packers periodically teetered on the financial abyss, forced to scrimp on everything, including the acquisition of players. Disaster was averted once again in 1949 when the debt-ridden Packers, on the verge of collapse, hosted a Thanksgiving Day old-timers' game, which generated $50,000, and then turned once more to their fans, raising $118,000 in capital from the sale of stock in a new nonprofit corporation.

Green Bay was in a league of its own. Unlike other NFL teams—dominated by autocratic owners like George Halas of the Chicago Bears, George Preston Marshall of the Washington Redskins, Art Rooney of the Pittsburgh Steelers, and Tim Mara of the New York Giants—no single person could control more than a fraction of the Packers, giving the franchise the most unusual ownership structure in American professional sports. A traditional owner, motivated by the capitalist impulse, might have moved the Packers away from the land of beer and cheese, but the way the team was organized—and repeatedly rescued—secured the town's chip in the big game. Long after the Pottsville Maroons, the Hammond Pros, the Kenosha Cardinals, and other small-town franchises vanished, unable to compete against the economic advantages wielded by the teams anchored to major cities like New York, Chicago, and Philadelphia, the Green Bay Packers—representing a community with a population at midcentury of roughly 60,000—somehow hung on, against the odds, their very existence requiring an asterisk in any discussion of major-league sports cities. This dichotomy infused proud Green Bay citizens—particularly the hearty souls who packed the taverns on snowy winter nights, smiling big, standing tall—with a level of emotional equity that no other franchise in America could quite match, especially with the knowledge that many rival fans in those faraway metropolises, conditioned to equate size with superiority, could not identify distant, tiny Green Bay on a map at the point of a gun.

It was a tale as old as the Bible, and the boys in Green Bay didn't even need a rock.

Then the magic faded.

The slide began under Curly Lambeau, the man who invented the Packers . . . the man who saved the franchise time after time by relying on nothing so much as his significant wits . . . the man who led Green Bay to six NFL championships, becoming one of only six coaches in league history to amass two hundred victories. Curly *was* the Packers, in a way no man ever would be again. But by the end of World War II, Lambeau was past his prime and increasingly out of his depth in a rapidly evolving game. After a dispute with the Packers' governing board, he resigned under pressure following a 2-10 disaster in 1949, providing a sad end to a remarkable run. You could almost hear the door slamming shut on the NFL's formative age. Even as the community stepped forward to save the franchise from folding, all the corresponding goodwill and civic pride could not prevent the team from sliding into a new era of mediocrity. The financially strapped Packers—the perennial home of the league's lowest payroll—lost two No. 1 draft picks to the rival All-America Football Conference during the tumble, unable to meet the market rate for the players' services.

Despite the presence of future Hall of Fame halfback Tony Canadeo—the first 1,000-yard rusher in NFL history—the Packers' demise deepened under Gene Ronzani, a former Bears star who presided over seasons of 3-9, 3-9, 6-6, and 2-9-1. The most enduring act of Ronzani's regime—in fact, one of the most pivotal moves in franchise history—was his decision to hire Jack Vainisi as the team's first full-time scout, but it would take many years for the points to show up on the scoreboard. Lisle Blackbourn, who had been a successful high school coach in Milwaukee for more than twenty years before moving on to Marquette University, took over as head coach in 1954. His first two teams finished with records of 4-8 and 6-6.

"The Packers were really struggling as an organization," recalled longtime franchise historian Lee Remmel, who started his career covering the team for the *Green Bay Press-Gazette* in the 1940s. "The glory days were starting to fade into the history books. People around the league were starting to question whether Green Bay really belonged in the NFL."

Some assumed it was just a matter of time before the clock ran out on the Green Bay experiment.

Next stop, Pottsville.

After an exhibition game in 1951, Washington Redskins head coach Herman Ball pulled rookie defensive end John Martinkovic aside and said, "I've just traded you to Green Bay."

Shocked, he looked Ball squarely in the eyes.

"Where the hell is that?"

"I honestly had no idea where it was," recalled Martinkovic, who arrived in Green Bay on an early morning train, half asleep, the smell of fresh milk wafting through the air. "It took forever . . . and that train stopped at every little town. I thought I would never get there. When I did get there, I was shocked at what a small town it was."

Among many NFL players unaware of Johnny Blood, Don Hutson, and all those championship pennants snapping proudly in the winter breeze, Green Bay was not a team or a place. It was a sentence. No one wanted to be dealt to the struggling franchise located in a frozen, isolated land many derisively referred to as "Siberia."

"Folks around the league used to talk about Green Bay as the end of the earth," former Cleveland and Green Bay defender Willie Davis said with a laugh. "Who in the world wanted to go play at the end of the earth?"

At a time when their rivals played in landmark venues such as Wrigley Field, the Polo Grounds, and Los Angeles Memorial Coliseum, the Packers toiled at tiny City Stadium, the home field for adjacent Green Bay East High School. When it was dedicated in 1925, the place was a source of pride for the Packers and their fans. Thirty years later, it felt like an obsolete relic. Babe Parilli, the Packers' No. 1 draft pick in 1952, was stunned the first time he saw the facility, which featured wooden bleachers, antiquated locker rooms, and a decidedly minor-league vibe. The candle-power of the lights was so poor, Browns star Lou Groza once sent a kickoff booming so high that the ball could not be seen until it floated back to earth. "The place was a real liability," Parilli said. "It was hard for us to avoid the message it sent to the rest of the league." To placate some teams who resisted playing at such an inferior facility—and to prevent another franchise from invading their Wisconsin turf—the Packers began playing two or three home games each year at a larger stadium in Milwaukee.

The thriftiness that pervaded the organization sometimes was manifested in unusual ways. When Martinkovic was forced out of a game against the Colts with a bleeding gash on his lower lip—the result of a lethal elbow—the team doctor sewed up the wound as he sat on a sideline bench. Feeling around in his bag, the doctor realized he was out of anaesthesia. "So I just dealt with the pain of that needle coming in and out," Martinkovic said.

He played the rest of the game with a throbbing lip, the cure more painful than the injury.

"In those days you played the game because you loved it, and I really loved playing the game," said Martinkovic, who earned $4,500 as a rookie. "You certainly didn't play to get rich."

Mary Martinkovic would always remember the combination of determination and fright that marked her first drive north from her hometown of Hamilton, Ohio, how she delicately steered along the icy two-lane roads, trying not to lose control of the attached one-wheel trailer packed with everything the newly married couple owned.

"Rookies never had wives because they couldn't afford to get married," recalled John Martinkovic's bride. "They had to work a year or two . . . playing football and doing whatever they did in the off-season . . . and save up their money first, so they could afford to have wives."

Playing pro football was still considered a part-time, seasonal job, and virtually every player in the league toiled in a less high-profile position during the off-season to make ends meet. Because the city was so small, many Packers were forced to find jobs elsewhere between seasons, and since few were prosperous enough to own homes, this made it tough to find houses or apartments to rent for five or six months. Some wound up renting single rooms in houses or living in motels.

Ann Forester, whose husband Bill was drafted out of SMU in 1953, would always remember a conversation with the neighbor lady across the street, who said with a sense of wonder, "I look over there and just think of that glamorous life you're leading. . . ."

Forester laughed and said, "And I look over at your house and think, Wouldn't it be wonderful to live *that* kind of life . . . where you never have to move!"

All the moving back and forth could be tough on the wives and children, so some families lived in other cities the year-round, visiting only for big games or other special occasions. Many players and wives grew to love Green Bay, seduced by its various charms.

The bond among teammates and families was tight, and could be seen when husbands and wives gathered after games at The Surf Club, a little dive on the edge of town where they celebrated—or, more often, consoled—each other by performing skits concocted by the ladies while munching on cold cuts and sipping on beer. When the team traveled by train to play road games, Packers lucky enough to have wives and girl-friends often carried picnic baskets stocked with fried chicken and sand-wiches.

After several years working as an expeditor at General Electric in Cincinnati, Martinkovic landed a good job selling cars for a Buick dealer in Green Bay, allowing him to bring his wife to northern Wisconsin full-time.

"It was that job, not my position with the Packers, that really allowed us to put down stakes in Green Bay," he said.

Long after the Humpmobile became a distant memory, as Bart Starr waited for someone to give him a chance, the National Football League was still mired in the dark ages.

Until Cleveland Rams owner Dan Reeves moved his struggling fran-chise to Los Angeles in 1946—threatening to disband the team if the re-location was not approved by the other owners—the NFL extended no farther west than Chicago and no farther south than Washington, D.C. For many years to come, it would be national in name only. Several large cities that would one day identify themselves as big league at least partially be-cause of the presence of an NFL team—great booming metropolises like Boston, Houston, Atlanta, St. Louis, Minneapolis, and Denver—remained outside the league's footprint. The high cost of travel, years of shared struggle, and the lack of a leader with strategic vision made the NFL own-ers cautious, complacent, and vulnerable to competition.

A four-year war with an aggressive rival with deep pockets exposed the NFL's weaknesses but ultimately, it survived the threat from the All-America Football Conference, merging three former AAFC teams into the NFL in 1950: the dominant Cleveland Browns, as well as the San Francisco 49ers and Baltimore Colts. The Colts folded the next year, un-able to pay the bills, although another Baltimore entry of the same name would hit the field two years later. In an era when even the savviest own-ers struggled to field a winning team without going broke, a group pur-chased a franchise for Dallas but closed after just one season, unwilling to sustain the mounting losses.

Heading into the 1956 season, the NFL consisted of twelve teams divided into two conferences:

EASTERN CONFERENCE	WESTERN CONFERENCE
New York Giants	Chicago Bears
Washington Redskins	Green Bay Packers
Cleveland Browns	Los Angeles Rams
Chicago Cardinals	Baltimore Colts
Pittsburgh Steelers	San Francisco 49ers
Philadelphia Eagles	Detroit Lions

In contrast to college football, the NFL was firmly committed to the two-platoon system. Some rugged players still went both ways, but the sport was evolving into one of increasing specialization and skill, which produced a faster, more creative, more nuanced game. In an era of bone-crushing defenders such as Chuck Bednarik of the Philadelphia Eagles, Art Donovan of the Colts, and Lou Groza of the Browns, several highly publicized collisions gave the league a collective black eye, contributing to the misguided belief that the sport was becoming more violent. It was *always* violent. Blood, mangled body parts, and the possibility of disfigurement remained part of the equation in a sport predicated on aggressive young men slamming into each other.

"You never thought about [getting hurt]," said former Baltimore and Green Bay guard Fuzzy Thurston. "You couldn't let yourself go there."

Forced to defend his sport as the criticism of rough play mounted, Commissioner Bert Bell pushed for a new dead-ball rule, which essentially ended the action as soon as any part of a ballcarrier's body, except his hands or feet, touched the ground. "Professional football as played in the National Football League is a rough, highly aggressive game, but it isn't a dirty game," he insisted.

It was also a time when technology and ingenuity were conspiring to produce significant advances in equipment that would make the game safer.

In *America's Game*, Michael MacCambridge's history of professional football's rise, the author described a visit by Cleveland head coach Paul Brown to the headquarters of the Riddell sports equipment company in Chicago. "Give me something that will fit across the front of a helmet and will be about as big as my little finger, with tensile strength," Brown instructed one of Riddell's technical consultants. "I want it so it can withstand a stray foot, or a deliberately thrown fist or elbow, and take away the inclination to punch someone. But keep it light enough to weigh less than an ounce." Riddell soon began manufacturing the face guards according to Brown's exacting specifications, and they quickly became commonplace across the league. Brown's invention earned him millions in royalties through the years.

The NFL championship was decided by a single game between the winners of the two conferences. In the first half of the 1950s, the Cleveland Browns emerged as the model for the modern professional football organization, appearing in six straight title games and winning championships in 1950, '54, and '55. Two other franchises produced consistently powerful teams during the period. The Detroit Lions advanced to three consecutive championship games and walked away with trophies in 1952 and '53. The Los Angeles Rams, featuring an explosive offense built around quarterbacks Norm Van Brocklin and Bob Waterfield and wide receiver Elroy "Crazylegs" Hirsch, faced the Browns in three title games, losing in 1950 and '55 and capturing the crown in 1951.

As offenses became more sophisticated, two quarterbacks stood above the crowd: Cleveland's Otto Graham and Detroit's Bobby Layne.

Discovered playing intramural football while on basketball scholarship at Northwestern, Otto Graham became the master of the T formation in a remarkable decade with the Browns. His coach, Paul Brown, called Graham "the greatest player in the game's history." The biggest star of the age, he became the highest paid NFL player of his time, earning a reported $25,000 in 1955. Poised and precise, blessed with a powerful arm and uncanny instincts, the dutiful Graham implemented Brown's powerful offense with machinelike precision. Of his vaunted passing ability, he once said, "I threw the ball hard enough to get it in there and soft enough to catch it."

It was a serious injury to Graham's face, after an apparent late hit in the first half of a 1953 game against the 49ers, that prompted Paul Brown to craft the first crude face mask, which Graham reluctantly wore, providing some protection for his fifteen stitches. But many players resisted the progress of rubber and plastic. Bobby Layne, Graham's most able competitor, refused to wear a face mask, even after they became standard issue across the league.

A free-spirited Texan with a reputation as a party animal, Layne starred for his home state Longhorns before being wooed by both the NFL and AAFC. His career languished before the soon-to-be defunct New York Bulldogs dealt him to the Detroit Lions in 1950, in what would turn out to be one of the shrewdest trades in the history of pro football. Recognizing his unusual gift for plundering defenses—often by improvising—head coach Buddy Parker gave Layne a virtual free hand, and he routinely delivered. A clutch performer, Layne was known for a degree of toughness and competitiveness that inspired his teammates. "Bobby could get more out of the players around him than any quarterback I ever saw," said longtime teammate Harry Gilmer, the onetime Alabama star. "He had a knack for knowing how to push a player, how to make 'em want to play. But he was a wild booger!"

The evolution to a more strategic game elevated the importance of coaching, and no man could match Paul Brown's cerebral, innovative, meticulously organized approach.

Brown, who won a national championship at Ohio State in 1942, was dismissed by many NFL snobs during the AAFC days, when Cleveland's talent level was so clearly superior to the rest of the league and his teams won four straight titles. But he quickly silenced the skeptics by transferring his dominance to the NFL. His offense was a marvel of efficiency. With Brown on the sideline and Graham under center, Cleveland won 81 percent of its games (57-13-1) during the first six seasons of the decade. Often described as the most influential coach in the history of the game, Brown was the first to emphasize film study, playbooks, and the grading of players; the first to call plays from the sidelines; the first to devise detailed pass patterns; the first to introduce intelligence tests for players; and the first to create a sophisticated approach to scouting.

In various ways, Brown put the *professional* in professional football, helping set the stage for a whole new era.

"Whether they know it or not, nearly everybody in football has been affected by Paul Brown," longtime NFL Commissioner Pete Rozelle said. "His wealth of ideas changed the game."

A stern disciplinarian whose enormous expectations dominated the

Cleveland organization, Brown often told players who failed to perform up to his standards, "Keep it up and I'll trade you to Green Bay!"

Green Bay.

In the language of professional football in the age of Otto Graham and Bobby Layne, it was a punch line and a warning.

Jay Berwanger, the University of Chicago halfback who was awarded the first Heisman Trophy in 1935, never knew quite what to do with the distinctive hunk of bronze. For years, his aunt Gussie used it as a doorstop.

A powerful runner who once rammed into University of Michigan lineman Gerald Ford so forcefully that it left a lifelong visible scar on the future president of the United States, Berwanger was surprised when the Eagles selected him as the No. 1 overall pick in the first National Football League draft, conducted inside a ballroom at Philadelphia's Ritz-Carlton Hotel on February 8, 1936. He had never given much thought to playing professional football, because playing professional football was not yet an automatic course of action for college athletes heading out into the world. The draft, the brainchild of future Commissioner Bert Bell, was intended to streamline the sometimes chaotic process of player acquisition and give weaker teams a fighting chance by allowing the selection of athletes in reverse order of the previous year's standings. When Berwanger made it clear that he would not move to Philadelphia just to play football, the Eagles traded his rights to the Chicago Bears. He asked the Bears for the enormous sum of $25,000 over two years, and when George Halas decided that was simply too much money, Berwanger took a job as a foam-rubber salesman.

Riley Smith of Alabama, selected second overall by the Redskins, became the answer to a trivia question: He was the first drafted player to sign and play in the National Football League. Teammate Paul "Bear" Bryant, who often mockingly referred to himself as "the other end" on the Crimson Tide's outstanding teams of the day, opposite the great Don Hutson, was the 31st overall pick, in round four, by the Brooklyn Dodgers. He opted to go straight into coaching.

Over the next two decades, as the sport slowly gained stature and stability, NFL owners learned not to waste their picks on players who had no intention of playing professional football. Jay Berwanger was a special case, but through the years, many No. 1 picks failed to pan out for one reason or another, proving that, despite the inevitable sea of statistics utilized to justify one selection over another, the draft was more of an art than a science. When the downtrodden Pittsburgh Steelers invested the first overall selection of the 1956 draft on Colorado State quarterback Gary Glick, they did so with great hope, not realizing he was destined to become nothing more than a journeyman defensive back, a forgotten name in NFL history. Likewise, the Packers could not have predicted that their first pick, University of Miami running back Jack Losch, would be out of football less than two years later, pursuing a career as a fighter pilot in the United States Air Force—or that one of their many late-round gambles would turn out to become one of the greatest quarterbacks of all time.

On the morning of January 18, 1956, after the second day of the draft, someone from the Green Bay organization called Bart Starr to inform him that he had been selected by the Packers in the 17th round, the 200th overall player taken.

"I was so happy . . . just knowing I was going to get the opportunity to compete," he said.

Starr stopped by to thank Johnny Dee for his help, but at that moment, he could not yet fully appreciate the life-altering impact of one man's act of faith.

How do you thank a man for opening the door to your future?

Dee, then in the midst of one of the greatest seasons in the history of Alabama basketball, later returned to Notre Dame as head coach and spent many years as an administrator for the city of Denver. George Linn's magnificent shot would forever be connected to him, but his involvement in Starr's career, an unlikely, largely unknown lob into the distance, was a testament not only to Dee's athletic judgment but also to his generosity.

Ears Whitworth very nearly destroyed Starr's football career.

Johnny Dee saved it.

Nine quarterbacks were selected before Starr, and except for the No. 2 overall pick, Earl Morrall, who would bounce around the league for more than a decade before leading the Baltimore Colts to the Super Bowl, and No. 186 George Welsh, who would eventually find success as a head coach at Navy and Virginia, the chosen were destined for football obscurity.

Only one quarterback drafted in 1956 was bound for Canton.

By the time Packers assistant coach Ray "Scooter" McLean arrived in

Tuscaloosa to sign him, Starr had been presented with another option: The Canadian Football League's Hamilton Tiger-Cats offered him roughly $7,500 to come north of the border and play the 1956 season. Several Alabama athletes of the era continued their careers in the CFL, including his friends Tommy Lewis and Harry Lee, but in addition to bristling at the thought of playing in all that Canadian ice and snow—he was not yet personally acquainted with the climate in northern Wisconsin—Starr was motivated by the desire to see if he could survive in football's most competitive arena, despite the daunting odds.

In the previous twenty drafts, only seventeen players out of a total of 213 chosen in the 17th round or later had ever played a down for the Packers. No quarterback drafted so late had ever survived the final cut. Not a single one.

Starr's cause was aided by a set of equally formidable statistics reflecting one unassailable fact: Green Bay was one of the weakest teams in the league. Since capturing the NFL championship in 1944, when Hutson was nearing the end of his career and Canadeo was in his prime, the Packers were 47-80-2, with eight straight nonwinning seasons.

At least he wasn't trying to make the Browns or the Rams.

When McLean offered a $6,500 contract—$3,500 less than Johnny Dee was earning as Alabama's head basketball coach—Starr politely asked for $7,500. Cherry had suffered a miscarriage, and he was still trying to pay off the medical bills, so an extra $1,000 would come in handy. He had no particular desire to play in the CFL—at that moment, he probably would have paid the Packers for the privilege of trying out—but since Hamilton had offered more money, he could at least use the competition to drive up his price. McLean telephoned Green Bay for approval, and Starr happily signed the contract, thinking they had struck a deal for $7,500. Months later, when it was too late, he would discover that the $1,000 he received upon signing the contract was an advance against his entire $6,500 compensation for the year, not a bonus.

It seemed like a moot point, because no one expected him to make the team.

The first order of business was consulting Rand McNally.

"I had never heard of the Green Bay Packers and I didn't know where

Green Bay was," Cherry Starr confided with a chuckle more than a half century later. "So my mother and I . . . we pulled out a map . . ."

They wanted to be ready when Bart made the team.

In May, when he graduated from Alabama and received his Air Force ROTC commission, Bart felt a special kind of pride when his father saluted him for the first time. When he returned the salute and handed his old man a ceremonial dollar, the Master Sergeant looked down at his son's second lieutenant's bars and smiled a father's smile. "You might outrank me, but I'm still the boss," he said as he gave his boy a hug.

In the world Starr was about to enter, his demanding father was his secret weapon.

As the phenomenon of Elvis Presley swept the country, the Starrs moved all their belongings—including a prized black-and-white television and their fifteen-dollar bedroom set—to Cherry's parents' house on the outskirts of Jackson, Mississippi, where Bart switched into training mode. His back was not bothering him anymore, thanks to the help of a Tuscaloosa chiropractor, Dr. John Robinson. The way things ended in Tuscaloosa had dented his confidence, particularly in his passing ability, and he knew he needed to work on his technique and strengthen his arm, so utilizing three old footballs procured from Johnny Dee—the Whitworth regime had been unwilling to help him in this regard—Starr spent several hours each day for a month throwing the balls through a specially built A-frame stationed in the backyard. Each day, he could feel himself growing stronger. His loving wife stayed by his side, shagging balls and offering encouragement.

"I lost seven pounds running around that yard," Cherry said.

After being traded from San Francisco to Pittsburgh, defensive back Bobby Luna, Starr's former Alabama teammate, gave him his old football shoes, which he took to his first training camp. "Back then you had to furnish your own stuff," Luna noted, "and I was glad to be able to help my old friend."

When Starr arrived in Green Bay for the first time in late June, he was immediately struck by the spartan facilities, especially the locker room, smaller than his father's garage, and the training room, dominated by an antiquated whirlpool with a rusty pipe. The bleachers of City Stadium made Alabama's Denny Stadium look like the Rose Bowl.

But it was the NFL, and in his mind, nothing else mattered.

"I felt, given the opportunity, I could make the team, even though I was pretty sure the guys I was competing with were bigger, stronger and more talented," Starr said. "I was never better prepared, and wanted to make that team more than anything."

Green Bay seemed like a big city compared to Stevens Point, the small town in central Wisconsin where the Packers convened for training camp. Five rookies arrived late, after playing in the College All-Star Game against the defending NFL champion Cleveland Browns. Starr was already there. He was not on anyone's all-star team or anyone's radar screen. When the equipment manager issued him a number 42 jersey—a numeral reserved for running backs—it was clear that the coaches expected little of him.

"No one knew who the hell Starr was," said fellow rookie Forrest Gregg, an All-American lineman at Southern Methodist who was drafted in the second round. "He was just another guy trying to make the team."

Back in Jackson, Cherry struggled with the separation, unaware of the long odds facing her husband. "I really had no idea what a competitive situation it was . . . that nobody thought he would survive," she said.

The message of the jersey hit Starr hard, but instead of sulking or protesting the slap, he embraced it as a motivational tool. No one knew his name. No one believed in him. No one expected him to make it out of camp.

Starr was not the most gifted player at Stevens Point, but he was incredibly well prepared, focused, and efficient. Being overlooked served only to harden his resolve, tapping into his hidden strength: the intense desire, cultivated by his father, to prove himself worthy . . . and to prove all those people wrong.

His old man was still in his head, and now more than ever, this was a source of psychological energy he could tap.

He would show them.

He would show them all.

On the first day of practice, Starr took the field as the holder on a field-goal kicking drill and was surprised when the center snapped the ball way left. The second snap soared over his head, and the third tumbled into the dirt, leaving the rookie perplexed.

"I didn't know what to think," Starr said.

Finally, the snapper raised up out of his stance, turned around, and approached his holder.

"Rook," he said to Starr, "my name is Jim Ringo. You may not remember me, but I was the center on that Syracuse team that you guys at Alabama beat the hell out of in that Orange Bowl. And I just want you to know: Today I get even!"

Then the All-Pro center laughed, settled into his stance, and started snapping perfect balls to Starr.

Like several other veterans known for their sense of humor, Ringo always seemed to be plotting his next practical joke to pass the time in a place with little to do besides eat, sleep, and play football. One day, when running back Al Carmichael returned to his room and went to sleep, Ringo taped his door shut so he would be late for an upcoming team meeting. When Carmichael woke up, he was trapped, causing him to miss the meeting and draw an automatic fine.

Meanwhile, Starr and the other rookies—and various nervous veterans—were consumed with earning jobs. The air was thick with fear and dread, as the weekly cuts began eliminating players who had failed to impress the Packers' coaching staff. Long before *Survivor*, *The Apprentice*, and *American Idol* introduced the tension of the competitive elimination process to the larger population, it was a difficult fact of life in the zero-sum world of professional football.

"I really thrived on that challenge," Starr said. "I didn't see it as pressure. I saw it as a challenge."

But, like all the rookies, Starr worried about every little mistake, wondering if the coaches might seize on some slipup as an example of his inability to make the grade in the NFL.

As Starr struggled to make the Green Bay coaches notice him, veteran Detroit Lions end Leon Hart made the papers for threatening to retire unless management met his demand for a three-year contract and a significant raise. "I can make more money staying out of football," noted Hart, who owned a street-paving business. "But I want to play football more than anything else."

Many players marveled at his nerve.

With veteran Tobin Rote firmly established as the Packers' starting quarterback and the team able to carry only two into the fall, Starr found himself competing with incumbent Paul Held and two other rookies for a single place on the roster. Unimpressed with Held's play the previous year, Blackbourn was still not sold on him as Rote's backup. Starr quickly caught his eye, especially after he tossed a winning touchdown on the final play of an intrasquad game in Janesville. "Starr's long suit has been his sharp-shooting, even under rush conditions," Art Daley reported in the *Green Bay Press-Gazette*.

When Blackbourn narrowed the quarterbacks to three, Starr, feeling more confident every day, called his bride and uttered the sentence she had been nervously awaiting: "Pack the car and head this way."

In the first preseason game against the Philadelphia Eagles at Milwaukee's Marquette Stadium, both Starr and Held saw significant action off the bench—especially after Rote was elbowed hard and forced to the sideline—but Starr was more impressive, leading the Packers to two touchdowns and completing three of four passes for 31 yards as Green Bay claimed a 27–6 victory. The coaches noticed how the players responded to Starr's quiet confidence and cool head.

As Blackbourn wandered around the locker room, lightheartedly shaking hands with his players, Tobin Rote spotted Starr walking through the door and shouted in his direction. "Way to go in there, boy!"

Remarking on his professional debut a few moments later, Starr told a reporter, "I was a little bit nervous . . . but once you get hit once or twice, it's just like anything else."

Three weeks later, on the day of the final cut, as the 1956 regular season opener against the Detroit Lions loomed, the Packers released Held and kept Starr, who had surprised everyone but himself by clearing the first of many hurdles on the way to football immortality.

Quiet, respectful Starr was not the sort to gloat or celebrate such an achievement around his new teammates—or the unlucky athletes packing their bags—but he felt the greatest sense of accomplishment of his young life. "I was just on cloud nine," recalled Starr, who by then had been issued a No. 15 jersey.

"I don't think there's any doubt that if I hadn't spent that time working out [in Jackson], I would not have been prepared for that experience," he said. "Because I was not the most talented quarterback in camp. Not even close."

The work ethic that made the difference for Starr then—and would pay dividends in the years to come—was inexorably linked to his father's tough love pressure and the feelings of inadequacy connected to his late brother.

At the same time, Bart was starting to learn about a different sort of love. Cherry, who drove up from Jackson with her mother in a brand-new Chevrolet, presented as a gift to Bart by her parents, was a strong-willed woman who believed deeply in her husband. In her own way, she somehow made him believe even more firmly in himself, and this quality, this gift, would prove as instrumental in his rise as Ben Starr's psychological warfare.

While driving all over town looking for a place for the young couple to live, Cherry happened upon a small house on a quiet street. Noticing the FOR SALE sign in the front yard, she telephoned the number on the sign, found out that the elderly lady who had lived there had recently died, and charmed the lady's family into renting it—for one hundred dollars per month—for the duration of the football season.

"We were really lucky to find that place," Cherry recalled, noting that the couple had about three hundred dollars in the bank at the time. "You wouldn't believe how hard it was for players to find decent places to live."

One Packer was not so lucky.

Several weeks after the Starrs left Tuscaloosa, the still-gathering civil rights movement reached the University of Alabama when Autherine Lucy attempted to become the first African-American student to enroll at the all-white campus. While the Montgomery bus boycott, launched by Rosa Parks's defiant refusal to give up her seat for a white man, continued with no resolution in sight—making a household name of the young preacher leading it, Martin Luther King, Jr.—the attempted integration of the state's leading university enraged white supremacist groups, including the Ku Klux Klan, who threatened violence to prevent such "race mixing." Several days after Lucy signed up for classes, she was expelled, supposedly for her own safety, a controversial and fateful surrender to the forces of hate that would keep Alabama all white for another seven years.

Professional football was integrated almost from the beginning, in the 1920s, but after the fog of Jim Crow descended across the league, effectively banning African Americans for many years, the color barrier in the NFL was permanently shattered in 1946, when former UCLA star Kenny Washington signed with the Los Angeles Rams. Like most of the league's other teams, the Green Bay Packers integrated slowly, tentatively. When Starr arrived in the summer of 1956, the only African American on the team was Nate Borden, a defensive end who had been drafted out of Indiana University the previous year. Like many other players, Borden struggled to find a suitable place to live, but his situation was magnified when he tried to move into a local motel. Apparently unnerved by the thought of a black man living down the hall, the other Packers in residence threatened to move out en masse if Borden was allowed to rent a room. Humiliated, Borden and his wife—among no more than a few dozen blacks in the entire town—were forced to live in a shack that Starr recalled "was little more than a shanty."

"I couldn't believe he was being treated that way by his own teammates," Starr said.

Instead of ignoring the situation, Bart and Cherry befriended the Bordens, who became frequent dinner guests at their home.

"They were very sweet people who were having a very difficult time," Cherry said.

In time, other teammates warmed up to the Bordens; new black faces would join the Packers, and their little corner of the world, like other segments of American society, slowly began to dismantle the barriers that had separated them for so long.

With Rote taking most of the snaps, Starr saw only limited action during his rookie year, completing 24 of 44 passes for 325 yards, 2 touchdowns, and 3 interceptions. The Packers stumbled to a 4-8 finish.

The thrill of earning a place on the roster soon faded as Starr began moving his own personal goalposts, anxious to play a significant role in a winning organization.

"I feel sorry for rookies," Starr told a reporter several years later. "A rookie is sort of an outcast . . . that's not really the word . . . but it's just that the system is so much advanced from college. If you don't have the veterans helping you can get down in the dumps real quickly."

Several veterans befriended Starr and tried to show him the ropes, including Rote, a gutty performer with a powerful arm who became a mentor, teaching him various lessons about playing the position. After observing him in practice one day, Rote pulled the rookie aside and gave him some advice: "Your arm isn't strong enough and you won't last long if you don't improve. You don't have to throw the ball 75 yards, but you must put enough zip on it to make the defense respect you. If they don't, the opposing defensive backs will eat your receivers alive."

Taking the criticism to heart, Starr created a personal workout regimen to increase his arm strength.

Three weeks after the season ended, on January 3, 1957, Starr was called to active duty in the United States Air Force, placing his professional football career in jeopardy.

Before he entertained the serious possibility of playing in the NFL, Starr had prepared for, and dreamed of, a life in the military. His ROTC commission left him with a military commitment to fulfill at some point, like a large number of professional athletes during the era. When he was called up and assigned to Eglin Air Force Base in Northwest Florida, "we thought he was going to be two years in the service, at least," Cherry said.

Service football was still a big part of the military in those days, so after pilot and former Georgia star Zeke Bratkowski returned to civilian life, the commander at Eglin needed a quarterback, and he pulled some strings to have Starr assigned to his base. But then he flunked his physical. The back problem that had caused him so much trouble in Tuscaloosa convinced the Air Force doctors that he was not physically fit for duty, and the commanding general refused to grant a waiver, leading to his discharge after a few months.

Ironically, Starr's bad back saved his pro football career.

The time in sunny Florida was not a total waste: By the time they headed north, Cherry was pregnant.

Back in Green Bay, Bart landed an off-season job selling tires. The Starrs became friends with Eddie Ginsberg, the owner of a local auto-salvage firm, and his wife, Louise, who had converted part of their attic into guest quarters, which included a tiny living room, bedroom, bathroom, and kitchen. It was a perfect space for Bart and Cherry, and they jumped at the chance to rent the cramped but reasonably priced apartment. "They were so generous," Cherry said. "We just loved it there."

The day before veterans reported to camp, Starr was standing on the first tee at Town and Country Golf Club, looking out at the short par four, holding his driver, waiting, along with Packers fullback Fred Cone, for Tobin Rote to tee off.

"Why are you hitting a two-iron?" Starr asked.

"I don't want to knock it over the green!"

Starr admired Rote's cockiness . . . and his athletic judgment.

Before he could hit the ball, Jack Vainisi, the boy wonder of the Green Bay front office, ran up to the green and told Rote, "You've just been traded to the Detroit Lions."

"Tobin was furious," Starr said. "I don't think I ever saw him so mad."

Rote threw his two-iron in the bag, grabbed his driver, and mashed a monster tee shot. The ball bounced off a house thirty yards past the green and landed up against a garden hose.

After the round, Rote packed his bags and moved to Detroit, where he would be forced to compete against Bobby Layne, one of the leading quarterbacks in the league.

The Packers also traded for onetime starting quarterback Babe Parilli, forcing Starr to battle his boyhood hero, the man who had tutored him during that formative summer in Lexington.

"It was awkward at first," Starr conceded.

Parilli, who had supplanted Otto Graham in Cleveland before suffering an injury, quickly put his former pupil at ease as both men contended vigorously for the starting position. "I never felt like we were competing," said Parilli, who wound up sharing the duties with Starr in 1957. "There was never any animosity between us."

Working with him on a daily basis six years after their first encounter, Parilli noticed very little different about him. "He seemed like the same young man," Parilli said. "Very mature, and he never made too many mistakes. I think that was his biggest asset: He didn't beat himself."

But Starr also was not able, at that point, to grab the Packers by the throat and lead them consistently to victories.

In a large organization with a complicated mesh of personalities, the man from Alabama became defined by his reserved personality. "He wouldn't say shit if he had a mouthful," said Packers defensive end John Martinkovic.

Everyone liked him, but some privately wondered if he was too nice, too timid to ever be a winning quarterback.

Liz Blackbourn, greatly influenced by Rams offensive mastermind Clark Shaughnessy, ran a complex system his quarterbacks struggled to master. "It was very convoluted," Starr said. "Too many numbers and formations to remember . . . which eats at your confidence after a while."

In various ways, Blackbourn appeared to be in over his head in the National Football League. Discipline gradually eroded. The previous season, Starr had watched Blackbourn send in a substitute, only to have Tobin Rote force the player off the field, reversing his head coach's decision in front of the team.

When Blackbourn walked up to John Martinkovic in the showers after a game and told him, without a hint of emotion, that he had been traded to the New York Giants, "They had to hold me back. I wanted to punch him."

"The guy had no business being a head coach in the NFL," said former Notre Dame star Paul Hornung, the 1956 Heisman Trophy winner, who brought his glowing celebrity to Green Bay after the Packers selected him as the bonus pick in the 1957 draft. "He was way out of his league. Then again, the whole organization was in pretty sorry shape."

After years of grumbling about their inadequate facilities, the Packers and the city of Green Bay floated $900,000 in bonds to build a modern 32,500-seat stadium on some farmland on the northern edge of town. The sparkling new bowl was a sight to behold, especially compared to the facility they were abandoning across town. On the opening Sunday of the season, with Vice President Richard Nixon presiding over the dedication of the new City Stadium—renamed Lambeau Field in 1965—the Packers upset the defending Western Conference champion Bears, 21–17.

The following Saturday, Cherry was rushed to the hospital with labor pains. Bart stayed with her all day and all night, pacing the floor, holding her hand, but still no baby. The next morning, the obstetrician advised Bart to go about his work, so he reluctantly went off to start his Sunday routine. He played poorly as the Lions beat the Packers 24–14, but his son, Bart Starr, Jr., was born that evening, and he would never forget the feeling of holding his child in his arms for the first time, or the look on his wife's face.

Soon after Bart Jr.'s arrival, the Ginsbergs knocked out another wall in their attic and built a room for the new baby.

In the autumn of 1957, the whole world held its breath in amazement—and fear—as the Soviet Union launched Sputnik, giving birth to the space age. Buddy Holly and the Crickets scored the first of their hits, "That'll Be the Day," as rock 'n' roll tightened its grip on youth culture. President Dwight Eisenhower, in the first year of his second term, reluctantly used federal troops to assist in the desegregation of a high school in Little Rock, Arkansas. After Bobby Layne broke his ankle, onetime Green quarterback Tobin Rote led the Lions to a 59–14 rout of Cleveland to capture the NFL championship.

And the Packers kept losing.

When Blackbourn was fired after a 3-9 season, his fourth straight loser, the Packers promoted one of his assistants, Ray "Scooter" McLean. Everyone liked Scooter—he often played poker with his Packers—but he was an inept leader who was unable to earn his players' respect.

"Scooter was a great guy but he just wasn't a head coach," said Packers tight end Gary Knafelc.

Stories circulated about players going over McLean's head, to members of the Packers' executive committee, and demanding playing time. The McLean regime featured very few rules—he actually created a curfew based upon the honor system—and as a result, discipline virtually disappeared as morale plummeted to a new low.

"The guys on that team didn't give a shit about anything," Paul Hornung said. "It was sad."

Despite some good young talent, the Packers' offense was horrible. Like Blackbourn, McLean ran a complex scheme and could not figure out how to utilize Hornung, a multitalented performer who was tried at several different positions. Starr and Parilli shared the quarterback job and proved equally unimpressive. Players were pulled in and out of games at McLean's whim, without any sort of rationale, as a dark mood descended across the entire team.

After three disappointing seasons in the league, Starr felt increasingly frustrated, miserable, lost.

"I lost confidence in my passing," Starr said. "I wasn't sure about the plays I called. Every time I was intercepted, it would kill me. It would have me worried the rest of the game."

McLean, a career assistant who never aspired to be a head coach, resigned after a 1-10-1 finish, the worst in Packers history, disappearing back into the anonymity of a staff job with the Lions.

More than ever, the Packers seemed like an anachronistic organization drifting aimlessly toward a dismal future.

The most humiliating loss of the most dreadful season came in week six, when the Baltimore Colts drilled the Packers, 56–0. The quarterback who led the assault had negotiated a road of rejection and hard luck even Starr could appreciate: Cut by his hometown Pittsburgh Steelers, he came to the attention of Colts head coach Weeb Eubank while working construction and playing for a semipro sandlot team. Johnny Unitas was one tough bird, and with a football in his arm, he was an artist.

Three days after Christmas, as the Green Bay Packers' governing board struggled about what to do with their coaching vacancy, a capacity crowd packed Yankee Stadium and a national television audience gathered around black-and-white sets connected to rabbit ears to watch the New York Giants and the Baltimore Colts battle for the 1958 NFL championship. Television had been part of the equation for nearly a decade, but when Johnny U led the Colts to a dramatic 23–17 victory over the Giants in sudden death overtime—culminated with Alan Ameche's one-yard plunge—professional football achieved a critical mass no one could have predicted. Forty-five million people—a staggering number for the day—watched the climactic finish, capturing the imagination of a wide swath of the American public, including many who had never paid much attention to professional football.

"There was such an electricity surrounding that game," remarked Chris Schenkel, the master of Midwestern understatement who called the action for CBS. "Suddenly, everyone was talking about the NFL . . . like they had just discovered it."

In years to come, historians would seize on the game as a defining moment in professional football's dramatic rise to prominence in American sport and culture. As counterintuitive as it seemed then, the timing of this awakening could not have been better for the lowly Green Bay Packers.

Like most of his teammates, Starr watched the game with a combination of awe and frustration. "I was very impressed with Unitas and was starting to study him very closely," he said. "You could not help being impressed with the way he led that football team." But he hated playing for a losing team, and even as he watched the landmark game, the Packers' ineptitude was never far from his thoughts. "We needed a leader."

Paying close attention to the game and its aftermath, former Green Bay mayor Dominic Olejniczak, president of the Packers board of directors, sought the counsel of various football people in his search for a new head coach. According to biographer David Maraniss, it was Jack Vainisi—the man responsible for bringing Bart Starr to Green Bay—who first contacted Vince Lombardi, the lead offensive assistant for the New York Giants. "I don't have the authority to make this call," Vainisi said, "but I'm curious to know whether you're interested." The confidential answer was in the affirmative, and while Olejniczak continued his search—which produced an awkward entreaty from team founder Curly Lambeau, who had retired to California after a dismal two-year run with the Chicago Cardinals—Vainisi began pushing for Lombardi. The intrigue of the next several weeks included a long list of better-known names, including University of Kentucky head coach Blanton Collier and University of Iowa head coach Forest Evashevski.

When Green Bay announced its choice on January 28, 1959, the consensus feeling among many fans was reflected in the reaction of board member John Torinus, who asked, in all apparent candor, "Who the hell is Vince Lombardi?"

For years, Paul Brown and many others across the league had looked down their noses at Green Bay, bathing the franchise in ridicule.

They did not know it yet, but the vocabulary of professional football was about to change.

FOUR

FOUR LITTLE WORDS

The first clue was sealed in his memory.

When Bart Starr picked up a copy of the *Green Bay Press-Gazette* on the morning after Vince Lombardi was introduced as the new head coach and general manager of the Green Bay Packers, the name did not immediately register. Like the vast majority of Green Bay fans, Starr knew little about his new boss beyond the most recent line on his résumé: offensive assistant for the New York Giants. But when he saw a photograph of Lombardi in the paper—his piercing eyes smiling through eyeglasses, exposing the gap between his two front teeth—something clicked in his mind.

The memory was still fresh and vivid: After leading the Packers to a touchdown in a preseason game against the Giants at Boston's Fenway Park in 1958, Starr was jogging off the field when he noticed a burly assistant coach with graying hair screaming "at the top of his lungs" toward the New York defense, castigating the unit for allowing the score. The man's intensity was hard to miss—even in a meaningless preseason game eventually won by the struggling Packers—and Starr was struck by the fact that an offensive coach could be so animated about the defense.

The face was unmistakable.

It was *him*, a realization that landed "like a lightning bolt."

When Starr suddenly realized the same figure who caught his eye in Boston was staring out from the front page of his morning paper, he knew the Green Bay Packers, burdened by the weight of eleven consecutive nonwinning seasons, by the accumulated gloom produced by all those years of futility, poor discipline, and low expectations, were in for a rude awakening.

Several weeks later, the new coach convened his quarterbacks and a few other offensive players for a three-hour meeting inside a classroom on the second floor of the Packers' headquarters, the first session of what amounted to a spring mini-camp.

"Good morning," he said, scanning the room where the athletes sat quietly in folding chairs. "I'm Vince Lombardi."

Nothing about the Packers would ever be the same.

From the first moments, Starr and his teammates could tell the new man was different, which was good because they desperately needed a large dose of different. His demeanor was direct, confident, cerebral, commanding. He never raised his voice. The way he spoke and comported himself reminded Starr of a military officer, and for a young man shaped in such a mold, this seemed like a very good sign.

"Immediately you had a strong feeling about the quality of the man," Starr said.

After Lombardi walked around the room handing out new playbooks and took up a position near the blackboard, chalk in hand, he said, "We're going to take a giant step backward, gentlemen."

The first milestone in the transformation was a dramatic simplification of the offense. As he asked the players to empty their sculls full of Scooter McLean's mush, they noticed that the new playbook was less than half the size of the old one. The point was clear: They were going to do a few things and do them all well.

In contrast to McLean's unnecessarily verbose wording, which often left his quarterbacks overwhelmed, Lombardi introduced a new play-calling terminology boiled down to two digits: one number for the formation, another for the hole. The new system transferred the calling of blocking assignments from the quarterback to the offensive linemen and gave the quarterback much greater latitude to react to the defense.

"This was such a radical change," Starr said. "He threw out all the crap. And you're thinking: Man, does this make sense or what?"

As he diagrammed several plays, Lombardi was able to manipulate the chalk without losing eye contact with his players, a little detail that impressed Starr.

Then, in what amounted to a verbal mission statement, he clarified the purpose of *his* Green Bay Packers.

"Gentlemen," he said, "we are going to relentlessly chase perfection . . . knowing full well that we won't catch it, because nobody is perfect . . ."

Starr was on the edge of his seat, soaking up the message like a sponge.

". . . but we're going to relentlessly chase it, because in the process, we will catch excellence."

Perfection.

Excellence.

The words tumbled in Starr's mind as Lombardi paused and moved closer, close enough to see the fire in his eyes. Starr would always remember the pause, the perfectly timed theatricality of it, the way it heightened the sense of anticipation pervading the room.

"I'm not remotely interested in being just good."

In a moment pregnant with possibility, gleaming with the sort of ambition the Packers had sorely lacked, the pulsating life force of Vince Lombardi reached deep inside Bart Starr and grabbed him in a way no one had ever grabbed him before. He was so fired up he wanted to stand up and cheer.

"We were all just blown away," he said. "It was so inspiring . . . such an exciting moment."

When they took a break for lunch, Starr rushed downstairs to a pay phone and placed a long-distance call to Cherry at their off-season home in Birmingham. "Honey," he said excitedly, "we're going to begin to win."

In his insightful biography of Lombardi, *When Pride Still Mattered*, David Maraniss wrote that Lombardi's arrival in Green Bay "completed a cycle of football mythology." Indeed, the hiring seemed connected to a sweeping parade of giants: Curly Lambeau started it all by playing for Knute Rockne at Notre Dame, then returning home to Green Bay to launch the Packers and coach at Green Bay East High School—where one of his greatest players was "Sleepy Jim" Crowley, who subsequently went off to Notre Dame to play for Rockne, becoming one of the famed Four Horsemen of the 1920s—before moving into coaching himself, including a stint at Fordham, where one of his greatest pupils was Vince Lombardi, who was clearly influenced by the Green Bay bloodline long before he ever aspired to coach the Packers.

Beneath the surface lay another connective tissue linking Lombardi, Rockne, and the man who wanted to be his quarterback: Paul "Bear" Bryant, who tried to lure Starr to Kentucky by providing Babe Parilli as his tutor, was coached at Alabama by Frank Thomas, who played for Rockne at Notre Dame, where he was the roommate of George Gipp of "win one for the Gipper" fame.

Who needs Kevin Bacon when you can play *Six Degrees of Knute Rockne*?

Born to Italian immigrants in 1913, the same year as Bear Bryant and Woody Hayes, the year that unknown Notre Dame upset powerful Army and ushered in the age of the forward pass, Vincent Thomas Lombardi grew up in the vibrant and ethnically diverse Sheepshead Bay section of Brooklyn, the eldest son of a meat-shop owner. Like Starr, Lombardi was greatly influenced by his father's overarching sense of discipline, although his happy upbringing in the great melting pot of middle-class New York lacked the pathos that defined Starr's youth. Like his mother, he was a devout Catholic who attended Mass every day and tended to view the world through the prism of right and wrong, forever determined to position himself at the foot of the cross.

About the time Starr was learning to walk, Lombardi cracked the starting lineup as a five-foot-eight, 183-pound guard for Fordham, then a college football power that routinely attracted large crowds and generated frenzied, often romanticized coverage from the New York press. During the heyday of the Fordham Rams, when the home of Broadway and the Yankees was known more for college football than the pro game, Lombardi gained a measure of fame as a member of the mighty Seven Blocks of Granite, even though previous and subsequent units actually proved more impenetrable, won more games, and, therefore, seemed more deserving of the formidable title.

The philosophy underpinning Lombardi's approach to the game began to take shape during his days at Fordham, when, like his teammates, he struggled to fight through pain and exhaustion not just because he loved playing, but also because he felt a sense of obligation to give his all. In later years, when he often told his players "Fatigue makes cowards of us all," they knew he was speaking from personal experience.

As a young man, Lombardi was never defined by the game, at least not in the way so many high achieving athletes seemed to be. "The importance of Fordham in Lombardi's life was far greater than learning what it took to play a game," Maraniss asserted. "From the Jesuits he acquired a larger perspective: duty, obedience, responsibility, and the exercise of free will were the basis of a philosophy that shaped the way he looked at himself and his world."

He began his professional life as a notoriously demanding Catholic-school teacher of physics, chemistry, and Latin, who found his calling on the football field, first as an assistant, then as head coach, winning four parochial school state championships. Even as he transitioned into the life of a full-time assistant coach with Fordham, the United States Military Academy, and the New York Giants, he remained a teacher at heart. In the laboratory of the classroom, he developed a knack for reducing even the most complex subjects to their most basic elements so they could be more easily understood, a skill that would serve him well on the football field. Like all good teachers, he reveled in the joy of watching young people struggle and persevere until they finally got it, especially students with modest abilities who learned they could compensate—and even outshine more talented but less motivated peers—by unleashing the critical link between desire and achievement.

His greatest pupil, the man who was destined to become the foremost conduit for his particular genius, awaited him in Green Bay.

Bart Starr needed Vince Lombardi, but Vince Lombardi also needed Bart Starr.

Before they could make history together, they needed to test each other. And in time, the teacher would be forced to learn a valuable lesson from the student.

Like Starr, Lombardi admired the military and was shaped by its culture and value system. He idolized General Douglas MacArthur, relished the opportunities he had to brief him on the progress of the Army football team, and carefully studied his leadership style. When he arrived at West Point in 1949, the Cadets, led by the brilliant coaching of Colonel Earl "Red" Blaik, remained one of the most powerful football programs in the land. Behind the dynamic running duo of Doc Blanchard and Glenn Davis—"Mr. Inside" and "Mr. Outside," respectively—Army stormed to consecutive national championships in 1944–45. Then came a near miss in '46, when 74,121 fans packed Yankee Stadium to watch Frank Leahy's

No. 2–ranked Notre Dame Fighting Irish battle the No. 1–ranked Cadets to a memorable 0–0 tie, preventing Army from becoming the first team in college history to win a third consecutive national title. The cheating scandal that shook the very foundations of the honor-bound academy in 1951 decimated the football program, and although Lombardi helped Blaik rebuild, Army football would never be quite the same. Profoundly influenced by his five years on Blaik's staff—eventually becoming the colonel's most senior and trusted aide—Lombardi coopted many of his mentor's methods, especially with regard to discipline, organization, film study, intolerance of mistakes, and what Maraniss called "the meaning of football itself," a concept destined to loom large in the shaping of the Lombardi legend.

Frustrated by his inability to land a head coaching position, Lombardi was lured to the struggling Giants in 1954, becoming one spoke in the most unusual triumverate in the history of the National Football League. Head coach Jim Lee Howell was a distant figure who delegated almost complete defensive authority to Tom Landry, a young Texan who seemed mature beyond his years, and similar control of the offense to Lombardi, who was middle-aged, ambitious, and impatient. Somehow, it worked. Lombardi's powerful offense, built around Frank Gifford, one of the most explosive halfbacks of the era, moved the chains with remarkable efficiency, turning heads throughout the league. (Even Paul Brown noticed: The man who uttered "Green Bay" like a curse word, later recommended Lombardi to the Packers' administration.) When the Giants captured the NFL championship in 1956 and lost the epic sudden death game in 1958, few football fans knew the names of Lombardi and Landry. But Howell could not shroud their talents for long; the year after Lombardi left for Green Bay—under the condition that Giants owner Wellington Mara, a close friend and mentor, could try to entice him back, when the top job became available—Landry became the first head coach of the expansion Dallas Cowboys.

When he arrived in Green Bay in the dead of winter in 1959, with the snow piling high and the temperature frequently plunging well below zero, far removed from New York and all of the familiar trappings of his life, forty-five-year-old Lombardi began to assess the hand he had been dealt. To his surprise, the Packers were filled with talented young players, thanks largely to the heretofore unrecognized efforts of Jack Vainisi, the Notre Dame man who had first approached him about taking the job and who would one day be credited with acquiring seven future inductees into the Pro Football Hall of Fame and various others who contributed to the Packers' dominance. When the thirty-three-year-old Vainisi died suddenly of a heart ailment in 1960, slumped over in the bathroom of his home, just as the curtain was rising on the new era, he remained an obscure figure. But Bart Starr would never forget what he did for him: Vainisi gave him a chance, believing in him when practically no one else in the world thought he could make it in pro football.

The cast of characters already on the Packers' payroll included receiver Max McGee; offensive linemen Forrest Gregg, Jerry Kramer, and Jim Ringo; running back Jim Taylor; linebackers Ray Nitschke and Dan Currie; defensive tackle Dave "Hawg" Hanner; and multitalented Paul Hornung, who had been so poorly utilized by the previous staff that he was considering giving up football to go full-time into the real estate business.

"I was so frustrated . . . ready to quit," Hornung said. "Sure didn't want to be part of another losing team that didn't have any pride."

As he began studying film from the 1958 season, Lombardi decided that Hornung, a strong and determined runner who reminded him of Frank Gifford, was the key to his offense. In a phone call to the former Notre Dame star, he was blunt: "You're either going to be my left halfback or you're going to be out of football."

"Right away, I liked his confidence, the way he laid it on the line," Hornung said. "He talked about winning and was very convincing. That was the kind of coach I wanted. All of the sudden I was excited about playing football again."

By saving Hornung's football career, Lombardi unwittingly intertwined his future with Bart Starr, even as he became convinced, after watching more film, that Starr was not capable of becoming a winning quarterback in the NFL.

This conclusion was understandable considering Starr's poor performance during the disastrous 1958 season: He completed a career-low 49.7 percent of his passes for 875 yards, tossing 12 interceptions and just 3 touchdowns. With Starr and Babe Parilli alternating, the Packers averaged a paltry 16 points per game.

In fact, during his first three years in the league, Starr's statistics looked like those of a man who might soon be selling tires the year round: During the miserable Blackbourn and McLean days, he completed 219 of 416 passes for 2,689 yards, 13 touchdowns, and 25 interceptions, offering no hint of the greatness that loomed in his future.

After assessing the whole team, he told reporters, "The first thing I need is help at quarterback," which landed with a thud at Starr's feet.

"Under the circumstances, I couldn't blame Coach Lombardi for doubting me," Starr conceded.

As he negotiated several trades and moved players around the field, searching for the right winning formula for the 1959 season and beyond, Lombardi called flanker Gary Knafelc aside and told him he was moving to tight end.

"Coach," Knafelc said, "I haven't hit anybody in five years."

He was joking, but Lombardi was dead serious and flashed an irritated look before saying, "Where would you like to go?"

Knafelc swallowed hard.

Not wanting to wind up like receiver Bill Howton—who had been banished to Cleveland, after a tense closed-door meeting with Lombardi—Knafelc, who had just bought his first home in Green Bay, suddenly warmed up to the position change, becoming a mainstay at tight end, where he proved very adept at hitting people and catching passes.

"We all learned very quickly that Coach Lombardi was no Scooter McLean," Knafelc said.

Traded from the defending NFL champion Colts to the Packers heading into training camp, Fuzzy Thurston drove through the night from Baltimore to Wisconsin, stopping in Madison for an evening to see his wife and newborn baby before continuing his journey north. When he walked in to the locker room and introduced himself to his new coach, Lombardi snapped, "I know who you are! You were due in here yesterday! Where the hell were you?"

Dealt to a rigorously demanding universe defined by the enormous expectations of Vince Lombardi—"a notably direct man who professes a dislike for subtleties," in the words of *Sports Illustrated*'s Tex Maule—Thurston quickly learned to speak the native language. "Coach Lombardi was a very driven individual . . . if you wanted to survive in his world, you had better be prepared to come to work on time, work your butt off, and be able to take a certain amount of abuse," he said.

Like all his teammates, Thurston adapted to the meaning of Lombardi time: Sometimes, meetings started *before* their appointed time, and no one wanted to be late. Showing up on time was a symbol of commitment to the larger cause and no one wanted to send the wrong signal to the boss. "I learned the message that first day," Thurston said. "All these years later, I'm always twenty minutes early for whatever I do."

During his initial meeting with the entire team on the first day of training camp at St. Norbert College, Lombardi expanded on the theme he first broached with the small offensive group: He was there to make the Green Bay Packers the greatest team in professional football—admired, emulated, feared—and anyone who was not prepared to be relentless in the pursuit of victory could head for the exit.

The process of transforming the culture of the Packers started with a renewed focus on discipline, which included a strict adherence to curfew and other rules, such as a dress code for road trips, because Green Bay was going to be first-class all the way, in look and deed. The new man made it clear that he was going to be in their face on the practice field, pushing them to push themselves, to play and act like champions, and he would not be shuffling cards and boozing with them into the wee hours. Because he was not their buddy.

Inspired by the message, Starr could not escape the irony that the very ambition that fired him up and renewed his sense of purpose was now endangering his job.

After Lombardi acquired Chicago Cardinals veteran Lamar McHan during the off-season and named him the Green Bay starter, Starr found himself competing with Parilli and Joe Francis, a onetime single wing tailback who had been drafted out of Oregon State in 1958, for the two remaining quarterback slots on the roster. When Starr, fighting for his professional life, threw an interception in the first scrimmage of the year, he was introduced to Lombardi's volatile temper. "One more like that," he yelled, "and you're through!"

Long before Vince Lombardi emerged as an American archetype, as closely connected to professional football as John Wayne would forever be to westerns, he began rebuilding the Packers with an unusual combination of inspiration and fear.

Even casual football fans would become aware of his most famous quotation: "Winning isn't everything; it's the only thing."

Through the years, as his legend grew, this one particular phrase was embraced by a long line of coaches and players who saw it as the ultimate expression of surging ambition in a zero-sum game; and scorned by many others, mostly far removed from the sport, who believed it reflected a dangerous win-at-all-costs mentality.

Looking back on the relationship that shaped his life, Starr expressed the belief, echoed by several of his teammates, that Lombardi's most ubiquitous pronouncement has always been misunderstood. "He meant *the will to win* is the only thing," Starr insisted. "He was talking about making the effort to win, because he believed making the effort was the key. If you did that, the winning would eventually take care of itself."

In Starr, Lombardi found a man completely receptive to—and, in fact, hungry for—the message inherent in this and many other soon-to-be familiar phrases.

After the painful experience of his senior year at Alabama and the aimlessness of the Blackbourn and McLean years in Green Bay, Lombardi's forcefulness and sense of purpose reinvigorated Starr.

Like his coach, Starr believed football was a sport in which success was closely connected to desire, effort, and persistence, making the game a mirror of life itself. He was eager to buy into a rigidly disciplined system because he was a rigidly disciplined young man who did not have to be sold on the transformative power of hard work, consistency, and diligence.

Lombardi's combination of intellect and bombast proved to be the perfect catalyst necessary to reveal and develop Starr's hidden legend.

In the years ahead, even as Lombardi's practice field rants caused every man on the roster to simultaneously cringe and reach, his ability to teach life lessons in the framework of football touched a powerful nerve with his quarterback.

Winning is not a sometime thing.

Leave no regrets on the field.

Teamwork is the primary ingredient of success.

The harder you work, the harder it is to surrender.

The greatest glory is being knocked to your knees and then rising again.

In time, the quarterback would be able to recite such verities in his sleep, investing in each the belief that the powerful intangible of attitude could be harnessed to enormous effect in the cause of building a winning team.

With each passing year, Starr would grow closer still to Lombardi—until the man seemed less like a coach and more like a second father figure.

Like many of Lombardi's old Latin students, Starr needed to be coached. But in the early weeks of their relationship, as he watched him move around in the pocket and struggle to implement his new system, Lombardi saw nothing to alter his original, film-based assessment.

"Lombardi didn't think Bart was good enough or tough enough to be his quarterback," said offensive tackle Forrest Gregg.

Convinced that Lamar McHan could lead him to the promised land, Lombardi pushed Starr to the margin during training camp. Anyone could see McHan had a stronger arm and was more mobile. He was also more polished, confident, and assertive than Starr, who seemed tentative and mistake-prone. Starr kept his job when veteran Babe Parilli was cut, but would always believe his survival was closely linked to his age, and he was probably right, because Parilli, four years older, was clearly past his prime.

"Bart didn't fit the mold Lombardi wanted in his quarterback," said tight end Gary Knafelc, who became one of his closest friends on the team. "He really didn't take Bart seriously."

When Lombardi asked his staff to evaluate each player on the squad, all expressed doubts about Starr as the starting quarterback. "I do not believe we can win with him," one insisted. "Not a consistent passer or a take-charge type of player."

While the playbook was significantly scaled down, the new offense required the quarterback to read the defense to a much greater degree, to be much more proactive in adjusting to the coverage. With each passing day, Starr worked relentlessly to master his keys even as he focused on improving his mechanics. To be the sort of quarterback Lombardi wanted him to be, he needed to learn how to think like his coach, to become his alter ego on the field, and to react in the blink of an eye to what he was seeing, applying his knowledge to the situation like a bolt a lightning before the conditions changed. This was an intricate, multilayered process that equated to mastering a new language. It would take time.

With McHan leading the way, fullback Jim Taylor hitting his stride, halfback Paul Hornung making one big play after another, and the defense displaying a new ferocity, the Packers won their first three games—their best start since the championship season of 1944—before losing the next five, including a 20–3 road defeat at the hands of Lombardi's old team, the New York Giants. When McHan, hobbled by an injury, struggled and was pulled out of the game, Starr thought, *This was going to be my big chance . . . I had worked real hard all week and thought I had everything down cold.* But Lombardi inserted Joe Francis instead, leaving Starr standing on the sideline, fearing that his professional football career might be slipping away. "It was the first time in my life I really felt sorry for myself," he said.

On a team filled with party animals, especially playboy running buddies Paul Hornung and Max McGee (who left a string of broken hearts and swizzle sticks from Los Angeles to New York), and accomplished drinkers like Fuzzy Thurston and wannabes like Dan Currie (who once challenged Thurston to a martini-drinking contest and wound up sprawled on the floor of some high-brow establishment in San Francisco), Bart Starr, devout Christian, seemed a little dull. Teammates rarely saw him consume more than one beer or glass of wine, probably because he always felt an obligation to be in complete control. This need to restrain himself, to always set a good example, was a big part of his sense of self. But after Lombardi refused to use him against the Giants, Starr went out on the town with tight end Ron Kramer, another future All-Pro who was also underachieving, and, the frustration eating at him, began drowning his sorrows, apparently consuming a total of four beers. "The only thing I do remember about that night is that it was the first and only time in my life that I have been drunk," he said.

Drunk?

Bart Starr?

Reminded of the story, Thurston, who spent the better part of a decade protecting Starr and growing to love him like a brother, laughed heartily and said, "Four beers! Oh my! Can you get drunk on four beers?"

The very competitiveness that caused Starr to temporarily give in to his frustrations also motivated him to keep working hard, and in time, his dedication began to pay off.

When McHan suffered injuries to his shoulder and leg, the choice between Francis and Starr was difficult, a matter of significant debate among fans and media. Art Daley, who covered the Packers for the *Green Bay Press-Gazette*, wrote, "The club doesn't really have a No. 2 quarterback but Francis is a better athlete than Starr." When Francis proved ineffective, Lombardi, more out of desperation than faith, turned to Starr, who started the last five games and led the Packers to four straight victories and a 7-5 finish—Green Bay's first winning season since 1947. During the winning streak, Starr completed an impressive 52 of 79 passes for 699 yards, and 6 touchdowns.

"You could see Bart slowly gaining confidence," said offensive tackle Forrest Gregg.

The breakthrough came on the road in the season finale against the San Francisco 49ers, when everything started to click as he led the Packers to a 36–14 rout. For weeks, Starr could feel his confidence gathering as he became increasingly comfortable with the offense, as the accumulation of Lombardi's teaching began to congeal in his mind. "Suddenly, it seemed like everything was in slow motion," he said.

When friend and landlord Eddie Ginsberg died suddenly, his widow Louise called Bart and Cherry in Birmingham with the offer of an off-season job. After his fourth season in professional football, Bart was earning slightly more than $10,000 from the Packers and working in the insurance business on the side. The job overseeing the renovation and leasing of an office building in downtown Green Bay, which Ginsberg had started but failed to see completed, was a perfect fit for the meticulous and dutiful Starr, who was determined to do right by his deceased friend and reduce Louise's worries. The Starrs opened a tiny restaurant on the first floor of what they christened the Edlo Arcade Building, where the quarterback's beautiful and charming wife sold egg salad sandwiches, soups, and other prepared foods.

Like many middle-class couples of the day, the Starrs felt a significant achievement when they were able to purchase their first home, a modest but comfortable three-bedroom house with a big basement, located on a quiet street less than a mile from Lambeau Field. The purchase price was $21,500, which seemed like an awful lot of money. "We didn't know if we could afford that or not," Cherry said. It was a milestone event in their lives because it was something they had earned after years of sacrifice and struggle, and they would never forget the feeling it stirred. Long before prominent athletes were showered with multimillion-dollar contracts right out of college, providing a life of immediate luxury, indulgence, and disconnection from the general population, the Starrs were deeply embedded in the larger culture of hard work, striving and traditional American values.

Embracing the life of devoted husband and father, Starr became the consummate family man. His relationship with Cherry was incredibly close and loving. During their first year of marriage, he started a ritual of leaving a little note on her pillow most every night—"the sweetest little messages," she said—a habit he would continue for the entirety of their marriage. He never failed to open the door for her, and when the situation permitted, he called her on the phone several times a day, just to hear the sound of her voice.

"Bart is the kindest person I have ever known," Cherry said.

Like many others, it was difficult for Lombardi to reconcile the image of a man of such kindness, a man so polite, so nice, with the requirements of an NFL quarterback. Starr never whined or complained, but Cherry could see the difficult time he was having while trying to establish himself during Lombardi's first year. "It was pretty clear Coach Lombardi didn't believe in Bart in the beginning," she said. Cherry made a good home for him and when few others recognized his potential, she believed in him, fortifying his confidence in himself.

Unconditional love can be a powerful force, especially for a man who negotiated adolescence while interpreting his father's mixed signals.

Bart Jr. was a precocious three-year-old when they moved into the new house. While Bart adopted his old man's sense of discipline, he endeavored to be a different sort of father. Theirs was a happy home full of laughter and togetherness. Never for a moment did Bart's sons ever doubt his love or fail to receive his unwavering support.

Ben and Lulu often drove up from Birmingham, especially for big games, but especially after the birth of their first son, Bart and Cherry began to notice a change in the Master Sergeant. Sometimes Ben acted like a totally different person; with his grandson in his arms, filling up his world, he could absolutely melt.

At some point, Ben Starr decided there was something he needed to say, but he was not quite ready. Not just yet.

In the warm afterglow of the 1958 championship game, the National Football League roared into an exciting new era enabled by television.

The first man to truly appreciate the potential of the medium as a revolutionizing force on the business of professional football was an aristocrat from Philadelphia who once owned the Eagles, partied with movie stars, and somehow squandered an enormous inheritance from his father, the former attorney general of Pennsylvania. His name was De Benneville Bell, but everyone called him "Bert." Bell, who played quarterback at the University of Pennsylvania around the time of World War I, eventually was forced to sell the Eagles. Appointed the NFL commissioner in 1945, he ran the league out of his Philadelphia home.

Like the leaders of professional baseball and college football, the NFL owners saw television as a threat because it manufactured an unlimited number of free tickets, causing untold thousands of paying customers to stay home and save their money. When the powerful Rams televised their entire home slate in 1950, just as the television craze reached critical mass in Los Angeles, attendance plummeted by nearly 50 percent, producing a cascade of red ink. Bell mitigated this problem by instituting a blackout rule—eventually protected by the federal courts—which prevented the telecasting of home games. Predictably, attendance stabilized and started to climb. The struggling, doomed DuMont Network, which aggressively pursued sports programming in the early 1950s, was the first to recognize the potential of professional football, starting with the Rams' thrilling 24–17 victory over the Browns in the 1951 league championship game, the first to appear on national television. After the demise of DuMont, the championship game moved to NBC, but throughout the television explosion of the fifties, the various clubs negotiated their own deals with local affiliates and ad hoc regional networks, a haphazard system that prevented any sort of consistency and exacerbated the financial disparities between the strong and weak franchises. In 1953, while the Rams reportedly earned about $100,000 for the rights to televise their away games, the Packers, located in the league's smallest television market, pocketed about $5,000, adding to their financial woes, making it even tougher for little David to compete with all those Goliaths.

After hearing about a radical proposal to share Major League Baseball's television revenue floated by St. Louis Browns owner Bill Veeck—who was branded "a damned Communist" by Dodgers owner Walter O'Malley—Bell became intrigued with the idea and began pushing for a single NFL television package in which all franchises divided the revenue equally. Like the draft, he saw such a plan as a way to enhance the league's stability by reducing the competitive gulf between the haves and have-nots, but the owners repeatedly rebuffed him.

The magic of the 1958 title game significantly enhanced professional football's leverage with the networks, but it took the sudden death of Bell—from a heart attack, while watching an Eagles game at Franklin Field in 1959—and the birth of the rival American Football League to push the NFL toward its future.

Especially after Johnny U's climactic winning drive set the nation's heart atwitter, the pressure from outside the league to expand started to mount, but several potential owners were politely told to go away, keep their money, and mind their own business. The old guard was not interested in adding franchises. To George Halas, George Preston Marshall, and Art Rooney, a dozen teams was plenty. Who needed Kansas City or Denver? This recalcitrance provided an opening, and a group led by Texas oilman Lamar Hunt, the son of one of the richest men in the world, formed the AFL, which announced plans to launch in 1960, featuring teams in Boston, Buffalo, Dallas, Denver, Houston, Los Angeles, Oakland, and New York. The difference between the old AAFC and the new AFL could be condensed to one word: television. The leaders of the new league still had a lot to learn about professional football, but when they signed a five-year, $8.5-million contract with ABC, the struggling No. 3 network, the weight of all the associated revenue, promotional value, and credibility instantly transformed the AFL into a serious competitor for the hearts, minds, and wallets of football fans all across America.

Fortunately for the NFL, the owners replaced Bell with a man of singular vision who understood the power of television. Pete Rozelle, who started his career as a publicity man for the Rams, was the surprise, compromise choice for the new commissioner in January 1960, weeks after the AFL's first draft and weeks before the rival league's blockbuster television deal hit the papers. Affable, intelligent, and savvy, Rozelle would become the most influential man in the history of professional football, deftly negotiating a series of minefields while transforming the NFL into the country's most popular sporting attraction by harnessing television's unique and consolidating hold on the American public.

Like Bell before him, he could see the destructive force of a system that allowed free market forces to drive a financial wedge between the various franchises, how the disparity between the 1960 television revenue of the Giants ($350,000) and the Packers ($75,000) threatened the whole league's strength—especially at a time when every single AFL team was guaranteed a six-figure paycheck from ABC. Despite heated opposition, Rozelle leveraged all of his significant charm and salesmanship to convince the owners to pursue a unified television deal and to pool the revenue equally.

After negotiating a two-year, $4.6-million deal with CBS in 1961, Rozelle drew a flag from U.S. District Court Judge Allan K. Grim, who ruled the NFL's actions a violation of his landmark 1953 television judgment. Long before Rozelle entered the scene, when the major sports leagues and the National Collegiate Athletic Association struggled to develop sensible television policies without decimating ticket sales, the Grim decision had allowed the NFL to pursue a black-out policy as a tactic to protect home attendance—but only in the narrowest terms. Grim's decision did not grant the NFL carte blanche against the federal antitrust laws. When the matter of the NFL's new league-wide deal—featuring what some legal scholars interpreted as an illegal cartel—came before him eight years later, his judicial whistle stopped the new commissioner cold, rendering all his intense lobbying moot and threatening his ambitious plans.

Undeterred, Rozelle took his case to Congress; fought for and won a special antitrust exemption, which allowed him wide latitude to sell a league-wide plan; and signed a new contract with CBS for the same terms.

The deal paved the way for a new era in the NFL, a new era when television would become an active partner in selling the NFL to the American public—selling it like soap, beer, and automobiles, selling the sizzle, drama, blood, sweat, heartbreak, and untrammeled joy of all those

Sundays punctuated by bodies colliding in the mud and balls soaring like bullets toward outstretched hands streaking for six.

It may have even prevented the ultimate demise of the Green Bay Packers.

One of the reasons Rozelle was able to sell the deal to those who had the most to lose from it was by suggesting that, if the trend was allowed to continue, small-market teams such as the Packers might reach a point where they could no longer compete. Instead, the new system leveled the playing field; by the late '60s, the Packers would be earning more than $1 million per year from the league-wide television deal, a revenue stream that allowed the team to reach solid financial footing for the first time in its history while mitigating the various other advantages wielded by the big city teams.

The timing of all this could not have been better for Green Bay, because just as the NFL learned how to use television, just as television learned how to use the NFL, the Packers bolted out of the shadows, led by an unlikely young man from Alabama who reflected something profound about the game and the American experience.

As the country turned a page and looked toward the sixties, eager for new heroes, Bart Starr and the Packers were ready for their close-up.

"Damn you, Starr!"

The scream thundered across the practice field.

Infuriated by an interception thrown during a training camp scrimmage, Lombardi began belittling the quarterback mercilessly in front of the entire team.

"Throw it away! Eat it! Do anything! But not a turnover!"

Starr took the tongue-lashing without saying a word, even though the ball was tipped by a defender before being picked off.

By the summer of 1960, every member of the Green Bay organization was well acquainted with Lombardi's volatile temper. He was a tough, intimidating, often abusive figure who scared the hell out of his players, and they knew better than to cross him. He deftly used the fear he cultivated to great effect. "Some days," guard Fuzzy Thurston said, "I just hated him."

Every day, before heading to his office, Lombardi attended Mass, causing Packers defender Henry Jordan to quip, "If you'd ever heard him chew our asses out, you would know why he had to be in church every morning!" (Jordan was the same jokester who once insisted, "Lombardi treats us all the same: Like dogs!")

In explaining his philosophy, Lombardi said: "Men want to follow . . . it gives them security to know there is someone who cares enough to chew them out a little bit or to correct their mistakes."

Like many coaches, Lombardi believed athletes performed at their peak under the exertion of maximum pressure, but he also understood not all individuals respond to the same methods. Leadership takes many forms, some far removed from—and, in fact, neutralized by—a fiery coach screaming at the top of his lungs, the threat of implied doom dangling in the breeze. Gradually, he learned which Packers needed to be pushed and which should be left alone. "He was on my ass all the time, because he knew I needed it and because he knew I could take it," Paul Hornung said.

Starr, perhaps the most self-motivated of all the Packers, could take the abuse, but he was also very sensitive to the psychology of the game. Because he was a quarterback who needed to cultivate the confidence of his teammates, he became increasingly concerned that Lombardi's frequent outbursts were undermining his ability to effectively lead, so after practice he went to see his coach in his office and closed the door.

"Coach, I've been with you a year now, working my butt off to be the leader you demand . . ."

His tone was respectful but firm, commanding Lombardi's full attention.

"That ball was tipped. It wasn't a clean interception . . ."

"You're right."

Surprised by the concession, Starr plowed upfield, determined to move the chains.

"Coach, if you're going to blister me in front of the team, at least have the guts to apologize in their presence as well. I want them to know I have your respect."

The coach was shocked. Beyond the limitations of his relatively unimpressive arm and the learning curve he experienced in mastering the new offense, Lombardi had been disturbed by Starr's lack of assertiveness, which he interpreted as a weakness in his leadership style. Part of this no doubt derived from his polite, well-mannered way off the field, which caused Lombardi to question his ability to be a cut-throat force between the white lines.

But now . . .

Now the low-key young man was sticking up for himself.

Instead of resisting the challenge, Lombardi accepted it as a sign of the quarterback's maturation.

"Okay," Lombardi said.

By displaying confidence in himself, Starr gave Lombardi a reason to have more confidence in him.

Starr called the moment a real turning point.

"I think Coach Lombardi was very impressed that I would come to him in such a manner and force the issue," he said.

Lombardi also knew Starr was right, because it was crucial for the rest of the team to see the quarterback as an extension of himself on the field. Rarely would the coach ever yell at him in front of the team again. If he needed to correct Starr, he would call the player into his office and handle the matter privately.

Word of the act quickly spread across the team, causing some who were still straddling the fence about to Starr to develop new appreciation for his leadership skills.

As the 1960 season began amid great expectations, the Green Bay defense was bolstered by two key acquisitions: free agent safety Willie Wood, a onetime Southern Cal quarterback, and former Cleveland tackle Henry Jordan. All of the pieces were coming together, including the emergence of 1959 third-round draft pick Boyd Dowler as an explosive and steady receiver. Starr was still battling McHan for the starting quarterback job, a competition that the former Cardinals star resented.

"Lamar didn't hate Bart as a person. It was impossible to hate him as a person. But he loathed him as a football player," Hornung said. "He was very bitter . . . just couldn't believe Lombardi would even consider playing Bart over him, because he was convinced he was so much better."

Despite McHan's more impressive natural talents, the studious, always well-prepared Starr, who put in long hours in front of a projector and always took copious notes in meetings, made it a race by proving more productive and making fewer mistakes than the former Arkansas All-American. He won the starting nod for the season opener, but after an unimpressive outing in the Packers' 17–14 loss to the Bears, Lombardi turned back to McHan, who led Green Bay to three straight victories, including a 35–21 upset of the defending NFL champion Colts.

Toward the end of the first half in a game against the Steelers at Forbes Field, with the Packers leading 12–7 on the strength of his four field goals, Hornung walked back to the huddle and collared McHan.

"I can get open on the fly outside," he said.

The outside fly pattern, known internally as "39," created a one-on-one situation that played to Hornung's strengths if he could beat the linebacker and if the throw was made on time.

When the ball was snapped and McHan started his drop, the Golden Boy ran a perfect route, slipping past the linebacker and into the open.

"He put a beautiful pass right on the money . . . and I dropped it," Hornung said. "I mean it was six points! It went right through my hands."

McHan was livid. It was not the first pass one of his receivers had dropped, but it was the most costly.

Frustrated by McHan's inability to punch the ball into the end zone, Lombardi started Starr in the second half. Seizing the opportunity, he played the entire half and was impressive, leading the Packers on one long touchdown drive as Green Bay scored a 19–13 victory.

"That's the day I *made* Bart Starr," Hornung said with a laugh nearly a half century later. "I still kid Bart: *You owe me, baby!* If I hadn't dropped that pass, Lamar starts the second half and maybe he becomes the quarterback who leads us to all those titles."

In describing Starr's methodical progress, Lombardi subsequently talked about him slowly growing in "stature" and "confidence," but perhaps more than anything else, he proved more poised than the hotheaded McHan—on and off the field.

On the airplane ride back to Green Bay, McHan, irate over being pulled out of the game, drank just enough to lead him down a troubled path. During a postgame team meal at a local restaurant, as the quarterbacks and a few others ate dinner in the back room with the coaches, McHan confronted Lombardi loudly, used an ethnic slur, and stormed out.

On his way out the front door, he spotted tight end Gary Knafelc, one of Starr's best friends, and yelled in his direction. "Why don't you go back there and eat with your girlfriend!"

Soon, McHan was nothing more than a memory—benched and then traded—and Starr began his twelve-year run as the Packers' starting quarterback.

Beyond the obvious implication that Lombardi could not tolerate a player—especially a quarterback—who cussed him and challenged his authority in front of the team, he saw McHan's emotional behavior as a significant weakness. In an oblique reference to the situation several years years later, Lombardi said, "Your quarterback has to be stable . . . and Bart is that." Starr never lost his cool, which was one reason the team responded better to his leadership. In contrast to his early years with the Packers, when one errant pass bothered him to the point of distraction, he was developing a powerful sense of mental toughness that belied his nice-guy image, fortified by Lombardi's newfound faith in him.

"This does a lot for a person," Starr explained, "to know that someone has the confidence to gamble on you. Believe me, that year I had nothing on my mind except justifying his decision."

In the first quarter of a late-season game against the Bears, middle linebacker Bill George broke through the Packers' line with a full head of steam and slammed into Starr. His flying elbow caught the quarterback's lip, which began spewing blood as Starr tumbled to the ground.

The Bears' game plan was familiar and sound football: Get to the still-green quarterback, rattle him, put him on his back, make him expend precious mental energy thinking about your next visit.

Looking down at his bloody victim, George began taunting him.

Climbing off the grass with a determined look, Starr got right in the mammoth defender's face.

And cussed him.

Tackle Forrest Gregg might not have believed it if he had not witnessed it with his own eyes and ears. "Bart didn't talk like that. It was so out of character."

No one, especially George, expected such a forceful reaction from such a quiet man. Like many people, he had underestimated Starr's toughness; he thought he could get into the quarterback's head by mangling his body, but every time he was knocked down, Starr pulled himself off the ground and methodically went back to work.

Is that all you got?

Poise and toughness could be a lethal combination, and Starr was learning to flex both muscles.

All day long, the fearsome Bears defense kept chasing Starr but he coolly stuck in the pocket, made some pinpoint throws for big yardage, and took the punishment as the Packers crushed the hated Bears, 41–13. The way Starr handled the pressure convinced all who saw it that the seemingly meek and mild quarterback was one tough customer.

With the increasingly confident Starr leading the way, skillfully leading an offense based around a powerful ground game—exemplified by the Packer Sweep—and punctuated by pinpoint, mostly high-percentage passes, the Packers finished 8-4, clinching the Western Division title with a 35–21 victory over the Rams in the season finale.

Prior to the game at Los Angeles Memorial Coliseum, roommates Starr and Knafelc somehow became confused about the time and showed up a few minutes late for the bus to the stadium, which they knew would result in a stiff fine. An irritated Lombardi gave Starr a dirty look as they stepped on the bus: "That'll cost each of you fifty bucks."

For the rest of the day, Starr's timing was impeccable. Growing in strength and confidence, he hit 8 of 9 passes for 201 yards and 3 touchdowns, while calling an impressive game.

Three snaps into the third quarter, Knafelc was knocked out; he eventually came to and played the rest of the game in a mental fog. He was still in a daze when Lombardi walked through the door of the jubilant locker room, yelled, "Forget the fines," in the direction of the tardy boys, and walked out without remarking on the most significant Packers victory in sixteen years.

"Thanks a lot, you old son of a bitch!" the loopy Knafelc said, fortunately out of Lombardi's earshot.

Starr fell to the floor, laughing uncontrollably.

When Knafelc started pulling out of his daze some time later—he would always remember looking into a locker-room mirror, having a terrible time tying his tie as the fog lifted—Starr told him about his comment. "No! I didn't say that! Tell me I didn't say that!"

At a postgame party in the home of a relative who lived in the area, Knafelc watched the tightly wound Starr, forever in control, reward himself with a second glass of champagne.

"It was the first time I ever saw Bart really relaxed," he said. "He didn't let himself relax very often. He had worked so hard to get to that point . . . and was so happy."

Happy but still hungry.

Back in the NFL Championship Game for the first time since World War II, the Packers faced the powerful but aging Philadelphia Eagles, led by quarterback Norm Van Brocklin, a grizzled veteran pushing thirty-five who was widely admired for his passing skills. "Best arm I ever saw," said the Packers' Hornung. In what would turn out to be his last season, the man known affectionately as the Dutchman had thrown for more than 2,400 yards and 24 touchdowns while leading the Eagles to a 10-2 finish.

The newspapers emphasized the old-versus-new theme, giving the 1960 NFL Championship Game the feel of a historic turning point, which it proved to be. Praise for the Packers' defense and the running tandem of Hornung and Taylor was high, but Starr, who had thrown only 4 touchdown passes in an abbreviated year as the starter, was still attracting little respect. "I think the Packers are a better team than Philly," assessed Giants head coach Jim Lee Howell, "but they are a little weak at quarterback."

Weak.

The word stuck in Starr's throat.

Striking a contrarian view, Green Bay legend Don Hutson told sportswriter Lee Remmel, "I think Bart Starr has been the unsung hero of this Packer team. I think he's done just a phenomenal job of calling the plays . . . Taking nothing away from Paul Hornung and Jim Taylor, who have been great, [but] you can't win in the NFL without good quarterbacking."

Before dawn on the day after Christmas, four chartered flights departed Green Bay's Austin Straubel Field in what was billed as the city's "biggest airlift in history." Some two hundred fans paid more than one hundred dollars each for the round-trip ticket to Philadelphia—about what many of them spent on their monthly mortgage payments—traveling on one Douglas DC-6 and three Convairs, among the most advanced and comfortable propeller-powered aircraft of the day. Similar plans for a chartered train were announced in the press, but the modern air operation—which delivered the fans in Philly in about four hours—apparently attracted all of the paying customers. It was 1960, and the train age was fading in the modern glow of the fast-approaching jet age.

The bitter December cold turned Franklin Field into a sheet of ice in the days before Christmas, thawing only slightly by kickoff as the temperature hovered just above freezing, creating what Starr described as "the worst footing I ever encountered." The slick field played into the Eagles' plan to slow down Green Bay's running game—especially by taking away the outside, where Hornung was most dangerous—and force Starr to pass. Despite the conditions, Taylor and Hornung combined for 166 yards, and Starr, facing the league's stiffest pass rush, completed 21 of 34 for 178 yards. It was an afternoon of missed opportunities: In the first half, the defense forced two turnovers inside the Philadelphia 25, but Starr was unable to punch it in either time.

"I was really in awe of [Van Brocklin] that day," Starr said many years later, adding, "I moved the ball well but I missed on the big plays. Van Brocklin made the big plays. And that was it, really."

By the fourth quarter, the sun was out and the field was turning to a less treacherous mush, which was both good and bad for Green Bay. Max McGee caught the Philly punt team napping, turning a fake into a 35-yard gain. "It definitely wasn't a gamble," he explained. "I could see ten yards [of daylight]." Five plays later, Starr hit McGee with a 7-yard touchdown strike, staking the Packers to a 13–10 lead. But Ted Dean, a rookie among all those veterans, took the ensuing kickoff, skillfully followed a series of blocks designed by the coaching staff to exploit weaknesses in the Green Bay unit, and returned it 58 yards to the Packers' 39. Van Brocklin completed just 9 of 20 passes on the day, but he called a very good game, especially at the end when the Packers expected him to put the ball in the air. Instead, he pushed toward the end zone on the ground, culminating with Dean's 5-yard touchdown run, giving the Eagles a 17–10 lead midway through the fourth quarter.

Two drives later, with 1:10 remaining, Starr took over at his own 35 and marched the Packers downfield with a series of passes. Six plays later, with a first down on the Eagles' 22, no time-outs, and the clock showing eight seconds, enough time for one more play, Starr hit Jimmy Taylor, who eluded one tackler at the 15, bounced off another near the 12, and kept moving forward toward the goal line. Taylor, a ferocious runner who punished anyone who tried to stop him, lived up to his reputation with the world championship on the line, using his powerful body like a weapon, pumping his legs and barreling toward for the end zone "like an enraged beer truck," in the words of New York sportswriter Red Smith. But at the 9, rookie defender Bobby Jackson stopped his progress, soon to be joined by the bruising veteran linebacker Chuck Bednarik, who had gained a measure of fame earlier in the year for his thunderous lick on Giants halfback Frank Gifford, which caused a concussion and hastened a premature end to Gifford's splendid career. Bednarik wrestled Taylor to the ground as the game ended.

"We didn't cash in when we had the opportunities," a dejected Taylor said.

"There were a lot of little things that hurt us," said Starr, determined to learn from the experience, determined to remember the hurt of watching a championship slip away.

Especially after breaking down the film, Lombardi was discouraged by Starr's inability to spot a wide-open McGee in the end zone in the first half. The touchdown could have been the difference in the game; not seeing McGee was the mistake of a young quarterback still learning to master many aspects of his position. But Lombardi also appreciated the way he had rallied the troops in the closing moments, defeated not by the Eagles but by the clock.

After telling the assembled newsmen, "I'm very proud of our ballclub . . . I think they played a great football game," Lombardi walked through the doors of a somber Packers locker room, wearing a defiant expression and delivered a message none of the assembled athletes would ever forget.

"The biggest tragedy of this loss is that you guys didn't realize you were good enough to win," he said.

Somehow they knew he was right.

Reaching the championship game in only his second year, Lombardi could tell that his players were still working through the process of developing the sort of swagger he knew they needed to compete consistently for the NFL championship.

Now they knew how it felt to be in the big game.

Now they knew what it took to win.

"We will win it all next year," Lombardi vowed. "We will never lose another championship game."

Reflecting on the scene half a century later, Starr said, "I'm not sure we said much to each other about what Coach Lombardi told us as we headed home, but it was what we were thinking to ourselves. Instead of being knocked down by the loss, we were suddenly lifted up. It was a tremendous moment."

Long after it was all over, when those remarkable years of his life had been consigned to history and legend, men and women of all ages often approached Bart Starr with one question above all others.

How tough was Vince Lombardi?

"I always say, 'He was very, very tough, but compared to my father, he was a piece of cake,'" Starr said.

Sometimes the curious fans think he is joking, but his answer is not only candid, it is critical to understanding the arc of his life, because in ways that Lombardi could never understand, Ben Starr prepared his son for the demanding man from Sheepshead Bay.

The essential element in Starr's rise was not high expectations, rigid discipline, or intellectual diligence, although all three of these characteristics played important roles in his life and career.

There was a more primal force at work.

Doubt.

By doubting Starr's athletic abilities, by making him feel unworthy, Ben Starr and Vince Lombardi gave him something to prove.

Their doubt was a source of enormous power, and he tapped this electric force to motivate himself while negotiating the arduous journey from anonymity to legend.

Doubt made Bart Starr Bart Starr.

Even as he taught Starr how to become a winning quarterback, the pupil taught the master how the combination of desire, intelligence, toughness, poise, perseverance, and attitude could trump superior athletic ability.

Bart Starr needed Vince Lombardi, and Vince Lombardi needed Bart Starr.

"Bart was the one guy you couldn't replace," Hornung said. "His net worth to those teams was immeasurable. It took Lombardi a while to realize it, but Bart was the one indispensable player."

After the 1960 season, Lombardi, still not completely sold on Starr, made an overture to the expansion Dallas Cowboys about trading for Don Meredith, a strong-armed quarterback with good mobility. How serious he was, no one can say, but Dallas had no intention of dealing Meredith anyway. News of the development somehow reached Starr, and if Lombardi's intention was to motivate his quarterback, he succeeded, because instead of pouting, Starr endeavored to work harder to win his coach's faith.

Doubt.

As professional football moved into the sixties, six other franchises loomed as legitimate contenders.

In the Western Conference, Green Bay's primary competition came from Johnny U's Baltimore Colts, who had captured consecutive NFL championships in 1958–59, and the Detroit Lions, who had finished just a game behind the Packers in 1960. The fortunes of the Lions, who won three titles in the fifties, turned dramatically after they traded quarterback Bobby Layne to Pittsburgh in 1958. Infuriated at being discarded after an injury, Layne predicted his old team would not win "for fifty years." He was more right than he would ever know: Detroit was headed for a mighty fall that even the menacing defender Alex Karras could not prevent. In time, Lions fans would seize on the quarterback's parting shot as evidence of "The Curse of Bobby Layne." Slowly, Detroit sank into a morass of mediocrity stretching into the twenty-first century.

The most important yardstick for the Packers continued to be their bitter rivalry with the Chicago Bears. While Lombardi personified a new age of football, the domineering George "Papa Bear" Halas remained the most visible link to the NFL's formative age. Like Green Bay's own Curly Lambeau, Halas once did it all: player; coach; promoter; owner. According to legend, he even manned the ticket booth in the early days of the Monsters of the Midway. While the sport slowly grew up, Halas remained a dominant figure on and off the field, exerting tremendous influence on the overall direction of the NFL even as he endeavored to bring championships to Chicagoland. After leading the Bears to five league titles and shepherding the sport through a series of innovations, including the advent of the T-formation offense—featuring the spectacular passer Sid Luckman—the legendary Halas walked away from the field for the third time following the 1955 season. But he could not stay away—not for long. Three years later, the sixty-three-year-old Halas returned to the sideline, planting the seeds of a team that would emerge as a significant threat to Lombardi's ambitions in the early sixties.

"Vince Lombardi loved George Halas because he had been one of the founders of the league," said Packers center Bill Curry.

Lombardi was a man who respected his elders, but he was determined to own Papa Bear on his way to dominating the league. His respect for Halas's standard of excellence motivated him all the more, infusing the rivalry with a renewed intensity and creating the climate for a whole new era of grudge matches, including several Green Bay blowouts. No man hit harder or pursued more relentlessly than the incomparable linebacker Dick Butkus, who joined the Bears in 1965. Even though the Bears eventually faded while the Packers hit their stride, Green Bay's 13–5 edge in the series during the period proved central to Lombardi's historic run.

In the Eastern Conference, defending league champion Philadelphia loomed as the primary target for all, but the Eagles were a franchise in decline, their fall soon to be exacerbated by the retirement of quarterback Norm Van Brocklin. Despite losing lead assistants Vince Lombardi and Tom Landry, the New York Giants were still a talented and powerful team behind new head coach Allie Sherman. After many years of domination, Paul Brown's Cleveland Browns, featuring the powerful running of Jim Brown, were engaged in a contentious battle with the Giants and Eagles to get back to the title game. It was only a matter of time before a new contender out of the East, the expansion Dallas Cowboys, climbed out of the cellar to supplant the dynasties of old.

But none of these title chasers was a match for the team Lombardi was building in the frozen north country.

In 1961, the Packers put it all together. The defense, featuring future Hall of Famers Ray Nitschke, Willie Davis, Herb Adderly, Henry Jordan, and Willie Wood, was punishing and opportunistic. The offense, featuring future Hall of Famers Bart Starr, Jim Taylor, Paul Hornung, Jim Ringo, and Forrest Gregg, was potent and efficient.

With Starr completing 58.3 percent of his passes for 2,418 yards and 16 touchdowns, Taylor rushing for 1,307 yards and 15 touchdowns, and the defense leading the league in yards allowed and turnovers, the Packers dominated, finishing 11-3 to win the Western Conference crown by three games over second place Detroit.

"There were a lot of pieces to the puzzle, but the difference was having a guy come in and take charge and lead," said defensive end Willie Davis, traded from Cleveland in 1960. "That guy was Bart Starr. He took charge. The team responded to his leadership."

With Starr slowly growing in effectiveness as a play-caller, Green Bay crushed contenders Chicago (24–0) and Baltimore (45–7) in consecutive weeks in early October. The following Sunday in Cleveland, the Green Bay defense held Jim Brown to 72 yards as the Packers' offense approached perfection: Jim Taylor rushed for 158 yards and four touchdowns and Starr completed 15 of 17 passes for 272 yards and a 45-yard touchdown strike to Max McGee. In a pivotal November rematch with the Bears, Starr threw three touchdown passes to key a 31–28 Packers victory— including a 53-yarder to tight end Ron Kramer.

Hardly anyone knew the quarterback played much of the season with a torn abdominal muscle.

By late November, the Western Conference race was over.

In his first full season as the Green Bay starter, Starr achieved something no one thought possible only two years earlier: While most of the major award selectors anointed either Y. A. Tittle or Sonny Jurgensen as the first-team All Pro quarterback, *The Sporting News* chose Starr, validating his arrival as a big-time player. In the years ahead, he would make second-team All-Pro twice (1962 and 1964) and only once capture unanimous first-team All-Pro status (1966.)

As Lombardi and Starr plotted an assault on the NFL championship, the whole country was obsessed with the space race, giving the potentially cataclysmic cold war with the Soviet Union the texture of a sporting event. When Alan Shepard, Jr., blasted off from Cape Canaveral, punched a hole in the sky, and splashed down safely in the Pacific Ocean, becoming the first American in space, the whole country was with him, in a way future generations would not be able to fully appreciate: strapped in like a copilot, fully invested in his perilous journey. Four years after the engineering marvel of Sputnik shocked the world, the Soviets managed to remain one step ahead throughout 1961, but then President John F. Kennedy changed the game, announcing the audacious goal of sending a team of Americans to the moon by the end of the decade . . . and returning them safely to earth.

A year later, as the space race accelerated and he endeavored to keep the country on message, Kennedy cleverly tapped into a football analogy, reflecting the prevailing realities of the old Southwest Conference, where Darrell Royal's Texas Longhorns ruled the day. "Why does Rice play Texas? We go to the moon!" he thundered. "We go to the moon and do the other things . . . not because they are easy, but because they are hard."

It was a time of ambition and optimism, and like many others, Vince Lombardi and Bart Starr somehow felt like disciples in a larger cause.

Hosting its first championship game—the others, in the prehistoric days, before television, face masks, and Lombardi, had always been played on the road or in Milwaukee—little Green Bay felt like the center of the football universe on December 31, 1961, when the long-powerful New York Giants came to town. Everyone wondered how the favored Packers would be affected by the bitter cold—their bitter cold. "This would be an ideal spot for Eskimos . . . it is hardly an ideal spot, however, for a football game involving any people less hardy than inhabitants of the Arctic," Arthur Daley surmised in *The New York Times*.

It was 20 degrees at kickoff, and in 1961, some people thought this was cold.

"Welcome to Titletown USA."

The message, with some variation, was tattooed across the city like a civic logo, dominating storefronts, billboards, and perfectly manicured lawns. On the bus ride from the airport to their downtown hotel, the visiting players from the nation's largest metropolis, conditioned to their less prominent profile in the life of a large, bustling, and diverse city, marveled at Green Bay's single-minded pride.

During the off-season, New York had acquired the services of veteran quarterback Y. A. Tittle, who led the Giants to an impressive 10-3-1 season and the Eastern Conference championship. Confronted with the ubiquitous signage, Sam Huff, the outstanding Giants linebacker who led a menacing defense, yelled out to his teammates, "Look, they spelled Tittle wrong!"

Fortunately for Green Bay, President Kennedy was a football fan who admired Lombardi. Like linebacker Ray Nitschke, receiver Boyd Dowler, and several other players across the league, Paul Hornung was an Army reservist who was called to duty during the fall of 1961, in a broad mobilization of forces in response to the Soviets' construction of the Berlin Wall, one of the most provocative acts of the escalating cold war. After Nitschke and Dowler were dismissed, Hornung remained with his unit at Fort Riley in Kansas and missed two late-season games. Lombardi, who had publicly endorsed Kennedy for the White House in 1960 and was personally courted, unsuccessfully, by the president, a Navy man, to return to West Point as head coach, appealed directly to the White House. In a later era, Kennedy's intervention might have caused scandal—he actually picked up the phone and called Hornung's commanding officer—but granting a weekend furlough to one truck-driving private so that the nation's two leading professional football teams could be at full strength to decide the championship of the free world hardly seemed like a threat to national security. In the context of the times, when so many invested football with meaning and significance, when the game reflected so much about the American way of life, the act seemed as patriotic to some as Alan Shepard's bumpy ride to glory.

The first heroes of the day began their work at 5 A.M., bundled tightly but still shivering as they removed twenty tons of hay they had previously placed above a massive tarpaulin to prevent the ground from freezing solid. Some isolated spots managed to freeze, but the field was overall in good shape, thanks to the diligence of the grounds crew, preventing a repeat of the slick conditions experienced during the 1960 title game in Philadelphia.

The weather was so cold, and the availability of television coverage protected from the elements so attractive, that roughly one thousand tickets went unsold, producing a crowd of 39,029, slightly below City Stadium's capacity.

"Scarcely a minute passed in which one shivering soldier or another in this cold war could not be observed taking courage from a hip flask or a plain pint bottle," reported Robert L. Teague in *The New York Times*. "This was a spirited crowd in more ways than one."

Emboldened by a dominant year—and a previous victory over the Giants—the Packers took the field with a quiet confidence.

"There was no doubt in my mind who was going to win that football game," said Willie Davis, a punishing pass rusher. "After losing to the Eagles the previous year, we were a team on a mission."

The Giants began beating themselves on their first series: Usually dependable Kyle Rote dropped two passes from Tittle, a sign of things to come. After Starr methodically drove the Packers 80 yards, culminating with Hornung's 6-yard touchdown run, Henry Jordan tipped a Tittle pass into the arms of teammate Ray Nitschke, the first of four interceptions for the struggling Giants. Six plays later, Starr tossed the first of three touchdown passes, a 13-yard strike to Boyd Dowler, and the rout was on. By halftime the Packers held a commanding 24–0 lead. Green Bay's 37–0 victory was over long before the final gun and could have been worse, if Lombardi had not pulled his starters early in the fourth quarter to prevent further embarrassment of his old team.

The oddity of little Green Bay clobbering gigantic New York so convincingly struck a blow for small towns across America. "It was like Cedar Rapids of the Three I League beating the Yankees in the World Series," remarked *Sports Illustrated.* No one realized it was a preview of coming attractions, the opening act of the most dominant seven-year run in the history of the NFL.

The biggest hero of the day was the immensely talented Hornung, who tied an NFL postseason record with 19 points, scoring 1 touchdown, 3 field goals, and 4 extra points.

But it was also a transformative afternoon in the life of Bart Starr, who silenced all doubts about his playing abilities, completing 10 of 17 passes and calling a virtually flawless game. Lombardi's decision to use Jim Taylor, hobbled by a bad back, mostly as a decoy proved to be a master stroke, and Starr engineered it brilliantly. The first of his two touchdown passes to tight end Ron Kramer illustrated his mounting sophistication at the controls: Calling a flood pass to the right from the New York 14-yard line, he coolly waited in the pocket until Kramer convinced linebacker Sam Huff to bite on a fake, then delivered a perfectly timed strike across the middle to Kramer, who outran the safety into the end zone. In the detailed notes he kept about every game, Starr wrote, "Kramer's speed put him 'on top' of safeties before they knew he had the ball."

A proud Lombardi told his players, "Today you were the best team in the history of the National Football League."

After being presented with a brand-new red Corvette as the game's Most Valuable Player, Hornung stood in the steamy home locker room, his curly blond hair matted with sweat.

"Give all the credit to our offensive line and that guy right there," he told a reporter, pointing to Starr, standing in front of the next locker, smiling a champion's smile.

"There's the guy," Starr insisted, pointing back toward Hornung, before heaping praise on the offensive line and the defense.

After he showered, combed his hair, and put on his coat and tie, Bart walked out into the cold and smiled broadly as he spotted Cherry and his parents, who had driven up from Alabama. As his wife and mother rushed to embrace the quarterback of the 1961 NFL champions, Starr could see his father lingering a few feet away, tears streaming down his cheeks.

The old Master Sergeant struggled for words but the tears got in the way. Finally, Ben reached over, wrapped his arms around his boy and said, "I was wrong, son."

Bart, who had spent the afternoon dodging colossal defenders, was stunned to the point of disbelief by a four-word sentence. He hugged his father tightly, not wanting to let go.

FIVE

CHASING PERFECTION

"Does anybody know anybody famous?"

The question hung in the air, colliding with the smoky smell of pork barbecue, as Larry Watkins's mind raced with ambivalence.

He looked around at his friends gathered in the dining room of Sprayberry's Barbecue, a landmark in the small town of Newnan, Georgia, waiting for someone else, anyone else, to speak up.

On a winter night in 1962, the leaders of the local Jaycees had agreed to take on the ambitious project of raising money to build a new high school football stadium. The suggestion to generate funds with a banquet featuring a prominent guest speaker, someone well known who could draw a crowd, was greeted with significant enthusiasm but stalled when they began to grapple for a name.

When it became clear that the civic leaders were about to strike out, Watkins, an executive with the local Playtex plant, reluctantly stood up and cleared his throat.

"Well, guys," Watkins said, "I know Bart Starr."

"Bart Starr?"

"You know Bart Starr?"

"*The* Bart Starr?"

Three years after his future in professional football teetered precariously on the tightrope of Lombardi's enormous expectations, Bart Starr began 1962 as one of the most recognizable athletes in America. More than 30 million viewers had tuned in to watch the Packers crush the

Giants to capture the 1961 NFL championship. He lacked the sizzle of teammate Paul Hornung or the stature of rival Johnny Unitas, but his name and face were known far and wide, causing every man within earshot of Watkins to snap to attention.

"You're crazy," insisted another Jaycee, Hugh Farmer, Jr. "You can't get Bart Starr to come to Newnan!"

A decade after the National Football League's championship games began appearing on coast-to-coast television, four years after the epic 1958 title showdown, fans across American were following professional football more closely than ever. Newspapers and magazines offered an intellectual connection to the sport, but television provided a visceral spark that reached into living rooms across the country and pulled fans into the drama. More than a window into the action, TV manufactured real-life heroes. Vince Lombardi's Green Bay Packers just happened to come along at the perfect time to lead and benefit from the revolution, propelled by an earnest 17th-round draft choice who played the game with an unusual combination of ferocity, determination, and humility. Television captured Starr's everyman, blue-collar, clean-cut essence, making him a powerful example for what a professional quarterback should be at a time when the country was still discovering the game, still enjoying the first blush of attraction.

Torn between wanting to help his community and not wanting to impose on an old classmate who was probably being bombarded with similar requests, Watkins explained that he had been a year behind Starr at Montgomery's Sidney Lanier High School but had not spoken to him in nearly a decade.

"I'll call him," Watkins told his colleagues, "as soon as I can figure out some way to get his number."

When the local manager of the telephone company suggested they could utilize his facilities to locate Starr's home phone number—and save on expensive long-distance fees—the meeting quickly reconvened to his headquarters several blocks away. To their surprise, the Starrs' number was listed in the phone book.

As he placed the call, his index finger carefully tracing the digits, one after another, around the rotary dial, Watkins rehearsed the pitch in his head.

When Cherry Starr answered, she recognized his name immediately and said sweetly, "Well, hello, Larry! It has been a long time! How are you?"

After chatting for a few moments, catching up on each other's lives, Cherry put Bart on the phone. Watkins apologized for the intrusion and then explained the situation. Immediately receptive to the idea of helping in the effort, to the shock of the men huddled around the telephone, Starr told Watkins he could schedule a trip to Newnan, located about thirty-five miles southwest of Atlanta, to coincide with one of his frequent visits to his hometown of Montgomery, where he volunteered his time to help the Young Men's Christian Association (YMCA), led by his old friend Bill Chandler. After some back and forth discussions, they set a date for May 1, 1962, five months after he was honored by his hometown with an event billed as Bart Starr Day in Alabama's capital city.

"Everyone was so excited," said local business leader Hershall Norred, who commemorated the appearance with a cartoon in *The Newnan Times-Herald*. "Getting Bart Starr to come speak to our little fund-raiser was a huge event for the whole town."

Like thousands of communities all across the country, especially in the Deep South, Newnan embraced high school football as the ultimate expression of local pride, which Starr understood from personal experience. The Jaycees' ability to enlist such a prominent sports figure in the push for a new stadium invested the effort with even greater urgency. Ticket sales moved briskly, at the princely sum of fifteen dollars each, including a barbecue dinner. For weeks, hand-drawn banners trumpeting Starr's visit hung from city streets near the courthouse square, which remained the center of commerce in an era before chain restaurants, shopping centers, and interstate highways, when Atlanta and the urban world still seemed distant.

On the very day Starr drove himself from Montgomery to Newnan, something happened a world away that was destined to have a dramatic impact on thousands of towns all across America: The first K-Mart department store opened in Garden City, Michigan, presaging the coming era of shopping centers and malls. State transportation officials in Atlanta were drawing up plans for the interstate highways to connect the rural areas of Georgia with its fast-growing capital city, creating the infrastructure for a sprawling suburban ring that would consume Newnan and other towns like it, sealing the future in asphalt. That very month, astronaut Scott Carpenter became the second American to orbit the earth, following the pioneering trajectory of the heroic John Glenn, who mirrored Starr's clean-cut, precise, and humble bearing.

After rendezvousing with Watkins and his other hosts for the day, Starr toured a local manufacturing plant and sat for a live radio interview with local radio and newspaperman Johnny Brown.

Somewhere along the way, the meticulous quarterback realized he had forgotten to pack a change of underwear. When he walked through the front door of Joe Carasco's men's shop on the south side of the courthouse square, teenage clerk Bill McNabb, alone in the store, recognized him immediately and was struck by "how friendly and down-to-earth he was."

"I'll never forget the thrill of selling Bart Starr a pair of Jockey underwear," McNabb said with a chuckle, recalling the youthful memory as he approached retirement age.

McNabb even asked him to sign the sales receipt, which he kept as a souvenir.

When fellow Newnan High School junior Bobby Lee took a break from working behind the counter of his father's pharmacy across the street and walked into Joe Carasco's, he was shocked to see his friend chatting with the quarterback of the Green Bay Packers.

"I was just stunned," Lee said. "We all knew Starr was coming to town . . . it was a big deal . . . but to see him standing there . . ."

Not wanting to disturb the discussion, Lee pretended to browse the store until Starr walked out the front door, then finally approached his buddy excitedly.

"What were y'all talking about so seriously?" Lee demanded.

"Gold Toe socks."

Then the store reverberated with their nervous laughter.

Several hours later, when the crowd began to gather for the evening's festivities at the National Guard Armory, Newnan High junior Billy Alford, a devoted fan of the Baltimore Colts, walked into the lobby and said, loud enough for Starr and others to hear, "I wish they could have gotten Johnny Unitas instead."

The official party ignored the smart-ass comment, but in the years ahead, even as Starr piloted the Packers to one championship after an-other, he would grow accustomed to life in Johnny U's shadow.

A full house packed the Armory to hear Starr deliver an inspiring speech about professional football, Vince Lombardi's leadership, and the importance of setting goals and working hard—kicking off the Jaycees' three-year fund-raising campaign to build Drake Stadium on the Newnan High School campus. The ovation was long and loud, and the Newnan crowd walked into the shadows marveling about the nice young man who seemed like such a wonderful example to the younger generation.

When one of the Jaycees presented Starr with an honorarium check, he immediately endorsed it and gave it back.

No one in the audience was happier to be wrong than the once-skeptical Hugh Farmer, Jr., who helped host the quarterback on his visit. For years to come, whenever one of the Atlanta newspapers ran a picture of Starr, he always carefully cut it out and saved it, never forgetting how one famous man's kind gesture helped his hometown.

In an age when many sports stars wore the label of role model—some uncomfortably, others hypocritically—Starr embraced the distinction, which reflected who he was even when the cameras and flashbulbs were not around: an authentically decent, kind, humble, principled man who held himself to high standards of personal conduct. He also saw the term and its implications as part of the job: "[Professional athletes] have an exceptional ability to be role models and I think it's sad when they are unwilling to do so." To a greater degree than many others, he felt an ob-ligation to live up to the image, because he understood that he and other athletes represented something to the country. The speech in Newnan, and countless other acts like it through the years, reflected his genuine de-sire to help a former classmate and a community while also demonstrat-ing his sense of duty to be the stand-up guy who walked the talk.

"Bart has always felt motivated to prove something . . . that's what makes him tick," explained his teammate and lifelong friend Gary Knafelc. "Going out of his way to do things for people, this is part of that same motivation . . . to be the best, not just the best quarterback [but also] the best role model. His image has always been very important to him. He's always Bart Starr. Always. I've often wondered if he ever got tired of being Bart Starr all the time, but the reality of it is, that's not some mask he puts on. There's not a phony bone in his body. He really is that person."

The regimented sense of discipline engendered by his father, coupled with a value system that struck a harsh distinction between right and wrong, colored his life in various ways. For many years, he roomed with Henry Jordan on the road and Gary Knafelc during training camp; both men quickly discovered that Starr was the sort of man who lined up all of his pencils in a row, hung his shirts in the closet neatly, facing the same way, and always endeavored to meet his own great expectations for himself in even the smallest details of life. Knafelc would never forget the morning when Starr discovered that his neatly packed dress shirt had somehow acquired a wrinkle, requiring him to find an iron with all the urgency of delivering a bullet in the face of an oncoming rush.

Zeke Bratkowski, his longtime backup, often was amused watching the care with which Starr replaced a divot during a friendly game of golf. "You'd think he had an agronomy degree, the way he takes the dirt and pats it down just right. He has a whole routine," Bratkowski said. The process offers two important clues about Starr the person and Starr the athlete: The sense of obligation (in this case, to help maintain the course) and the power of structure as a habit (the replacement and the patting just so, all in the same way every time) loomed large in his success on and off the field.

"You're talking about a very special human being," said Packers defensive end Willie Davis. "Everything I ever witnessed about Bart Starr was first-class and high-class. When you live your entire life that way, as Bart did, [the accumulation of] all that consistency has a momentum all its own."

It would be easy to reduce Bart Starr to some wholesome caricature, but do to so would be missing the larger point of his life: He was a fighter who was defined by his remarkable tenacity.

More than any athlete of his time, the overachieving Starr reflected something noble in the American character: Desire as the great equalizer.

"Nobody has ever played the game with more love than Bart Starr," said Packers offensive guard Fuzzy Thurston. "He gave it all he had on every down."

Becoming a national figure at a time before cynicism and relativism, when most Americans still believed in institutions like government and the military, when traditional values remained a powerful cultural glue, Starr epitomized a nation of dreamers and strivers who struggled, sometimes failed, and kept fighting while holding firm to a set of principles. Like millions of Americans who chased their own goals far from the spotlight, he knew how it felt to be knocked down in humiliation—and the sort of inner strength it took to climb off the ground and keep reaching for some distant, invisible horizon. Like the butcher down the street or the salesman across town who dreamed big, worked long hours, and played by the rules, he was living proof that achievement was closely linked to attitude, effort and persistence.

Anyone with a set of eyes could tell he was not the most physically gifted quarterback in the league—that he possessed neither Sonny Jurgensen's rocket arm nor Fran Tarkenton's scrambling ability—but he learned to compensate by marshalling other forces, making his entire career an object lesson in the transformative power of optimism, hard work, and resolve.

It was the firmament of competition that lifted him, and in this respect as in others, he symbolized something fundamental about a country so profoundly shaped, and indeed, enriched, by the friction of struggle and rivalry: Sometimes superior skill is no match for indomitable will.

"Bart was a tremendous competitor with an amazing will to succeed," said Packers center Bill Curry. "Lombardi kept looking for someone better but Bart kept demonstrating, time and again, that he was the man."

The doubt empowered the tenacity, enabling Starr to exploit his intellect, work habits, consistency, and toughness to transcend his limitations.

He was one of us, in ways most of us never realized.

After watching the Packers capture their first championship under Lombardi, Pittsburgh Steelers quarterback Bobby Layne, nearing the end of an outstanding career, told a reporter that Bart Starr had the easiest job in professional football. "All he has to do is hand off the ball to Paul Hornung and Jim Taylor," Layne explained, giving voice to a widespread perception.

Buffeted by such conventional wisdom that suggested he was little more than Lombardi's robot, Starr moved into a new era of his career, firmly established as the Packers' starting quarterback but trapped in the shadow of his coach and the team's more celebrated offensive weapons. Having Hornung and Taylor certainly made his job easier, liberating him from a certain amount of pressure to win games strictly with his arm, but many failed to recognize the full measure of Starr's offensive leadership, particularly his growing confidence and alacrity as a play-caller. "Starr is definitely an underrated quarterback," said Norm Van Brocklin, the former Eagles quarterback who became head coach of the expansion Minnesota Vikings in 1961. "He carries out a game plan perfectly. And he can improvise when he has to."

As the Packers began the pursuit of a second consecutive title in 1962, Lombardi kept encouraging Starr to improve his mechanics and his decision-making but he no longer doubted the man's ability to win. He knew, because he saw. Better than anyone else, Lombardi understood the quarterback's enormous role in the Packers' success. "Bart Starr with that analytic mind, retentive memory and inner toughness . . . ," he said in 1962, "is great at picking that defense apart and adjusting."

Even as Green Bay became the model professional football franchise of the era, Lombardi pushed the Packers relentlessly in pursuit of perfection. In the film room, he was a stickler for the smallest imperfections, such as an offensive guard pulling slightly out of synch or a poorly timed connection between quarterback and receiver. Because he worked directly with the offense and acted as his own offensive coordinator, Lombardi spent a large amount of time analyzing Starr's performance and figuring out how to help him improve his mechanics, play-calling, and understanding of the opposition.

"[Lombardi] really gets you ready for a game," Starr said. "He repeats and repeats and repeats . . . until finally you can recognize the other's teams defenses in your sleep."

Each night during the season, before drifting off to sleep, Starr read through his notebook containing the gameplan as well as the tendencies of opposing defensive players, further solidifying his visualization of every matchup, pattern, and defensive look.

In the darkened film room on a Tuesday late in the 1962 season, Lombardi saw something disturbing and stopped the projector.

"On your quick passes, Bart, you should always look at your quick man first," he said. "You'll have a quick man open first, and a slower man later."

"Yes, sir," said Starr, carefully taking notes.

Two days later, while scrimmaging on the practice field, Lombardi watched Starr call the same pass play, fade into the pocket and find primary receiver Gary Knafelc covered by defender Dan Currie. Reacting in the blink of an eye, Starr fired a strike to Gary Barnes on a slant for a big gain.

"That's the way, Bart!" Lombardi yelled. "Very good!"

Such minor tweaking between teacher and pupil played a large role in the Packers' success, demonstrating the studious Starr's ability to absorb feedback and apply it to the proper situations.

"I loved going to meetings with Coach Lombardi," Starr said. "You never grew tired of [those meetings] because of what a great teacher he was. It was always intellectually challenging, and I enjoyed that aspect very much."

Lombardi focused his keen eye for detail to every player on the offense but his relationship with Starr emerged as the most important and influential of his professional career. Starr's ability to soak up Lombardi's coaching and push himself to become a great player was the catalyst to an entire era of Packers football: Once he mastered the system and began to think like Lombardi, his accumulation of knowledge, confidence, forcefulness, and skill lifted Green Bay to an entirely different level, transforming the Packers' offense into a marvel of efficiency.

"The dirty little secret of those days," said Packers offensive tackle Steve Wright, "was that during the week it was Lombardi's team, but on Sunday, it was really Starr's team."

On Sunday, Lombardi trusted Starr as he leveraged the combination of their collective knowledge. Lombardi developed the game plan, but Starr called the plays, read the defense, checked off at the line of scrimmage, fought off clawing bruisers intent on slamming him to the turf, and delivered perfectly timed passes, applying the accumulation of his education with a level of consistency that often amazed his teammates. He was not Lombardi's robot, but the two men were in one another's heads at all times, creating a powerful symbiosis.

"Lombardi had such great confidence in Bart," Hornung said.

Starr was the perfect instrument for Lombardi because he was such a good student of the game, because he worked so hard, because he could take the intense mental strain associated with Lombardi's methods, because he was so unflappable on the field, because he so seldom made mistakes, because he could take a jarring lick without losing his nerve, and, ultimately, because he approached the game with the same sort of zealous pursuit of victory as his coach.

"Bart and Coach Lombardi thought the same way about football—that was the secret," Gary Knafelc said.

Though polar opposites in background and temperament, the mild-mannered, devout Southern Protestant and the bombastic, equally pious New York Catholic learned to understand, trust, and admire each other.

The complexity of their relationship could be seen during one of Lombardi's frequent classroom tirades, when the volatile coach began berating his team. "Nobody around here takes responsibility for poor play! Nobody but me . . ."

A forceful voice rang out from the back of the room. "That's not true, sir! I take responsibility . . . let's get it right!"

No one on the team except Starr could have gotten away with correcting Lombardi in such a manner, but the coach knew his hyperbole had crossed a line. He quickly conceded the point.

Lombardi's deference toward Starr caused some members of the Packers to joke about a fictitious rant, inevitably ending with the qualifier: "Oh, not you, Bart, honey!"

In truth, Starr was just as susceptible to being corrected by Lombardi as anyone else on the roster, and when he believed it was warranted, he accepted it dutifully. But the coach never lost sight of the need to handle his quarterback differently.

"I respected Coach Lombardi enormously but I wasn't afraid of him," Starr said.

Always respectful toward the boss—calling him "sir"—Starr slowly evolved from compliant to assertive, exemplified by the day he marched into the head coach's office and politely but firmly demanded a significant raise after a successful season.

"A couple of years ago, I'd have signed anything you gave me but now you've taught me to be more aggressive . . ."

"So that's it," Lombardi said with a grin, before approving the raise. "I've created a monster."

Through the years, Lombardi lifted a long line of athletes to new levels of performance and ambition, in football and in life, but what he accomplished with Starr constituted an entirely different realm of influence. Exploiting a mysterious but powerful chemistry between the two men, Lombardi somehow transformed Starr from a man who doubted himself into a supremely confident athlete who inspired the confidence of others. He made Starr a leader, and so much of the Green Bay Packers' success flowed from this simple fact.

The transformation was most pronounced when Starr stepped onto the field. In contrast to his early years with the Packers, when his flagging confidence sometimes inspired doubts among his teammates, Starr's mastery of Lombardi's offense infused him with a commanding self-assurance, allowing him to dominate the huddle not with the force of his personality but with the power of his knowledge. The calm, quiet, focused way he conducted himself in the huddle—whether the Packers were ahead or behind—contributed to the sense of pervasive inevitability that defined those Green Bay teams.

"Believe me, nobody questioned Bart, nobody doubted Bart, and that was a reflection of all Lombardi's training that flowed through him," Bill Curry said. "Not only did we believe he was going to get the job done, that guy across the line probably believed it, too. You can't overestimate the power of that."

Defenders who initially doubted Starr because of his relatively modest arm gradually gained respect for the other assets that made him a winning quarterback, especially his ability to react to the defense and change the play at the line of scrimmage. "You don't have time to think at the line of scrimmage," he explained to a reporter during the period. "It must be second nature by then." No quarterback of the era utilized the audible as effectively. The systematic approach developed by Lombardi and the consistency of Starr's implementation played to his strengths—especially his prodigious memory—while reflecting the sport's mounting sophistication. In the years ahead, every quarterback in the league would feel the need to master the audible like Starr, which required an incredibly detailed knowledge of the opposition.

Following in the footsteps of Paul Brown, who revolutionized the game in various ways in the 1950s, Lombardi placed a premium on film study. He was determined to perceive, analyze, and correct every weakness in his own team and identify the slightest vulnerability in the opposition. This analytical approach to the game accentuated Starr's strengths, because, like Lombardi, he viewed the game from a cerebral perspective and was able to exploit his significant intelligence to figure out how to recognize defenses and attack their weaknesses. Being a devoted family man actually aided his career and the Packers' success: Instead of hitting the town at night, basking in his celebrity and feasting on the pleasures attached to it, Starr fed his insatiable desire for victory by taking canisters of opposition film home several nights a week. ("When the coaches took bed check," Paul Hornung once remarked to Jerry Kramer, "they never checked Bart's room. He was always there.") In the early years of the Lombardi regime, he often transported the film to Gary Knafelc's house, where they projected the movies on the wall and searched for clues.

"Dedication made Bart a great football player," Knafelc said. "You could see his dedication in the way he watched film obsessively, before most people in the league watched much film. He was very astute at picking out the tiniest things . . . Those little things gave us openings. And he knew how to take advantage [of weaknesses] better than any quarterback I have ever seen."

The dedication gradually made Starr smarter, and his intelligence emerged as an increasingly powerful weapon in the Packers' arsenal.

Empowered by the accumulation of Lombardi's repetition, Starr learned to recognize a safety overshifting on a zone coverage, creating the opportunity for a big pass play, and to interpret the all-important movement of the middle linebacker. If, for example, he saw the middle linebacker going back at a 45-degree angle, moving hard to the corner, he immediately recognized this as a strong side move, which opened up opportunities for a quick-thinking quarterback.

Even as the accumulation of live game experience with Lombardi's system helped him grow into the position, it was through obsessive film study that he was able to learn what to look for in the opposition and among his own players—determined to avoid the critical mistake he made in the 1960 championship game, when he failed to see a wide-open Max McGee.

"Bart was very self-critical, more than anybody I ever knew," said

Packers defender Willie Davis. "Was tougher on himself than anybody had a right to be."

Next to the film projector in his basement, Starr kept a blackboard. In later years, he and longtime backup Zeke Bratkowski spent hour upon hour drawing up hypothetical situations and testing each other with hypothetical adjustments.

Lombardi called very few plays. ("Perhaps a total of nine in nine years," Starr said.) Even when he sent in a play, his quarterback, who had been studying their so-called ready list all week, was charged with the authority to change it. "Coach Lombardi was very rigid and disciplined in the way he approached an opponent and what he wanted to do," Starr said. "But he was also extremely flexible. Not too many people realize how flexible he could be. In our meetings . . . not only did he encourage, he demanded . . . that when we didn't get what we were looking for, based on what we were calling . . . that we audible."

Once he reached the line of scrimmage, Starr looked out over the defense and made a quick search for tells, comparing the way the opposition lined up against the memories rattling around in his head from watching hours and hours of film.

If he decided to keep the play he called in the huddle, Starr yelled out "Set," a series of meaningless numbers to confuse the defense, and then "Hut," or several "Huts," depending on the snap count previously determined in the huddle. If he saw something that caused him to change the play at the line, Starr yelled out, "Set! Three!" and then the new play number.

Even as many bought into the simplistic notion that Starr's primary job was to hand off to Hornung and Taylor—a perception backed up, at first blush, by the statistics, as Green Bay routinely ranked first or second in the league in rushing—players and coaches who studied film began recognizing his play-calling skills, particularly his performance as a check-off master. "[Starr] calls automatics as good as anybody in the league," said Giants head coach Allie Sherman.

Sometimes replacing a run with a pass or a pass with a run, Starr's brainy leadership became the central force in Green Bay's powerful, ball-control offense. The combination of the Packers' potent running game and Starr's mounting skills as a play-action passer kept defenses constantly guessing.

Compared to Tom Landry's still-developing system with the Dallas Cowboys or the already powerful Chicago Bears, Lombardi's offense was rather simple. It was all about execution, consistency and minimizing mistakes, which played to Starr's strengths.

The dominant offensive line of the early 1960s—Bob Skoronski and Forrest Gregg at the tackles; Jim Ringo at center; Jerry Kramer and Fuzzy Thurston at the guards; and either Ron Kramer or Gary Knafelc at tight end—was fortified in the crucible of a practice routine known as "the Nutcracker drill," a test of wills against the Packers' most determined defenders . . . and, ultimately, against Lombardi's enormous expectations. Learning to fight through the pain for every ounce of physical and mental strength, the linemen proved very adept at providing plenty of time for Starr to maneuver in the pocket while becoming widely studied across all levels of football for springing Green Bay's signature running play, the Packer Sweep.

Typically called out of a split back formation, the Packer Sweep reflected Lombardi's emphasis on power, precision, and teamwork. The play worked perfectly only if every man did his job—eleven men thinking and acting as one—and Lombardi drew it up on a chalkboard with all the sobriety of a physicist sketching the blueprint for an Atomic bomb. Starr's most important duty was to call it at just the right time; the defense knew it was coming again and again during a typical afternoon, but if he could belie his own tendencies and keep the defense on its toes, the run was even tougher to stop, especially if he could influence the strong side linebacker. To accomplish this, it was critical that he faked the handoff up the middle just right. Choreographed with all the intricacy of a ballet—from the tight end's crucial block of the linebacker, who had to be isolated from the ballcarrier at all costs; to Jim Taylor's assault on the end; and the lead blocking of Kramer and Thurston, who headed upfield, forearms extended, clearing the path of defenders drawn into the developing play—the Packer Sweep was a thing of beauty when everyone accomplished their mission with the proper technique at the right time. "I bet we ran that play no less than fifty times a day," Thurston said. "There were so many variables . . . and Coach Lombardi was going to make sure we were sharp at all times."

The scholarly quarterback took great delight in mastering every detail of this and other plays, which could be seen in his meticulously drawn, and annotated, playbooks and notebooks. For instance, in describing the sweep, he wrote: "Note: weak side offensive tackle pulls just as guards. Tackle's responsibility is to cut off anyone who 'leaks' through."

When Paul Hornung took the handoff from Starr, most fans focused on the Golden Boy's "run to daylight," as his coach was fond of calling the freedom he granted for his runners to find the open seam. At the peak of his playing career in the early 1960s, Hornung's ability to run, cut, and find the daylight made him one of the most explosive backs in the NFL. But the Packer Sweep was anything but glamorous or one-dimensional. It was smash-mouth football at its very best, and Hornung's often brilliant running was merely the predicate in a complex and meticulously crafted sentence.

The success of the sweep empowered Starr's play-calling options. "When the defense was expecting the sweep, we'd line up in that same formation and run a trap inside or a quick toss or even a weak side sweep," he said. "It worked for us even when we weren't running it, because the defense respected it so much."

Forced to guard against Hornung's outside freewheeling and Taylor's punishing inside running, opposing defenses made themselves vulnerable to Starr's knowledge and his underrated arm. Unlike Johnny Unitas or Y. A. Tittle, he rarely threw the ball way downfield with abandon but was the master of precise short and intermediate range passes. Many assumed this reflected a lack of confidence in his arm, but in reality, it had as much to do with his determination not to foolishly gamble his finite drives. This quality—Lombardi called it his "conscientious conservatism"—reflected both strength and weakness. Lombardi sometimes tried to convince Starr to be more daring: "He doesn't throw for those home runs often because, where Unitas or Layne or Tittle will take a chance with an offensive man and a defensive man going down the field together, he has to be sure that his offensive man has that defensive man beaten." The same sort of desire for control that motivated him to have one or two sociable beers and stop also informed his play-calling, where his ego never overwhelmed his judgment. To be sure, there were times when the Packers would have benefited from a quarterback who rolled the dice more on an occasional long pass that required him to thread the needle. "If I could just get him to be a little more daring," Lombardi once said, "he'd be everything." But ultimately, what Lombardi perceived as a weakness more often than not turned out to be a strength, because Starr completed a high percentage of his shorter passes and typically threw fewer than half as many interceptions as the league's other leading quarterbacks. What some interpreted as blandness was instead a very methodical, precise, and risk-averse approach to moving the ball down-field, scoring points and winning games.

"Bart was determined not to beat himself," Hornung said. "That seems like a small thing, but it was huge."

Way ahead of the rest of the league in creating a timing game between quarterback and receiver, Lombardi exploited Starr's intelligence and consistency by teaching him how to produce precise passing lanes for Max McGee, Ron Kramer, Boyd Dowler, and the backs. When Gary Knafelc lined up at left end, ran a post route exactly 14 yards, made a hard, leaning fake to the inside, and planted his right foot, Starr put the ball in the air, knowing Knafelc was about to make a second fake before reaching his final destination. If both quarterback and receiver accomplished their task, the ball landed within Knafelc's grasp, without concern for an approaching defender.

"If I have a defensive man on my outside shoulder when I make my fake, he's not going to catch the ball," Knafelc said. "He may tackle me after I catch the ball, but there is about a five- or six-yard area where Bart can safely throw it to me . . . without fear of getting it picked off."

By building his passing game around such high-percentage situations, Starr maximized his margin for error and gave the defense very few chances to capitalize on his mistakes. "You had to hope one of them screwed up," said former Steelers and 49ers safety Bobby Luna, "and that didn't happen very often."

Starr typically threw a soft pass and rarely needed to put tremendous zip on the ball. But in contrast to his first years in the league—when Tobin Rote saw his lack of arm strength as a weakness, and he worked hard to improve his velocity—the championship era Starr was capable of drilling the ball when the situation warranted it, especially when confronted with a blitz or when he was flushed out of the pocket and needed to dump it off quickly.

Asked many years later to compare his arm to latter-day Packers quarterback Brett Favre, Starr laughed and said, "Oh my heavens! Brett could throw the ball farther standing on his knees than I could standing!"

But he was one of the most fundamentally sound quarterbacks who ever played the game.

Especially after Lombardi's teaching began to sink in, Starr offered a textbook example of how to play the position, starting with his authoritative signal-calling at the line of scrimmage. ("My wife has said that I am pretty much a Dr. Jekyll and Mr. Hyde," Starr once said. "I'm not very loud around the house, but in the fiftieth row of our stadium she can hear me as if I were just across the room.") In addition to the practicality of clearly communicating to his offense, the forcefulness of his delivery also exuded confidence to a defense searching for the slightest vulnerability. "You can tell from the way he rattles off those numbers that he knows what he's doing," said longtime Giants linebacker Sam Huff. "The way Starr barks those automatics, you'd think he was reading the numbers out of a book."

Every move in his routine was practiced over and over again, carefully choreographed and analyzed for the slightest imperfection, from the way he gathered the ball from his center: right hand up, left hand down, fingers slightly spread; to the manner of his handoff to an approaching running back: determined to keep his body between the defender and the ball, lessening the possibility of a fumble-causing tackle in the backfield; to the process of his passing stroke: never losing sight of the need to follow through with a full extension of his arm.

The precision of his mechanics reduced the likelihood of error and empowered him to exploit this mastery in a variety of ways, especially with regard to the all-important fake, a skill he first began to learn during the summer session with Babe Parilli. Being so fundamentally sound and creating such a consistent picture for the defense was central to making his fakes believable. Without the ability to so convincingly fake, he would never have been such a potent play-action passer. Take away the play-action pass and the entire offensive scheme begins to unravel.

Just when a defense was crowding the line on third-and-short, determined to stop the run, Starr loved to fake up the middle and throw downfield. Time after time, defenses were victimized—often for big yardage.

"It's amazing how often that worked," said Packers defensive back Tom Brown, who watched in admiration. "Somehow he really had a knack for fooling defensive backs . . . knowing just when to do it."

A good example of this tactic could be seen in a comeback victory over Detroit in 1965. Facing a third-and-one from the Green Bay 24, Starr faked to the fullback and then hit a streaking Carroll Dale with a perfect pass across the middle. "A great call," Dale surmised, because "the field position called for a run." Caught off guard, the defensive back had rushed toward the line of scrimmage, creating a seam for Dale. "I just stepped behind him, delayed for a second, then took off downfield," Dale explained.

By the time the defensive back starting giving chase, he was fifteen yards downfield, racing 76 yards for the go-ahead touchdown.

"Every time we did that," Starr said years later, "we were taking advantage of the other team's respect for our running game. People sometimes talked about that sort of play as a gamble, but it was really a high-percentage option, because we were taking advantage of a weakness in the defense."

In contrast to the popular notion of the successful quarterback as an instrument of raw power, Starr was more like an exacting surgeon with steely nerves and a prodigious intellect delicately wielding a scalpel, not a hammer, at a defense's weaknesses.

Even though the Packers' line was the one of the best in the game, Starr often took thunderous hits. During the early days, when someone missed a block and Detroit Lions bruiser Alex Karras slipped through to clobber the quarterback, Lombardi watched in horror: "I thought it was the end of my team." But he pulled himself off the grass and went back to work. Starr's lack of scrambling ability made him a target vulnerable to defensive predators such as Alan Page of the Vikings, Dick Butkus of the Bears, and Merlin Olsen of the Rams. "I saw him take some awful punishment and walk back to the huddle like it was nothing," Forrest Gregg said. "He was one of the toughest athletes I've ever been around."

As Starr prepared to play one game with a severe rib injury, he casually asked teammate Gary Knafelc to come talk to him in the training room while he received a shot for the pain. "I'm sitting there and the doctor shoves this needle in his stomach and it looks as big as a saber," Knafelc recalled. "I'm supposed to be there to help him, and I'm about to get sick just watching that big needle being plunged into Bart's body."

The metamorphosis from mild-mannered civilian to fearless quarterback often astonished his teammates, but when Starr strapped on his game face, he was a different person.

"He'd cut your heart out on the football field," said Zeke Bratkowski.

The fierceness Starr displayed—and the shots he sustained—endeared him to his teammates, making them believe in him even more forcefully as Lombardi, who once doubted his ability to summon this critical quality, watched with a sense of gathering admiration.

The same intensity that made Starr such a competitive quarterback spilled over into the rest of his life. After big snowstorms, it was not enough for him to climb out of bed early and use his snowblower to clear the driveway in front of his house. He often kept right on blowing in the frigid air until every driveway in the neighborhood was powder free, which struck him as the neighborly thing to do.

"[The neighbors] wouldn't even know he was out there," Cherry said. "That's just Bart."

As the Starrs moved into the 1960s, with Kennedy in the White House and the nation prosperous and at peace, life was good. No longer struggling, Bart earned a salary exceeding $20,000 and also began attracting the attention of advertisers who paid him handsomely for endorsing their products, placing the family firmly in Green Bay's upper middle class. Especially after the dramatic exchange with his father following the 1961 championship game, he felt a sense of peace about the relationship that had proven so instrumental in driving him to success in professional football but also caused tremendous heartache.

"I don't know if [that moment] changed how they related to each other . . . but it certainly made Bart feel loved, in a way I'm not sure he had ever felt from his father," Cherry said.

By the time the Packers chased their second NFL championship, five-year-old Bart Jr. and his friends in the neighborhood began awakening to the fact that his father had an unusual job. But no one made a big deal about living across the street from the Packers' quarterback. Even as he learned his ABCs and his numbers while growing up in a safe, family-oriented community, Bart Jr. was taught to keep his father's celebrity in the proper perspective.

"Dad often explained to me: He did what other people did . . . worked hard for his organization, gave it his best effort, just like our neighbors, who might be restaurantuers or insurance executives or real estate agents,"

Bart Jr. said. "The only difference was that he was better known, that his job put him in the limelight. Because Dad never thought of himself as better or worse than anybody else because of his profession, I never did, either. He shaped the way I thought about all that from a pretty young age."

On the third martini at a Manhattan hotel bar, Pete Rozelle looked Ed Sabol in the eye and took a leap of faith. "All right," he said, "I'll give you a shot."

Then he paused before blessing their agreement with a memorable warning.

"Don't screw it up!"

Sabol smiled a salesman's smile and shook the commissioner's hand, unwittingly launching the NFL into an entirely new realm.

Two years into his tenure, Rozelle had succeeded in raising the NFL's profile by moving the league's headquarters to New York, expanding to fourteen teams with the addition of franchises in Dallas and Minneapolis, and consummating the first unified television plan while fending off competition from the increasingly aggressive American Football League. Baseball and college football still mattered more than professional football, but the NFL was on its way. When Blair Motion Pictures, Inc., out of Philadelphia, bid three thousand dollars for the film rights to the 1962 championship game—double the previous year's contract—he was intrigued enough to take a cocktail-hour meeting to size up the fledgling company's owner, even after reading that the man had never filmed a professional football game. In his application, Sabol, a onetime overcoat salesman who had already made a fortune but aspired for something more, was candid: His only experience filming football at all had been shooting his son's high school games on an inexpensive sixteen-millimeter camera.

But Ed Sabol was some kind of salesman and Rozelle, still inventing the new-age NFL, was a good judge of character. He had a feeling about the guy.

After sealing the deal, Sabol telephoned his twenty-one-year-old son Steve, then a running back at Colorado College, where he was majoring in art. "I can see by your grades that all you've been doing is going to the movies and playing football," Ed said, springing his pitch. "So . . ." Steve Sabol signed on as a runner for the title game, still several months away.

"The fact that my dad could make such a deal with no experience and for such a small amount of money demonstrates how different things were in those days," said Sabol, the longtime president of what would become NFL Films. "The curtain was rising on a whole new era."

As Blair Motion Pictures started planning for the big game, the first to ever be filmed in color, Vince Lombardi's Packers stampeded through the 1962 season, finishing 13-1 and outscoring the opposition by 415–148. One of the most dominant seasons in league history included blowout victories over the Eagles (49–0), Rams (41–10), Vikings (34–7) and Bears (49–0 and 38–7).

The defense, led by safety Willie Wood, who intercepted a league-leading nine passes, and fellow All-Pros Willie Davis, Herb Adderly, Dan Currie, Ray Nitschke, Henry Jordan, and Bill Forester, smothered opponents, finishing first against the run—allowing just 4 touchdowns—and second against the pass while causing a league-best 50 turnovers.

Jim Taylor won the rushing crown with a career-best 1,474 yards and 19 touchdowns and was named the NFL's Most Valuable Player.

While Taylor soaked up most of the ink, Bart Starr quietly played one of the greatest seasons of his career.

In the first Bears game, he scored 2 touchdowns and threw just 3 incomplete passes.

In a 17–6 victory over the Colts, he outdueled the iconic Johnny U, hitting Ron Kramer for a 25-yard touchdown pass that proved to be the difference.

While many aspects of his steady leadership could not be reduced to easily digestible statistics, an October game against the second-year Minnesota Vikings at Metropolitan Stadium in Minneapolis offered a powerful example of Starr's team-strengthening evolution.

The game quickly turned into a rout as unbeaten Green Bay built a 27–0 lead in the second quarter on the strength of two Starr touchdown passes, a Paul Hornung run, and two Jerry Kramer field goals. It was never close, but Fran Tarkenton made it fun to watch. The elusive former University of Georgia star, who would one day lead the lowly Vikings out of the wilderness and to three Super Bowl appearances, dipped and dodged and made some terrific throws.

When all the numbers were totaled at the conclusion of Green Bay's convincing 48–21 victory, the two quarterbacks had produced nearly identical passing stats:

Starr completed 20 of 28 for 297 yards and 3 touchdowns.

Tarkenton completed 18 of 29 for 288 yards and 2 touchdowns.

But there was one difference—one glaring difference:

Tarkenton tossed three interceptions.

Starr threw none.

Throwing a certain number of interceptions has long been accepted as the price of putting the ball in the air and moving the chains. With high reward comes high risk. This was especially true in the sixties, before the advent of more sophisticated passing offenses that tended to reduce the number of errant balls. Even the best quarterbacks of the day often tossed more interceptions than touchdowns, making Johnny Unitas's 32-touchdown, 14-interception performance during his MVP season of 1959 a marvel of both potency and efficiency.

In 1961, Starr established himself as one of the most efficient passers in the league, tossing just 16 interceptions against 16 touchdowns for a passer rating of 80.3. Among full-year starters, only Cleveland's Milt Plum (10) tossed fewer than Starr. The great Unitas was intercepted 24 times while throwing 16 touchdowns. Philadelphia's Sonny Jurgensen scored 32 touchdowns but was intercepted 24 times. Washington's Norm Snead was picked off 22 times and scored just 11 touchdowns—no wonder the Redskins finished in the cellar.

In Starr's first full year as the Green Bay starter, his aerial precision proved to be an enormous asset for a franchise in ascendance.

But in 1962, he elevated his game to an entirely new level.

In a year when eight different quarterbacks tossed 20 or more interceptions—including New York's Y. A. Tittle (33), Philadelphia's Sonny Jurgensen (26), Chicago's Billy Wade (24), and Unitas (23)—Starr led the league with 9.

Even after factoring in the difference between the number of balls each man lofted into the wind, Starr's interception percentage (3.2) proved to be less than half of Tarkenten's (7.6) or Jurgensen's (7.1), and far below Unitas (5.9), Wade (5.8), and Tittle (5.3).

Beyond the controlled violence of all those bodies slamming together, beyond the meticulously crafted strategies and tactics honed on practice fields and in projection rooms, football has always and will always turn at least partially on what amounts to a glorified math problem: Every minus is a plus for the other guy.

Decades later, while leaning on Starr's low interception rate to make a case for his greatness, particularly in big games, noted NFL researcher Kerry Byrne of the Cold Hard Football Facts Web site condensed his complex mathematical formula to a memorable line: "We want zeros, not heroes."

"Quarterbacks who avoid throwing interceptions are more successful in the postseason than quarterbacks who toss touchdown passes," Byrne concluded.

Starr helped the Packers win in many ways but perhaps most powerfully by not beating himself.

Like all good teams, Green Bay willed a certain amount of its success in 1962 by virtue of its impressive plus-22 giveaway/takeover ratio—by turning the ball over far fewer times than the opposition. No single man was more responsible for the electric force of this stat than Starr, who so rarely made the sort of mistakes that turned into somebody else's plus.

Yes, it was the success of the Packers' powerful running game that allowed him to throw just 285 passes in 1962, compared to Billy Wade's league-leading 412 attempts. But it was also the way he managed his assault: By carefully picking his spots, edified by Lombardi's teaching, which helped him hit those precise holes in time and space, Starr completed a league-best 62.5 percent—nearly five points higher than second-place Frank Ryan of the New York Giants—for 2,438 yards and 12 touchdowns, achieving an NFL-leading 90.7 passer rating.

By dramatically increasing his completion percentage (by 4.2 points) and reducing his interceptions (by 56 percent), Starr gave Lombardi's surging Packers a certain mathematical momentum.

Beyond the raw numbers, Starr was making the Packers better because he was growing smarter and more comfortable in the job. Exploiting the widespread respect defenses developed for Taylor's running ability, he demonstrated a new boldness in the way he attacked short-yardage situations, reflecting an elevated level of sophistication and confidence in his play-calling.

"So much of what Bart did got overlooked that year just like it did many times," Taylor said.

By November, the word Lombardi introduced during the first meeting with his quarterbacks was being tossed around with increasing frequency.

Perfection.

8-0.

9-0.

10-0.

As the Packers relentlessly chased perfection, the whole league buzzed with the prospect of the first undefeated season in NFL history, which seemed like a distinct possibility as fans across the country tuned into CBS television on Thanksgiving Day.

This particular Thanksgiving, unlike any other since the end of World War II, Americans celebrated with a special sense of blessing and relief.

For twelve tense days in October, after American military forces discovered offensive Soviet missiles in Cuba, the world teetered on the brink of nuclear holocaust. When President Kennedy took to the airwaves to brief the nation about the grim situation—including his decision to impose a naval blockade of the communist-backed island—the news united Americans of all walks of life in gloom and fear. Some dug bomb shelters in their backyards. Others obsessively followed the developments through television, radio, and newspapers. Many went to church to pray.

When Soviet premiere Nikita Khrushchev blinked, agreeing to remove the missiles even as Kennedy reluctantly contemplated a full-scale invasion, the whole country exhaled and slowly returned to other pursuits, including the professional football season.

The history of Thanksgiving games dates to the earliest years of the NFL as several franchises, including the Detroit Lions, attempted to capitalize on the holiday to lure fans to the stadium on their day away from work. Starting in 1956, television began the process of transforming the gimmick into a national tradition. By 1962, professional football seemed as central to the Thanksgiving experience as turkey and stomachaches.

The widely anticipated showdown at Tiger Stadium between the Lions and the Packers, the two best teams in the Western Conference, arrived seven weeks after a hard-fought defensive struggle at home. Detroit appeared to have the first game won until quarterback Milt Plum foolishly passed into a crowd on third-and-long in the closing minute and was intercepted by Herb Adderly, who streaked up the sideline, putting the Packers close enough for a winning field goal.

Several times the powerful Lions defense came up with big plays to keep Green Bay out of the end zone, but a good example of Starr's play-calling acumen could be seen in the second quarter, when he checked off to take advantage of Detroit's shift into a 4-3 zone. On the play known internally as Swing Pass Inside Delay, tight end Ron Kramer forced the left linebacker wide, Jim Taylor took the middle linebacker to the left, and the right linebacker pursued Max McGee deep. With the safety occupied by Boyd Dowler, Paul Hornung was wide open over the middle. Starr hit him for 13 yards and a crucial first down inside Detroit territory, demonstrating once more the power of his accumulating knowledge. But the drive eventually fizzled, and Hornung's field goal attempt fell short.

Thanks to Adderly's big play, the Golden Boy got another chance with thirty-five seconds left, the Packers trailing 7–6.

In the moments before the whistle, as the capacity City Stadium crowd of 38,669 waited in anticipation, Dan Currie took a knee and wiped Hornung's kicking shoe with a towel as Starr moved into position. The snap floated cleanly into Starr's hands, he instantly turned the ball and placed it on the ground at the 21, and Hornung planted his foot firmly. The perfect boot allowed Green Bay to escape with a 9–7 victory, the narrow margin serving only to make a very good Detroit team hungry for a second chance.

"Let's remember this," Lombardi told his players in a noisy postgame locker room, raising his voice above the chants of *Adderly! Adderly!* "We were the better team. We made mistakes, and let's not forget it. Let's stop making mistakes."

The rematch six weeks later quickly turned into a rout. The record national television audience of more than 30 million was stunned to see the Lions jump out to a 26–0 lead as the menacing Detroit defense, led by Alex Karras, stuffed the Packers' running game and sacked Starr eleven times. Anticipating the pressure, Lombardi had devised a game plan in which Starr dumped the ball off quickly, but Detroit routinely smothered the Packers' receivers on the line of scrimmage. "Detroit was a helluva football team and they didn't like us very much," recalled Green Bay tackle Bob Skoronski. "Those defensive backs played heads-up on our receivers, leaving Bart with few good options." In the fourth quarter, Starr rallied Green Bay for two touchdowns to make it respectable, but the humbling 26–14 loss shattered all the talk about the Packers' invincibility.

The defeat could not be assigned to one culprit, but offensive guard Fuzzy Thurston felt a terrible burden. "I had just buried my beloved mother on Friday, and I was in a bad place," said Thurston, who missed several blocks as Starr took a beating from the Lions' pass rush. "I felt horrible about it, but Bart handled it so well . . . told me not to worry about it. I never forgot the kindness he showed toward me that day."

Instead of launching into a locker-room tirade, Lombardi soft-peddled the defeat, ascribing it to overconfidence.

"You didn't think we were going to win them all, did you?" he told a surprised press corps.

Privately, he seethed.

Lombardi had just lost his chance at perfection—but recognized the opportunity to reinforce something critical about the game and the larger world it reflected.

The greatest glory is being knocked to your knees and then rising again.

Lombardi repeated this phrase often, until it rang in the head of every single Packer, like a ubiquitous radio jingle.

Of all the lessons Lombardi endeavored to teach his players, few struck so fundamentally at the collision of football and life. What he tried to explain to his players was that being humbled—having some sort of setback—was inevitable in life, but that the real measure of a man was how he reacted to being knocked down. Would he wallow on the ground feeling sorry for himself? Accepting his ultimate defeat? Or would he climb off the turf and go back to work, infused with a renewed determination to transcend the setback?

For an example of the power of rising again, he needed look no further than his own number 15. Time after time, football kept knocking Starr down, but he continued to fight back.

"You learned so many things about life while playing for Coach Lombardi," Starr said. "One of the most important was to persevere. If something bad happens, don't panic. Go back to basics. Work hard. Don't let one failure get you down."

In contrast to the early years of his professional career, when one intercepted pass burrowed into his psyche, causing him distraction and doubt, Starr was now fortified by a steely mental toughness that allowed him—

forced him—to quickly separate from such a setback and move forward with fire and resolve.

In ways that never showed up in the statistics, the force of his will, energized by Lombardi's, strengthened and propelled the Packers.

Lombardi used the Detroit loss to motivate the Packers to push harder in the weeks ahead, while analyzing and learning from the weaknesses exposed by it. Reputation meant nothing. Only performance counted. If the Packers failed to play their game, to execute, fight, claw, and scratch on every play, they could and would be beaten. It was just that simple. In this sense, Lombardi's philosophy was vindicated even in defeat. Instead of collapsing, as some teams in such positions have been known to do, Green Bay stormed through the next three weeks, playing once more like a champion while crushing the Rams, the 49ers, and then the Rams once again to capture a third straight Western Division championship.

Perfection remained elusive, but the 1962 Green Bay Packers personified excellence.

In the weeks leading up to the 1962 NFL Championship Game at Yankee Stadium, Lombardi installed a sign leading into his locker room:

HOME OF THE GREEN BAY PACKERS
THE YANKEES OF FOOTBALL

The message was clear. Since his first days in Green Bay, Lombardi had filled every room he entered with his seething ambition to build not just a winning team but a dynasty. Now his Packers had a chance to take a pivotal step in this direction, in a storied venue poorly suited to football but home to the most successful franchise in the history of professional sports, where the exploits of Ruth, Gehrig, DiMaggio, and many others represented a collective gold standard for winning. He was a New Yorker who admired everything the Yankees represented, so when the players walked into their dressing room and saw the sign, they required no clarification. The boss was telling his men to act like the champions he knew they were.

A different sort of sign hung in the home locker room of the 12-2 New York Giants, champions of the Eastern Conference. It contained not a word but two numerals: 37.

Since the 37–0 drubbing at the hands of the Packers in the 1961 title game, the Giants had been hungry for revenge. Defensive end Andy Robustelli spoke for many of his teammates when he told a reporter, "If we win this game it won't be enough. We have to destroy the Packers and Lombardi. It's the only way we can atone for what happened to us last year."

With better weather conditions, the sort of temperature befitting a professional football championship game in the civilized world, many Giants and their fans believed powerful New York would be able to bring the small-town Arctic wonders down to size.

But the weather was not better. It was worse. Much worse.

When Cherry Starr stepped off the bus at the stadium on the morning on December 30, all bundled up to resist the bitter cold, she was wearing a favorite white fur hat. A stiff gust of wind pulled the hat off her head, into the sky, and toward an uncertain future.

"I never saw that hat again," she said. "Somebody's probably still wearing it."

At game time, the temperature registered 20 degrees; it dipped as low as 10 in the second half. But what made the situation so unbearable was the whipping wind, gusting up to 40 miles per hour.

"It was very, very cold, but it wasn't as cold as the Ice Bowl," Starr said. "That wind . . . that wind was something else. It really had a big impact on the game."

The wind was so severe, it actually toppled the heavy sideline benches before kickoff.

Throughout the game, in an age before sideline heaters, players from both teams huddled around a series of metal oil drums stuffed with trash and doused with lighter fluid, giving the big game the feel of a Depression era sidewalk.

When he walked onto the frozen field for his first NFL game, Steve Sabol watched as Giants quarterback Y. A. Tittle warmed up with Frank Gifford, Lombardi's onetime offensive linchpin who had returned to the lineup after missing the 1961 season with a severe head injury, and the explosive receiver Del Shofner, who entered the game with 12 touchdown receptions. Nearing the end of a brilliant career, the bald-headed Tittle was capping one of his most impressive seasons, having thrown for 3,224 yards, second only to the young bomb-thrower Sonny Jurgensen. His ability to throw short and long was widely admired. (In 1963, the three-time league MVP would throw an NFL record 36 touchdown passes.) As he watched from the sideline, Sabol was shocked when a gust of wind hijacked a Tittle pass intended for Frank Gifford and violently slammed it toward a sideline bench.

"There was such an expression of despair and surprise on Tittle's face," Sabol recalled. "You could tell he realized he was in for a long afternoon."

Starr experienced a similar moment of truth. The initial game plan called for him to emphasize the pass to exploit weaknesses in the Giants' defense, especially its tendency to blitz. "But you couldn't in this weather . . . You couldn't throw long because you weren't sure where the ball would go." When he saw the wind whipping across the field so severely, he conferred with Lombardi and advised a change to a more conservative approach. Because Green Bay was a team that typically relied on the run, the Packers could win by simplifying the game plan and concentrating even more on the ground. But New York's running game was much less productive, which played into Green Bay's hands.

When Willie Wood prepared to kick off for the Packers as the NBC cameras zoomed in on him, a gust swept across the field and lifted the ball off the tee. Frustrated, he placed the ball on the tee again. And the same thing happened. Finally, he called on a teammate to hold the ball and he kicked it into the distance.

Both teams tried to pass, but more often than not, the ball was sucked into the invisible vortex, rendering most aerial adventures risky or even futile. The result was an ugly, bloody, frigid test of wills dominated by two defenses determined to inflict maximum punishment upon each other.

Jim Taylor was a great runner who also liked to hit people, making the 1962 championship game a perfect showcase for his value to the Packers.

Taylor's propensity for going out of his way to slam into defenders when he ran upfield with the ball perplexed his coach, but the Packers learned to appreciate the logic associated with his running style. He went looking for a fight because he wanted the opposition to respect him. Any man who ever collided with Taylor—which his coach once admiringly compared to "bumping into a cast-iron statue"—could not help respecting him, especially the next morning, when wake-up calls were delivered by twinges of pain.

On the Packers' first series, Taylor took a handoff from Starr and plotted a course toward Giants linebacker Sam Huff, a ferocious tackler with a reputation for punishing licks. (In 1960, as professional football's profile began to soar, the CBS television network aired *The Violent World of Sam Huff*, a documentary that took viewers closer than ever before to the action, catapulting Huff to a new level of fame.) Taylor slid on the slippery ice, Huff pushed him out of bounds, and they tumbled to the ground, knees and elbows flying. Climbing off the hard ground spitting blood, Taylor limped back to the huddle and asked for the ball, forcefully demonstrating what he was all about. On a day when any sane person wanted to go home, Jimmy Taylor wanted the ball. Again and again.

"They kept running me out of bounds, because I couldn't cut too well on that field," said Taylor, who carried the ball 31 times for 85 yards. He called it "the hardest-hitting game I ever played in my life."

Play after play, the Giants punished Taylor, two and three and four blue shirts gang-tackling him, slamming him into the concrete-hard frozen dirt, thinking about that number, that cursed 37, focused on revenge. Down ten pounds from his normal playing weight, the Louisiana bruiser looked weak, even before all the violence began. He was suffering from hepatitis, which doctors would not discover until later. But Taylor always climbed off the ground, sometimes spitting blood, always prepared for another adventure in pain.

"The lasting image of that game in my mind is the ferocity and anger of Jim Taylor . . . his barely restrained rage as he ran with the ball," recalled a wide-eyed Steve Sabol, who walked the sidelines making sure the cameramen always had fresh magazines of film and maintaining the piss bucket, because no bathrooms were located nearby. "Taylor just got the shit kicked out of him all day long . . . There was all this trash-talking between him and especially Sam Huff . . . Tons of profanity when they tackled him. I had never experienced anything like that."

All day long, when Huff tackled the determined Packers fullback, he yelled, "You stink, Taylor! You stink!"

In the second quarter, when Taylor broke through a seam and rambled seven yards for the game's only touchdown, giving Green Bay a 10–0 lead heading into the half, he turned to Huff. "How do I smell from here, Sam?"

"Did everything I could to that son of a bitch!" Huff said afterward, adding, with a measure of admiration, "Taylor isn't human. No human being could have taken the punishment he got today."

Starr completed several clutch passes, but it was his steady hand at the controls, methodically driving the Packers close enough for three Jerry Kramer field goals and not doing anything foolish, even as the Giants clobbered him, that paved the way for victory. Hornung contributed several big plays, including a perfectly executed option pass to set up Taylor's touchdown, but an injury prevented him kicking. Kramer, who spent most of his time clearing a path for Starr and the running backs, assumed the kicking chores and became the Packers' most prolific scorer, nailing field goals of 26, 29, and 30 yards, a remarkable feat considering the wind.

The Giants' only touchdown resulted from a special teams failure in the third quarter when Max McGee, subbing for the injured Bowd Dowler, was forced to punt out of his end zone. Erich Barnes charged through to block the kick and Jim Collier fell on the ball, giving New York new hope as the cold intensified.

In the fourth quarter, Tittle skillfully drove the Giants from deep in his own territory to the Green Bay 33, aided by a costly pass interference penalty. But the Packers' defense, led by game MVP Ray Nitschke—a menacing force at middle linebacker who recovered two fumbles and dropped an interception in his hands only because his fingers "were so numb I couldn't feel the ball"—stiffened and held. The last of Kramer's field goals sealed the Packers' 16–7 win and a second consecutive NFL championship.

In later years, Lombardi cited his team's performance as example of character and will to win, but in the locker room, still trying to thaw out, he said simply, "I'm real satisfied with the win. Defensively, we were superb."

Remarking on the experience many years later, Starr said, "Playing in such difficult conditions is one of the things that brought us all together as a team. We went through something very trying as a unit that made us believe in each other even more . . . made us even stronger."

In the years to come, the 1962 Green Bay Packers would often be proclaimed as one of the greatest teams in the history of the National Football League, but for Starr and many others who still had plenty of championship football to play, the goalposts kept moving, as the accumulation of all they had learned produced new reservoirs of desire, skill and resolve.

When he opened the door to the Packers' locker room, a sideline pass dangling from his neck, Steve Sabol suddenly entered a different dimension. He was a strong, tough, streetwise athlete who thought he understood what professional football was all about, but then he saw Ray Nitschke's face, which looked like a mask of dried blood. On one side, a doctor was administering more than a dozen stitches to Jim Taylor's busted lip. On the other side stood Bart Starr. As the quarterback pulled off his shoulder pads and removed his uniform, Sabol was struck by the sight of massive purple welts covering his entire torso.

"It looked like Bart had been in a fight for his life," Sabol recalled.

Deeply affected by the scene, Sabol began to realize the enormous difference between college and professional football, particularly the physical toll wrought by such violent trauma. The wheels in his head began turning as he wondered how many Americans truly appreciated the inherent drama of the sport as he was experiencing it.

"I didn't know this was the beginning of my life's work . . . that I would be part of this for the rest of my life . . . and have a chance to help make it grow," he said.

Ed Sabol was so jittery about his company's big chance, he had spent much of the game in the press-box men's room, dealing with a nervous stomach. His worst fears were confirmed when he learned that two of the firm's six cameras froze, several boxes of film cracked, and one cameraman suffered frostbite.

A veteran of the Normandy invasion and the Battle of the Bulge, the elder Sabol reunited with his son outside the locker room, as they both tried to get warm. "Christ! This was like being in the war again . . . except I wasn't being shot at!"

Lightbulb.

Drawing a parallel to the new D-day epic *The Longest Day*, being hailed as one of the year's best motion pictures, Sabol decided to call their film *Pro Football's Longest Day*.

Featuring the narration of CBS announcer Chris Schenkel and scored with a John Phillips Souza–style march, *Pro Football's Longest Day* premiered several weeks later to great fanfare for a select audience of invited guests—including Giants Frank Gifford, Del Shofner, and Alex Webster, and various influential media and advertising officials—at Toots Shor's, the famed Manhattan watering hole.

The opening scene featured Bart Starr with a toboggan cap pulled over his head, standing in front of Green Bay's City Stadium, looking wholesome enough to sell soap.

"I remember something Coach Vince Lombardi told us when he first came to Green Bay," Starr said, starring into the camera, the hint of a smile rising across his lips. "He said, 'Fellows, there are planes and trains and buses leaving here all the time. If you don't produce for me, you're going to find yourself on one of them. . . .'"

About 15 minutes into the 25-minute film, a waiter tripped over the electric cord and the projector tumbled to the floor, landing in a pile of cocktail sauce and crabmeat. While the quick-thinking Pete Rozelle stood up and began conducting an impromptu press conference, preventing the dignitaries from making a hasty retreat, Steve Sabol got down on his hands and knees, pulled the print out of the gooey mess, and re-threaded the machine so they could complete the screening.

"It was a total disaster," Sabol said.

Despite the embarrassing gaffe, Rozelle and others liked the film and green-lighted Blair Motion Pictures, already over budget on the project, to begin showing it across the country. Throughout the first half of 1963, the Sabols and others screened it for Kiwanis and Rotary clubs, Mason lodges, and other small groups, sometimes aiming a projector toward a dangling bedsheet, winning new fans for professional football with each clicking sprocket.

The film was a long way from the sort that would one day make NFL Films such a powerful force, but it marked the first tentative step in the creation of a new NFL mythology, exemplified by the excellence of the Green Bay Packers and featuring a quarterback whose greatest skill was leadership.

Like all competitive organizations, Lombardi's Green Bay Packers consisted of many different kinds of individuals united by a common cause. Starr and playboy bachelor Paul Hornung were polar opposites but genuinely respected and liked each other. Lombardi learned that Hornung and best buddy Max McGee could party hard and still perform at full speed the next day, so he often looked the other way when they missed curfew. But he never cut them an inch of slack: The duo paid the price for their activities with severe fines, and both knew better than to make any excuses when they were expected to do their jobs.

"Like Max McGee, Paul Hornung was as dedicated and unselfish a player as we had on that football team," Starr said. "The only negative was, he didn't like curfew. If you weren't an insider, you wouldn't know he had broken curfew, certainly not by the way he performed on the field."

For many years, the cumulative fines assessed to Hornung and McGee funded the annual team party.

But Hornung made one mistake that could not be solved with a fine. After a widespread investigation into alleged gambling activities by players on several league teams, the commissioner confronted Hornung with evidence that he had bet on NFL games and suspended him indefinitely, along with Detroit Lions defensive star Alex Karras, on April 17, 1963. The news exploded off the sports pages, becoming a huge national news story and causing Lombardi to consider resigning from the Packers. That Hornung—who grew up practically in the shadows of Churchill Downs—gambled was hardly news, but like all NFL players, he knew better than to bet on league games, which was strictly forbidden in every player's contract. While there was never any suggestion that he altered the outcome of a game, he understood the perils of starting down a road that could leave an athlete vulnerable to gamblers. The integrity of the entire sport was on the line, and to his credit, Rozelle understood the need to act swiftly. Even as many wondered if the two high-profile players were being turned into scapegoats, Hornung took his punishment like a man, admitting his crime and vowing to keep his nose clean so the commissioner would eventually give him another chance.

"I made a terrible mistake," Hornung told reporters who followed him to a golf course when the suspensions hit the wires. "I realize that now. I am truly sorry."

The news was a body blow to the Packers' bid for an unprecedented third consecutive title and a devastating revelation to Lombardi, who felt personally betrayed by a young man he thought of as a son. When camp opened, Lombardi was determined to prove that no man was indispensable, even if the man was a beloved figure and arguably the most talented athlete on the roster. Tom Moore proved to be an able substitute. But he was not Paul Hornung. Losing the season opener to Chicago 10–3 put the Packers in a mighty hole, because the Bears, rivals for supremacy in the Western Conference, were headed for one of their best years of all time.

In week six, the 4-1 Packers suffered an even more devastating blow when Starr went down with a critical injury during a 30–7 road victory over the St. Louis Cardinals. Flushed out of the pocket, he scrambled out of bounds, where he collided with defensive back Jim Hill and fell awkwardly, snapping a bone in the back of his right hand. After swinging a fist at Starr and bumping him, Hill was ejected from the game. When Starr, shaken up on the play, leaned down to pick up his helmet, he could not lift it. "That's when I realized my hand was hurt," he said. Although he had played much of the 1961 season with a torn abdominal muscle, hiding it from Lombardi, it was impossible for him to play with a broken throwing hand. Doctors advised Lombardi that Starr, who had started forty-four straight games for the Packers, would be out for three to four weeks.

"I almost went crazy sitting it out," he confided later.

While backup John Roach took the reins and led the Packers to victories over the Colts, Steelers, and Vikings, Lombardi negotiated a trade for another quarterback, former Rams starter Zeke Bratkowski.

When she heard about the acquisition, the name immediately rang a bell with Cherry Starr.

Several weeks before, Cherry had been shopping in a downtown Green Bay department store when she noticed two large men fumbling over the ladies' sweaters. She could tell they were football players, and since she knew all the Packers, she assumed they were members of the Los Angeles Rams, in town for a game against the Packers the next day. Always friendly and outgoing, she introduced herself to the men, who turned out to be Charley Britt, whose bleach blond hair marked him as an out-of-towner, and Zeke Bratkowski, who was having a difficult time selecting a gift for his wife, Mary Elizabeth, known to one and all as M. E.

Zeke Bratkowski?

Now it was coming back to her.

In addition to having been the All-SEC quarterback at Georgia when Bart was at Alabama—Zeke barely edged him out for the nation's best punting average in 1953—Bratkowski's return to civilian life and professional football was directly related to Starr's Air Force activation. She would never forget the story in the local Florida newspaper, illustrated with a pair of cleats, asking the rhetorical question: Can Bart Starr fill Zeke Bratkowski's shoes?

As the dots connected in her head, Cherry gently steered him away from the sweater he had selected. "It was not very attractive," she recalled.

When she offered to help him find a nice present for his wife, he gladly accepted. Two days later, when he arrived back in Los Angeles and gave M. E. the sweater, he confessed that he had received some help picking it out.

"I knew about Bart Starr, of course, but that was the first time I ever heard Cherry's name, and it was because she took the time to do something nice for me, even though she didn't know me," M. E. said.

One of the most celebrated quarterbacks in the history of the tradition-rich University of Georgia program, Bratkowski twice led the Southeastern Conference in passing under Wally Butts and was drafted in the second round by the Bears, the 17th overall selection. His promising career with the Bears was interrupted by his stint as a jet pilot in the service, and after being traded to the Rams for former Vanderbilt star Bill Wade, he soon wound up playing behind the potent arm of the young Roman Gabriel, destined for greatness on the powerful team assembled later in the decade by George Allen. A few short years after Paul Brown wielded the words "Green Bay" and "trade" like a knife, the scene was dramatically different when word reached Bratkowski that he had been dealt from the 1-6 Rams to the 6-1, two-time defending NFL champions.

Green Bay now equaled excellence.

"I couldn't wait to get packed," he said.

After a long day of flying to reach Green Bay, requiring several plane changes, Bratkowski arrived one night after practice and checked into his room at the Holiday Inn. Not long after he settled in, the phone rang. It was Starr, welcoming him to the club and inviting him to come over to his house to watch film, launching a weekly habit that would take on all the markings of a ritual.

The two quarterbacks clicked immediately, united by their intense desire to win, similar personalities, and a shared military background, which gave both men a very precise and disciplined view of the world.

Several months later, when the school term ended, M. E. moved east with the children and was befriended by the lady who had selected one of her favorite sweaters. They were sisters from the start.

In the years ahead, the Starrs and the Bratkowskis became the best of friends, sharing each other's joys, challenges, and heartbreaks. "When we first met, it was like we had known each other our whole lives," Cherry said.

The first call from Starr surprised Bratkowski, but he quickly learned what a special organization Lombardi had built. Beyond the undeniable talent of athletes like Hornung, Taylor, McGee, and Nitschke, Green Bay dominated for one simple reason: It was all about the team. Somehow, Lombardi skillfully sublimated all of those egos into the larger purpose of winning. "The whole atmosphere was team, team, team," Bratkowski said, "and that was really refreshing."

No single person personified the team-oriented approach quite like Starr, whose first impulse was not to be threatened by the new quarterback, but instead, to embrace his skill and knowledge to help the team's pursuit of a third straight league championship.

In most cases, the reserve quarterback tends to be an athlete either on his way up or out. Backups want to start; the very ambition that drives them to be good enough to make a roster often produces tension, rivalry and sometimes undercutting of the starter. But the tandem of Starr and Bratkowski was unusual in the history of the National Football League. "Zeke wanted to win as much as I did," Starr said. "It was all about the team."

Starr learned the measure of Bratkowski soon after he arrived from Los Angeles, when the new No. 2 discovered how to tell when the Pittsburgh Steelers were going to blitz. Bratkowski brought the tip-off to Starr's attention and spent much of the second half signaling him from the sideline, providing vital help in a close game that turned into a rout. Unlike his experience with the volatile Lamar McHan, Starr and Bratkowski became extremely close teammates and friends. "We got so close . . . like brothers," Bratkowski said. "We spent so much time together, we almost thought like one person."

Good enough to start for many NFL franchises, the very precise Bratkowski—shaped by his experience as an Air Force pilot, where "if you hit the wrong button, you die"—instead became defined by his backup role with the Packers. The special bond Starr developed with Lombardi gave him a certain amount of job security, but instead of keeping Bratkowski at a distance, Starr endeavored to teach him and learn from him. Instead of weakening Starr, the arrival of Bratkowski made him a better quarterback as the two men pushed and supported one another in the years ahead.

More than four decades later, Packers quarterback Brett Favre would strike a dramatically different tone, telling reporters, "It's not my job to be a mentor" to the young backup Aaron Rodgers. When Rodgers supplanted the record-setting Favre and led Green Bay to its thirteenth NFL championship in 2010, the lingering tension between the two men provided additional context to a long-ago quarterback partnership.

With Starr still healing and Bratkowski not up to full speed on the offense, Roach struggled in the rematch against the Bears, who won a decisive 26–7 victory over the Packers at Wrigley Field, taking a pivotal lead in the Western Conference race. Whether the outcome would have been the same with Starr in the lineup, no one could say, but Lombardi fully appreciated that the Packers were a far different team with Starr at the helm than without him.

Like millions of Americans, Starr was preoccupied with his own life during the third week of November. The doctors had cleared him to return to the lineup against the cellar-dwelling San Francisco 49ers at Milwaukee's County Stadium, and as he moved through drills early in the week, he could feel his battered arm growing stronger. On Friday, a few minutes after a team meeting was adjourned, someone ran in with the news: President Kennedy had been shot. Like the rest of the country, Starr felt a sense of profound sadness and wondered how such a thing could have happened, unable to fully comprehend that the assassination had slammed the door on an era in American history.

After the commissioner decided to go ahead with the weekend's games, Starr returned to action two days later, leading the Packers to a 28–10 victory over the 49ers. "Starr's the boy who hurt us the most," said San Francisco head coach Jack Christiansen. "He's the most underrated quarterback in the league and he's liable to be the best." Beyond the 10 of 14 passes Starr completed for 107 yards, Jim Taylor alluded to the edge that the Packers had missed the most: "Bart did a magnificent job of play selection." Starr led Green Bay to two more victories and a tie but the Packers' 11-2-1 finish left them in second place behind the 11-1-2 Bears, who captured the league championship with a 14–10 victory over the Giants.

The country was still in a daze when the Packers and Cleveland

Browns took the field at Miami's Orange Bowl on January 9, 1964, for something called the Playoff Bowl, a glorified consolation game between the second-place winners of the two conferences. Devised by Pete Rozelle primarily as a way of squeezing more money out of the television networks and giving the league a bit more exposure at a time when the postseason was otherwise limited to the championship game, the Playoff Bowl was contested every year from 1960–69, destined to be swept into the history books by the NFL-AFL merger. Of the meaningless game, the Rams' Roman Gabriel once famously said, "You're playing for third place in the NFL, which is like playing for third place in a war." Lombardi's disdain for the game and what it represented was well known: "A hinky-dinky football game, held in a hinky-dinky town, played by hinky-dinky players. That's all second place is—hinky dinky!"

The fourth renewal of the event was most notable for a gimmick employed for the first time in an NFL game by CBS director Tony Verna.

In the early days of television, the same quality that made football perfectly suited to the medium—live action in a controlled setting—also reflected its inherent limitations. Live meant live. One play happened and then it was gone. Viewers, like fans in the stands, never got a second look at a pivotal play. Fans of the day did not yet know what they were missing, but Verna, who had been directing NFL and college games for several years, began wrestling with a solution to this constraint at a time when few others even recognized the existence of a problem.

After several weeks of preparation, including the retrofitting of a bulky and expensive videotape machine designed for use at the network studios, and overcoming a variety of technical obstacles, Verna invented what one day would be known as instant replay while directing Navy's 21–16 victory over Army at Philadelphia's Municipal Stadium on December 7, 1963.

"Ladies and Gentlemen," play-by-play man Lindsey Nelson told the viewing audience as Army quarterback Rollie Stichweh reappeared on the screen, dashing once more into the end zone, as if by magic, "what you are seeing is a tape of Army's touchdown. This is not live, but something new . . ."

Thanks to Verna's inventive mind and persistence in making instant replay a reality, the experience of watching football on television would never be the same.

Since NBC owned the rights to the NFL championship game, Verna's first chance to display his creation came during the Playoff Bowl, where he replayed about a dozen snaps in Green Bay's 40–23 victory over the Browns, as Starr hit 15 of 18 passes for 259 yards and 3 touchdowns. By the next season, fans would start to expect instant replay as part of the NFL experience, setting the stage for the most memorable moment of Starr's career.

Even after beating a Cleveland team led by the powerful running of Jim Brown, the sting of finishing second loomed across the entire Packers organization, where winning indeed was the only thing. But on February 1, 1964, Bart's frustration turned to joy when Cherry gave birth to their second son, Bret Michael Starr. The boy was healthy and the mother came through it all like a champ, glad to have the father nearby for the entire process. Nine days later, when a record television audience tuned to CBS to watch The Beatles make their first appearance on *The Ed Sullivan Show* and the whole country seemed to be caught up in Beatlemania and the British Invasion of American popular music, Bart and Cherry were consumed once more by dirty diapers and 3 A.M. feedings, and loving every minute of it.

The fear always lingered in the back of Cherry's mind. She understood how rough football could be. Bart always tried to shield her from his pain, but the evidence often was tattooed all over his body. Sometimes he climbed into bed at night and winced, and she knew. Like all successful professional football players, he learned to play through the pain, and she tried not to think about the punishment he absorbed every time some massive defender slammed him to the ground. But in the back of her mind lingered the fear that he might one day be seriously injured.

"The anxiety was always there," she said. "The night before a game, I always had a hard time sleeping and that was one of the reasons . . . worrying about something happening to him."

Ten weeks into the 1964 season, with the prodigal son Paul Hornung back from suspension, Cherry was watching the Packers–49ers game from San Francisco on television when Bart was knocked cold by a thunderous hit, sprawled motionless on the field. Out came the stretchers. Half a continent away, she watched helplessly as her husband was carried off the field, her mind racing.

After leading Alabama to the SEC championship in 1953, Starr was sidelined by a crippling back injury and a coaching change as the Crimson Tide descended into a dark age. *(Courtesy of the Paul W. Bryant Museum)*

During Alabama's loss to Rice in the 1954 Cotton Bowl, Starr, playing both ways, raced up the field with an interception. *(Courtesy of the Paul W. Bryant Museum)*

After initially doubting his ability to become a winning quarterback, Vince Lombardi learned to appreciate Starr's cool head and his intense desire to win. *(Lee Balterman/ Getty Images)*

Above: During Bart's sophomore year at Alabama, the quarterback eloped with high school sweetheart Cherry. The couple celebrated their 57th wedding anniversary in 2011. *(Courtesy of the Starr family)*

Right: Determined not to beat himself, Starr once threw 294 consecutive passes without an interception, which stood for many years as an NFL record. *(Courtesy of the Paul W. Bryant Museum)*

Often overshadowed by flashier quarterbacks, Starr nevertheless finished his career with the highest completion percentage in league history. *(Focus on Sport/Getty Images)*

Green Bay's powerful running game was mechanical in its precision, but many failed to appreciate Starr's masterful play-calling skills, which kept the opposition guessing. *(George Silk/Getty Images)*

Scrambling was not Starr's strong suit, but he was a competitor who hated to take a needless sack. *(Vernon Biever/Getty Images)*

Although he was often dismissed as a robotic extension of his coach, Starr called nearly every play for the Packers, fortified by Lombardi's careful instruction and his obsessive film study. *(Vernon Biever/Getty Images)*

The unusual relationship between Starr and longtime backup Zeke Bratkowski loomed large in Green Bay's historic run during the 1960s. *(Vernon Biever/Getty Images)*

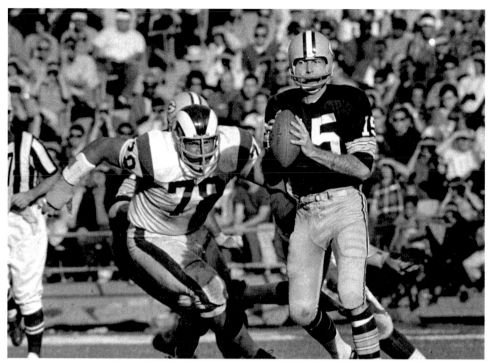

Known for his poise in the pocket, Starr frequently released the ball just before sustaining a devastating lick from a blitzing defender . . . such as Rams tackle Roger Brown. *(Vic Stein/Getty Images)*

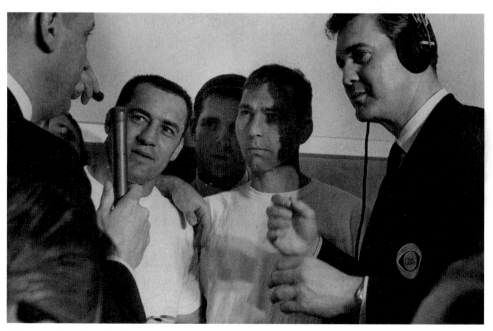

After leading the Packers to victory in Super Bowl I, MVP Starr and teammate Jim Taylor answered questions for CBS's Pat Summerall and NBC's George Ratterman. *(Vernon Biever/Getty Images)*

Years after turning down the chance to play for Paul "Bear" Bryant at Kentucky, Starr watched with great satisfaction as he restored the Alabama program to national prominence. *(Courtesy of the Paul W. Bryant Museum)*

Like teammate Paul Hornung, Starr felt a profound sense of loss on the day when Vince Lombardi was laid to rest. *(Vernon Biever/Getty Images)*

Despite the pressures associated with serving as the Packers' head coach and general manager, Starr was the consummate family man for (*left to right*) Bart Jr., Cherry, and Bret. *(Courtesy of Starr family)*

Burdened by his own inexperience and a franchise sorely lacking in draft choices, Starr produced just a single playoff victory in his nine years at the Green Bay helm. *(Ronald C. Modra/Sports Imagery/Getty Images)*

More than 45 years after John Gillespie's fateful telephone call, which launched one of the greatest causes of their lives, Bart and Cherry remained very involved in Wisconsin's Rawhide Ranch for troubled boys. *(Courtesy of Rawhide Ranch)*

Long after he stepped away from the football field, Starr often went out of his way to accommodate his many fans. *(Courtesy of University of Alabama Sports Information/Kent Gidley)*

After moving to Birmingham following several years in Phoenix, Bart and Cherry were able to watch their granddaughters, Shannon *(seated in middle)* and *(left to right, on floor)* Jennifer and Lisa, grow up. *(Courtesy of Starr family)*

"I was really panicking . . . not knowing if he was alive or dead," she recalled.

Several minutes later, Starr woke up in the locker room and began talking and moving around. The team doctor telephoned his frantic wife. "I was so relieved," she said. "It was the most considerate thing for the doctor to do . . . to think of me at that moment."

Starr was back in uniform two days later.

The next Sunday, before a packed house in Milwaukee, an example of Starr's gutsy game management could be seen as the Packers trailed the Browns 14–7 in the third quarter.

Facing a fourth and one from his own 44-yard line, with the Browns lined up in a goal-line defense, Starr faked perfectly to Jim Taylor, causing the middle linebacker to commit as Taylor bulled into the line. Starr then lofted a short pass just over the line to flanker Max McGee, hitting him in full stride. McGee caught the ball cleanly and ran into the distance as the home crowd roared.

"I sort of shuddered in the huddle [when Starr called the play]," McGee explained later. "I was nervous waiting for the ball to come down. It was up there an awful long time."

Exploiting the Browns' respect for Taylor and their belief that he would play the percentages, the quarterback demonstrated his ability to gamble big and turn the opposition's strength into a weakness. This was not the act of a robot.

"The call was Bart's," Lombardi conceded. "We certainly didn't plan to pass from there . . . it was a helluva play."

The play also caught the Browns completely by surprise as McGee raced down the field, into the secondary and toward an apparent touchdown. A defender tripped him near the goal line; he tumbled into the end zone, and the officials ruled him down at the one. On the next play, Taylor bulled his way in for the tying touchdown.

"I've called it before on fourth down," Starr explained, "but never from that far away. We were a long, long way out."

Seven days after being carried off the field on a stretcher, the resilient Starr was named the NFL Player of the Week for his performance in the 28–21 victory over the Browns.

Even as Starr led in passing percentage for the second time in three years—completing 59.9 percent for 2,144 yards, 15 touchdowns and just 4 interceptions—the Packers stumbled out of the gate and finished a disappointing 8-5-1, second once again, this time behind Baltimore. Two of the losses came at the wire to the Colts, the first one a 21–20 nail-biter secured by a rare Starr interception.

With the Colts already tagged with one loss to the powerful Bears, Green Bay had the chance to knock Baltimore into a mighty hole in the tight Western Division race. Heading toward a climactic finish, a missed extra point loomed large, but after the defense forced a turnover and Green Bay picked up a first down, putting the team near field-goal range, Starr called a time-out to discuss the situation with Lombardi, who wanted him to throw a flood pass to tight end Ron Kramer.

In the huddle, believing he had a better idea, Starr overruled his coach, as he often did. Just before he lofted a pass for Max McGee, who was faking across the middle and heading for the sideline, a fast-approaching Colts defender hit his elbow, veering the ball way off course. It never came anywhere close to McGee, who was wide open, and instead was intercepted by Don Shinnick. Game over.

In the dressing room, Lombardi blasted his quarterback. Starr took it like a man, but after a torturous night of replaying the tipped pass over and over again in his head, he vowed to put it behind him. This was a sign of maturity for a quarterback still growing and learning. "If I can point to one turning moment in my career," Starr said several years later, "it was that play."

In the frustrating year of 1964—culminated by a Playoff Bowl loss to the Cardinals—the aging Packers played inconsistently and lacked the fire that had produced those back-to-back championships. They needed a renewed focus and some new blood. But thirty-year-old Starr was just hitting his prime.

SIX

RESPECT

The pungent aroma of sweat filled the bus as rookie center Bill Curry moved up the aisle and found a seat near the back. Every muscle in his body ached.

Prior to the 1964 season, Lombardi traded All-Pro center Jim Ringo, who had been a key figure in the first two championships, to Philadelphia. The circumstances of Ringo's departure long ago became part of the Lombardi legend. According to one account, apparently perpetuated by the old man himself, Ringo's decision to become the first Packer to hire an agent—and the representative's demand of a significant raise— caused Lombardi to send him packing in a fit of rage. While it was true that Lombardi did not like the idea of a third party intruding on the player-coach relationship, the move apparently was something he had been contemplating as one way of injecting new blood into the team. Whether Ringo's hiring of the agent actually prompted the trade, no one could say with absolute certainty, but the possibility of cause and effect was useful for Lombardi because it made other Packers think twice about hiring one, helping perpetuate the boss's air of dominance and the all-important focus on the team concept. After experimenting with coverted tackle Bob Skoronski and rookie Ken Bowman during the disappointing 1964 season, Lombardi opened training camp at St. Norbert College in 1965 still looking for a reliable center, which gave Curry, drafted in the 20th and final round out of Georgia Tech, an opportunity to make the roster.

Like every other player on the bus leaving the practice facility, Curry was looking forward to catching a couple of hours' rest back at the team hotel. In no time at all, they would have to climb back on the bus, return to St. Norbert, and resume Lombardi's bone-rattling quest for another championship.

"I was so exhausted . . . just starting to learn what Coach Lombardi was all about. Then something happened that taught me a great deal about my quarterback," Curry said.

As Starr started to walk up the steps of the bus, he noticed a crowd of children standing nearby, screaming his name.

"Bart! Bart! Bart!"

When Starr walked away from the bus and approached the crowd, Curry and many other players watched with a sense of frustration.

"The rest of us were hiding on the bus, trying to avoid those kids," Curry said. "We just wanted to get out of there, because we only had a little time to rest before we had to come back. But Bart didn't think that way."

When Starr signed the first autograph, the entire crowd of perhaps a hundred young people converged on him, pushing and shoving each other, angling to get close to him, shake his hand, ask him a question.

"Okay, stop the pushing!" he said in a booming voice. "I'll stay here and sign something for everybody. No need to push!"

Like the other Packers, Curry soon learned that Starr took his relationship with the fans very seriously. When someone asked for his autograph or a moment of his time, he was genuinely gratified by the attention and felt an obligation to treat each and every person with respect. This could be seen as Starr, despite his fatigue—despite his teammates' impatience—stood in the sun for more than half an hour, speaking to every kid like he was the most important person in the world.

The scene also reflected the mind-set that played a significant role in Starr's success: His determination to do the little things that ultimately make the difference between winning and losing, to go above and beyond even when no one is looking, to act like a champion at all times.

Because winning is not a sometime thing.

———

The change happened slowly, imperceptible to most casual observers, but by the middle of the 1965 season, the trend was unmistakable. As Jim Taylor and Paul Hornung aged and lost a step—Taylor's rushing average fell from 5.0 to 3.5 in one year and the Golden Boy was slowed by an injury—more of the offensive load fell to Starr, just as the quarterback was reaching his physical and mental peak. The ball-control offensive philosophy remained, but as Green Bay slipped to tenth in the league in rushing, Starr was called upon to win more games with his arm, and he rarely disappointed, completing 55.8 percent of his passes for 2,055 yards and a career-best 16 touchdowns to lead the Packers to a 10-3-1 finish in 1965.

Even as he became a more daring figure in the air, Starr's efficiency remained high. In fact, during a stretch from the middle of the 1964 season through the middle of the 1965 season, he threw 294 consecutive passes without an interception. The number jumps off the page, testifying to a level of consistency rarely experienced in professional football. That Starr could negotiate such a long stretch without making a single throwing mistake, without once putting the ball slightly off the mark while being rushed by a menacing defender, seems almost inconceivable. This reflected not only the maturation of his increasingly deft passing touch, but also the careful application of all his knowledge as a play-caller. Starr had always made very few mistakes; now he was gradually increasing his degree of difficulty but still committing few errors. (The record stood for sixteen years, until Cleveland's Bernie Kosar reached 308 straight passes without being picked off in 1990–91. New England's Tom Brady eventually surpassed Kosar, accumulating a streak of 319 during the 2010 season.)

For his entire professional career, Starr had been pursuing Colts star Johnny Unitas. He idolized Unitas, meticulously studied film of him, and tried to emulate him in many ways. "He was such a special player . . . my hero and then my rival," he said. "We became great friends. I was grateful for the friendship that developed." Like Starr, Johnny U was a furious competitor who had fought his way into the National Football League. Like Starr, Unitas knew how it felt to be rejected. Like Starr, he was defined by a certain tenacity that made teammates love him and opponents admire him. Like Starr, he was a team man who cared little about statistics, money, or fame but lived to win. Even though Unitas emerged as a major sports figure while Starr was still waiting for Lombardi to rescue him from obscurity, most of their respective careers occurred against the relief of professional football's dramatic rise in the sixties, as each man, in his own way, symbolized what it meant to be a professional quarterback. While Starr's place in the limelight was shrouded by Lombardi's magnetic legend, the Colts' head coaches—first Weeb Eubank, who eventually moved on to the AFL's New York Jets, and Don Shula, who later gained his greatest fame with the Miami Dolphins—always seemed smaller than the towering Johnny U. No matter how much Starr accomplished—including a career 13–9 head-to-head advantage in the series—he always seemed to be caught in Unitas's enormous shadow.

Frequently named to the same Pro Bowl team, the two men became friendly during the early 1960s, when Unitas often told teammates, "The only player I ever talk money with is Bart Starr, because we're in the same business. I respect him and I think he should know what I make."

Many years later, after both men retired, they stayed in touch and sometimes played golf together with their two juniors. "There was such mutual respect between these two men," recalled Bart Jr. "Dad just admired Unitas so much."

On a trip to Birmingham for a charity event, Unitas took a liking to Jim 'N Nick's Bar-B-Q, a local chain with an outlet just up the road from Bart's and Cherry's house, so Starr made a habit of sending him a shipment each year for Christmas. Unitas reciprocated with some of Baltimore's finest crab cakes.

Long before the days of barbecue and crab cakes, Unitas made Starr a better quarterback by giving him someone to chase.

Ted Williams had Joe DiMaggio.

Muhammad Ali had Joe Frazier.

Bart Starr had Johnny Unitas.

During the second week of the 1965 season at the newly dedicated Lambeau Field, with the Colts and Packers tied 10–10 in the third quarter and the early lead in the Western Division race up for grabs, Green Bay faced a fourth-and-one from its own 12. Remarkably, to the astonishment of every soul in the stadium, Starr decided to go for it.

In the huddle he called a trap, featuring Elijah Pitts up the middle, but never intended to hand the ball off.

As Pitts bulled forward, shocked when the quarterback failed to stuff the ball into his arms, the defense bit on the fake, made all the more realistic by the halfback's genuine follow-through, and Starr darted around right end for a 19-yard gain and a crucial first down, setting the stage for Green Bay's 20–17 victory.

Who is that quarterback and what has he done with Bart Starr?

What made the call so perfect was that it seemed completely out of character—like something the daring Johnny U might do—demonstrating Starr's ability to turn his reputation as a mechanical quarterback who assiduously followed a game plan into a defensive vulnerability: One moment he's a classical musician, following Lombardi's chart with precision, striking each key just so. The next he's improvising like John Coltrane—using his brain to turn even the sloppiest slugfest into a test of intelligence and nerves.

So you think you know me, huh?

Writing in *The Detroit News*, Pete Waldmeir became one of the first members of the national media to suggest the full measure of Starr's ascendance: "For five years Bart Starr has been just inches away from becoming another Johnny Unitas. Yesterday he crept right up next to the Baltimore Colts' fabulous quarterback . . ."

To an entire generation of Colts fans, this was, of course, blasphemy. No one played the game like Johnny U, who typically threw at least twice as many touchdowns in a season as Starr—and once tossed a TD in forty-seven consecutive games, one of the greatest records in the history of professional football.

Starr was too focused on leading his team to another championship to get caught up in the comparison, but hearing his name uttered in the same breath as his idol—even if he ultimately lost the argument in a country mesmerized by Unitas's aura—was the sort of accomplishment that transcended statistics.

Comparing the two quarterbacks, Detroit Lions safety Bruce Maher said, "Unitas may be able to burn you faster because of his arm, but Starr will frustrate you to death. He will find the weakness in your defense and keep after it until you adjust. Then he will find the new weakness. And when you do something about that, he'll go back after the old weakness."

The nuance of Starr's adjustments often eluded fans, but coaches learned to recognize his skill.

"You can't take any kind of gamble against him," said San Francisco defensive coordinator Dick Voris. "Any gamble produces a weakness and he always finds it. For instance, if you blitz him, he'll let you come within inches and then flick the ball out on a screen pass for a big gain."

Beyond their various strengths, Unitas's style of play tended to make him a more exciting player, contributing to a more emotional connection with the fans. Because Starr led a more conservative, methodical offense dependent on exploiting defensive vulnerabilities, he could be fully appreciated only if you saw the game through a more calculating, cerebral lens.

"Bart is a fine quarterback," Unitas once said, "but he calls plays to control the ball and I gamble. I throw any time. He throws when the odds are in his favor. But he's a heck of a passer. Look at his statistics. Or the scoreboard."

But then, at just the right moment, he could surprise you, mocking his own reputation with a fourth-and-one from his own 12.

A month after the victory over the Colts, Starr rallied the undefeated Packers from a 21–3 halftime deficit against Detroit by throwing touchdown passes of 62, 32, and 76 yards to key a 31–21 victory over the stunned Lions. Hitting 15 of 23 passes on the day for 301 yards, he piloted a long drive to clinch the win in the fourth quarter, faking to Jim Taylor and scoring the go-ahead touchdown on a quarterback keeper.

No longer the dominant Packers of old, aging Green Bay endured a season of highs and lows and plenty of adversity in 1965. After struggling in midyear losses to the Bears and Lions, Starr told reporters he was grateful to Lombardi for sticking with him during a mini-slump. "I really stunk up the joint the last couple of weeks," he said. "I know I've been pressing too hard."

Two days after losing to the last-place Rams in November, Lombardi walked into the meeting room and tore into his team.

"Goddammit! You guys don't care if you win or lose! I'm the only one who cares!" he thundered. "I'm the only one who puts his blood and guts and heart into the game!"

He went on like this for several minutes, berating the players' performance, questioning their desire.

Finally, offensive tackle Forrest Gregg bolted out of his chair, breathing fire. "I want to win! It tears my guts out to lose! We lay our ass on the line for you every Sunday!"

Then Starr jumped up . . . and Bob Skoronski . . . and Willie Davis—

each man challenging their coach's perspective, each man proclaiming their absolute commitment to the cause.

All the while, the wheels in Lombardi's head kept turning.

He was wearing the mask of an enraged tyrant, but inside, he was smiling, because he knew he had his players right where he wanted them.

Lombardi understood how much Gregg, and Starr, and Skoronski, and Davis, and all the rest wanted to win. He had watched every last one of them spill their blood from Pittsburgh to San Francisco and back in the cause of winning championships for the Green Bay Packers.

But did *they* remember how important it was to them?

Sometimes, Lombardi pushed his players to reach. Sometimes, he pushed them to see if they would push back.

"We were practically in tears because he had challenged our very being," Starr recalled. "I think he had a definite purpose in doing so. He could see we were about to be deeply involved in some sort of slump, and I think maybe this was his way of jacking us up and out of it."

Every man in the room walked out of the room determined to prove the old man wrong—which was exactly what he wanted.

"Lombardi was the master," Davis said with a laugh. "He knew what to say to get in our heads."

After beating the Vikings and the Colts, a 24–24 tie against the 49ers in the last game of the regular season forced the Packers into a playoff with the Colts for the Western Conference flag. On the first play from scrimmage, Starr dumped the ball off short to Bill Anderson, who was hit hard and fumbled in midair to the Colts' Don Shinnick, who started running upfield for a touchdown. Starr gave chase but was blocked to the ground by Jim Welch, a collision that broke one of Starr's ribs, preventing him from raising his arm high enough to pass. Forced into duty in the most critical situation of his career, Zeke Bratkowski was impressive, hitting 22 of 39 passes for 248 yards to lead the Packers to a thrilling 13–10 victory in sudden death. Don Chandler, acquired from the Giants during the off-season to replace Hornung, who was no longer able to kick, sent the game into overtime with a controversially close field goal. Many Baltimore fans believed the boot sailed wide. Then he nailed one to win it that left no doubt, setting up a showdown with the Browns for the NFL championship.

The 1965 season had taken shape against the backdrop of the rapidly widening war in Vietnam, which hit especially close to home for Starr, who might have been shipped off to the fight the communists, given a different twist of fate. By the fall, 120,000 American boys were on the ground and President Lyndon Johnson's advisers were privately telling him, behind closed doors and away from the earshot of the press, that it could take half a million troops to achieve their objective. It was also the year of the Watts riots and the Selma-to-Montgomery march that would forever be known as Bloody Sunday, paving the way for the passage of the Voting Rights Act, the climactic legislative initiative of the civil rights movement. Still, most Americans were too caught up in the space race, Beatlemania, and another exciting football season to linger much on Selma, Watts, or Vietnam.

The question of whether Starr could start against the Browns hung like a dark cloud over the entire team. "That whole week leading up to [the championship game] we were wondering how in the world he was going to be able to play," recalled then eight-year-old Bart Jr., who spent the week listening to the fears of his mother and his paternal grandparents, in town for the big game. "On Wednesday and Thursday, he still couldn't lift his arm up very far at all and he was in terrible pain. I remember asking him about it and he just said, 'Come Sunday, I'll be ready to go.'"

On Friday, Lombardi was cagey with reporters: "If I told you Bart was going to start, I might be wrong. And if I told you he wasn't going to start, I might not be telling the truth. I just won't know for sure until he warms up on Sunday."

Defending champion Cleveland earned its way back into the championship game, allowing its owner, Art Modell, to feel justified in the most controversial decision of his tenure. In 1963, after watching the once mighty Browns slip to the middle of the pack, failing to make the title game for five years in a row, and clashing on several personnel issues, Modell fired Paul Brown. Despite his numerous innovations, victories, and championships, Brown was just another employee, even if his name was quite literally stamped on the entirety of the franchise's history. The point was clear for all to see: If you could fire Paul Brown you could fire anybody.

But Brown was not just another coach, so instead of sending out résumés and trying to land another coaching job, he soon began lobbying the NFL for an expansion team of his own. (In 1968, after the NFL-AFL merger was announced, his Cincinnati Bengals joined the AFL, with Brown as principal owner, general manager, and head coach.)

In his place, Modell hired his longtime assistant, Blanton Collier, who had fled to the NFL after following Paul "Bear" Bryant at the University of Kentucky and failing to live up to the Wildcats' newly elevated standards. Collier adopted many of Brown's methods but emerged as a less dictatorial force, running a much looser shop than Brown—or, for that matter, Vince Lombardi—while making much better use of the team's greatest offensive weapon: the incomparable Jim Brown.

Throughout the first half of the sixties, the Packers' Jim Taylor and the Browns' Jim Brown dominated the league's rushing statistics. Brown, considered by many the greatest runner in the history of football, was not the sort to invest too much energy thinking about the competition, but Taylor was obsessed with Brown. Invariably, after every game, he wanted to know how many yards his Cleveland rival had amassed. Taylor had a terrible time remembering names—he called everybody "Roy"—but he kept a running tally of his stats and Brown's in his head at all times.

"I'm always aware of Brown," Taylor said. "When we meet head-to-head, I want to do better than he does. I think about it."

With Brown playing the final game of his remarkable career and Taylor not too far behind, the competition reached a climax in the 1965 championship game.

Determined to avoid the distractions of Green Bay, the Browns stayed overnight in Appleton, thirty miles away, so when a snowstorm hit the next morning, dumping four inches of powder on the roads, the Cleveland team wound up negotiating a very treacherous commute to Green Bay.

When Bart Jr. climbed out of bed to see the snow falling outside his window, he wondered if his father would be able to play.

Cherry was a bundle of nerves when he walked out the door, headed for the stadium.

"Don't worry, honey," he said with a smile. "You don't have to play today."

The Master Sergeant had no doubt. He knew how much it meant to his boy. He knew Bart would dig deep.

In an age before flak jackets, the trainers taped Starr's ribs as tightly as possible and gave him some shots to lessen the pain, and he told Lombardi he was good to go. Every time he raised his right arm to pass in warmups, the pain was intense. But he desperately wanted to play.

"He didn't want anybody to know how bad it was, especially Coach Lombardi," said Bratkowski, who was ready to step in.

While few knew the extent of Starr's injury, the rushing battle occupied most minds at kickoff, when a temperature of 33 degrees created a slushy, slippery field.

The Green Bay defense never thought in terms of stopping Jim Brown. He was too good, too powerful, too athletic, too determined. The idea was to slow him down and hold him to a reasonable number.

But Ray Nitschke, the Packers' menacing middle linebacker, was not a reasonable man when he wiped the grease beneath his eyes. Like his teammates, Nitschke was focused on taking away the inside lanes where Brown typically churned for big yards.

"Jim Brown was such a force," said end Willie Davis, the Packers' defensive captain. "The weather helped, but our defense did some kind of job on him. Nitschke deserved a lot of credit. He was all over Jim Brown."

Benefiting from the sloppy field, which limited his ability to cut, the Packers neutralized Brown, holding him to 50 yards on 12 carries, one of the least potent days of his record-setting career.

The heroes were plentiful in Green Bay's 23–12 victory over Cleveland, which gave the Packers their third NFL championship in five years. Don Chandler cemented his already memorable season by kicking three field goals. In addition to the tremendous defensive effort, Jim Taylor and Paul Hornung somehow found the footing that Brown could not, rushing for 95 and 105 yards, respectively.

"Just a couple of old-timers trying to hang on," Taylor said happily in the afterglow, arm in arm with Hornung.

Between the weather and his aching ribs, Starr found himself maneuvering in some of the most difficult conditions of his career, but he played one of his gutsiest games, completing 10 of 18 passes for 147 yards, 1 touchdown, and 1 interception. The offensive line gave him good protection but he still took some shots. "I just tried to block [the injury] out and do the best I could," he said.

On a drive into Browns territory in the first quarter, he faded into the pocket and lofted a pass toward Carroll Dale, but the wet ball slipped off his hand, falling from the sky way short of its target. Alert to the situation, Dale stopped his route, came back toward the ball, caught it, and ran into the distance, turning what might have been a busted play into a 47-yard touchdown, staking the Packers to a 7–0 lead.

"You need good luck in this game . . . and teammates who are there to help you," Starr said.

But it was not just his arm that helped clinch another title.

Forever cognizant of the way defenses reacted to the Packers' tendencies, Starr had spent much of the week analyzing the Browns, which led him to set a trap in the first half by concentrating on the weak-side sweep to great effect. "We wanted to make them aware . . . to make them overshift to the weak side," he said. Then, when the Packers drove into Cleveland territory in the third quarter, he sprung the trap. First, he faked Taylor to the weak side and handed off to Hornung, who raced for a 20-yard gain, putting the Packers in scoring position at the Cleveland 15. Two plays later, after planting the seed of doubt, he came back to the weak side by giving the ball to Hornung, who started to his left and followed the blocks by Jerry Kramer and Forrest Gregg into the end zone for a 13-yard touchdown, giving the Packers a 20–12 lead.

"Their defense played a fine game, but we created the right climate in their defensive thinking, and it was time to take advantage of it," Starr explained.

Rebounding from two near misses, Lombardi's Green Bay Packers took a forceful step into the history books, surpassing the trophy runs by Paul Brown's Cleveland dynasty and Bobby Layne's Lions, who each needed six years to claim three.

When word reached the locker room that Taylor had been voted the title game MVP for the second time, Hornung flung his jersey to the floor in disgust. "To pick anybody but Bart Starr is ridiculous," he said loud enough for several reporters to hear.

Gratified by the way his team had fought back all season, Lombardi said, "It came so hard, all year long. Everything was hard. The season. The playoff. Everything . . ."

These were not the 1962 Packers, those young bucks who dominated their opponents so completely, very nearly becoming the first team in NFL history to finish unbeaten.

But this team . . .

This team knew how it felt to be knocked down and what it took to climb off the deck and keep fighting.

"This team," Lombardi said, "has more character than any other team I've had. This may not be the best team I've had but it has the most character."

Character.

He didn't mention Starr by name.

He didn't have to.

The war started on television but quickly spread to the acquisition of talent.

By the mid-1960s, the competition between the established National Football League and the upstart American Football League was escalating out of control. Most NFL coaches and players looked down their noses at what they perceived as the AFL's inferior product, but the new league was fundamentally changing the sport. No longer the only game in town, the NFL was forced to compete directly with an aggressive and in many cases well-heeled rival for the services of the nation's leading college players, driving salaries to astronomical levels.

The same force that made the AFL a serious competitor also aided the NFL in protecting its turf. Proven correct on the issue of television, Pete Rozelle negotiated a new deal with CBS guaranteeing the NFL $14.1 million per year starting in 1966, a stunning level of growth that reflected the country's newfound fascination with the sport. Over the span of seven years, the Packers' television revenue had skyrocketed from $75,000 to slightly more than $1 million per year, helping the franchise mitigate many of the inherent financial disadvantages of playing in such a small market, achieving for Curly Lambeau's brainchild the sort of stability it had never approached. For all the hand-wringing and talk of self-sacrifice that preceded the owners' original decision to create a unified television plan, it was not, as some feared, a socialist impulse Rozelle was peddling. It was pure capitalism, because he understood that the product wasn't the Steelers or the Browns or the Rams as individual entities. No. The product was the National Football League collectively in all its competitive glory, contending for the hearts and minds of the American viewing public.

Then something truly unexpected and remarkable happened at the intersection of capitalism, television and culture. The Green Bay Packers became America's Team.

Long before the Dallas Cowboys adopted the label, the Packers emerged as a defining force in the new-age NFL, setting a standard for excellence while attracting fans from coast to coast.

The Colts already boasted a significant national following, thanks to the mystique of Johnny U and a favorable contract with NBC prior to the advent of the league-wide package. The Giants, Bears, and Browns all owned big swaths of the landscape. But Lombardi and the Packers staked a powerful claim all their own.

Without a doubt, some of this phenomenon could be directly attributed to television's power to validate any sort of success, shattering the ancient barriers of geography, and causing fans all across the country to be able to choose their own team, reflecting the latest permutation in the great American tradition of reinvention. Living in Mississippi but making the conscious decision to identify with the Pittsburgh Steelers was part of the same impulse that drove pioneers West: Beyond the obvious, it was a search for identification and meaning. This process predated television—after all, radio coverage a generation earlier caused far-flung fans across the continent to cling to the New York Yankees and Notre Dame football—but television made it more practical and visceral. After the heart-pounding 1958 title game, multitudes across the country gravitated to the Colts. But Lombardi's Packers represented an entirely new level of nationwide fascination.

Some people loved the Packers. Some people hated the Packers. But everyone who loved football respected Lombardi's success and the gold standard the Packers represented.

"People always talk about the 1958 championship game and how it turned the country on to pro football, but I say it was Vince Lombardi's Packers," said longtime NFL Films president Steve Sabol. "The '58 game was like the first flickers of lightning before a thunderstorm. The appeal of the Packers during the sixties was just phenomenal . . . and lifted the whole NFL."

Television sold the Packers not just as a powerful football team, but also as a universal representation of teamwork, precision, and small-town values, led by a demanding figure who seemed like a cross between John

Wayne and General George S. Patton, forever connecting the dots between the virtues of football and the American experience. In an increasingly urban country, in which New York City and the Northeastern corridor appeared to set the agenda for everything, many saw each Green Bay championship as a victory for small towns across America, proof that bigger was not necessarily better, that David could fell Goliath, that any obstacle could be surmounted, given the proper concentration of hard work and desire. Green Bay and New York may not have belonged in the same sentence, but somehow, tiny Green Bay kept whipping gigantic New York's smug butt . . . and somehow this demonstrated the greatness of a land built on upward mobility, where performance ultimately trumped pedigree, where the romance of small towns represented something deeply embedded in the American psyche. This undercurrent in the Packers' appeal was especially vivid given the context of the day, when Americans were still predisposed to believe in their collective nobility, when the frenzied race to beat the Russians to the moon was not just a technological contest with significant implications for the epic cold war. It was a reflection of everything we believed about ourselves.

Amid all this drama and symbolism, Bart Starr sometimes appeared to fade into the background. In contrast to Lombardi's unusual combination of bombast and eloquence, Starr remained the same quiet, respectful, and earnest young man who had arrived in Green Bay intent on winning a place on the roster, when hardly anyone believed he could. In the early days, he was easy to overlook. In the glow of Green Bay's first championships, reporters often stumbled over him to crowd around the charming Hornung or the ferocious Taylor. New York sportswriter Phil Pepe called Starr "the forgotten man of the Green Bay Packers, the anonymous quarterback."

But this invisible man—discarded by his college coach, drafted as an afterthought by the lowliest franchise in the league, doubted by his father and the coach who emerged as a father figure—was on his way to becoming the most successful quarterback in the history of the National Football League.

Television made Starr and the Packers national figures but it was the dramatic storytelling of NFL Films that began to capture the passion of the sport and transform Lombardi, Starr, and others into iconic figures.

After surviving the embarrassing night at Toots Shor's, Ed Sabol slowly gained Rozelle's confidence and eventually convinced him to purchase Blair Motion Pictures, which became NFL Films. The new company was formed to create highlight reels of every team in the league and quickly began producing a syndicated television program, extending the NFL's brand into other days of the week and the off-season even as the league began moving aggressively into the realm of merchandising. The ultimate objective was something more profound. Rozelle wanted to create a new mythology for the league, fostering a more meaningful connection with a nation of impressionable eyeballs. He found a kindred spirit in Steve Sabol, whose entire perspective of professional football had been demonstrably altered by his experience at the 1962 championship game.

Important as it was in spreading the sights and sounds of the NFL, television still approached the game from a distance. Compared to the live action on the field, the wide, sweeping camera angles and the lack of innovations viewers would one day take for granted gave the televised experience an antiseptic feel.

"I wanted to show the violence . . . the snot flowing . . . the spit . . . the blood . . . the cursing . . . the struggle," Sabol said. "The idea of capturing the game the way the players experienced it had a tremendous appeal to me."

When the younger Sabol graduated from college and went to work under his father at NFL Films, helping produce a series of well-crafted but rather conventional films and programs, he began to develop ideas for how to create something more powerful. Ed Sabol's business savvy and entrepreneurial guts put NFL Films in business and set the tone for all that was to come, and his son's artistic sensibilities, which he believed in, led the fledgling unit to an entirely different realm. In 1965, Steve began producing a film featuring a microphone attached to Philadelphia Eagles head coach Joe Kuharich; a series of very stylistic, quick-cut shots from close-up, field-level angles; a focus on the punishment endured by quarterbacks, including Bart Starr; a sophisticated musical score by Sam Spence; and the narration of a Philadelphia television newscaster who was being phased out of his full-time job by the dictates of the fast-approaching plastic age. John Facenda knew very little about football and nothing at all about the Sabols or what they were attempting, but $250 to read a script sounded like a pretty good deal to him.

"We had the confidence of ignorance because neither one of us knew much about filmmaking," Sabol said. "There was nobody around to tell you if this was good or bad."

When *They Call It Pro Football* premiered in 1966, it caused an intense reaction by nearly all who watched it. The film was raw, up close, and dramatic, pulling the viewer closer than ever before to the pain, the blood, the struggle behind every down. The combination of Sabol's carefully worded narrative and innovative production; Facenda's rich, commanding instrument of a voice; and Spence's cinematic score set a new standard in sports documentaries. Some of the owners hated the film—believing the intimacy it revealed had removed the veneer from the sport—but Rozelle and many others loved it *because* it showed the game as it was. "This is not a highlight film," he said gleefully. "It's a real movie." Like Sabol, Rozelle was convinced that the truth reflected in the film would make the game even more compelling, especially when the story was told in such a sophisticated way. By the time NFL Films managed to syndicate it to television stations across the country, thousands of Americans had already caught a glimpse of *They Call It Pro Football* at local civic clubs, infusing it with the hip buzz of an underground film.

More than any other single event, the premiere of what Sabol proudly called "the *Citizen Kane* of sports films" gave rise to a new NFL mystique, just in time to capture the climactic years of the Lombardi era.

While the Sabols concentrated on documenting and aiding the NFL's rise, the popularity of the rival AFL—and the intense competition among the three broadcast networks—prompted NBC to steal the AFL contract away from ABC, consummating a contract worth $7.5 million per year starting in 1965. Determined to maximize its investment, NBC took the unprecedented step of advancing several hundred thousand dollars to several different AFL teams to cover the price of competing against their NFL counterparts in the bidding war for college players.

During this period, when the NFL office instituted a so-called babysitting program aimed at preventing NFL draftees from being poached by the AFL, recently retired Packers linebacker Bill Forester and his wife, Ann, were entertaining a prominent receiver and his bride at dinner one night when the ladies slipped off to the powder room.

"They've offered us $80,000," the nervous woman confided when they were alone. "We don't know what to do. Is that a lot?"

Ann Forester was shocked. "Oh, my goodness gracious sakes alive!" she said, her Texas vernacular spilling through her excitement. "You're talking to the wrong person. That would be astronomical for us."

Even after playing for eleven seasons with the Packers, Bill Forester never reached $20,000 per year. But the war between the leagues—and the television money helping to fund the combat—kept pushing salaries to new heights.

Back in 1961, when the pro football feud was still gathering steam, a friend in the business called Paul "Bear" Bryant, the University of Alabama head coach who was then on the verge of his first national championship, and told him about a hotshot quarterback he needed to see to believe. The player had failed an entrance exam at the University of Maryland and suddenly was back on the market, so Bryant dispatched one of his most trusted assistants, Howard Schnellenberger, to the coal-mining country of western Pennsylvania with instructions to bring the young man to Tuscaloosa for a visit. Various other schools were hot on his trail, including Notre Dame, but after more than a week on the road, Schnellenberger finally managed to convince him to get on an airplane and head south. By this time, he was running out of money. In an era before credit cards or ATM machines, the modestly paid Alabama coach was forced to write a rubber check for the player's plane ticket and, when the Birmingham airport was fogged in, he wrote another rubber check for a hotel room. Digging through his pocket the next morning, he found fifteen cents, with which he bought the young man a cup of coffee as they set off for Tuscaloosa.

Fortunately for Schnellenberger, Joe Namath did not want any breakfast.

Because Alabama was such a high-profile program, the pro scouts became aware of Namath's potential soon after he took over the Crimson Tide's starting quarterback job as a sophomore in 1962.

At first glance, Al Davis could hardly believe his eyes. Davis, then a young assistant coach for the AFL's San Diego Chargers, returned from a trip to Tuscaloosa and told head coach Sid Gillman, one of the fathers of the modern passing game: "I saw a guy who tips the field."

"What do you mean?"

"This son of a bitch is so good he plays like he's going downhill."

Endowed with the quickest release any one had ever seen, plus outstanding mobility and athleticism, Namath also was blessed with a charisma that defied description. By late in the 1964 season, as he led Alabama to the national championship, the clamor for his services exacerbated the intense competition between the NFL and AFL. The St. Louis Cardinals wanted him badly, but the AFL's struggling New York Jets, who saw him not just as a quarterback but as a much-needed box office attraction, wanted him even more. The resulting $427,000 contract, much of which was deferred to reduce tax liabilities, was the richest in the history of professional sports, making Namath a household name all across America.

Upon hearing the shocking number, Frank Ryan, the quarterback of the fast-fading New York Giants, said, "If he's worth $400,000, I'm worth a million."

Namath was worth every penny to the Jets and the AFL, simultaneously infusing the upstart league with credibility and forcing the NFL to meet the competition.

The Packers were not immune to the escalation.

After selecting Paul Hornung as the bonus pick in the 1957 draft, Green Bay signed him to a three-year, $54,500 contract, including a first-year salary of $15,000 and a signing bonus of $2,500.

Eight years later, searching for Hornung's replacement in the wake of the Namath tsunami, the Packers selected Texas Tech halfback Donny Anderson in the first round and eventually signed him to a three-year, $600,000 contract. The following year, the Packers inked first round pick Jim Grabowski of Illinois, designated to take Taylor's place, to a three-year, $400,000 deal. The two bonus babies joined the team in 1966, Anderson delayed by a year because he was playing his redshirt season for the Red Raiders.

The disparity between the rich rookies and the established players making considerably less caused significant grumbling all across the league. But it was pure economics. In time, the veterans lucky enough to stick around for a few more years would benefit from the rising tide.

When the AFL crossed a once sacrosanct barrier and began trying to entice NFL veterans, several prominent players signed big contracts, including Rams quarterback Roman Gabriel and Bears linebacker Mike Ditka. Neither man ever played a down in the AFL but both exploited the competition to win significant raises.

"I was never approached but I would never have entertained the idea anyway," said Starr, who earned about $40,000 in 1966, and would see his salary reach $100,000 by the end of his playing career in 1972. "I was very, very happy in Green Bay and with Coach Lombardi."

Because of his prominence on such a successful team and his wholesome image, Starr saw his opportunity for outside income increase steadily in the mid-1960s, including lucrative sponsorship deals with Vitalis and Lincoln-Mercury, which allowed him to significantly augment his Packers salary. (During a prominent television commercial of the day, the quarterback turned to the camera, holding a can of shaving cream. "Hi, I'm Bart Starr. And I want to tell you: I take it off with Noxema.") The rapid growth in the NFL also fueled an escalation in the bonuses paid to participants in the championship game. The winner's share jumped from $5,000 in 1961 to $25,000 in 1967, providing additional incentive for Starr's heroics.

Like Motown, James Bond, and the Mercury Seven, the war between the NFL and the AFL became part of the fabric of the sixties, a smash-mouth example of the greatest zero-sum game of them all: free-market capitalism. Whether on Wall Street or at the 50-yard line, money was just another way to keep score. Like Bart Starr and Johnny Unitas, Coca-Cola and Pepsi, and Chevrolet and Ford, the NFL and AFL elevated one another by chasing each other.

But it had to end.

By the spring of 1966, a growing number of owners in both leagues wanted peace. The merger agreement announced by Pete Rozelle on June 8, 1966, hit players and coaches in both leagues like a punch in the gut. Al Davis, who had recently taken over as the AFL commissioner, vowing to bury the NFL, felt blind-sided and betrayed by the actions of his own owners, who signed away his job and his cause. Many of the details were yet to be worked out—and Rozelle would be forced to do some serious deal-making with the antitrust watchdogs in Congress, directly resulting in the birth of the New Orleans Saints—but the first step toward a fully merged National Football League in 1970 would be an NFL-AFL championship game in January 1967.

Rozelle could make them merge but he could not make them like each other, at least not with the stroke of a pen. The bitterness built up over six years would take time to cool, so the looming championship game immediately became the repository of all the disdain and contempt many NFL players, coaches and officials harbored for the rival league. They desperately wanted to teach the AFL a lesson.

Even as Starr's career unfolded against a dramatic backdrop, Cherry knew how to keep him loose.

One night after a particularly bitter loss, Starr walked through the front door of his house and eventually made his way to the master bedroom, where his wife was sitting up in bed, reading a newspaper. When he leaned down to give her a kiss, she pulled back the newspaper, revealing a face adorned by a Groucho Marx mask, complete with fuzzy mustache. A smile quickly rose across the quarterback's previously sullen face and he laughed out loud.

Watching him press so hard every day, Lombardi sometimes worried about Starr's stress level. Turning down the noise from time to time was Cherry's job. She knew how to push his buttons.

"Mom had a way of making Dad laugh, even in the most difficult times," said Bart Jr.

When Starr came home one night in a rare foul mood to find Cherry cooking supper and toddler Bret on the floor nearby, having a good time tearing up a magazine, his wife asked, sarcastically, "Where is it are you going tonight, in such a good mood?"

Sheepishly, he said, "I'm getting a Mr. Nice Guy Award."

She just started laughing.

"Well, you certainly deserve it tonight!"

She had a way of picking at him that somehow eased his mind, pulling them closer through the years.

The epitome of a charming Southern lady, Cherry often delighted in telling slightly racy jokes, which seemed contrary to her image but became a big part of her fun-loving persona. "Bart started out so serious, with that military background, but Cherry was such a cutup. She gradually brought him out of his shell," said their friend M. E. Bratkowski. "She will say things and he will pretend to be embarrassed, but he loves her sense of humor."

People unaccustomed to her humor often were taken aback by it at first, such as one particular league meeting many years later in Hawaii.

Walking through a buffet line, Cherry surreptitiously placed a gigantic rubber roach atop a salad bowl. When Norma Hunt, the wife of longtime Kansas City Chiefs owner Lamar Hunt, started filling her plate and suddenly saw the very authentic-looking bug inches away, she started screaming, "Kill that roach! Kill it!"

As Cherry lingered off to the side, enjoying the fruits of her gag, a large native Hawaiian man who worked for the restaurant rushed into the room, knocked the roach to the flood, and began stomping it, forcing Starr's wife to come clean in order to protect her precious property.

"No! Stop! That's my roach!"

One night during dinner, when Madeline Harlan, wife of the Packers' president, was consumed by a conversation and unaware that she had been served, Cherry carefully slipped the roach onto her plate. Everyone else at the circular table was aware of the joke and saw Cherry plant the fake bug, but when the very-proper Madeline finally picked up her fork, glanced down at her plate and saw the roach, she screamed violently and jumped up, knocking over her chair as everyone roared.

"Madeline was the perfect one to pull that on, because she's such a lady," Cherry said, adding, "She was a great sport about it."

Noticing Cherry's habit of eating off Bart's plate, a friend sent her a fork with a shaft that expanded to several feet long. Recognizing the implement's potential for mischief, she hid it in her purse one night when they hosted a fund-raising dinner for the Birmingham Humane Society. After the main course was served, she pulled the fork out of her purse and used it to reach across the table to lift the meat off the plate of a local politician she had never met. He was dumbfounded.

"You should have seen the look on his face," she said. "He didn't know what to think! But it broke the ice . . . and then I put the meat back."

While waiting for a plane at the Phoenix airport, Cherry struck up a conversation with a man seated next to her. When she told the man she lived in Green Bay, he asked, "Have you ever seen Bart Starr?"

"Oh, I've seen him from time to time," she said.

"Have you ever had a chance to talk to him?"

"Yes, on many occasions," she said, then leaned in to whisper, "As a matter of fact, I slept with him last night."

The man didn't know what to say—until Mrs. Bart Starr finally introduced herself with a hearty laugh.

Because of Cherry's fondness and compassion for all types of animals, the Starr household sometimes took on the feel of a zoo. Dogs, cats, rabbits, snakes. Even a pet ant.

"Okay, come here, Bart!" she once yelled out to her eldest son, summoning him to the kitchen to watch her place a grain of sugar and then see an ant show up for dinner.

Young Bart observed the science experiment with a sense of amusement. "Mom," he said, with all the mock concern a very bright teenager could summon, "this is really starting to fall into some area where we don't want to go. This ant can find its own food!"

Laughing at the scene from his childhood, Bart Jr. said, "Mom's compassion for animals really knows no bounds."

Waking up out of a sound sleep one night, Bart bolted up in bed and announced, "Cherry! There's a rat in bed with us!"

Stirring from her slumber, Cherry said, "Oh, Bart, honey! You had a bad dream. Go back to sleep."

A few moments later, the quarterback barked again. "Cherry! I know that rat just ran across me. It's in bed with us!"

"Oh, Bart! Stop it!"

When Cherry turned on the light, she discovered that Ralph, one of Bret's two pet rats, had somehow escaped from its cage in the basement and was running around the bed being watched by the two Peekapoo dogs sleeping at the foot of their king-size mattress.

"Ralph was real sweet . . . intelligent . . . and clean," Cherry said. "He liked me a lot. He just came to see me."

The next morning, Bart, who was not quite so fond of Ralph, made sure the door to his cage was securely fastened.

While Cherry's sense of humor rubbed off on their eldest son, who became a master of comical voices, Bart Jr. also inherited his father's brainy intensity. The father created a sense of structure for his boys and a sense of expectation: They were to treat people with respect, act like gentlemen, be honest, work hard, and live within their parents' rules. When they needed a spanking, they got a spanking. When they needed to be grounded, they were grounded.

"The thing I remember most from my dad growing up is how he used to say, 'If you just live a clean, simple life well grounded in proper values, that's the lowest stress life you can imagine," Bart Jr. said. "Where it gets complex and stressful is if you're trying to hide this, juggle that, avoid this . . ."

Determined to foster a climate filled with incentive and accountability, Bart rewarded his first born with a dime for every perfect grade he earned in school.

"Bring home a hundred and we'll divide by ten," he often said, until Bart Jr. could hear the phrase in his sleep.

Like his father, who toiled in a world where a drive that ended on the 1-yard line was nothing but a time-consuming failure, Bart Jr. received nothing for a 99, which made him work all the harder for those precious 100 grades. The system helped frame Bart Jr.'s life, making him very driven and studious. When the father won one particularly important victory, the son demonstrated his pride and the edification wrought by his dad's teaching by leaving a prize on the old man's pillow.

A shiny dime.

First came a knock at the door.

Sunday school was in full swing on a bright summer morning in 1962, when a member of the church cracked the door, interrupting John Gillespie in midsentence.

"This is Jerry and he would like to attend your class," said a member of the church, ushering the young boy to an empty seat.

Gillespie welcomed him and continued with his Bible lesson at the small interdenominational church in Appleton, Wisconsin.

The following Sunday, Jerry returned for Sunday school, stayed for the church service, and lingered in the parking lot as Gillespie prepared to leave.

"Son, is there something I can do for you?"

"I was just wondering . . ." Jerry said.

"What is it, son?"

"I was just wondering if I could go home with you this afternoon."

Gillespie did not know what to say.

Puzzled but wanting to reach out to the young man who seemed lonely and shy and apparently had been left without anywhere else to go,

Gillespie told him they would have to check with his parents. When Jerry explained that he didn't have a father and that his mother was working, Gillespie and his wife Jan, both in their twenties and with two young children of their own, took Jerry to his house, where they carefully pinned a note to the front door for his mother, explaining the situation, and asking her to call them when she returned home.

"In those days, people didn't go around abducting children," Jan said. "So we didn't think too much about carrying a boy home from church with us."

When the mother called and Jan asked when she would like to pick up her son, she said, "Maybe he would like to stay with you for a few days." Suddenly, the Gillespies realized they were caught up in something more complicated than a Sunday school stray. A short time later, Jerry's mother showed up at the Gillespie house with a suitcase full of his clothes, a cardboard box filled with other personal items, and a pair of ice skates.

Ice skates.

In the middle of summer, she was dropping off ice skates.

"The mother explained that she had just gotten remarried and that her husband had given her thirty days to get rid of two of her three children," John said.

Their hearts sank, especially when they began to consider how it must feel to be abandoned by your very own mother at such a tender age.

"It was so sad," Jan said. "I didn't judge the woman . . . she was an alcoholic who had married an alcoholic. She was trying to do the right thing."

Instead of calling the authorities and washing their hands of the situation, as many other young couples might have done, the Gillespies took Jerry into their home. For about eighteen months, he lived with the Gillespies and their other children, becoming part of their family. "He was always very quiet but he slowly gained confidence," Jan said. "He was a good little boy who needed to be loved. We loved on him the best we could." Eventually, he moved back in with his mother but Jerry never forgot the power of the Gillespies' precious gift. Many years later, after becoming a successful small business owner, he welcomed his elderly mother into his own home and cared for her in her old age, forever coloring their lives in a circle of irony.

Jerry never met Bart and Cherry Starr, but the tragedy of his youth unwittingly launched the most enduring cause of their lives.

The experience with Jerry prompted the Gillespies to take in several other foster children, each escaping some sort of trouble, each yearning for the proper combination of discipline and love. "We didn't realize there were so many who needed help . . . until Jerry came into our lives," Jan said. At some point, they felt the tug of a calling and began dreaming of creating a ranch for troubled boys.

In the fall of 1965, John Gillespie, who operated his own land-planning business, received a telephone call from a potential client who wanted to subdivide a 500-acre tract in the countryside of central Wisconsin, near the small town of New London, so he could sell it. The asking price was $200,000. When John and Jan drove out from Appleton, met the elderly man, toured the picturesque, isolated estate along the Wolf River, and walked through its eleven-bedroom lodge, they were immediately struck by the same thought.

"This would make a great boys' home!" John said, as Jan nodded in agreement.

The elderly man's eyes lit up. "Yes, it certainly would."

The owner of the land was already predisposed to seeing his land used for such a purpose but he could not afford to donate it. He was, however, willing to sell it very cheap: $69,000, coinciding with the amount of money he needed to purchase an apartment building to help fund his retirement. John, only a few years out of college, had very little money, so after brokering a deal with the man, he borrowed five hundred dollars from his skeptical father-in-law to put down as a deposit, buying some time to develop a plan to purchase the property. The Gillespies moved into the lodge with two foster children, started the process of incorporating as a nonprofit organization, and began trying to raise money to fulfill their vision.

"Hardly anybody took us seriously," John said. "Most people thought it was a nice idea but . . ."

Early in the process, Jan began suggesting that her husband approach one of the most prominent celebrities in Wisconsin for help, but he resisted. "You don't just call Bart Starr," he said.

"Why not?"

"Well, first of all, I'm sure he has an unlisted number. And why would he believe in us?"

Jan was insistent. As their frustration mounted and the clock kept ticking on their option, with very little progress toward purchasing the land, she periodically peppered him with the same question: "Did you call Bart Starr?"

"If God is in this and it's bigger than us," she finally said, "why wouldn't you at least try to get in touch with him?"

More out of a desire to put an end to his wife's badgering than any realistic belief that he could actually reach the quarterback of the Green Bay Packers, John called information and, to his astonishment, located Starr's listed telephone number. When he nervously dialed the number, a man answered after two or three rings.

"Can I speak to Mr. Starr," he said.

"There's no Mr. Starr here. Bart's here," the man said pleasantly.

"Well, can I speak to Bart?"

"This is Bart."

Fumbling for words, Gillespie explained that he and his wife were attempting to start a youth ranch and asked if he could make an appointment to meet with him to discuss it.

"How about today?"

Floored by Starr's response, Gillespie dropped everything and immediately drove from the ranch to Green Bay with his wife on that summer afternoon in 1966, walking through the Starrs' front door as Cherry was busy cooking supper. Not wanting to intrude on their meal, the Gillespies promised to be brief, but Cherry insisted they stay for supper.

"It was pretty incredible that these people had never met us but had already planned for us to have dinner with them after one brief telephone conversation," Gillespie recalled.

Wielding a three-ring binder while seated on a couch in the living room, John outlined the plan.

When John began talking about the need to establish a foundation of Christian faith for the boys, Cherry nodded in agreement.

"Oh, Bart," she said excitedly, "this is what you and I believe!"

When John moved on to the need to develop a strong work ethic in the children, Cherry nodded enthusiastically.

"Oh, Bart, this is what you and I believe!"

Finally, when Gillespie outlined the importance of establishing a sense of structure for the boys and Cherry once more said, "Oh, Bart, this is what you and I believe!" Bart placed his hand over the ring binder and said firmly, "Cherry, don't tip our hand until we see the bottom line."

When John finished his sales pitch, Bart asked, "What do you want from us?"

What their organization needed most acutely was to be able to leverage Starr's name. No one knew John and Jan Gillespie, and even the people who had helped them so far tended to view their quest as a nice little idea with very little hope of ever succeeding. But everyone in Wisconsin, and millions across America, knew Bart Starr and held him in high esteem. When he spoke, people listened.

After John explained that they desperately needed help setting up a nonprofit board and raising money, Bart turned to Cherry, who nodded her head, and he turned back to John with a smile. "I guess we're on board."

This unlikely encounter turned out to be a defining moment in the lives of Bart and Cherry Starr, revealing much more about their character than a lifetime of athletic accomplishments, producing a legacy destined to positively impact thousands of troubled teenage boys.

"Bart and Cherry gave us instant credibility," John said.

Starr did not squander his fame.

He did not hoard his fame.

He invested his fame in building an organization framed by love and generosity.

Bart was never the sort to seek publicity for his various charitable endeavors or the other random acts of kindness that colored his life, but he and Cherry understood that making people aware of Rawhide Boys Ranch's mission was central to its success, so from the start, they became the public face of the charity, using Bart's celebrity to attract attention to the cause.

"Bart and Cherry are such wonderful people," Jan said. "They have such big hearts. Without their critical help, Rawhide never would have gotten off the ground, or survived those difficult early years."

About three months after their first meeting, with the final deadline fast approaching and the future of Rawhide Boys Ranch hanging in the balance during the early weeks of the 1966 football season, John sent the Starrs an urgent letter. When Cherry opened it, she was shocked to see a succinct message, scrawled across the page in huge letters:

Dear Bart and Cherry:

Help!

Sincerely,
John Gillespie

"I called Bart [at the practice facility] and told him things were desperate [and that] he needed to deal with this immediately," Cherry said.

Even though he was consumed with winning a fourth NFL championship, Starr took the time to help save something he believed in.

After learning from John that the organization required $20,000 by the following week to avoid losing the land for good, Starr obtained Lombardi's permission to address the team. He outlined the plan and asked those who were interested in helping to join him for a luncheon the following Monday at The Left Guard, the steakhouse owned by lineman Fuzzy Thurston, who had already agreed to spring for the food. If they could raise $20,000 by the close of business on that day, the First National Bank of Appleton had agreed to mortgage the rest. If not, the owner of the property would be forced to take it back. Far from the adoring crowds, Starr faced a clock fast ticking to zero with no possibility for overtime, even as he juggled the game plan for the following Sunday.

More than a dozen Packers showed up, each bringing along a prominent businessman interested in donating to the cause. After Gillespie and Starr made their pitch, the players and their friends began writing checks. Painfully aware of the looming 5 P.M. deadline as the group began to disperse, Gillespie was approached by one older gentleman who had waited for the others to leave.

"Would you mind me asking you how much you've collected?" the man said.

"No, not at all," said Gillespie, who quickly added up the checks, which totaled $14,000.

J. O. Johnson, one of the businessmen who had been brought to the meeting by a player, nodded his head, sat down at a nearby table, and wrote a check for $6,000, putting them over the top.

Less than a week after the situation had appeared hopeless, the Gillespies rushed to the bank with the checks and completed the purchase of the land before the deadline, culminating one of the most important drives of Bart Starr's life.

By the time John Gillespie's letter arrived, Starr was in the middle of the greatest season of his career.

All of the Packers' championship seasons have a special place in Starr's heart, but even though he has always been too modest, too team-oriented to see his career through a personal lens, 1966 represented a breakthrough. This was the year the country stopped overlooking him, when his long journey out of the shadows began to reach a certain critical mass. After leading the Packers to an impressive 12-2 season and a fifth Western Division championship—marred only by narrow losses to the 49ers (21–20) and the Vikings (20–17)—Starr was named the NFL's Most Valuable Player.

"I am proud and grateful but it really should be a team thing," he told Art Daley of the *Green Bay Press-Gazette*. "It would be better to cut up something like this and pass it around to each member of the team. This is our philosophy. It is not how much it benefits the individual but how much it benefits the team."

The award came in a year when he tossed just 3 interceptions—translating to an NFL record low 1.2 average per attempts—while leading the league in completion percentage (62.2) and passer rating (a career-best 105.0). He threw for 2,257 yards and 14 touchdowns, averaging a staggering 9.0 yards per attempt—nearly a yard more than his previous best season, 1962—amid a growing realization that his value to the greatest dynasty of the age transcended his arm.

In a year when Cleveland's Frank Ryan tossed a league-leading 29 touchdowns and Washington's Sonny Jurgensen topped the charts with 3,209 yards, the decision to award Starr with the league's most coveted individual honor demonstrated not only how far he had come, but also how the media had learned to see beyond the traditional measurements of quarterbacking greatness and recognize the achievements of a slightly different sort of offensive master.

As NFL Films moved into a new era shaped by the ethos of *They Call It Pro Football*, the Sabols produced a highlight film emphasizing the importance of the calculated risk, which turned into a virtual tribute show to Bart Starr, the master of third-and-short and the play-action pass.

After losing to the Packers 20–7 on a sleety Sunday late in the season—victimized by an 83-yard touchdown bomb on third-and-one, proving that, yes, indeed, Starr could go deep—San Francisco head coach Jack Christiansen said: "He's probably the best quarterback in football today and before he gets through he may be recognized as the greatest of them all."

But even during his MVP season, Starr continued to be underrated by some. While shadowing the quarterback for a profile, *Sport* magazine's Dave Wolf observed a telling moment: on the morning of a big game on the road against the Baltimore Colts in early December, in the hotel room he shared with Henry Jordan, Starr tossed a crumpled newspaper clipping on the desk. Circled in red was a quote from Colts cornerback Bobby Boyd: "Bart Starr is not a good passer. You seldom see him throw the ball more than 12 yards. If they must throw they have problems. If we can get them two touchdowns down, we're going to beat them."

Instead of sulking about Boyd's insult—or ignoring it—the forever controlled Starr quietly used it in his own way, drawing strength and motivation from another man's doubts. Green Bay beat the Colts, 14–10, to clinch the Western Division championship.

Then Don Meredith whipped back into his life like a long-spinning boomerang.

Six years after Lombardi tried to interest the expansion Cowboys in a trade for Meredith, the cocksure former Southern Methodist star led Dallas out of the wilderness and to the Eastern Conference championship in 1966, earning a berth to the NFL Championship Game against the Packers, bidding for their fourth title in six years. The deal might have altered a large portion of NFL history, but now Dandy Dan, for all his obvious skill, was chasing Bart.

Starr never mentioned the Meredith situation and harbored no ill will toward his counterpart. But he had a very long memory, and although he needed no extra motivation with the NFL championship on the line, he certainly didn't want to give Lombardi any reason to second-guess his long-ago decision.

While the Packers headquartered in frigid Tulsa to prepare for the big game, a Dallas sportswriter reported that Lombardi was considering retirement. He hit the roof and denied the report. "I have no intention of quitting," he insisted. Now the Packers had reason to wonder, which might have been a distraction, but they were coached by Vince Lombardi, who did not allow distractions.

No longer the patsies who finished 0-11-1 during their debut season of 1960 and struggled for the next four years, the Cowboys were strong and talented on both sides of the ball and extremely well coached by the placid, cerebral, fundamentally sound Tom Landry. No coach in the NFL had spent more time studying Lombardi's offensive system than his former New York Giants colleague, who was anxious to build his own dynasty in Dallas.

The future was emblazoned with a silver star, but at the Cotton Bowl in sunny, mild Dallas on the first day of 1967, the next great NFL franchise would learn the value of patience.

In one corner of the end zone, amid a sea of cowboy hats and sunglasses, a crude handmade sign attested to Green Bay's increasingly national constituency:

FROM CONNECTICUT
GO PACKERS

Attacking Landry's innovative Flex defense, led by strong, quick tackle Bob Lilly, represented a significant challenge for the Packers. "Their scheme was so unique and their personnel was so good," Starr said. "We came in with tremendous respect for that Cowboys defense." Fortunately for the Packers, Lombardi had spent significant time studying his old colleague's invention, eventually devising a simple but incredibly effective way to mitigate some of its strength: Normally, Green Bay ran the sweep to the right almost exclusively out of the red formation (when the fullback lined up directly behind the quarterback) and to the weak side out of the brown formation (when the halfback and fullback lined up split behind the quarterback). Against the Cowboys, Starr flipped the tendency, and time after time, this change caught Dallas by surprise, giving the Packers a tactical lift in a hard-fought affair Green Bay led 21–17 at the half.

Meredith attacked the Green Bay defense aggressively, completing 15 of 31 passes for 238 yards.

Playing one of the greatest games of his career, Starr completed 19 of 28 passes for 304 yards and four touchdowns: 17 yards to Elijah Pitts, 51 yards to Carroll Dale, 16 yards to Boyd Dowler, and 28 yards to Max McGee.

The scoring play to Dowler was something to behold.

As Starr faded into the pocket, All-Pro Dallas linebacker Chuck Howley somehow broke through, grabbed the quarterback by the ankles and began to pull them together, exerting the full force of his 228 pounds. Still looking downfield, fighting against the laws of physics to stay vertical, Starr spotted Dowler in the end zone, gliding near the goalpost, and rifled a perfect pass just in front of him, in the narrow zone just outside the reach of an approaching defender.

Six points.

It was the sort of play that clearly demonstrated Starr's unusual combination of tenacity, concentration, poise—and delicate touch.

The nuance of Starr's cool-headed leadership usually escaped public view, but one moment captured by the NFL Films cameras was impossible to overlook. When Starr found Dowler in the end zone, he made an amazing catch, holding on to the ball even after being tackled low and spinning head-over-heels, landing on his previously injured shoulder. As Dowler hobbled off the field, an enraged Jim Taylor got in the defender's face and started berating him for what Taylor thought was a cheap shot.

"You chickenshit!"

The film crew captured Starr quickly squeezing between Taylor and an official, forcefully leading his teammate out of trouble and off the field. "Jimmy! It's okay! It's okay!"

Seconds later, Hornung whispered to his buddy: "Way to go, Bart!"

Without Starr's intervention, the hard-charging Taylor, whose rage was both a strength and a weakness, would have been thrown out of the game. More than a skilled offensive master, Starr often was forced to be the enforcer of Green Bay's disciplined, rigidly efficient operation, maintaining the proper balance between emotion and reason, keeping his players hungry but focused.

With the Packers leading 28–20 in the fourth quarter, Starr faced a third-and-19 on the Dallas 28 when Max McGee whispered, "I can beat Livingston on a zig-out. Give me a shot."

Starr, who had already converted twice on third-and-long on this drive, and was 7 of 10 on the day, nodded and called the play.

During their preparation, Lombardi and Starr had noticed that a Dallas cornerback tended to overplay the middle when defending a post route. They planned to exploit this weakness at some point, and now was a perfect time. McGee faked to the middle—"sold him on the post route," Starr said—before breaking outside, where the quarterback found him wide open with a clear path to the end zone. Lilly blocked the extra point, giving Green Bay a 34–20 lead with less than seven minutes left.

But Dandy Don was not finished.

Facing third-and-20 from his own 32-yard line, Meredith hit tight end Frank Clark with a 68-yard touchdown bomb, pulling the Cowboys within 34–27. When the Dallas defense rose to the occasion, sacked Starr, and forced a punt, giving Meredith one more stab, he quickly led the Cowboys downfield. After a long pass and an interference call, Dallas faced a first-and-goal on the two with 1:52 to play, needing a touchdown and an extra point to force sudden death.

"We didn't have a very good game defensively," said linebacker Lee Roy Caffey, one the young guns who had been acquired from Philadelphia in the Jim Ringo trade. "But down there, man, it was love, pure love. We knew we could stop them. We got together and said we couldn't let the offensive team down. They had played such a beautiful game."

Three plays later, when Meredith rolled right on the option, Dave Robinson chased him toward the sideline, forcing an off-balance throw, and Tom Brown intercepted his desperate fourth-down pass in the end zone, preserving Green's 34–27 victory for its fourth NFL championship in six years.

To make the game-winning play, Robinson, a former Penn State star, disregarded his assignment. In such a situation, the pursuing linebacker is coached to front the quarterback and make him commit. But after watching Meredith slip away to complete an earlier pass, he now followed his instincts and ran the quarterback down, well aware of the peril.

"The danger is, if I missed him, he could have walked into the end zone," Robinson said.

Fortunately for Green Bay, he didn't miss. Brown watched the wobbly pass sail across the goal line, catching it cleanly. "Dave made an outstanding play," Brown said. "But there was nothing spectacular about mine. My wife could have caught that ball."

Despite saving Green Bay's championship, Robinson was penalized by Lombardi when the film grades were handed out.

"I got a minus two on the play, because I didn't do my assignment correctly," Robinson said. "But I would have done it again. I respected Vince's system, but at that moment, I was more interested in the W."

In the triumphant Green Bay locker room, aging Fuzzy Thurston, forever associated with the Packer Sweep and all it represented, spoke for many others: "This game will prove for all time, for all history, the greatness of my teammates. This is the big one for all of us."

Walking through the door, a grinning Starr yelled out, "How sweet it is!"

In the era of catchphrases such as "Sock it to Me!" on *Rowan & Martin's Laugh-In,* when television and other instruments of popular culture promoted a new level of cultural shorthand, millions of Americans routinely tuned to CBS on Saturday nights, watching the larger-than-life Jackie Gleason walk on stage in Miami Beach, take a big gulp from what everyone assumed was a potent adult beverage, and blurt, with sinful delight, "How sweet it is!"

But it was never about the drink.

Just as it was sweet to be the Great One at the summit of his career, when the world was his for the taking, Starr now relished his view from the top in the age of the Green Bay Packers, professional football's reigning dynasty.

Hornung, who spent the day on the sideline with a pinched nerve in his neck as Elijah Pitts took his place, could sense the end of an era when he put his arm around Starr. "I've never seen you any better, especially in a pressure game," he said above the noise, and Starr thanked him and started praising his offensive line and the defense.

In the game's aftermath, statisticians started to connect the dots, discovering what Hornung and his teammates had known for years: Starr was a money player who performed at his best in big games, especially the postseason. Not only was Starr 4-1 in the NFL championship game, with four straight victories, he had thrown 9 touchdowns and just 1 interception while completing 57 percent of his passes.

"I didn't go into the game planning to pass so much," he said. "You just do what the other team permits you to do."

After taking a few hours to savor their latest conquest, the Packers prepared to defend the honor of the entire National Football League in Super Bowl I.

The gamesmanship started even before the Packers clinched the ticket to Los Angeles.

Hank Stram, the forever quotable head coach of the Kansas City Chiefs, became so caught up in his team's 31–7 rout of the Buffalo Bills in the AFL championship game, he yelled out, "Pour it on, boys! There will be a lot more when we tear apart the NFL."

Lombardi, upon hearing the line, pretended to be amused. "Good for Stram," he said, smiling wide. "If he said anything else, I wouldn't have any respect for him."

The first Super Bowl was all about respect: one team determined to preserve it, the other eager to earn it.

Officially known by the unwieldy, unglamorous title of the AFL-NFL World Championship Game, the first showdown between the two leagues gained the unofficial designation in the press, but in the beginning, it seemed like an exercise in hype—"the greatest buildup since *Gone with the Wind*," surmised *The New Yorker*—colliding forcefully with the enormity of the Packers' mystique.

No doubt aided by the assumption that mighty Green Bay would wipe the field with outmatched Kansas City, the sale of tickets—available for as little as six dollars—failed to live up to expectations. Only 61,946 showed up at Los Angeles Memorial Coliseum, leaving more than 30,000 empty seats at the giant bowl and forcing a blackout on local television. Some enterprising local fans found a way to circumvent the TV ban by buying—or fashioning, from spare parts—high-powered antennas capable of tuning in distant San Diego stations.

After more than a decade of technological, logistical, and financial obstacles, the transition from black-and-white television to color gained steam as the big game approached. The big three networks converted the last of their scripted shows to color in the fall of 1966 as local stations across America began the expensive process of upgrading and producing local programs in the new format. Fewer than 10 percent of the nation's television homes contained a color set, but by 1972, the figure would surpass 50 percent. At a time when the sight of NBC's peacock spreading its wings like a rainbow and the accompanying phrase "in living color" seemed as familiar as Walter Cronkite's stoic face, color TV and the Super Bowl—which featured a jet pack rider streaking across the field during the pregame frenzy—felt like part of the same modern force sweeping the country toward the future. Out with the old, in with the new.

Fourteen years after the crowd at Dr. Major Mills's house marveled at the technological achievement embodied in the fuzzy reception of Alabama's first televised bowl game, many Americans would remember Super Bowl I on January 15, 1967, as the first football game they ever watched in living color.

The shotgun marriage happened so abruptly, the only logical solution was to allow both CBS and NBC to broadcast the game—for the princely sum of $1 million each—a solution that frustrated both networks while contributing to the unprecedented nature of the event. Like the teams, the television rivalry produced unavoidable tension, exacerbated by the decision to force the sharing of one video feed, produced by CBS. "It was a good lesson in humility," said the venerable Curt Gowdy, who handled the play-by-play duties on NBC. With CBS splitting the game between regular Packers announcer Ray Scott—who worked the first half—and Jack Whitaker, the coverage featured significant differences. Like the Packers, CBS—the longtime home of the NFL, which was stronger in the largest markets—was a heavy favorite. Expecting a monster rating, the networks convinced advertisers to pay as much as $40,000 for a 30-second commercial.

Despite the chest-thumping arrogance of many NFL leaders, the upstart league had come a long way in a relatively short period of time and played a competitive brand of football. Worried about overconfidence, Lombardi brought the Packers west several days before the game and set up camp in the coastal resort town of Santa Barbara, far from the distractions of Hollywood. Pressing hard while leading a series of grueling practices, determined to get his players' attention, forever stressing Kansas City's talent, he threatened exorbitant fines for the smallest infractions. The Packers had never seen their coach so stressed, no doubt exacerbated by the large media crush descending on the Santa Barbara Inn, pushing cameras, microphones, and flashbulbs into the players' faces. "We had been playing in championship games for years but we had never seen so many media people in our lives," Starr recalled. Feeling the burden of the entire National Football League on his shoulders, Lombardi wanted to be certain the Packers were prepared and focused, despite the conventional wisdom undercutting his mission. "He made sure we didn't take the Chiefs lightly," recalled Willie Davis.

Some time later, Lombardi confided to longtime *Sports Illustrated* football writer Tex Maule, "I knew if we went out and lost to Kansas City, no one would remember those championships. The only thing anyone would ever remember about the Packers was that they had lost to the Mickey Mouse league in the first Super Bowl."

The possibility that one game—"a game played on a stage," in the words of Kansas City fullback Curtis McClinton—could dent the mystique of the Packers and cause their magnificent run to be tarnished, dominated the mind of every Green Bay player. One game could destroy all they had built in capturing four championships in six years, and also call into question the superiority of the NFL. So, it was not just a game. Rather, it was a referendum on the entirety of Vince Lombardi's life.

With oddsmakers favoring Green Bay by 13 and a half points, Stram wanted to keep his players loose, so he mocked the insult being thrown about by many sportswriters: issuing Mouseketeer caps to his Kansas City players, who mugged for the cameras and expressed confidence in their ability to make a statement on behalf of the AFL.

"Lombardi, the mystique, even the idea that maybe this was the greatest team of all time . . . sure, all that was on our mind," recalled Chiefs linebacker Johnny Robinson. "Were we in awe? I think apprehensive would be a better word."

Among the more colorful characters on the Chiefs was hard-hitting cornerback Fred "The Hammer" Williamson, who repeatedly went out of his way to disparage the Green Bay organization, causing more annoyance among his teammates than the Packers. "We thought it was funny," said guard Fuzzy Thurston. "The guy was in love with the sound of his own voice."

The merger agreement, still little more than a piece of paper, had not really ended the war. It had merely moved the competition from boardrooms and living rooms to the field, which represented a tremendous achievement for the rebel AFL, founded by men who could not buy their way into the NFL.

"Everyone has waited for this game for a long, long time," Starr told a reporter during the frenzied buildup. "You'd have to call it an historic occasion . . . To be a member of the first team to represent our league is a deep privilege . . . There is a great deal at stake."

Reflecting on the scene four decades later, Starr said, "We felt a tremendous responsibility in representing the National Football League. I'm not sure we understood this was the beginning of something so big for the whole country."

On the night before the game, after moving headquarters to the Los Angeles Sheraton Town House, flanker Max McGee risked Lombardi's wrath—and a stiff fine—by sneaking out after curfew. Like many of his teammates, he had grown restless in Santa Barbara, and the lure of a little action after being cooped up for a week was too much for him to resist. In a year when Starr had spread the ball around to a group including Jim Taylor, Carroll Dale, Marv Fleming, Boyd Dowler, and Elijah Pitts, the veteran McGee, no longer starting, had caught just 4 passes. After joining the Packers during the Blackbourn regime and playing such an important role in the early years of the Lombardi dynasty—leading both the 1961 and 1962 championship teams in receptions—the thirty-four-year-old McGee was now the eldest of the Green Bay receivers and clearly past his prime. He was just sort of playing out the string and often joked that the only reason Lombardi kept him around was to make sure Paul Hornung got up on time. His running buddy was about to get married and stayed in for the night, yet another sign of the Packers' advancing age. After an evening on the town with a new honey, McGee walked through the lobby of the hotel sometime after 7:30 A.M. and encountered Starr, who had taken the elevator downstairs for breakfast and a newspaper.

"Good morning, Max," Starr said, noticing his teammate needed a shave as he moved toward the elevator. McGee rushed back to his room to wake up Hornung, hoping to catch perhaps an hour's sleep before the team gathered to begin the biggest day in the history of professional football.

The night before, in the lobby, McGee had collared announcer Ray Scott, whose football roots stretched to the old DuMont Network in the early fifties. "I don't know if I'll get in the game, but if I do, they'll never get me out!" he said with an old warrior's appetite for one more moment of glory. "Ray, I've found me a cornerback I'll have for breakfast, lunch and dinner!"

When CBS color commentator Frank Gifford landed a pregame interview with Lombardi, his old coach said, "Every owner in the league is calling me . . . telling me, 'You've got to not only win, but win big.' You know, this is a really good football team. This isn't just a bunch of Humpty Dumpties."

As he leaned in close with the microphone and put his arm around Lombardi, Gifford could feel him trembling.

The Packers had watched reels and reels of film on the Chiefs, but with very little knowledge about the competition in the AFL, they lacked the frame of reference to adequately assess Kansas City's strength. Quarterback Len Dawson, halfback Mike Garrett, defensive tackle Buck Buchanan, and fullback Otis Taylor were big-time players who had been drafted high by NFL teams before signing with the Chiefs.

Far from the oppressive cold of northern Wisconsin, the teams took the field on a sunny day with the temperature reaching 72 degrees by kickoff. Instead of his familiar overcoat, Lombardi walked the sideline in a short-sleeve, white dress shirt, tie slightly ajar, clutching the game plan in his right hand.

When Boyd Dowler reinjured his shoulder on the opening series, Lombardi could see Starr needed a replacement flanker.

"McGee!"

The former Tulane star was sitting on the bench next to Hornung, talking about the bachelor party he planned to throw for his buddy. When Lombardi screamed his name, he came running, only to realize he had left his helmet in the dressing room. Defensive line coach Dave "Hawg" Hanner came to the rescue, provided headgear, and he ran onto the field, playing the first series wearing someone else's helmet.

Surprised to see his old favorite target, especially under the circumstances, Starr put him to use several plays later. Facing a third-and-three from the Chiefs' 37-yard line, Starr sent McGee on a quick slant. As six-foot-seven, 287-pound Buck Buchanan broke through the line, he lunged to avoid him, but the agile Chiefs tackle slammed Starr just as the ball took flight, causing it to veer slightly off course, in the direction of defensive back Willie Mitchell. Alert to what was happening, McGee reached back with his right hand, stabbed the ball, and gathered it to his chest, making a catch worthy of a highlight reel. Then he raced into the open for a 37-yard touchdown. Six points.

"That was some kind of catch," Starr said.

As the Packers' offense trotted off the field, the coach remained completely unaware that McGee had been out till dawn.

"Max was the kind of guy who could stay out all night and still be sharp the next day, which was pretty amazing to me," Starr said. "He was a great competitor."

After Dawson led the Chiefs downfield to tie the game, the Packers knew they were in for a battle.

The game might have been out of reach at the half, if an illegal procedure penalty had not nullified one of Starr's most memorable plays: Suckering Fred "The Hammer" Williamson on the sort of fake that worked time and again for the Packers through the years, he hit Carroll Dale with a spectacular 64-yard touchdown pass. It was a tough day all around for Williamson, who was nailed so hard in the fourth quarter by Donny Anderson, the rich rookie, he had to be carried off the field, no longer talking trash about the overrated Green Bay Packers. "I guess Anderson must have hit him with his wallet," quipped Fuzzy Thurston.

At the half, with Green Bay leading 14–10, Lombardi made some adjustments and told his team they had learned all they needed to know about Kansas City. Now it was time to put them away.

When the Packers' defense started blitzing, Dawson was toast. On the first series of the third quarter, the pressure led to an errant ball picked off by Willie Wood, who raced 50 yards to set up a touchdown by Elijah Pitts. For the rest of the game, Ray Nitschke, Lee Roy Caffey, and Dave Robinson relentlessly chased the Kansas City quarterback, who finished with 211 yards but was unable to find his way back to the end zone.

After going to school on the Chiefs' defense in the first half, Starr kicked into high gear after intermission. Skillfully picking apart the Kansas City secondary and making good use of his well-honed play-action skills, he completed 16 of 23 for 250 yards, 3 touchdowns, and 1 interception, his first miscue in 174 passes. Starr converted a stunning 12 of 15 third-down opportunities. Taylor, Pitts, and Anderson pounded away on sweeps and traps, the sort of basic football that had defined the Packers throughout their run at the top.

The game quickly turned into a rout. Green Bay's 35–10 victory convinced all of the Packers' greatness, including a record television audience surpassing 51 million. CBS, as expected, won the ratings war. How the performance reflected the relative strengths of the two leagues remained a matter of some debate, but one man from Kansas City was blunt: "The only difference I can see between the NFL and the AFL is Bart Starr."

With McGee back in the lineup, it seemed, for one afternoon at least, like 1962 again. His 7 receptions for 138 yards included a 13-yard touchdown in the fourth quarter, when he once again bested corner Willie Mitchell, making his conversation with Scott the night before eerily prescient.

"Just shows you what a great athlete, what a great competitor, Max was . . . playing like that after being out all night," said Hornung, who spoke with authority on the subject.

Unable to play because of his neck injury, the Golden Boy had suited up for his final Packers game, providing a bittersweet subtext to Green Bay's triumphant moment. The game also marked the end of the line for the ferocious Jim Taylor. Prior to the season, Taylor, nearing the end of a brilliant career, had pushed too far in his demands, finally angering Lombardi with his decision to play out his option. Lombardi felt personally betrayed.

When Starr was named the Most Valuable Player of the first Super Bowl—and presented the keys to a silver 1967 Corvette convertible, awarded by *Sport* magazine—he expressed humility and gratitude. "I accept this on behalf of the other thirty-nine members of the Green Bay Packers," he said, adding, "It may sound corny to some, and I don't care if it does: At Green Bay we eat, cry, and live as forty people. Any award or acclaim for an individual comes from the efforts of all forty players plus the coaches and it's in that spirit that I receive this honor."

Some no doubt believed Starr was merely spouting the company line, but the way he accepted the award accurately reflected the way he approached his role as the leader of an organization that succeeded because it thought and acted as a team.

"It reads hokey on paper," remarked New York columnist Jimmy Cannon. "But this was a guy talking about the way of his life."

More fulfilling than the award and the car was what Lombardi, having vindicated the entire National Football League, told the media.

"I don't know where the story began that Bart couldn't throw the long pass," he said. "That's ridiculous. He can throw with anyone . . . The attention hasn't always been on him because we've done other things. He didn't get the credit. But he was the same old Starr. He was terrific today . . . and I'm delighted that he's finally getting the recognition he has long deserved."

Starr was a team player who saw himself as one piece of a complex puzzle, but sometimes even a team man needs a pat on the back, especially the sort of humble leader who would be the last one to ask for it.

Respect was the order of the day, but the larger battle between the NFL and the AFL was no match for the dramatic journey of one man who walked into the shadows with a new set of keys.

"It took the Super Bowl with a super television audience to convince the world what the Packers already knew: Bart Starr is a Super Starr," Phil Pepe opined in New York's *World Journal Tribune.*

. In the year when the sport began counting in Roman numerals, unwittingly consigning all that had come before to an increasingly prehistoric context, like black-and-white television, Bart Starr became the first major football hero of the new age. Subsequent generations of knowledgeable fans, steeped in NFL lore, could be forgiven for knowing little about Sammy Baugh, Otto Graham, Bobby Layne, and Y. A. Tittle, but Starr's name was now forever etched as a grandfatherly figure in the modern history books, studied feverishly by young boys wielding flashlights after bedtime, internalized for a lifetime like multiplication tables and the alphabet.

Named to the Pro Bowl for the fourth and final time of his career, Starr showed up for his first meeting the next day with Los Angeles Rams head coach George Allen, the head coach of the Western Conference all-stars. He was on top of the world. *How sweet it is!* Playing in the Pro Bowl was an enormous honor and Starr took the experience very seriously. Then Allen dropped the bomb: He was starting Johnny Unitas.

Starr took the news like a man, practiced hard all week and enjoyed his time with Unitas. But he was crushed.

Even after the greatest season of his life, Starr was still trapped in Johnny U's shadow.

Equally troubled by the slight, Cherry ran into Allen while checking out of the team hotel on the morning of the game. The forecast called for rain; her husband was not starting, and she was headed home.

Allen went out of his way to assure Cherry that he was starting Unitas because Bart had just finished a grueling championship game and Super Bowl. "I thought Bart would enjoy not having to worry about the game," Allen explained.

Regardless of Allen's reasoning, both husband and wife were annoyed, especially considering that the Packers, led by their league MVP quarterback, had beaten Johnny U's Colts twice during the 1966 season.

"Coach," she said, "I'm not going to hold a grudge. I like you very much and so does Bart. But I want you to know, Bart has a memory like an elephant."

Some months later, a fan dropped a letter in a mailbox addressed only to "The World's Greatest Quarterback."

No city, no state, no street address.

When Bart walked through the door one night, Cherry told her husband the postman had delivered an unusual letter, showed him the envelope, and then, with the sort of comic timing even Bob Newhart could appreciate, sprung her punch line.

"This was obviously intended for Johnny Unitas," she said with a wink, and they enjoyed a good laugh.

SEVEN

THE COLDEST WAR

Ray Nitschke's thunderous voice cut through the roar of the crowd.

"Don't let me down!"

Screaming at the top of his lungs as he ran off the frozen Lambeau Field turf, the ferocious, tenacious Nitschke challenged the offense with four little words that hung heavily in the frigid air.

"Don't let me down!"

After forcing the Dallas Cowboys to punt with less than five minutes remaining, Vince Lombardi's Packers faced a defining moment in their age at the summit of professional football. The situation was dire. Green Bay trailed Dallas 17–14 in the 1967 NFL championship game, and thanks to the efforts of a determined defense, the Packers had one last chance to somehow pull out a third consecutive NFL title as the offense jogged onto the field. Chuck Mercein would never forget the sight or sound of the emotional Nitschke cheering on his teammates, his animated face bloodied and full of passion, stabbing the air with his massive arms.

"I took it personally," said Mercein, a fullback recently acquired from the New York Giants. "I didn't want to let him down."

Bart Starr was too focused on the task at hand to allow Nitschke's emotion to ensnare him. No matter. He knew it was all on his shoulders now, the burden of responsibility, the mantle of leadership, and he required no external motivation beyond the caldron of simmering desire that had propelled him to this critical, desperate moment. Ray Nitschke? Bart Starr didn't want to let *himself* down.

On the coldest, most unbearable championship day in the history of professional football, Starr convened his huddle and carefully studied the faces of the men gathered around him. A large scratch was visible on his left cheek, the result of a collision earlier in the game. Like every man on the field, he had spent the entire day fighting off the effects of partially numb fingers and toes, slipping and sliding on the icy surface, struggling to stay vertical, trying to put the frigid air out of his mind.

The combination of the slick field and Dallas' menacing Doomsday Defense had stymied the Green Bay offense for much of the second half, but as millions of Americans sat on the edge of their seats in toasty living rooms, witnessing an event they would never forget but never be able to fully comprehend, the Packers needed to drive 68 yards in the most challenging conditions imaginable. The scoreboard, sponsored by the Original Pabst Blue Ribbon Beer, showed 4:54 remaining.

One way or another, the clock was slowly running out on the Green Bay dynasty. The only question was how it would all end.

Like every soul in the stadium, Starr was miserable and just wanted to win the football game, go home, and thaw out. But as he looked around at the steely eyes gathered around him, staring at their leader with a common resolve, he felt lucky to be in such a position with such a group of dedicated men, lucky to be facing such a daunting task, with the opportunity to prove something and make history. This was the situation Lombardi had been preparing him for since the day they first met. All of the training and struggle had led to this moment, and he was ready.

"Nobody had to say anything," recalled halfback Donny Anderson, "because nine years of Vince Lombardi was in the huddle with us."

The road to this historic moment began in skepticism and doubt, when Lombardi inspired Starr to join him in the pursuit of perfection but wondered if he was good enough or tough enough for the task. Those days seemed distant and unfamiliar now, when Lombardi's fate, his place in the history books, his transcendence into a realm of legend and myth, rested largely on the leadership skills of the very same man.

After capturing NFL championships in 1961, 1962, 1965, and 1966, plus the additional achievement of winning the initial Super Bowl, the opportunity to become the first team in modern NFL history to win three consecutive titles—since the advent of the championship game in 1933—mesmerized Lombardi, even as he contemplated retirement.

"In '63, Vince was sort of quiet about going for three in a row," said linebacker Dave Robinson. "Like he didn't want to jinx it. But in '67, he was very public about it. You could tell how bad he wanted it. We all wanted it real bad."

Starr's circle had started all those years earlier with Johnny Dee, which made one moment early in 1967 incredibly fulfilling. On a Monday night in April, a crowd approaching five hundred gathered to honor Starr at the annual Green Bay Elks Sports Award Dinner, including Dee, who flew in from South Bend, Indiana, where he was the head basketball coach at the University of Notre Dame. Hardly anyone knew what a pivotal role Dee had played in the revival of the Green Bay Packers, but his affection for number 15 was unmistakable. "I classify Bart Starr as an inspiration," Dee said. "We need Bart Starrs; we don't have enough of them. I want to have somebody that I can point to and tell my two boys: 'I want you to be like him.' And if my two boys turn out to be like Bart Starr, I'll thank God every night the rest of my life."

When the time arrived for him to address the crowd, Starr paid tribute to his wife—referring to the raven-haired beauty as "this young girl," to her great delight—as well as his parents and his high school coaches. Then he paused and looked to his left on the dais, where Vince Lombardi was seated, taking it all in, waiting for his turn.

"I've told him this many times in private," Starr said as he stood behind the microphone, "but I want to say it publicly tonight. Coach Lombardi has influenced my life more than any other person . . . I'll never be able to thank him enough."

Then he choked up, stopped to regain his composure, and said, "I'm extremely proud to stand here as an athlete and to be honored by you. Words could never describe my gratitude."

When Starr took his seat next to Cherry, Lombardi walked to the podium, carefully read a resolution from the Alabama Legislature commending its native son, and then looked around the room, into the sea of coats and ties and fancy dresses. Most of the people in attendance were encountering Lombardi and Starr up close for the first time, and while the tall, athletic, and trim Starr looked about the way most expected, many were struck by the larger-than-life Lombardi's unimposing frame. They still saw him as a giant, nonetheless, so when the man who had turned the Green Bay Packers into a synonym for excellence began addressing the crowd, he owned the room.

"Bart Starr was voted the National Football League's Most Valuable Player this past season . . ."

He let this well-known fact linger in the air, pausing for dramatic effect.

"But he has been the most valuable player on this team for many years."

The room erupted in enthusiastic applause, very few of the clappers able to fully comprehend the long and arduous journey that preceded one of the most succinctly eloquent sentences ever uttered by a brilliant and demanding man.

One of the assets that made Starr such an exceptional athlete was his ability to keep pushing himself even after tremendous achievement. Staying in shape during the off-season was always a priority for the quarterback, who was obsessive about eating a well-balanced diet, his nearly six-foot-two frame rarely fluctuating higher than 200 pounds or lower than 190. The weight training revolution in professional football was still a few years away, so he spent much of his workout time jogging, usually with Bratkowski. His calisthenic regimen included exercises such as the "six-count burpee," intended to promote stamina, as well as "the windmill," good for stretching the upper body and legs, and "the wood-chopper," used to flex the back and hamstring muscles. After turning thirty-three, well aware of the creeping calendar, he added a new wrinkle: Running the steps at Lambeau Field wearing a specially designed vest weighted down with 15 pounds of lead.

"I've probably worked harder before training camp this year than I ever have," he told a reporter.

By the time the Packers convened for training camp and prepared to fulfill the defending league champion's duties in facing the college all-stars at Chicago's Soldier Field, hundreds of thousands of young people from across America and beyond were flocking to San Francisco for something billed as the Summer of Love, many following the advice of singer

Scott McKenzie and wearing flowers in their hair. The hippie movement was in full bloom. Spurred by illicit drugs, especially LSD—whose mind-altering properties were trumpeted by former Harvard professor Timothy Leary, who urged the younger generation to "turn on, tune in, and drop out"—the pilgrimage began much earlier but reached its zenith that summer, when the Haight-Ashbury neighborhood became a magnet for disaffected youth. Awash in both idealism and narcissism, the Summer of Love emerged as a powerful symbol of the generation gap then sweeping across the country, prompting young people of various backgrounds to challenge the prevailing social order in a variety of ways, particularly with regard to sex, drugs, religion, and the increasingly unpopular war in Vietnam. The counterculture espoused a disdain for traditional values and institutions, including what many saw as the oppressive force of authority, work, rules, consequences, and competition—everything Bart Star stood for.

Even as much of America looked upon the Green Bay Packers as an example of everything good about the country, the counterculture viewed such instruments of traditional America with ridicule and scorn. The admonition "Don't trust anyone over thirty" resonated like a Madison Avenue slogan but the tension surging across America was more than a math problem. Periodic rioting in major cities contributed to a perception that law and order was breaking down. (Halfback Jim Grabowski missed part of the exhibition season when his National Guard unit was mobilized to deal with unrest in Milwaukee.) The scourge of illicit drugs began to invade every city and town in the country, leading many people of all walks of life down the path of their own destruction.

At the heart of it all was the antiwar movement, which began modestly but by 1967 was a large and persistent force across the American landscape, particularly on college campuses, including the University of Wisconsin–Madison, which had a long history of radicalism. With more than 400,000 troops on the ground in Vietnam and the television news programs bringing the carnage into U.S. living rooms as never before, large numbers of young men facing the draft were defying compulsory military service by burning their draft cards or fleeing to Canada. On April 28, heavyweight boxing champion Muhammad Ali refused induction into the army, citing religious reasons. Nine years after Elvis Presley had been drafted, given a crew cut, and shipped off to Europe amid a flurry of flashbulbs and crushed female fans, the contrast with Ali saying no to his government was profound.

Instead of running off to Canada, Ali decided to stand on principle and take his punishment, causing Americans to debate, as never before, the meaning of patriotism. Two months later, he was convicted of draft evasion, sentenced to five years in prison, fined $10,000, and stripped of his boxing license. Ali, who avoided prison time while the case worked its way through the courts, eventually regained his title after the U.S. Supreme Court overturned his conviction three years later. But in 1967, his defiance drove a wedge through the county, illustrating as never before the collision between sports and culture.

Like many professional athletes of the day, Starr was disturbed by the tremors shaking the country, which mocked many of the beliefs he held dear, but he was focused on leading the Packers' assault on the history books.

Even as Starr finally gained recognition for his role in the Packers' success, a new sort of quarterback for a new age was preparing to take his place.

For the first three years of the decade, as the American Football League cut a swashbuckling path across the country, challenging the NFL's dominance, the New York Titans struggled, sometimes drawing as few as 7,500 fans to the ancient Polo Grounds while repeatedly finishing in the league cellar. Just when some AFL leaders favored abandoning New York altogether, a five-man group headed by Sonny Werblin bought the team, rechristened it as the Jets—striking a more modern tone, as the country headed at full-throttle into the jet age—and announced plans to move into gleaming new Shea Stadium. Then the Jets signed Joe Namath to the richest contract in the history of sports and the tectonic plates of professional football shifted.

Not only was Namath's incredible talent plotting a course for Super Bowl III and a place among the greatest quarterbacks of all time, the combination of his charisma and brash, flamboyant manner transformed him into a celebrity who transcended the sport. Perfectly timed to benefit from television, the antiestablishment movement, the sexual revolution, and the rise of professional football, Broadway Joe reflected and hastened a new age of assertiveness, independence, and stardom among professional athletes. In no time at all, Namath seemed bigger than the Jets, the AFL, even the institution of professional football.

Which made him the exact opposite of Bart Starr.

Starr wasn't cool like Joe Namath.

He didn't have long hair or date beautiful starlets.

He didn't star in pantyhose commercials or movies with Ann-Margret.

He didn't have a catchy nickname.

Half of the men in the country wanted to be Namath—especially off the field, where he was forever surrounded by leggy blondes—but when most of them looked in the mirror in the morning, they saw a guy more like Starr.

Starr didn't take your breath away. He won championships . . . and left the heavy breathing to others.

Broadway Joe was warming up in the wings, but in 1967, the stage still belonged to Bart Starr and the Green Bay Packers.

Nine years after forty men took the field for the first game of the Lombardi era, only eight remained: Starr, tackles Bob Skoronski and Forrest Gregg, guards Jerry Kramer and Fuzzy Thurston, middle linebacker Ray Nitschke, receiver Boyd Dowler, and receiver Max McGee. Thurston lost his starting position to Gale Gillingham but hung on to his job by playing special teams.

After the first-year New Orleans Saints signed free agent Jim Taylor and claimed Paul Hornung in the expansion draft—the Golden Boy was nursing a back injury and decided to retire, never playing a down in New Orleans—bonus babies Jim Grabowski and Donny Anderson took over the running game.

The most far-reaching change was the NFL's realignment: the two conferences were separated into two divisions, with Green Bay placed in the Central Division along with Chicago, Detroit, and Minnesota. The division winners would meet for each conference championship, representing the first expansion of the postseason beyond the league title game.

Veteran offensive guard Jerry Kramer agreed to keep a diary and work with journalist Dick Schaap to produce an insider's account of the 1967 season. The resulting book, *Instant Replay*, became a classic in sports literature, illuminating the climactic year of the Lombardi era with refreshing candor and often-powerful insights. His admiration for Starr was evident throughout. "[Starr's] got so much character, so much willpower," he wrote. "He's about as complete a person as I've ever known. He admires Lombardi tremendously, and the affection is mutual. When Vince bawls Bart out in a meeting, it's always about the receiver he didn't see, or the play he didn't call, never about putting out enough. I really think the only reason Vince ever criticizes Bart is just to show the rest of the club that he's impartial, that he'll even yell at his favorite."

Eleven years after he showed up for his first training camp with the lowliest franchise in professional football, shrouded in anonymity, Starr arrived at St. Norbert College in July 1967 as the undisputed leader of the sport's most dominant franchise. Far removed from his tense rookie year, his confident, playful side could be seen the night when he returned to his room, hid behind the door, waited for roommate Henry Jordan to walk through the door . . . and then jumped out and yelled, "Boo!" Jordan, one of the hardest-hitting players on the defense, was so startled, he jumped.

But when Starr entered the classroom or stepped on the field, he was all business, which Steve Wright quickly discovered during an exhibition game against the Pittsburgh Steelers. When Wright, a reserve tackle, missed a block and his man charged through to level Starr, landing a devastating lick to his face, the quarterback trudged back to the huddle and looked Wright in the eye.

"Steve Wright, you ought to be ashamed of yourself," Starr said. "I'll tell you one thing. If I see that guy in here once more tonight, I'm not going to kick him in the can. I'm going to kick you in the can, right in front of 52,000 people."

Recalling the incident, Wright said, "I felt about two feet tall. That was all Bart had to say. And I didn't miss another block."

It wasn't the fear of physical retribution that motivated Wright, but the thought of having let Starr down.

Like the veterans of championships past, the young bloods who joined the offense in the mid-1960s learned to appreciate Starr's quiet but forceful style of leadership. Raising his voice was not only out of character, it was unnecessary when he could exploit his presence in such a manner. Wright, who weighed nearly one hundred pounds more than Starr, was not fearful of being physically assaulted by his quarterback. He was afraid of disappointing him, which represented a much more powerful motivation in the rarified culture of the Green Bay Packers.

In the season opener, Starr faced tremendous pressure and played poorly, tossing four interceptions in the first half as the Packers fell into a 17–0 hole against the Lions before rallying for a 17–17 tie.

Two days later, Lombardi blamed guard Jerry Kramer for allowing his man, Detroit linebacker Alex Karras, to cause such havoc. "One man made us look like a bunch of dummies!" Lombardi railed during a team meeting. "One man tossed us around like a bunch of dolls!"

The next Sunday, despite better protection, Starr was even more off the mark, throwing five interceptions but benefiting from a strong defensive effort in a 13–10 win over the Bears.

Everyone wondered what was wrong with the Super Bowl hero, who had been picked off only three times in the entire 1966 season. "He didn't seem to be throwing the ball with the snap that he usually has," observed Bears safety Rosey Taylor. "When he followed through, he wasn't snapping the wrist."

As he watched the quarterback unwrap a maze of tape and bandages in the Packers locker room, sportswriter Brent Musburger smelled a rat. But Starr refused to discuss it. "I'd rather not talk about the injuries, if you don't mind," he told Musberger, the future CBS and ABC sportscaster who then wrote a sports column for the *Chicago American* newspaper. "I just don't like to make a big deal them of them."

To writers who covered the Packers and the NFL in those days, the refrain was familiar. Starr always downplayed or hid his injuries. Beyond some practical reasons, it also reflected something deeper: When Starr started his career, his personality caused some coaches and players to question his toughness so through the years, when he suffered various injuries, he never wanted give anyone an excuse to wonder about his mettle or ever think of him as a crybaby. This was another way for him to assume the full measure of the quarterback's responsibility—to lead not only by calling plays but also by sucking it up: leadership by denying pain's ability to cause paralysis. Like many other teams, the Packers gained a measure of mental strength when one athlete kept pushing through severe physical difficulty, causing all those competitive players to meet the ante. Not all players could withstand the same level of pain or perform effectively when their body suffered significant trauma. Eventually, everyone faced a wall, including Starr.

The way Starr blew off reporters also made an impression. Even after taking a significant beating, the quarterback was not the sort to snap at sportswriters who were just trying to do their jobs. "I don't want to be rude, but I just don't want to talk" was his way of pushing writers away, which contrasted dramatically with some of the more colorful phrases scribes heard through the years. "He was always such a gentleman," said Lee Remmel, who covered the Packers for the *Green Bay Press-Gazette.*

After the Bears game, Lombardi repeatedly denied rumors his quarterback was hurt. "He's in a slump," the coach said. "It happens to everybody sooner or later."

During a 23–0 victory over the second-year Atlanta Falcons at Milwaukee's County Stadium in week three, Starr dropped back to pass. Safety Bob Riggle and linebacker Tommy Nobis blitzed. Just as he cocked his arm to throw, Riggle hit him in front and Nobis clobbered him from behind.

"The blow was right behind my right shoulder," Starr recalled years later. "I had to leave the game because I couldn't even pick up the ball."

The man who inflicted the damage was already recognized as one of the sport's most intimidating defenders. After a brilliant career at the University of Texas, Nobis had been zealously pursued by the AFL's Houston Oilers and the NFL's expansion Falcons. In the new age defined by Broadway Joe's epic deal, when the competition for every prominent player represented a proxy war for the larger struggle between the rival leagues, the clamor for Nobis's services reached new heights. While orbiting the earth in Gemini 7, astronaut Frank Borman radioed home: "Tell Nobis to sign with Houston."

Moments after tumbling to the ground, Starr stood on the sideline as Domenic Gentile, the Packers' assistant trainer, took his arm and pulled it with great care even to his shoulder, trying to assess his injury. Then, as Bratkowski moved the team downfield, Gentile carefully lifted off Starr's shoulder pads and began massaging the shoulder. When the backup quarterback tossed a touchdown to Carroll Dale and jogged off the field, Starr paused the treatment long enough to clap and shake his buddy's hand. He was so frustrated at not being able to go back into the game, Starr was later seen kicking the ground and, at one point, welling up in tears.

Two days later, no longer able to hide his quarterback's distress, Lombardi reversed field. Concern that opposing defenses would attack the Packers' offense differently and go after the quarterback and possibly hurt him had caused Lombardi to deny, deny, deny. "Really, he's been playing under a severe handicap all year," the coach finally confessed on his weekly television show, revealing injuries to Starr's shoulder, ribs, wrist, and thumb. "I've denied it in order to protect him . . . not from the fans or from the newspaper, but rather from the opposition. He's certainly displayed a great deal of courage in playing."

Bratkowski started the next two games as Starr tried to heal, but he would be dealing with the lingering effects of the devastating blow for years.

Three days after the Packers' first loss of the year, to the struggling Minnesota Vikings, Lombardi walked into the meeting room and lit into his team. "I want to tell you this: I had another look at those movies and they stink! You didn't run! You didn't block! You didn't do a damn thing!"

On the same day, the antiwar movement at the University of Wisconsin turned violent. Protesting the presence of recruiters from Dow Chemical, maker of napalm, a controversial incendiary being used in Vietnam, several hundred students blocked access to the university's Commerce Building. The confrontation between protestors and police resulted in dozens of injuries on both sides, galvanizing opposition to the war on the Madison campus, which became a center of radical activism.

The distance between Madison and Green Bay seemed enormous, despite the interconnectivity between the two communities. The tension between the discipline and authority of the Packers and what struck many average Wisconsin citizens as permissiveness bordering on anarchy at the state's leading university reflected the forces starting to roil the country.

Deeply bothered by the student unrest, Lombardi often incorporated it into the speeches he gave on leadership. "I am sure you are disturbed like I am by what seems to be a complete breakdown of law and order and the moral code which is almost beyond belief," he said. "The prevailing sentiment seems to be if you don't like the rule, break it."

The decline in values also became a recurring theme in Starr's frequent speaking engagements. "Society today is so permissive it is an absolute catastrophe," he told attendees to one professional convention. "We are getting to the point where parents are apologizing for having to discipline their children . . . Anyone looking at a permissive society will be looking at a loser."

Popular culture still largely reflected the order and conformity of traditional America, but the premiere of *The Smothers Brothers Comedy Hour* on CBS on February 5, 1967, marked a turning point in U.S. television. Hitting the airwaves just as opposition to the Vietnam War neared a tipping point, the show's biting satire on the war and other sensitive subjects rankled network censors and pushed the boundaries of what was considered acceptable on American television. In a year when the leading prime-time programs included *The Andy Griffith Show, Gunsmoke,* and *Bewitched,* millions of Americans still arranged their schedules to watch the venerable *Ed Sullivan Show,* which, since the days of Elvis, had played an important role in introducing the biggest rock 'n' roll acts to mainstream America, including the landmark programs featuring The Beatles in 1964. Disturbed by the suggestive lyrics of The Doors' megahit "Light My Fire," Sullivan's producers instructed lead singer Jim Morrison to rewrite one line of the song during a widely anticipated guest appearance on the show. He reluctantly agreed but during the live performance on September 17, for reasons that have been debated ever since, he uttered the line—"Girl we couldn't get much higher"—and Sullivan hit the roof, vowing that the group would never make another appearance on the show. The event symbolized not only the tension between traditional America—reflected in the rigid standards of network television—and the increasingly forceful and edgy popular music scene, but also the dilemma television faced in embracing youth culture without proving impotent to tame it.

At the same time, NFL Films was busy producing a glowing documentary special on Vince Lombardi scheduled to preempt Sullivan's "really big shooo" and garner a huge prime-time audience, representing a tremendous breakthrough for professional football.

Lombardi's success made him a huge target. Many of his peers across the league resented the attention he attracted, which the film addressed. "Coach Lombardi is probably the most hated man in professional football," Paul Hornung observed. "Every coach wants to beat Lombardi more than any man." The connective tissue between Ed Sabol's sales job on Pete Rozelle and his larger vision, Steve Sabol's dramatic epiphany at the 1962 NFL championship game, the groundbreaking film, *They Call It Pro Football,* and the enduring legend of Lombardi's Packers was now validated by the power of prime-time television. As young people all across the country started to question everything associated with the older generation, especially authority, the success of Lombardi and the Packers as a reflection of establishment America was never more dramatically framed.

Starr, whose voice played a significant role in the film, observed that Lombardi "tells you that if you give anything less than what you have within you at any time, regardless of the situation, regardless of the consequences . . . you're cheating yourself, you're cheating your teammates, you're cheating professional football and you're cheating the fans who have made the game what it is today for you. But most of all, you're cheating your maker who gave you that God-given talent with which to succeed. . . ."

Still healing from the collision against the Falcons, and forced to wear tape on the thumb of his throwing hand, Starr returned to the lineup in week six, leading the Packers past the Giants, 48–21. "He's still hurt," Lombardi said. "He had deep receivers open twice and just couldn't hit them." But despite Bratkowski's solid play in his absence, the Packers were Starr's team and had missed much more than his arm. "Bart is our man," Forrest Gregg said. "With Bart back, we got a lift. We knew anything we ran would go."

Two weeks later, the Packers led the Baltimore Colts 10–0 in the closing minutes. But Johnny Unitas led a brilliant rally, exploiting an onsides kick and converting a gutsy fourth-and-six, to pull off a 13–10 victory.

On the subdued airplane ride back to Green Bay, Starr sat on the armrest of a seat near the back, where several of his teammates were playing cards. The disappointment was fresh but Starr, Kramer, and McGee were consumed with the bigger picture. "This man is one great coach," Starr said, as the other two nodded. "He's got a brilliant mind . . . I've never seen a more complete book on a team than Coach Lombardi had on Baltimore. It was really a beautiful thing to see."

The *Lombardi* film captured for posterity the coach sitting next to Starr at a rectangular table, with Bratkowski at one end and rookie Don Horn on the opposite side, all four men wearing plain white T-shirts as they pored over the specifics of one week's game plan. In these meetings, Lombardi and his quarterbacks discussed the reasoning for attacking the opposition's defense in one certain way, tailored to exploit the other team's personnel.

"This may make your 38 pretty good," Lombardi said about one particular defensive weakness as Starr scribbled a note in his ring-binder. "Your toss to that side . . . but not your pitch-outs."

Deadly serious one moment and lighthearted the next, Lombardi reached out and shoved Starr's head playfully as the quarterback laughed.

Even after becoming the dominant team of the sixties—*especially* after becoming the dominant team of the sixties—Lombardi drove the Packers relentlessly. The process began on Tuesday, always impacted by a steady stream of injuries and nagging hurts. Facing off against his own menacing defense, determined to disguise a coverage one moment and a blitz the next, caused Starr to stay sharp during the week as he implemented Lombardi's meticulously crafted game plan, and forced him to think through the process of how to attack in various live situations.

The delicate balance between intensity and restraint, crucial to any successful football team, could be seen on the Green Bay practice field when Starr was chased out of the pocket by his defense and hammered by six-foot-three, 240-pound Willie Davis.

"Davis!" Lombardi screamed, rushing to the scene. "Don't do something foolish! We need a tough practice but we don't need to lose a quarterback! Don't do something foolish! That's all I ask!"

How do you tell your defense to attack hard but not *too* hard?

Davis glared at his coach until the risk of his aggressive tackle began to sink in.

"When you're in that situation and you get a chance to lay one on somebody, you do it, I don't care who it is," Davis said. "It's hard to hold back after all the training you've been through."

Starr, clobbered but unhurt, climbed off the ground and went back to work as Davis and his teammates breathed a sigh of relief.

In a year when the Baltimore Colts finished a dominant 11-1-2 but lost the Coastal Division title to the 11-1-2 Los Angeles Rams, who won the head-to-head battle, Green Bay clinched the Central Division in week eleven before losing the final two meaningless games and finishing 9-4-1.

Hobbled by the various injuries, Starr suffered through one of the worst years, statistically, of his career: His completion percentage dipped to 54.8, his passing yards to 1,823, and his touchdowns to 9; and he very uncharacteristically tossed 17 interceptions. (This ballooning number required the proper perspective: High as it was compared to his own history, his 17 interceptions still ranked lower than five other quarterbacks, including St. Louis Cardinals slinger Jim Hart, who recorded 30.)

Two weeks after falling to the Rams by virtue of a blocked punt in the fourth quarter, the Packers hosted Los Angeles for the Western Conference championship in Milwaukee. Starr had not forgotten about George Allen's decision to start Unitas in the previous Pro Bowl, but he was more focused on the task of dealing with one of the most imposing defensive fronts in football.

The size, speed, and aggressiveness of Deacon Jones, Merlin Olsen, Lamar Lundy, and Rosey Grier—better known as the Fearsome Foursome—played a large role in the Rams' ascendance under Allen during the sixties. Bears great Dick Butkus once called it "the most dominant line in football history."

"One of the best rushes I've ever faced," Starr said. "The Rams' defense has almost completely thwarted many passing attacks . . . creating havoc among some of the most outstanding teams in the league."

A generation before Peyton Manning's six-foot-five body became the prototype for NFL quarterbacks, the nearly six-foot-two Starr (and many other contemporaries, including the six-one Johnny Unitas) often found himself at a disadvantage in dealing with the persistent pressure of six-seven Lundy, six-five Olsen, six-five Jones and six-five Grier (who was replaced in 1967 by six-five former Lions star Roger Brown).

"When they got any sort of penetration at all," Starr said, "and put their hands up in the air, it was like trying to throw out of the bottom of a barrel."

Years later, looking back on all the punishing defenders he faced, Starr said, "It's hard to pick just one . . . but I was always impressed with the consistency of Merlin Olsen. Oh my gosh, was he consistently good."

The Rams' line came hard and often, forcing quarterbacks to either flush out of the pocket or dump the ball off quickly. Jones, who eventually joined the tenacious Olsen in the Hall of Fame, proved especially difficult for quarterbacks to elude, becoming virtually synonymous with the sack, a term he coined long before the NFL recognized the stat. "Every quarterback we met was so ready for the rush that he threw the ball early," Olsen said. "We didn't always get him, but we put the thought in his head."

Olsen and the others were never far from Starr's thoughts two days before Christmas, but they sacked him just once and forced him to throw just one interception. Pressure? What pressure? As usual, the Rams' intense rush created not just peril but opportunity for a quick-thinking quarterback riding a wave of institutional knowledge and surging confidence. After spotting Roman Gabriel a touchdown, the Packers played their most complete game of the season, clamping down hard on defense and clicking effortlessly on offense. Benefiting from a dominating performance by his offensive line, which largely neutralized the Rams' front four, Starr was virtually flawless, hitting 17 of 23 passes for 222 yards—including a 17-yard touchdown to Carroll Dale—to key a 28–7 victory that sent Green Bay back to the title game for the sixth time in eight years.

Visiting fans from sunny Southern California walked into the Milwaukee shadows complaining about the cold weather, as the thermometer plunged to 13 degrees. Many bundled up and shivered.

They usually popped popcorn.

Several times each week during the season, Zeke Bratkowski arrived at the Starr house and retreated to the basement with Bart. One of them would roll down the screen and the other would hit the lights and flip the switch on the projector. While munching popcorn amid a celluloid whir, the quarterbacks searched for meaning and opportunity. In the darkness they followed the flashes of light.

This routine became intertwined in the context of Bart Jr.'s childhood. "I can't say I was able to observe the subtleties of the game just yet, but I was able to see how being a quarterback was about so much more than playing the game on Sunday," he said. While the sports world focused on Starr's machinelike efficiency on the field, his son grew up observing his obsessive film study, understanding from an early age the way the leader of the Green Bay Packers prepared assiduously, forever searching for an edge in the upcoming game as he went to school on every defensive player, learning their weaknesses as well as their strengths.

"This was fun to me," Starr said. "I thought of it as a game . . . trying to spot something nobody had noticed. Each day you feel like you're growing toward [eventual victory on] Sunday."

Even after spending a significant amount of time watching film at work, usually with Lombardi, Starr took the same films home and kept threading them through his own machine again and again, creating a detailed mental picture of the opposition's defense and how it had reacted to various situations.

"By the time Bart stepped on the field he had already played that game a hundred times in his mind," Bratkowski said. "It all started with what he learned watching film. By the time he took the field he was so incredibly prepared."

Far from the adoring crowds, the pivotal relationship between Starr and Bratkowski blossomed in the film room, where each team spoke a slightly different dialect of a common language and they worked together to interpret the nuances like so many consonants and vowels.

One year after escaping with a victory over Dallas to capture the 1966 championship, Starr was incredibly impressed by the strength and athleticism of Bob Lilly, the Cowboys' All-Pro defensive tackle. While watching film of the Dallas defense, Starr noticed that whenever an offense pulled a guard as the lead blocker for a fullback, Lilly invariably utilized his prodigious quickness to crowd the gap between the center and the guard.

"He was so good at pursuing laterally . . . in no time, he's right there on your butt," Starr said.

Lilly's quickness and aggressiveness was a major factor in the success of the Cowboys' Flex defense. But as the Packers prepared for the rematch against Dallas, Starr devised a way to turn Lilly's strength into a weakness—and planned to hold his ace until he really needed it.

Unlike his wife, Starr usually slept like a baby on the night before a game.

The pattern typically reversed on the night after a game, when Cherry fell asleep easily, spent and relieved, but Bart often stayed up late, consumed with critiquing his performance and looking ahead to the next week's opponent, sometimes even retreating to the basement to pore over film.

After a good night's sleep prior to the showdown with Dallas, Starr woke up, ate some breakfast and drove off with his father to attend an early service at First United Methodist Church. As soon as they walked out the front door, the cold air and the gusty wind assaulted both the quarterback and the proud father like a punch in the face. "Both of us were so cold, neither one of us mentioned it," Starr said. "Not one time did we talk about the weather. Not once."

On the morning before the game destined to be known in football lore as the Ice Bowl, the last thing Bart and Ben wanted to talk about was the weather.

The day before, when the Packers conducted their walk-through drills at Lambeau Field, the temperature had hovered near freezing, with sunny skies and no wind. Forecasters predicted a similar Sunday. But a blast of Arctic air unexpectedly descended on northern Wisconsin during the night, creating an unprecedented climate for deciding the NFL championship.

Preparing to shoot their sixth championship game, the Sabols of NFL Films asked for an early wake-up call in the downtown hotel room they shared. As usual, Ed slept fitfully, concerned about all the variables beyond his team's control. When the telephone rang sometime after 7 A.M. on December 31, 1967, the father was already awake, looking out the window into the darkness and going through preparations in his mind. His son, sound asleep, fumbled for the receiver.

"Good morning, Mr. Sabol," the operator said. "It is 16 degrees below zero and the wind is out of the north. Now, have a nice day."

Sixteen below?

Steve wondered if he was having a nightmare.

"Dad! You're not going to believe this!"

Temporarily living in the Northland Hotel in downtown Green Bay, Willie Davis took the elevator downstairs for breakfast and encountered an out-of-town sportswriter.

"Can you believe how cold it is?" the scribe asked the Packers' defensive captain, who was oblivious to the situation.

"No!" Davis protested. "It can't be that cold!"

Even after confirming the temperature, Davis found the figure difficult to fathom.

"I started wondering whether we would even play the game," Davis recalled. "I mean, it was so cold . . . there was a real question in my mind whether the game would—or should—take place."

Chuck Mercein heard the temperature on the radio but, still in bed and in a state of semiconsciousness, refused to trust his hearing, so he placed a call to the weather station at Austin Straubel Field. When the person on the other end of the line confirmed the temperature and said it could get even colder, Mercein was "in absolute disbelief." He showered, dressed and went to Mass. "Believe me, I did some praying," he said.

Willie Wood, the Packers' safety, was perhaps the most adamant that the game would eventually be called off. "No way we're playing in this shit!" he said, walking around the locker room as his teammates began to arrive. "This is just too damn cold to play football."

By the time the players learned that the game would go on as scheduled, Lombardi was steaming hot over one consequence of the cold. In an attempt to prevent the field from freezing, the Packers had invested $80,000 in a newfangled heating system, essentially a large electric blanket installed six inches beneath the playing surface. In the days leading up to the big game, the coach had delighted in explaining the features and merits of the electric marvel to out-of-town visitors. But now Chuck Lane, the Packers' publicity director, was presented with the unenviable task of informing Lombardi that the heater, which had been working just fine on Saturday, somehow malfunctioned during the night, allowing the field to freeze solid.

Like many failed car batteries—which left countless people stranded, forced to seek other modes of transportation, including extended thumbs— the heating system was never prepared for such cold conditions, especially with the intense and constant wind, which gusted up to 30 miles per hour, pushing the wind chill to a reported 46 degrees below zero at kickoff, when the air temperature was 13 below. "When the temperature dropped to 16 below and with that wind, it just couldn't hold it," explained engineer John Harrington, who installed and maintained the giant heater.

When the Cowboys took their pregame walk-through, discovering a playing surface that felt more like an ice rink, mammoth defensive tackle Jethro Pugh said, "That bastard Lombardi! He turned off his machine!"

While thousands of sturdy Packer Backers showed up at least two hours before kickoff, maintaining their usual pregame routine in the parking lot, huddling around makeshift bonfires, many other fans filed in to the stadium as near as possible to game time, including Cherry Starr. Before the age of luxury skyboxes at Lambeau and other NFL stadiums, players' wives were forced to shiver like everyone else. Ordinarily, the ladies of Green Bay approached Packer games like church and dressed to the nines. Cherry normally wore one of her finest and snazziest outfits for games, adorned by a stylish hat. But on the day of the Ice Bowl, over her dress she wore a fur-lined coat with a hood, boots, and mittens. On top of the coat she wore what was known as a "stadium bag," which resembled a sleeping bag with a zipper running up to the neck.

Despite her preparation, Cherry spent most of the afternoon unable to feel her fingers and toes. "I've never been so miserable in my life," she said. "The atmosphere was so cold, you could take a cup of coffee, throw it up in the air and it just vaporized . . . before it hit the ground."

M. E. Bratkowski would always remember how her face ached.

One of the most striking of the images captured for posterity by NFL Films shows rows upon rows of fans intently watching the action while bundled from head to toe, each person's breath flowing into the distance like smoke. The smart ones wore ski masks, making Lambeau Field look like a bank robbers' convention. Unlike the bitterly cold 1961 championship game, the game was a hard sellout, with the recently expanded stadium filled to its capacity of 50,861.

Ten-year-old Bart Jr. and his friends usually walked to the stadium, located less than a mile from their house, but not on the day of the Ice Bowl. After catching a ride with some adults, Bart Jr. and the boys—including Zeke and M. E. Bratkowski's two sons, Bob and Steve, as well as his good buddy Steve Crispigna, whose family owned Green Bay landmark Sammy's Pizza—huddled as best they could under sleeping bags while gulping hot chocolate. Every so often, they escaped to a nearby restroom, just to find shelter for a few precious moments from the relentless wind.

"It was unbearable, but we had to be there," said Steve Crispigna. "I get cold just thinking about it."

Forced into action on the morning of the game, the grounds crew quickly constructed small shelters, covered by tarpaulins, around both benches, to provide some protection for players standing on the sideline. Several small butane heaters pumped warm air through the glorified lean-tos, with limited practical effect.

Lombardi usually forbade his players from wearing additional layers below their uniforms because he understood how the added weight inhibited movement, but on this day, he allowed all to wear long underwear and some to wear gloves. Starr could not grip the ball with gloves, so he was forced to keep his hands exposed.

The press box protected the large media contingent from the wind but not from the cold. Reporters were forced to deal with condensation and ice forming on the windows, blocking their view of the field. Chuck Lane mitigated the problem by sending a member of his staff to a service station down the street for a container of antifreeze. Throughout the game, business manager Tom Miller squirted and scraped the windows to melt through the fog.

"The conditions were just miserable . . . but at least the windows were closed," recalled Green Bay sportswriter Lee Remmel.

Still, in an era long before portable computers, some writers discovered that the keys on their typewriters began to freeze, a problem even Lane's magic liquid could not solve.

Determined to experience the authentic feel of the game, CBS television play-by-play man Ray Scott insisted on opening the window to his booth, where he shivered alongside analysts Jack Buck and Frank Gifford, who picked up his coffee at one point during the game to notice it had frozen solid. "I think I'll take another bite of my coffee," Gifford ad-libbed, providing the broadcast's most memorable line.

In the frigid CBS truck parked behind the stadium, where a space heater provided little warmth, the weather was just another logistical challenge for veteran director Tony Verna. Like all national media people who descended on Green Bay during football season, Verna found himself being charmed by Lombardi in some instances—the boss loved to play bartender at his home, spinning yarns and slapping backs—and feeling his wrath at other times. Even in an era when Lombardi appeared on the cover of *Time* magazine as the personification of professional football, he was sometimes portrayed as a bully. Especially after a controversial piece by Leonard Shecter appeared in *Esquire* in the fall of 1967, painting Lombardi in an unflattering light, the coach was very conscious of his image. When Verna showed him fuming on the sideline—as he frequently did—Lombardi never shied away from giving the producer an earful. "He could be very sensitive to that stuff," Verna said. "He was always giving me a hard time." Despite television's central role in cultivating the mystique of Lombardi and the Packers, the coach often viewed TV people with a certain disdain, especially when they invaded his turf.

As Verna planned the postgame in Green Bay, he could not forget how Lombardi had pushed Jack Whitaker out of the locker room following the 1966 title victory, preventing CBS from capturing a dramatic moment. "I was determined not to let that happen again," Verna said, which was one reason he planned to have Gifford, one of Lombardi's favorites, in the Green Bay locker room, win or lose.

Four years after introducing instant replay, even Verna was surprised by how widely it had been adopted by the networks. "Very quickly the fans began to expect it, like it had always been there," said Verna, who was precluded from pursuing a patent on the invention because of his employment contract with CBS. In sharp contrast to the 1963 Army–Navy game, CBS now had the ability replay a variety of plays all over the field and to add the viewer-friendly elements of slow-motion and isolation, accomplished with equipment specially designed for remote purposes. "We were already light-years ahead of 1963."

The technological sophistication embodied in television and instant replay contrasted sharply with the timeless struggle against the elements, simultaneously demonstrating mankind's constant strive to innovate and the inevitable limitations of this impulse, thereby providing the most dramatic setting in the history of professional football.

Two days before the game, before anyone knew how cold it would be, Lombardi spent some time before practice impressing on his players the opportunity that lay before them. "I want that third championship," he said. "And I deserve it! We all deserve it!

"Lots of better ballplayers than you guys have gone through here. But you're the type of ballplayers I want. You've got character. You've got heart. You've got guts."

When Lombardi walked around the locker room just before sending his players out into the cold, he said, "It's our kind of day, boys. It's our kind of day."

Willie Davis, as tough and dedicated as any man on the roster, just looked at Lombardi, desperately wanting to say something but not knowing how to respond. "That was a crazy thing to say," Davis recalled. "The weather was horrible and there was a legitimate question about whether any game . . . especially a championship game . . . should be played in such conditions. You just couldn't help thinking about that, as you got ready to go out into that weather."

The Packers had learned to see cold weather as an ally, but in this case, the conditions were too extreme to benefit either team, casting Lombardi's comment in a haze of absurdity. But the larger point of Lombardi's message was lost on no one. He was not merely referring to the weather. He was speaking of the challenge to overcome the adversity of such difficult weather on the way to an elusive third consecutive championship. Beyond his very skillful manipulation of x's and o's and his masterful organization, Lombardi's metamorphosis from late-blooming coach to legend was closely linked to the way he invested the game with such meaning and the way he was able to transplant his philosophy into every member of the organization with an urgency approaching desperation.

"The Ice Bowl was an awful way to play a football game but so much of what Coach Lombardi believed was embodied in that game," said Fuzzy Thurston, the longtime leader of the Packer Sweep who had lost his starting job to Gale Gilllingham and spent most of the game on the sidelines, cheering his teammates.

Now was the chance to see how much his players wanted to make history . . . as the ravages of frostbite attacked their fingers and toes . . . as icicles dangled from their noses . . . as every breath placed enormous stress on their lungs . . . as every planted foot on the treacherous ice represented a precarious step into the unknown, causing many to slip, slide and eventually lose their balance . . . as every body slam to the frozen turf felt like a collision with concrete.

Now, in order to extend their dominance over the National Football League, Lombardi's Packers would be forced to conquer, or at least endure, an even more formidable opponent.

Nature.

Where have you gone, Joe DiMaggio?
A nation turns its lonely eyes to you.

One week before Bart Starr and the Green Bay Packers took the field to defend their NFL championship, American moviegoers began flocking to theaters to see Mike Nichols's epic film, *The Graduate*, featuring Simon & Garfunkel's "Mrs. Robinson," destined to become one of the hottest-selling, and most iconic, records of 1968.

To fully comprehend the Ice Bowl and Bart Starr's role in it, you must understand the cultural swirl of 1967 embodied so perfectly in the movie and the song.

Even as the younger generation began to question everything about American culture, including the predominance of traditional values, "Mrs. Robinson" exploded into the Zeitgeist, dripping with counterintuitive nostalgia. Cleverly using DiMaggio, the legendary former New York Yankees star, as a symbol of an era close enough to remember but distant enough to miss, Paul Simon mourned for the loss of a sports hero who epitomized dignity and grace, on and off the field. The subtext of the song begged a central question: By challenging everything, have we sacrificed something fundamental and good about American society?

"Mrs. Robinson" reflected a powerful sense of yearning for a simpler time then sweeping across the country, but beyond the two-dimensional characters of 45 rpm vinyl, America still had plenty of dignified sports heroes to celebrate in 1967. Including Bart Starr.

A generation later, in a world where many sports stars no longer felt an obligation to act like role models, casting the entire industry in a police-blotter haze of lowered expectations, fundamentally weakening the connection between athletes and fans, Simon could have updated his song:

> *Where have you gone, Bart Starr?*
> *A nation turns its lonely eyes to you.*

Like DiMaggio, Starr represented much more than the sum of his statistics.

Released three days before Christmas in 1967, *The Graduate* accurately reflected the tidal wave of disillusionment sweeping across America as many members of the baby boom generation struggled to find their place in a world shaped by their parents. The lurid affair between recent college graduate Benjamin Braddock (Dustin Hoffman) and his girlfriend's middle-aged mother (Anne Bancroft) proved shocking to Middle America, but the shattering of this cinematic taboo was connected to a larger and more profound point. Young Benjamin felt trapped by the weight of society's rules and expectations, not knowing what to do with his life.

While many Americans, especially the generation just reaching maturity, could relate to Benjamin's confusion and ambivalence in a world buffeted by cultural upheaval, the vast majority of the country—the group President Richard Nixon would later call "the silent majority"—lived in a world of certitude, framed by obligations, consequences, and boundless opportunity.

Bart Starr was not confused about his place in the world.

His mission was to be a good father, husband, and football player.

He worked hard, played by the rules, and earned his success.

He did not feel lost.

He felt blessed.

When he walked through the locker-room door and out into the cold on the last day of 1967, he knew he was where he was supposed to be, doing what he was meant to do.

His world made sense.

Through the years, as the mythology of the Ice Bowl took on a life of its own, some who were around for both began to suggest that the 1962 title game between the Packers and Giants, punctuated by a brutal wind, was actually colder, but Starr, like many others, refutes this notion. "I've never played in more difficult conditions than [the 1967 title game]," Starr said. "The Ice Bowl was the coldest, most challenging environment I've ever played in."

The Ice Bowl was the ultimate test of nerves and skill.

"It called on every bit of character . . . every bit of discipline . . . every bit of knowledge . . . you could bring to bear," said defensive captain Willie Davis.

Like several other players on both teams, the indomitable Ray Nitschke suffered frostbite. "I damn near froze my toes off," he said. "It was a miserable feeling."

After the frustrating loss to the Packers in the 1966 NFL Championship Game, Dallas quarterback Don Meredith spent the entire 1967 season focused on winning the big one. Some of the Cowboys expressed frustration that such a big game had to be played in such awful conditions, but Meredith was convinced the weather would make little difference—until he felt the reality of the bone-chilling temperature. "We really didn't know how cold it was until we got on the field," he said.

Some hid their discomfort better than others. Early in the game, Green Bay defenders noticed that Dallas receiver "Bullet" Bob Hayes always stuck his hands into his pants at the line of scrimmage when the Cowboys called a run—but kept his hands exposed when they passed. Hayes, the onetime Olympic sprinter known as the world's fastest human, never knew until later that he had inadvertently opened a window to his team's play-calling. The tell proved enormously helpful to the Green Bay defense.

On Green Bay's first offensive series, Starr led the Packers on a 16-play, 82-yard drive, culminating with an 8-yard touchdown pass to Boyd Dowler. Early in the second quarter, Starr called a perfectly time play-action pass and hit Dowler in the open across the middle for a 46-yard touchdown, giving the Packers a 14–0 lead. Indeed, it looked like Green Bay's sort of day.

Then the Doomsday Defense came alive.

"After you forgot about how cold it is and all the other thngs that are going through your mind, you just figure you've got to go play football," Cowboys cornerback Cornell Green said. "They weren't going to cancel the game . . . so you better . . . try to play and try to win."

Late in the second quarter, with Green Bay deep in its own territory, Dallas defensive end Willie Townes broke through the Packers line, chased Starr out of the pocket, and slammed him to the frozen ground—*hard*. The ball squirted out and George Andrie picked it up and rambled 7 yards for a Dallas touchdown. Starr rarely fumbled, and now he had fumbled at the worst possible moment in the biggest game. Two series later, Green Bay's sure-handed Willie Wood fumbled a punt, which set up a 21-yard field goal by Danny Villanueva. At the half, Green Bay clung to a 14–10 lead.

"We had control of the game until the time of those two fumbles," Lombardi said. "That gave them a tremendous lift."

In the third quarter, Dallas threatened twice but the Green Bay defense stiffened. One drive ended when linebacker Lee Roy Caffey ran down quarterback Don Meredith and forced him to fumble inside the Green Bay 20. Another resulted in a missed Villanueva field goal, after Caffey sacked Meredith to halt the drive. Those two plays alone validated Caffey's acquisition from Philadelphia in the Jim Ringo trade . . . and probably preserved Green Bay's championship. For the Green Bay offense, the third quarter was a blur of frustration, as the powerful Packers gained a net of just 10 yards. Starr, sacked eight times on the day, was constantly under pressure, trying to keep his footing, struggling to find a weakness in the Dallas defense.

In the new age of professional football just over the horizon, Tom Landry's trademark fedora and stoic expression were destined to become as iconic as Lombardi's eyeglasses and clinched teeth, but on this day, he walked the Dallas sideline wearing a white sweatshirt hood over a fur cap pulled low over his brow, making him look like a longshoreman who had gotten lost on the way to the docks. ("It was like being at the North Pole," Landry remarked.) A brilliant tactician, Landry knew as much about Lombardi's defense as any man in football, and after leaning heavily on the running of Dan Reeves throughout the day, Landry and Meredith set a trap for the Green Bay defense.

On the first play of the fourth quarter, Meredith handed off to Reeves, who darted to his left. Biting on the run, Willie Wood and Bob Jeter moved in to stop Reeves, who then stopped cold and lofted a perfectly thrown option pass to wide-open Lance Rentzel, who raced for a 50-yard touchdown and a 17–14 Dallas lead. "I don't think the Packers expected it," Landry said.

As the shadows began to creep across the field and the temperature started to plummet, Starr drove the Packers close enough for a 40-yard Don Chandler field goal attempt, but it missed short. Dallas was content to run time off the clock, but the icy conditions caused runners to lose their footing on three straight plays, forcing the Cowboys to punt and giving the Packers, who had barely moved the ball since the second quarter, one final opportunity to rally.

Bart Starr pounded the table with his fist.

The calendar zoomed forward, to a day when a man well into his seventies looked back on his life, all the way back to the defining moment of his football career, when he was thirty-three and at the peak of his athletic ability. As he chatted with a journalist all those years removed from his greatest glory, he pounded the table with his fist, not in anger but in still-surging amazement.

"I'm not exaggerating: By the end of the game, it was like this . . ."

Pound. Pound.

"The field was as hard as this table."

Don't let me down!

Like Chuck Mercein, Dave Robinson would always remember the urgency in Ray Nitschke's delivery.

"Nitschke had this sound in his voice that is hard to describe," Robinson said. "It was angry. It was defiant."

It was not a request.

It was a demand.

"You have to remember that the Cowboys had owned our offense the entire second half and truthfully, I had very little hope," Robinson said. "Nitschke was a very emotional guy, and my interpretation of what he was saying was: Look, we've been sacrificing our guts out there. Don't you guys go out and screw this up for us!"

When he jogged onto the field, past Ray Nitschke's fury, into the realm of professional football mythology, Starr gathered his troops, saying little before calling the first play.

Four decades later, he recalled, "I could see it in the faces of all those men. . . . Every man knew this was it. They knew everything was on the line. This was everything we had prepared for . . . all those years of hard work, boiled down to one drive."

Like many of his teammates, Starr had lost feeling in his fingers and toes.

No one understood Starr's journey better than All-Pro tackle Forrest Gregg, who had watched the quarterback's transformation with admiration while helping the Packers win four NFL championships. Gregg, nearing the end of a Hall of Fame career, said, "You could sense Bart's determination when he stepped in the huddle."

Center Ken Bowman recalled, "I've never felt so confident that we were going to score. Never had such a powerful feeling, before or since. We were going to do whatever it took. We were putting that ball in the end zone. I mean, you could feel it."

Among the varied and constantly changing cast of characters who made the commitment required to chase perfection in Lombardi's neatly ordered universe, Bowman, who eventually became a lawyer and a judge, was very nearly the direct opposite of the forever polished and respectful Starr. Bowman, a third-year man out of the radical hotbed of the University of Wisconsin, reflected the changes sweeping the country and the sport. More than any of his teammates, he was a child of the sixties and all that represented, and when he routinely showed up for work in cut-off blue jeans and a T-shirt, he could tell Starr—who always wore a dress shirt and nice slacks—considered his appearance inappropriate.

"He used to call me the river rat," said Bowman, who owned a home south of Green Bay on the Fox River. "He'd ask me, 'How was the swim up today?'"

Despite their differences, the professional bond between the two men was unmistakable, demonstrating Starr's ability to cultivate respect among a variety of personality types, which was central to his success. "We believed in him completely," Bowman said.

On first down from the Green Bay 32, Starr hit Donny Anderson on a swing pass for 6 yards . . . two eras of professional football connected by a single sentence.

In contrast to Starr, who had been forced to fight and scrape his way from obscurity to stardom against a headwind of low expectations, Anderson had arrived in Green Bay as a rich, celebrated rookie. Like Joe Namath and all the other new-age bonus babies, he represented an enormous investment for the Packers, presaging the coming age when millionaire players with agents wielded tremendous clout, when professional football no longer cultivated heroes quite like Bart Starr.

Anderson, who fancied himself a playboy in the mold of Paul Hornung, his predecessor at the halfback position, was still struggling to live up to the great expectations swirling around him. Some of his teammates doubted his desire, but when he collared Starr before the final drive and asked for the ball, the quarterback could see the fire in his eyes.

After Chuck Mercein rambled seven yards for a first down, Starr hit Boyd Dowler on a slant across the middle, picking up 12 yards and another first down. Dowler was slammed violently to the frozen turf and knocked out cold.

After Willie Townes slipped through the Green Bay line and tackled Anderson for a 9-yard loss on a sweep, putting the Packers in a mighty hole, Starr went back to the air, hitting Anderson for a 12-yard completion. Now it was third-and-seven, a possession down, at the Dallas 39, and the possibility of Green Bay's third straight title hung by a flimsy thread.

"This was history in the making, and you could feel it in the air," recalled NFL Films cameraman Steve Sabol, who was stationed at the Dallas 20 with a telephoto lens, which had frozen, reducing him to just another spectator. "I remember being very frustrated that I couldn't do my job but also appreciating how lucky I was to be there to see this monumental drive."

In the stands, Bart Starr Jr., was numb all over. "I remember looking down at the players, thinking: How are they functioning in this weather?" He believed his dad would find a way to win—somehow.

Vern Biever, the Packers' official photographer, somehow managed to keep his camera clicking. Hoping for a miracle finish, he decided to stay near the team bench so he could capture something dramatic of Lombardi. "I really didn't think there would be anything unique, from a photographic standpoint, at the goal line," he said. Just in case, he dispatched his teenage son John, who helped him on occasion and had a good eye, toward the Green Bay end zone.

Facing a stiff rush, Starr pumped once and then dumped a pass over the middle to Anderson, who raced 9 yards as Packer fans everywhere exhaled. First down. Clock ticking. Anderson's face would never adorn a plaque in Canton, but for those two catches in the waning moments of the Ice Bowl, for those two runs, for those two answered prayers, he would always be remembered.

Eleven men contributed to the success of the epic drive, carving for themselves a hallowed place in the storied history of the Green Bay Packers. But the moment truly belonged to Bart Starr, who calmly led the Packers downfield, making one good decision after another, propelling his team forward with the sort of radiating confidence that suggested inevitability.

"I never saw Bart perform better than he did on that drive," Forrest Gregg said. "He was just absolutely superb."

The day's unlikeliest hero was fullback Chuck Mercein.

"One of the great things about Bart was how he would listen to a receiver if he said, 'I can get open on this route,'" recalled former battery mate Gary Knafelc, by then retired and watching from the press box. "But you knew you'd better get open and you'd better catch the ball. Or you'd never see another one."

Mercein was the new guy in the huddle, but like Anderson, he wanted the ball.

One year after leading the New York Giants in rushing, Mercein, a former Yale star, had been cut at midseason by the Giants, then in the early stages of a long and painful slide. "I was miserable with the Giants," he said. "It was a bad situation." Humiliated, he feared that his professional football career might be over. When Otto Graham and the Washington Redskins agreed to sign him, he called his wife and told her to start packing the car. Then Vince Lombardi, who needed a temporary replacement for the injured Jim Grabowski, picked up the phone.

"Here I was just trying to hang on in professional football . . . and Lombardi calls and asks if I want to come play for the world champion Packers," Mercein recalled. "That was not a difficult decision."

Six games into his run with the Packers, Mercein had rushed a total of 14 times for 56 yards and caught a single pass for 6 yards, but in the huddle on that defining drive, he provided his quarterback with what he thought was essential information. "I'm open on the left side if you need me," he said, and the quarterback nodded and filed it away in his head.

"Out of respect, you wouldn't ordinarily suggest a play to Bart . . . because he was the boss and nobody questioned his judgment," Mercein recalled. More typically, one of the offensive players would wait until the ball turned over and provide him with this sort of intelligence on the sideline, but waiting was not an option now. "I'm thinking, we may be down to the end here . . . and I'm not going to get to the end of my life thinking we could have done this if only I'd spoken up."

With 1:35 to play and the clock running as the Packers faced first-and-ten from the Dallas 30, Starr faded into the pocket, planning to hit either Dowler or Anderson across the middle. But when he glanced left, he saw Mercein open. The defense was playing Mercein soft, giving him a wide berth while double-covering wide receiver Carroll Dale, so with the flick of his wrist, Starr lofted a swing pass to the former Giant, who jumped into the air to snare it. Struggling to maintain his balance, he barreled upfield, determined to stay vertical on the slippery grass, eluding two tacklers for a clutch 19-yard gain before falling out of bounds at the 11 to stop the clock.

"The Cowboys were not going to be beaten deep, which meant they were all flying back," recalled Dale, who made a useful decoy, considering he had caught thirty-five passes on the year for 738 yards, second only to Pro Bowler Dowler (54 for 836). "Bart did a great job of getting the ball to Mercein while he was still open."

"That play killed 'em . . . broke their back," Mercein said.

Then Starr played his ace.

One of Starr's greatest assets was his ability to exploit an opponent's strengths as well as its weaknesses, so when he approached the huddle with 1:11 remaining and the championship on the line, he knew the time was right to turn Bob Lilly's tremendous athleticism into a Dallas liability.

"I'd been saving it for just the right situation," Starr recalled.

Lombardi's sense of propriety did not permit him or his players to stoop to the vulgarity of referring to such a call as a "sucker play," but regardless of the nomenclature, the Packers needed to lure Lilly, destined for the Hall of Fame, into a trap.

The call was 54 Give.

Starr was betting that Lilly, seeing the Packers lined up in their Brown formation, with the fullback directly behind the quarterback, would bite on his fake to the halfback and the guard pulling, anticipating the sweep. He was also counting on Bob Skoronski to block the left end, taking him out of the play.

The call could have blown up in his face, if Lilly had read the play differently.

"You're talking about a very, very gutsy call by Bart Starr," Mercein observed.

By the time Lilly crossed the line in pursuit of pulling guard Gale Gillingham, Mercein had the ball and was shooting up the middle, through Lilly's vacated hole. Because Skoronski had made a textbook block on Dallas end George Andrie, Mercein found a huge seam and headed for the goal line while the leader of the Doomsday Defense, arms spread, looked on from afar, isolated from the play by his own aggressiveness and skill. In normal conditions, Mercein might have scored, but the field was like a sheet of ice, especially as he approached the goal line. After gaining eight yards, he was tripped up at the Dallas 3.

"That's the greatest call I've ever made," Starr said. "It just worked like a charm. That, in my opinion, was the key play in the game, because it put us in position. . . ."

With the clock down to 54 seconds, Anderson took the handoff straight ahead to the 1, picking up the first down.

On the next play, Anderson lunged toward the goal, believing he scored, but the official ruled him short.

On second down, unable to keep his footing, he slipped for no gain, and the wheels started turning in the quarterback's head.

After calling his final time-out with 16 seconds left, Starr approached All-Pro right guard Jerry Kramer. "Can you get your footing for a wedge play?"

"Hell, yes!"

Having received the answer he wanted, Starr jogged to the sideline to confer with Lombardi. The possibility of sending dependable Don Chandler on for a game-tying field goal, and extending the game to sudden death overtime, was not discussed, because Starr was an extension of Lombardi—nine years of Lombardi in the huddle—and in this instant more than any other, winning was the only thing.

"If we can't get those two feet," center Ken Bowman remarked many years later, "we don't deserve the championship."

On the sideline, Starr expressed his doubts about trying another hand-off. "The backs are slipping and sliding," he told Lombardi. "But I'm upright. I can shuffle my feet . . . and sneak the ball in."

"Then run it!" Lombardi said forcefully. "And let's get the hell out of here!"

The Green Bay playbook did not feature a quarterback sneak, so when he jogged back onto the field and reached the huddle, Starr decided to keep his intensions to himself.

Calm and focused, he yelled, "Brown right, 31 wedge," which called for the fullback, Mercein, to run between the center and the guard. The burden for the play's success rested heavily on guard Kramer and center Bowman, assigned the chore of creating a wedge to drive Cowboys tackle Jethro Pugh off the line of scrimmage and allow an opening for Mercein.

One year after Dallas found itself in a similar situation, ultimately turned away at the goal line by an errant Don Meredith pass, the Cowboys' defense dug in, needing only to hold the line, survive the final 16 seconds, in order to win the franchise's first NFL championship.

With no way to stop the clock if the third-down play failed, Starr understood that he was wagering the championship on the ability of Kramer and Bowman to neutralize Pugh—and his ability to keep his footing and dart through the opening.

"I understood my responsibility," Kramer said. "If I don't get a great block, we don't do it."

An instant after the snap, Kramer slammed violently into the left side of the six-foot-six Pugh, standing him up, turning the defender's size into a weakness. Bowman then hit Kramer on his right, trapping him in the wedge as a green and gold wave surged across the frozen goal line. Mercein, expecting the handoff, instead watched in astonishment as Starr lowered his head, lunged behind the wedge, and sneaked into the end zone for the game-winning touchdown.

Young John Biever, who would later have a long and distinguished career at *Sports Illustrated,* snapped one of the most iconic sports photographs of all time because he was in the right place at the right time. The image of Starr sprawled in the end zone, at the bottom of the climactic pile, was made all the more memorable by the presence nearby of still-surging Mercein, who could be seen raising his arms high in the air. Some mistakenly, and understandably, believed Mercein was signaling touchdown but instead, he held his arms aloft to make clear to the officials that he had not pushed Starr, which would have justified a flag.

"I was really surprised when Bart didn't turn around and give me the ball," Mercein. "I was going hard and couldn't stop so I just instinctively threw my arms up. . . ."

Buried under the pile after blocking the end, Anderson said, "When I heard the cheer, I figured it was Chuck who scored. I didn't find out it was Bart until I got back to the bench."

Soon after Green Bay's 21–17 victory, as fans stormed the field, some climbing the triumphant goalpost, the second-guessing began in earnest. What if Starr had been stopped and the clock simply ran out? "We could have run it ten times and it would have worked every time," Starr insisted. "Under the circumstances . . . considering how Donny was slipping . . . it was the smart play."

As he began to thaw out, Lombardi told reporters, "We gambled. We won. It was as simple as that." Pressed for a deeper explanation, Lombardi said, "Want to know the real reason why we went for the touchdown instead of the field goal? Because I didn't want all those freezing people in the stands to sit through a sudden-death overtime. I've been accused of lacking compassion. But that just shows that I'm not without compassion." No one who knew Lombardi believed his explanation, but it made for a memorable quote.

Given the possibility that one of his defenders could have tackled Starr and ended the game, Tom Landry said, "It was a dumb call. But now it's a great play."

Years later, Ken Bowman found himself chatting with Jethro Pugh, who said he had expected Starr to pass. After all, an incompletion would have given the Packers time for one more stab or a game-tying field goal. "That's one of the reasons it was such a smart call by Bart," Bowman said, "because a quarterback sneak was the last thing the Cowboys expected. Bart made a lot of brilliant calls in his time, and that was one of the smartest."

Starr's decision to call his own number demonstrated his intelligence and his guts, two qualities deeply entwined in the Green Bay Packers' dominant run. But the more significant achievement was negotiating those first 67 yards across the frozen tundra.

No drive in the history of professional football compares to Green Bay's winning march in the Ice Bowl, which will endure as long as the sport is played as a monument to overcoming adversity with precision, power, imaginative play-calling, and steely determination. Those twelve plays provided an object lesson in everything the Packers stood for, especially the strength of eleven individuals fully committed to a single goal, empowered by the mighty surge of their collective will.

"We had fought our way back in a very difficult year, and the winning drive was a testament to everything Coach Lombardi had taught us," said Starr, who completed 14 of 24 on the day for 191 yards and 2 touchdowns. "It was a bunch of individuals coming together as a team to accomplish something in the most extreme conditions imaginable. Will over adversity. Every man doing his job . . ."

More than anything else, the climactic drive demonstrated Bart Starr's extraordinary ability to grab a team by the throat and lead it to victory.

In the difficult year of 1967, Starr did not win All-Pro acclaim or a place on the Pro Bowl roster. But with the magnificent final drive in the Ice Bowl, he became a legend nevertheless, claiming an iconic role for himself in the gathering mythology of professional football.

In the joyous, mercifully warm Green Bay locker room, as the Ice Age gave way to the Space Age, the CBS television crew spent several minutes interviewing Jerry Kramer as the country watched, over and over again, a replay of the quarterback sneak. Four years after Tony Verna introduced the innovation, instant replay truly arrived in the afterglow of the 1967 NFL Championship Game, feeding the insatiable desire of football fans to dissect, understand, and relive the climactic touchdown push, and, in the process, sealing the most dramatic moment of Bart Starr's career in a kind of cultural amber.

Ali.

Vietnam.

Haight-Ashbury.

Jim Morrison.

The Graduate.

And the Ice Bowl.

In a year when traditional America felt increasingly threatened by the changes roiling the country, the 1967 NFL Championship Game resonated beyond the sports pages, demonstrating to many why they loved football and invested it with such meaning.

For Starr, the extreme weather was more than a strategic challenge. It was a metaphor for his entire career.

In the dramatic shadow of the Ice Bowl, the enormity of Green Bay's larger achievement has often been lost. Becoming the first and only franchise in modern NFL history to win three straight championships—and five over seven years—elevated the Packers to a stratospheric level among football dynasties. As the leader of this assault on the history books, Starr became the most successful quarterback in league history. The 17th-round draft choice had endured the first several years of his career listening to fans and media insist he did not belong in the same sentence with great quarterbacks like Johnny Unitas, Y. A. Tittle, Bobby Layne, and Otto Graham. Now it was quite literally true. Three straight. Five in seven. Now Starr deserved his own paragraph.

"It would have been sweet, no matter how we accomplished it, but the way we fought back that year and the difficult conditions we faced against Dallas made it all that much sweeter," Starr said. "We wanted to do something no one had ever done . . . and the satisfaction of winning the third title in a row was just incredible."

After the thaw, the Packers went back to work, because they had one more big football game to play.

Especially after Super Bowl I, it was difficult for fans and media to see Super Bowl II as anything less than an anticlimactic exhibition game.

After the Ice Bowl, what could the Packers possibly have to prove?

All they could do was destroy their mystique, their unparalleled achievement, by losing to the AFL champion Oakland Raiders, which Lombardi exploited to great effect.

"The [Ice Bowl] was very draining," Starr said. "But we had a job to finish in the Super Bowl. We felt a tremendous responsibility."

Rumors of Lombardi's pending retirement swirled two weeks after the Ice Bowl in sunny Miami, infusing the Packers, who wondered, like everyone else, if it was true, with another reason to sock it to the Raiders.

Even though Oakland was established as a huge underdog, the anticipation for Super Bowl II eclipsed the first event in Los Angeles, as all 75,546 seats at the Orange Bowl sold out and CBS paid $2.5 million for exclusive television rights.

The determination was palpable in the Green Bay dressing room as Bob Skoronski, Willie Davis, Forrest Gregg, Max McGee, and Ray Nitschke took turns addressing their teammates. "It's the last game for some of us," McGee said, "and we sure don't want to go out of here and live the rest of our lives letting these guys beat us."

After Carroll Dale led the Packers through the Lord's Prayer, Lombardi stepped to the front of the room, full of emotion. "All the glory, everything that you've had, everything that you've won, is going to be small in comparison to winning this one . . . You got to be forty tigers out there. That's all. Just hit. Just run. Just block and just tackle. If you do that, there's no question what the answer's going to be in this football game . . ."

When they paraded through the door, with the uncertainty of Lombardi's future dangling in the ether, every man on the team understood the stakes: They were fighting to secure for the Green Bay Packers a special place in the history of professional football.

Super Bowl II was never in doubt, thanks in part to Starr's brilliance.

After stampeding through the AFL—and clinching the league title by crushing Houston 40–7—Oakland was determined to pressure Starr. Throughout the game, Oakland blitzed, and sometimes, Starr was forced to scramble. But more often, he made the Raiders pay, completing one big pass after another.

As he stood before a locker-room mirror following Green Bay's decisive 33–14 victory, wiping away the remnants of shaving cream from his newly smooth face, Starr told reporters, "I love it when they blitz."

Early in his career, when he was still unsure of himself, the blitz caused Starr trouble.

But now it played to his strengths.

Like the slippery ice of Lambeau Field, the blitz was just another obstacle for a man at the top of his game.

"They had a great pass rush and their linebackers did a superb job of putting added pressure on you," Starr said many years later. "We would get very excited about playing teams that liked to [blitz]."

With the Packers leading 6–0 in the second quarter thanks to a pair of Don Chandler field goals, the Raiders came hard and Starr read it perfectly, hitting Boyd Dowler for a 62-yard touchdown strike and a 13–0 advantage.

One of the best examples of his mastery came on a crucial third-and-one in the third quarter. With the Packers leading 16–7, the Raiders dug in to stop the run. Anticipating this, Starr faked a handoff and hit Max McGee, the old warrior, for a 35-yard bomb. "It's the threat of the run that makes the play successful," said Starr, who completed 13 of 24 passes for 202 yards. Seven snaps later, Donny Anderson's 2-yard touchdown run gave the Packers a commanding 23–7 lead.

"After three consecutive National Football League championships, everything hinged on this game," Starr said. "None of what we accomplished the last two games would have meant a thing if we had lost this one."

After preserving their place in the history books, the mood in the Green Bay locker room was more relief than jubilation.

Ever since the Ice Bowl, the players had noticed something different about Lombardi. He seemed more distant, more subdued. The reporters kept asking; he kept stonewalling. "What I think I will do is give Vince Lombardi a good, hard look," the general manager said of the head coach after Super Bowl II. "I will say this: The history of the Packers is in the future, as great as it has been in the past."

While his teammates celebrated, Starr, named the Super Bowl MVP for the second consecutive year, could be seen walking around the locker room picking up dirty towels and methodically tossing them into a hamper.

Fourteen days after Super Bowl II, Lombardi convened a news conference and introduced Phil Bengtson, his longtime defensive coordinator, as the Green Bay Packers' new head coach. The news led local sportscasts and sports pages all across America. Even though Lombardi planned to stick around as general manager, his decision to step away from the field at the summit—not unlike Ted Williams, who slammed a home run in his final at bat for the Boston Red Sox—ended an exciting chapter in the history of the Packers and the National Football League with the sort of dramatic symmetry that enhanced his already glowing legend.

But his quarterback, suddenly decoupled from the man who had helped make him a champion, was not ready to turn the page.

EIGHT

BLOOD AND GUTS

The razor strap was reinforced with serrated edges. Long before he could recite his telephone number, Peter Zukas knew every jagged notch wielded with anger by his alcoholic father.

"He'd beat on us . . . my brothers and sisters and me . . . till he got tired . . . till we were bleeding and begging him to stop," Zukas said, launching into a memory more painful than the original blows. "If somebody left a sock out, he'd go into a frenzy and work his way around . . . I got to where I would stand there and try as hard as I could not to cry. Didn't want to give him the satisfaction of seeing me cry."

His mother, who watched helplessly as her children were repeatedly abused, never escaped the guilt.

The cycle of anger engulfed Peter, swallowing him whole, pushing him onto the streets of Tomah and Green Bay, Wisconsin, to torment the neighborhood kids, brandishing a fist and then a switchblade with authority and alacrity, launching a life of crime, stealing cars, busting heads, dealing drugs. Like thousands of American adolescents during the late 1960s, Zukas fell into the quicksand of marijuana, LSD, heroin, and acid, seduced by the lure of feeling good or just feeling nothing at all. At eleven, he spent his first night in jail, left to rot by his old man, who wanted to teach him a lesson. The lesson did not take. At twelve, he joined the first of five different street gangs, gaining a reputation as a tough guy with a short fuse. At fourteen, after leaving home for good and impregnating his underage girlfriend, who was sent away to have the child, a judge sentenced him to serious time in a state reformatory, declaring him "a danger to society."

"I hated the world, hated being born," Zukas said. "I didn't trust anybody. The way things were going, it was just a matter of time until I killed somebody or somebody killed me."

The young punk with the chip planted firmly on his shoulder may have been the only person in the state of Wisconsin who had never heard of Bart Starr.

In the five years since they first ventured out to the woods near New London and dreamed of creating a refuge for troubled boys, John and Jan Gillespie—with significant help from Bart and Cherry Starr—had turned Rawhide Boys Ranch into a working reality embraced and supported by the citizens of Wisconsin and the state justice system. Thanks to John's intervention, Zukas won a reprieve from the reformatory in the summer of 1970 and wound up instead at Rawhide, where he was introduced to a rigidly disciplined routine full of work, study, and love in an rural setting isolated from the destructive drug culture, far removed from his father's oppressive right hand. The onetime dope dealer found himself handling a variety of mundane chores to meet the ranch's needs and to fill his time, but John could see that the boy's anger issues called for a more specialized prescription.

Several days into Zukas's stay, Starr drove out to the ranch for one of his frequent visits and introduced himself to the newest exile from the mean streets.

The encounter began with a firm handshake, which the boy, nervous as a wild animal, reluctantly returned. When Starr placed his arm around Peter's shoulder, like a father, like a friend, the young man pulled back. "I wasn't used to that," Zukas recalled. "Coming from the place I'd come from . . . I didn't know how to take all this buddy-buddy stuff."

As Starr took his measure of Zukas, looking him squarely in the eyes, he said, "I hear that you're an angry young man."

"So?" Zukas responded defiantly.

"I also hear you're a leader . . . but you're headed in the wrong direction."

Playing it cool, Peter listened but said little.

"I hear you like to bust people up on the street?"

"Yeah . . . So what?"

He saw no need to take any guff from this meddling stranger.

"You do that on the street and you're called a thug," Starr told him. "But you know what? You do that on the football field and they call you a hero. And playing football is tougher, because you have to follow the rules . . ."

Too consumed with his own rage to pay any attention to sports, Zukas was unimpressed when Starr pulled out a football and waved him back across the yard, perhaps 40 or 50 feet, and let the ball take flight.

The perfect spiral hit the boy in the chest, so hard that the impact knocked him on his rear end, breathless but impressed.

"First time I had been knocked on my butt in years," he recalled. "The guy had some power that was unbelievable. He had my attention."

As the conversation continued, Starr challenged Zukas to sign up to play high school football as a way to channel his anger, promising to help him learn the game.

"I don't know if you're tough enough to play football," Starr told the boy, purposely touching an exposed nerve.

"Oh yeah? I'm tough enough. Nobody's tougher than me!"

Thinking back on the pivotal encounter, Zukas said, "I was so full of myself. I was going to show him how tough I was."

When he met Peter, Starr was nearing the end of his playing career and occupied with various other business commitments, in addition to helping Cherry raise their two boys. He did not have a lot of free time on his hands, but he chose to invest some of his limited time in trying to reach a troubled boy who desperately needed a purpose and a friend. While Bart and Cherry's larger commitment to building and sustaining Rawhide as an institution reflected their sincere desire to make a difference, his direct involvement with Peter—and other boys like him through the years—contributed significantly to Rawhide's mission and demonstrated his humanity far beyond writing a big check.

Looking back on one of the thousands of boys who have called Rawhide home, Jan Gillespie said, "Peter was not a bad kid; like so many we've had through here, he just needed discipline and love. Bart saw something in Peter and really took him under his wing."

Several months later, in a conversation with some of his new teammates, Zukas happened to mention that a man involved with Rawhide was tutoring him on the finer points of the game—a man named Bart.

Bart Starr?
Sure.
Tell us another one, Zukas.
Bart Starr!

"They didn't believe me and I didn't know it was such a big deal . . . didn't understand why they wouldn't believe me, because I really didn't know who he was," Zukas recalled. "To me, he was just Bart. I didn't know he was some superstar quarterback."

As the relationship developed and Zukas found an outlet for his rage as a starting fullback/linebacker for New London High School, learning how to block and tackle and run and catch, how to experience the sheer joy of competition, how to feel the pride of accomplishment, how to be part of something larger than himself, the young man sometimes visited the Starr home in suburban Green Bay. On one such occasion, after Peter turned sixteen and obtained his driver's license, Bart tossed him the keys to his brand-new Lincoln and said, "Why don't you go gas it up?"

"To him that might have been an insignificant thing," Zukas said, "but to me it was huge. Not too long before that I had been *stealing* cars. I'd never [ridden] in a Lincoln, much less driven one. He was showing me that he trusted me. It was the first time an adult had ever showed me respect like that. Man, that was a big thing to me . . . a turning point in my life."

When he pulled up at a nearby gas station and told the attendant to fill it up and put it on Bart Starr's tab, he felt like a big man, like somebody, for the first time in his life.

While driving from Rawhide to Stevens Point for Starr's annual youth football camp several months later, Zukas learned, for the first time, the full measure of his friend's celebrity.

Noticing a Dairy Queen sign up ahead, Starr turned to his teenage companion. "I like chocolate Dairy Queen malts. How about you?"

Starr pulled the Lincoln into the parking lot and ushered his young friend through the front door. The whispers and pointing began almost immediately.

About the time Starr pulled out his wallet to pay for the ice cream, a sweet young lady approached him, tentatively, apologetically.

"Excuse me, but aren't you . . . ?"

When the quarterback smiled and humbly acknowledged his identity, the whole restaurant converged on him, shaking his hand, shoving paper napkins and pens in his face. Politely, he signed his name over and over and chatted with all who approached him, to the amazement of his travel companion.

"People were running out [of the Dairy Queen] and coming back with friends and relatives to meet him," Zukas said. "It was incredible. Until that moment, I didn't understand what a big deal he was."

After at least forty-five minutes of mingling with his fans, Starr looked down to see that his malt had melted in his paper cup. He chuckled and poured it out as they headed for the car and continued their journey.

"I asked him how he could [deal with] being mobbed like that and he said, 'You have to take care of those people. They're the reason I'm where I am. Without them, I wouldn't be here.' He was as sincere as he could be. I never forgot that."

When they arrived at the University of Wisconsin–Stevens Point, an even larger crowd surrounded the two-time Super Bowl MVP. One man asked Starr if he could see his Super Bowl ring so the quarterback took it off his finger, placed it in the man's hand, and turned to sign something for another Packer backer. While Starr moved on to other fans, happily signing T-shirts, programs, photographs, and odds scraps of paper, his priceless ring moved around the room, from one finger to the next. Finally, after perhaps half an hour, he turned around and the current ring bearer smiled and extended the palm of his hand.

"I guess this is yours," the man said with a laugh.

Like many others who interacted with him through the years, Zukas learned to appreciate Starr's remarkable generosity and lack of pretension. To him, Starr was not a famous football player; he was a kind man who fundamentally altered his view of the world.

In the shadows of his mind, Zukas would always be able to imagine how he might have died at the dark and desolate state reformatory in Wales, mortally wounded by a knife-wielding inmate or by the accumulated poison of his own desperation and self-loathing.

"Rawide and Bart Starr saved my life," Zukas said. "*Saved* my life."

Avoiding hard time in the Wisconsin penal system allowed Zukas to completely reinvent himself, becoming an honors student, president of his senior class, and a mentor to other troubled youths at Rawhide on his way to a successful and happy life as an electrician, father of two, and grandfather of three.

Somewhere along the way, the nightmarish image of his father's razor strap lost its power over him, forever tamed by other memories, like the triumphant view from the driver's seat in Bart Starr's Lincoln.

"Bart took an interest in me, mentored me, taught me what it meant to be a genuinely decent person," he said. "I'll never be able to repay him for what he did for me."

He stopped in midsentence, caught up in the rippling enormity of one man's act of kindness.

"There are three generations of people in my family who were saved by Bart Starr . . . who wouldn't exist without what he did for me," he said.

Even as Starr took an interest in Zukas as part of his larger commitment to Rawhide Ranch, he was struggling to deal with his rapidly aging and deteriorating body while adjusting to life without Vince Lombardi.

In 1968, as Green Bay entered a new era under the leadership of Phil Bengtson, Starr increasingly was seen as the public face of the franchise, much better known than his new coach.

In the weeks after Super Bowl II, two fifth-grade classes at a Methodist church school in Wauwatosa, Wisconsin, were polled to determine their favorite hero from a list that included Jesus Christ, President Lyndon Johnson, Queen Elizabeth, and several others. When the votes were counted, write-in candidate Bart Starr, to the astonishment of the teachers, tied Jesus. Winning may have been the only thing in Green Bay, but in this case, the deadlock forcefully demonstrated Wisconsin's unquestioned affection for its favorite athlete. Unfortunately, no provision was established for a sudden-death runoff.

In the tumultuous year of 1968, Starr's stature as one of the most accomplished and admired figures in American sports translated into even greater attention and clout. The overwhelming demand for him to address civic and business organizations collided with the reality of his increasingly tight schedule, which included new advertising campaigns for Pepsi-Cola and Dinty Moore Beef Stew. His continued endorsement work with the Lincoln-Mercury division of Ford Motor Company paved the way for him to cofound a dealership bearing his name in Birmingham, a long-term investment that would help secure his financial future. He chatted with Johnny Carson on NBC's *The Tonight Show* and filled one of the celebrity chairs on the *Match Game*. He even made his acting debut in the CBS drama *Gentle Ben*, explaining to young Clint Howard the importance of teamwork.

Gary Wetzel, a lifelong Packers fan, never saw Super Bowl II. In fact, he doesn't remember much from mid-to-late January in 1968. But he vividly remembers a bedside visit from Bart Starr.

Wetzel, a 19-year-old U.S. Army helicopter gunner who had grown up in Milwaukee, was nearing the end of his second tour in Vietnam when he was severely wounded on January 8, 1968. Despite losing his left arm to an exploding grenade tossed during an insertion, Wetzel performed valiantly, fighting off a large contingent of Vietcong and saving the lives of several of his fellow soldiers. By the time he was transported to a field hospital, Wetzel was desperately clinging to life, drifting in and out of consciousness as doctors treated his various wounds, including the amputation of what remained of his arm.

Several days after he arrived at an army hospital in Japan, a medical staffer yelled across the crowded ward: "Anybody from Wisconsin in here?"

"Yeah . . . over here," hollered Wetzel, bedridden, bloody, and tethered to a series of tubes.

After an orderly threw a sheet over his most glaring wound, a small group of NFL players began working their way through the ward, including the MVP of the recently played Super Bowl. A decade after his short-lived air force career, Starr had embarked on a Pentagon-sponsored goodwill tour of Far East hospitals, happy to lend moral support to the war effort.

"I was pretty low," Wetzel said many years later. "Still in that stage of trying to deal with what happened to me. But Bart's visit was a big moment in my life. He picked me up. He said some things that really made me feel better. Never forget it as long as I live."

Even as Vietnam divided the country, the trip touched the patriotic Starr deeply. "I was never prouder to be an American," he told a reporter back in Wisconsin. "I felt ten feet tall."

After returning to the states, Wetzel was shocked to learn that he had been awarded the Medal of Honor, placing him in an elite category of

American military heroes. Of the 246 MOHs awarded during the Vietnam War, only 92 were not bestowed posthumously.

Many years later, the happily married, Harley-driving, wise-cracking, Packer-loving Wetzel walked to the 50-yard line at Lambeau Field, representing a group of Medal of Honor winners, and waited to call the coin toss.

He nodded at Green Bay quarterback Brett Favre, who was standing nearby.

"No offense, Brett," Wetzel said, using his good hand to tap the chest of his bulging No. 15 Bart Starr jersey, "but *this* is my hero."

Especially after he began campaigning for Richard Nixon's successful White House run, speculation abounded that Starr might soon quit football and run for office on the Republican ticket. GOP operatives approached him about running for the U.S. Senate. Like many Americans, he was troubled by the direction of the country. In the years to come, he became an outspoken supporter of Republican candidates and causes, campaigning for, and getting to know, Gerald Ford, Ronald Reagan, George Bush, and George W. Bush. But Starr knew himself well enough to know he would never be happy as a politician, once telling a reporter, "The very nature of the system requires you to call on people to donate to your campaign to get elected, and when you do that you have lost your independence and are no longer your own man . . . I couldn't compromise my principles that way."

During a memorable visit to Dallas for a sports award banquet featuring several prominent college and professional players and coaches, a grinning Starr watched from the dais as Cowboys head coach Tom Landry, still stinging from the Ice Bowl, took the microphone and poked fun at the man who had blocked his path to the NFL championship. "How can you call 850 plays during the season and one quarterback sneak? That one call destroyed Vince Lombardi's whole philosophy . . . so he retired." After the laughs and applause subsided, Landry turned serious. "When Bart Starr retires . . . and I hope it's soon . . . I think he'll be recognized as the best all-time quarterback in pro football."

When his moment at the podium arrived, Starr, as usual, spent the whole time praising his teammates and coaches.

In the aftermath of the greatest run in the history of professional football, Bart and Cherry devised another way to help strengthen still-struggling Rawhide Ranch.

When *Sport* magazine presented him the keys to a shiny new red Corvette convertible for being named Most Valuable Player of Super Bowl II, Starr donated the car to Rawhide and exploited his connections with the Wisconsin governor, who engineered the necessary legal changes to allow a one-time-only lottery to benefit the quarterback's favorite charity. Over the course of three days, Rawhide sold 40,000 raffle tickets on the Corvette at one dollar each. "I was carrying suitcases full of one-dollar bills to the bank," Cherry recalled with a laugh. "It's like I was laundering money!" Thanks to the generosity of the Starrs and the people of Wisconsin who loved Bart, Rawhide Ranch was able to achieve a measure of financial stability.

"Time after time," Rawhide founder John Gillespie said, "Bart used his fame to help us."

Another measure of his notoriety could be seen a few weeks later, when several calls to the Associated Press office in Milwaukee prompted reports that Starr had, in fact, died. Journalists from the AP, the *Green Bay Press-Gazette,* and various other news organizations chased the story breathlessly before discovering that the quarterback was safe and sound in Miami, taping his episode of *Gentle Ben* and unaware of the rumor or how it had set newsrooms back home aflutter.

Like many of his aging teammates, Starr considered following Lombardi out the door. Within three years, virtually every starter from the glory days would retire or be traded, as well as backup quarterback and close friend Zeke Bratkowski. But even as the Packers' dynasty began to unravel, Starr felt an obligation to stick around and help longtime defensive coordinator Phil Bengtson. He also believed he had a few good years left.

"Although I'll miss that wonderful personal relationship with Coach Lombardi, I'm looking forward to playing under Bengtson," Starr told a reporter during the early weeks of the new regime. "He's a perfectionist like Lombardi. Extremely capable, dedicated, and thorough."

Bengtson was a knowledgeable, hard-nosed football coach who ran a taut ship, but he lacked his predecessor's charisma and strategic skill. He was also much less emotional. Without the domineering Lombardi, the entire tone of the Green Bay Packers changed, especially offensively, as Starr suddenly found himself navigating without the one man who had fundamentally shaped his development, guiding him to a level of achievement no one thought possible.

By the end of their historic run, Starr and Lombardi were so close, they could finish one another's sentences.

Now there was a void Bengtson could never fill.

In the years after his separation from Lombardi, Starr was confronted with his overriding sense of obligation to the franchise that had given him so much; his still-surging love of the game; the unmistakable aging and battering of his body, which slowly reduced his effectiveness; his still-powerful drive to win; and the gathering realization that he was surrounded by a team far removed from the glory days.

Pain was not always delivered by a crushing blow delivered by a hard-charging linebacker. Sometimes, it was the inevitable result of a life spent chasing something elusive, achieving enormous success and acclaim—and then grappling for how and when to walk off into the sunset. Sometimes pain arrived wrapped in layers of ambivalence.

Among the various changes sweeping through the country and the Packers in 1968 was the new assertiveness of the National Football League Players Association (NFLPA). Still struggling for unity, the players union struck for several days during training camp before returning to the bargaining table. Without the involvement of the Packers coaches, Starr directed two-a-day practices at a local high school.

Prior to another short-lived strike two years later, when many members of the union were vacillating, Starr stirred player reps from across the league by relating a conversation with Lombardi, who disdained the labor movement but admired loyalty. "Coach Lombardi called me in and said, 'I don't like unions and I sure don't like players associations, but if I were quarterback of the Packers, I'd sure as hell be a leader of the union.'" Lombardi had taught Starr many things, including the importance of standing up for his teammates when the situation called for leadership.

As Starr led the league in passing efficiency in 1968—completing an NFL-best 63.7 percent for 15 touchdowns and 8 interceptions—opposing defenses struggled, as usual, to stop him. After defeating the Packers 14–10, Minnesota Vikings head coach Bud Grant observed, "The thing about quarterbacks is that as long as their physical health holds up, they only get better and better. Is Starr getting better? Sure he is."

Starr missed parts of six games with injuries, but more often than not, he endeavored to play through a mounting list of ailments mostly shrouded from public view. With the leader of all those championship teams unable to prevent Green Bay from stumbling to a 6-7-1 finish—the team's first losing season in a decade—Lombardi watched helplessly from the front office, trying not to meddle with his hand-picked successor.

As the Packers slid from dominant to ordinary in 1968, the country endured a year unlike any other in its history, teetering precariously close to the brink. Assassins murdered civil rights leader Dr. Martin Luther King, Jr., and Senator Robert Kennedy while he campaigned for the Democratic presidential nomination. Rioting disrupted the Democratic National Convention in Chicago. Civil unrest gripped several major cities. The antiwar movement mobilized hundreds of thousands of protesters onto the streets, especially after the communists' Tet Offensive, which turned many Americans, including CBS News anchorman Walter Cronkite, against the divisive and bloody conflict in Vietnam.

The fall of the Green Bay Packers was just another storyline in a nation transitioning from one era to another, not quite sure what lay over the next hill.

Restless for another challenge, Lombardi tendered his resignation as general manager of the Packers several weeks into 1969, becoming head coach and GM of the struggling Washington Redskins. Before embarking on his new adventure, he called Starr into his office. Well aware that his quarterback had been taking—and saving—copious notes on every team in the league for years, Lombardi asked to borrow the whole lot, which filled an entire drawer in a filing cabinet. He took it all with him, photocopied every page, and sent the files back to Starr. "The nicest compliment he ever paid me," Starr said.

Even as he began wearing a protective vest, at the insistence of Bengtson, to safeguard his tender ribs—tweaking the contraption to "give me protection and also freedom of movement"—Starr brushed off talk of retirement and returned for the 1969 season, often leaning on one of Lombardi's favorite themes. "Our greatest glory in the Packer organization was not in never falling, but in rising every time we fell," he told a reporter during the summer. "I feel we've fallen now so we have to get back up."

But Vince Lombardi had left the building, rendering the once mighty Packers as anachronistic as Elvis. Their time at the top was over. Past tense. History.

The stage belonged to Joe Namath and a new generation of heroes now. Broadway Joe's ascendance to pop culture superstar reached a fever pitch in the days before Super Bowl III in Miami in January 1969, when he brashly "guaranteed" a victory by his New York Jets over the NFL's heavily favored Baltimore Colts. The verbal swagger of Namath's prediction assaulted the senses of many sports fans who expected humility and a certain amount of decorum and sportsmanship from their heroes. In this respect as in many others, Joe Namath was no Bart Starr. Seven months after Namath and the Jets delivered one of the biggest upsets in the history of American sports, culminating the unlikely rise of the American Football League and casting the looming merger of the two rival leagues in an entirely new light, Starr showed up for training camp feeling somewhat like the last warrior from the previous war. "At times I feel a little strange," he conceded to a reporter who noted all of the new faces surrounding him in the summer of the first moon landing and the cultural phenomenon of Woodstock.

With the retirement of Forrest Gregg, Jerry Kramer, and Bob Skoronski leaving big holes on the offensive line, the quarterback was forced out of the pocket, sacked, and battered more often in 1969, but still managed to once again lead the league in passing efficiency—completing 62.2 percent for 9 touchdowns and 6 interceptions—as the Packers finished an improved, but still disappointing, 8-6.

Years after the fact, Starr remained too diplomatic to criticize Bengtson, but linebacker Dave Robinson saw the one-time defensive master overwhelmed, especially after Lombardi moved to Washington and his successor was burdened with the additional responsibilities of general manager.

"Phil was a great coordinator," Robinson said, "but [in filling Lombardi's shoes] he was in over his head."

Clouded by all those losses, the magic was not always easy to see. But sometimes it was impossible to miss.

During a road game against the Pittsburgh Steelers in week seven, twenty-four-year-old backup Don Horn started in place of the injured Starr, who was beginning to look like a quarterback approaching the final gun. With the Steelers leading 24–14 in the third quarter and Horn struggling to find the end zone, Phil Bengtson, desperate for a victory, approached his veteran leader, who was walking the sideline while nursing a sore arm and shoulder, consumed by extreme pain every time he flexed his bicep.

"How do you feel? Do you think you can go in there?"

This, Starr realized, was not so much a question as a plea.

Dutifully, the quarterback said "I'll try," and trotted onto the field, not knowing whether his arm would hold out but determined to reach deep.

Tuning out the hostile Pittsburgh crowd, he completed one short pass. Then another. And still another.

The rush was intense, forcing him to unload the ball quickly. Hardly anyone outside the organization understood the level of discomfort he was enduring to raise his arm and put a good zip on the ball, because, as usual, he made it look easy. After a while, the Steelers' defense noticed that he was avoiding the long routes, which the injury prevented him from hitting. Still, the Steelers could not stop him. Somehow connecting on 7 of 10 passes for 168 yards—including a 43-yard touchdown strike— Starr rallied the Packers for a dramatic 38–34 victory.

"[The arm] has been bothering me for some time," Starr told a Pittsburgh sportswriter, before adding, "I'd just rather not talk about it. No useful purpose would be served. I'll talk about anything else."

As the hero struggled to lift a razor to shave his face, Horn, his underachieving understudy, looked across the winning locker room in admiration: "That's as well as I've seen him throw. He's the old master, no doubt about it."

The kid meant this comment as a compliment, but he could not possibly understand how it felt for the old master to be staring into the glare of his approaching thirty-sixth birthday, desperately trying not to think about how it would all end.

The speculation about Starr's future took on a new urgency three weeks later when he separated his shoulder once again while scrambling against the Lions, causing him to miss the final four games of the season.

Cherry Starr would always remember the last time she saw him.

In the spring of 1970, when Vince Lombardi returned to Green Bay to play golf with some buddies, he stopped by to see his old quarterback and the quarterback's bride. He was warm and relaxed. He looked good. After Cherry showed him around their big new house in suburban De Pere—quite a step up from the two-room apartment the Starrs had once rented—they settled for a visit in the den, as the old coach complimented

Cherry on her decorating touches and remarked how happy he was for their good fortune.

"Coach," Cherry said, turning serious, "we owe it all to you.

"This house never would have been possible with you, because you believed in Bart and gave him an opportunity. We'll always be grateful to you."

Suddenly, Lombardi's eyes welled up in tears.

Without saying a word, he pulled himself off the couch, walked over to Cherry, gave her a big hug, and then walked over to Bart and gave him a big hug.

As tears ran down his cheeks, Lombardi headed for the front door, and without saying a word, walked out. "He didn't want us to see him break up like that, so he just got up and left," Cherry said. "It was just the most tender moment. That's the last time I ever saw him alive."

Like his wife, Bart was touched by the scene, which belied the coach's bellicose stereotype. "Very few people saw that side of Coach Lombardi, but he was a man who could cry easily under the right circumstances," Starr said.

Cherry was right.

They owed everything to Lombardi.

The championships.

The money.

The fame.

The sense of accomplishment that only an overachieving underdog can know.

He made it all possible.

Lombardi doubted Starr when he needed to pushed, and believed in him when many others failed to see his true potential.

He made Bart Starr Bart Starr.

Without Lombardi in the equation, Starr probably would have been nothing more than a footnote in National Football League history.

"Coach Lombardi meant everything to me," Starr said nearly forty years after the memorable moment in his den. "I owe him so much for what he did for me on the field, for his teaching . . . his inspiration . . . but also for his off-the-field example, for his strength, his character. We should never be content, we should always be trying to improve, to grow, in every aspect of our lives, and that's something I took away from my time with Coach Lombardi."

Viewed from a larger lens, the life of Bart Starr offers a powerful statement about the American meritocracy, proving that a man can overcome the most daunting odds to achieve if success means enough to him. But such achievement never happens in a vacuum, and in Starr's case, Lombardi arrived in his life at just the right moment and supplied the perfect combination of high standards, inspiration, and instruction necessary to exploit his various physical and mental attributes.

Yet they easily could have missed each other if the dominos had tumbled differently. *Bubba's death. Don Shannon's injury. Falling in love with Cherry. His sweetheart's decision to attend Auburn. Johnny Dee's telephone call.* Beyond their immediate direct impact, these seemingly isolated events, bouncing off each other, caused Starr's life to veer toward a very different reality. Even the disastrous 1955 season in Tuscaloosa proved to be a critical prerequisite in his circuitous route to Lombardi. Minus the humiliation of his senior year, he might have wound up somewhere else, under very different circumstances. Ultimately, the struggle proved essential in bringing Starr and Lombardi together—and in shaping the quarterback's very demanding and humble sense of self, which made him such a perfect instrument for Lombardi.

Lombardi gave him a chance. He earned everything else.

While making a speech after moving to Washington, Lombardi was asked to compare the two leading quarterbacks of the sixties. "Johnny Unitas is a great, great, great quarterback," he said, "but Bart Starr is the smartest quarterback I've ever seen. Starr has done the winning . . . and the object of the game is to win."

By the time of this statement, the rivalry was mostly a memory. Both players were nearing the end. In the years ahead, the incomparable Johnny U, forever bathed in the glow of the 1958 title game, would often be cited as the greatest quarterback of all time. After being supplanted in Baltimore by Earl Morrall and then spending an unsatisfying year with the struggling San Diego Chargers, Unitas retired holding NFL records for attempts (5,186), completions (2,830), and total yards (40,239). But when it was all over, Starr owned more hardware (five league titles to Unitas's three), and was ranked higher in career passer rating, completion percentage, and interception percentage. While the country was mesmerized by the Lombardi mystique, Starr quietly staked his own powerful claim. Still, he remained trapped in Johnny U's shadow, forever victimized by the combination of Unitas's perpetual aura and the shrouding effect of Green Bay's ball-control offense and mechanical efficiency.

Starr needed Lombardi, but Lombardi also needed Starr.

The man from Sheepshead Bay certainly could have found a quarterback with a stronger arm, but it is difficult to conceive of a quarterback more perfectly suited to Lombardi's temperament and style of play. He needed a man who could withstand his extraordinary pressure without losing his poise, engender the confidence of his teammates, perform at a high level while making few mistakes, and maneuver in his very large shadow. It took a very special sort of athlete to play quarterback for Lombardi. It took a guy like Bart Starr.

Starr was not merely the quarterback who led the Packers to all those championships. He was the man who proved that Lombardi's philosophy, geared around simplicity and execution, could actually trump much more complex schemes led by more gifted passers, when empowered by the meticulous search for knowledge and the zealous pursuit of ultimate victory.

More than Hornung, Taylor, Nitschke, and all the rest, Starr validated Lombardi's particular genius.

"It's hard to imagine that football team without Bart," said Paul Hornung. "He was just perfect for Lombardi . . . like he had been born to play that role."

While Lombardi's impact on Starr's career is conceded by all, the inverse proposition is rarely discussed. No one can say how many championships the Green Bay Packers might have won with another quarterback, but the two men will forever be intertwined in the history books, fused for the ages by the enormity of their accomplishment and the complexity of their relationship.

Without Starr skillfully exploiting the talents of Hornung, Taylor, and so many others—converting all those third-and-shorts with perfectly executed play-action passes—and calmly leading the game-winning drive in the Ice Bowl, perhaps Lombardi never becomes Lombardi.

About three months after his memorable visit to the Starr home, Lombardi checked into Washington's Georgetown University Hospital, complaining that he had been unable to defecate for several days. Exploratory surgery confirmed the doctors' worst fears: the great football coach, symbol of American manhood and rectitude, was dying of colon cancer at the age of fifty-seven.

When the awful news began to circulate among Lombardi's former players as the time drew short, Bart and Zeke Bratkowski flew to Washington and rushed to the hospital.

"We knew we were going to say good-bye," Bratkowski said. "It was a very sad trip for the both of us."

When they walked through the door to his private room, the quarterbacks were unprepared to see their old coach looking so frail.

"It was tough," Starr recalled. "We didn't say much. We just hugged him and told him how much he had meant in all of our lives."

After a few awkward minutes, Lombardi signaled for Marie, his wife, to usher the men out.

"He didn't want us to see him like that," Starr said.

Slightly more than a month later, after Lombardi's death attracted headlines across the country, Starr joined former teammates Paul Hornung and Willie Davis as honorary pallbearers for the funeral at St. Patrick's Cathedral in Midtown Manhattan and the subsequent interment at Mount Olivet Cemetery in Middletown, New Jersey.

News crews descended on the scene outside the majestic church on Fifth Avenue, capturing for posterity the look of profound sadness on Starr's still-youthful face.

He knew how it felt to lose a brother.

Now he knew how it felt to lose a man who had helped transform him into a more powerful version of himself.

The first time hurt.

During a humiliating 40–0 loss to the Detroit Lions in the 1970 season opener at Lambeau Field, the Green Bay fans booed Bart Starr, who was having a bad day.

"That was disappointing," Starr said many years later. "But I understood the frustration of the fans. I was frustrated, too."

By 1970, when Green Bay slipped to a disappointing 6-8 finish that cost Coach Phil Bengtson his job, it was clear that the Packers were not merely rebuilding. They had fallen into a gigantic hole, and Bart Starr was not powerful enough to pull them out.

Surrounded by a young team far removed from the heady days of the Lombardi dynasty, Starr's body was starting to fail him. On a given day, he could still look like an All-Pro. He still read defenses skillfully. But his body did not always cooperate. "I know it was really frustrating for him not to have that full range of motion with his shoulder and his arm," Bart Jr. said. His passer rating slipped from 104.3 in 1968 to 89.9 in 1969 to 63.9 in 1970, as he threw more interceptions (13) than touchdowns (8) for one of the few times in his professional career.

"The first time I finish a ballgame, I'm going to have a bottle of champagne," Starr told reporters at midseason, after his sore arm prevented him once again from playing sixty minutes.

In discussing the final seasons of his playing career many years later, Starr said, "Several of us made emotional decisions to stay and help Coach Bengtson, and I've often regretted it, because I was hurting and I didn't perform well the next couple of years. I wasn't able to play up to my standards and that was very frustrating."

Throughout the last several years of his career, Starr benefited from the ingenuity of longtime Packers trainer Domenic Gentile who, in 1970, fashioned a taping regimen that minimized the discomfort in his passing arm. "Domenic deserves a lot of credit," Starr said. "That tape job got me to the point where I could throw the ball without pain."

Because of chronic rib problems, which made throwing more difficult, Starr compensated by changing his delivery, which caused him to flex different muscles. "The muscles he should have been using began to atrophy," explained Gentile, who eventually discovered that Starr's right forearm had actually become smaller than his left. "He had pain for four years and the more he tried to throw in a way that wouldn't cause more pain, the more he changed his delivery to a shot-putting motion that aggravated it."

One month into the 1970 season—the first year of the merged NFL and the first year of *Monday Night Football*—President Richard Nixon arrived in Green Bay to celebrate the quarterback's record-setting career. In a year when the antiwar movement exploded after the bombing of Cambodia, the fatal shooting of students at Kent State University, and the bombing at Sterling Hall on the University of Wisconsin campus— which killed physics researcher Robert Fassnacht and injured four others— Nixon was greeted at the Green Bay airport by a crowd of students hurling obscenities. The scene across town was dramatically different. As the featured speaker for the invitation-only tribute to Starr at Brown County

Arena, the president was among friends while lauding the quarterback's "leadership qualities" and "moral fiber," casting Starr as a shining example of his Silent Majority.

"If there is one thing that is being nonpolitical, it is being for Bart Starr," Nixon told the packed house of six thousand, which cheered him and the guest of honor enthusiastically. "He is a very, very, great football player. But more than that, he is not only the number one pro quarterback in this period, he is a number one American citizen when it comes to character."

The Packers designated the next day's game against the visiting Los Angeles Rams as Bart Starr Day, featuring a halftime tribute in which the quarterback walked to a microphone stationed at midfield as the crowd of 56,253 cheered wildly. "Today, I feel like the luckiest man in the world," he said, invoking the memorable farewell speech by the dying Lou Gehrig. "Now I know what that man felt like. I owe everything to a couple of people in Alabama and all you wonderful people up here. . . ."

The event—spoiled by the Rams' 31–21 victory—looked like a culmination, especially in the context of the most miserable Packers season since Scooter McLean, punctuated by the sight, in the next-to-last game, of Starr hobbling off the field after being clobbered by a menacing Bears rush. Some wondered how long the old hero could keep taking such a beating. But to the surprise of many, Starr, feeling an obligation to help smooth the transition to new head coach Dan Devine, returned for the 1971 season.

"I really love the game and I think I can play," he said. "I'll be the first one to know if I'm slipping and I don't feel that way."

In the dressing room during the run for the three-peat in 1967, Jerry Kramer's tape recorder captured a telling conversation between several Packers.

When Kramer said he was planning to retire soon, Forrest Gregg said, "You ain't gonna quit! You can't quit!"

"I sure as hell won't quit till you do!"

"I'm not going to quit till Bart quits," interjected Ray Nitschke. "And he ain't ever gonna quit."

No one was surprised when, four years later, Starr was the last man standing from the 1961 championship team.

When Cherry Starr rushed through the bathroom door and saw blood dripping from her husband's shoulder, her heart raced with fear.

"I saw that and . . . I was just scared to death," she said.

The frantic call from the housekeeper on that summer day in 1971 had reached Cherry at the beauty salon, when her head was buried deep in a shampoo bowl. *Come quickly. Bart is bleeding very, very badly.* In an instant, the quarterback's wife was out the front door, racing home in the family station wagon, her hair still dripping wet.

Even then, especially then, one devastating hit by Tommy Nobis continued to reverberate through Bart Starr's life.

More than three years after the Atlanta Falcons star knocked Starr out of a game with a separated right shoulder, the effects of the original injury lingered, never fully healing as the quarterback took similar shots to the same area, enduring varying degrees of pain and immobility. After a doctor at the Mayo Clinic in Rochester, Minnesota, diagnosed the chronic problem as a damaged tendon, Starr reluctantly agreed to undergo complex reconstructive surgery. By all accounts, the procedure went well. In time, Dr. Ed Henderson told his patient, he could regain full use of his shoulder and be able to throw the ball without pain.

But five days after the surgery, Starr stood over the lavatory in his master bathroom, watching blood from his still-fresh wound drip into the sink. He knew something was terribly wrong.

"With every heartbeat, blood was just spewing out," Cherry recalled. "It was frightening to watch."

Taking control of the situation, Cherry arranged to charter an airplane to Rochester, wrapped Bart's wound tightly with bath towels, and quickly drove her husband to the local airport. As they took off, the quarterback's wife applied pressure to the wound to keep it from bleeding.

"I was in danger of bleeding to death," Bart said.

By the time the plane landed in Minnesota, Starr was very pale and so weak from the loss of blood, he was unable to walk.

"He was gray," Cherry said. "And I was just so scared."

As Cherry squeezed his hand, paramedics wheeled him off the tarmac on a stretcher, bound for the Mayo Clinic.

The original procedure called for the doctors to cut a keyhole-shaped opening in a bone near the top of Starr's arm, severing the tendon, knotting it, and then inserting the knot into the hole. But when the Starrs arrived at the clinic, Dr. Henderson discovered that one of his assistants had neglected to seal an artery, meaning that Bart had been bleeding internally for nearly a week, causing him to lose nearly three pints of blood. Quickly, Henderson operated to close the artery and repair the damage.

"Thank God we got there in time to get [the situation] corrected," Starr said.

After learning about the quarterback's surgery, President Nixon placed a telephone call to the hospital but was unable to reach him. When Starr received the message and returned the call to the White House, Nixon was in a conference with chief of staff H. R. Haldeman concerning the efforts to ban the chemical DDT. He interrupted the meeting to take Starr's call.

"I know you're going to be back and you're going to be better than ever," the president said.

By the time Starr was reactivated on the Tuesday before Thanksgiving, the Packers—behind rookie quarterback Scott Hunter—were heading for a miserable 4-8-2 season. Starr's recuperation was only partially complete but he was anxious to help his team. "The arm was so weak following the operations . . . I had to learn to throw all over again," he said.

The following Sunday, he showed flashes of his old brilliance when he started against the New Orleans Saints. On a crucial third-and-short call, he evaded a stiff rush, rolled out of the pocket, and hit John Spills on the run for a 13-yard gain. Seemed like old times. Then Spills fumbled, negating the old warrior's great play. Later, Starr fumbled, tossed an interception, and struggled to hit receivers as the Saints walked away with a 29–21 victory.

He was not quite healed, not quite ready, but Dan Devine, the former Missouri coach, wanted him in the lineup. Three weeks later, in the season finale against the Super Bowl–bound Miami Dolphins at the Orange Bowl, Starr found himself missing receivers by five yards or more. Watching from the press box on a balmy day, Bud Lea, who covered the Packers for the *Milwaukee Sentinel*, noticed a telling detail: "Bart was wearing gloves. He never wore gloves." Not even during the Ice Bowl had he worn gloves. Now, as he struggled to control what remained of his arm, Starr needed all the help he could get. Feeling that he was hurting the team, he called a time-out, jogged to the sideline, and asked Devine to replace him. "Coach," he said, "we'd be better off with Scott."

But Devine refused to pull him out, and as Starr tried to make his old arm pop, unable to affect the Dolphins' 26–7 victory over the Packers, one of the great careers in professional football ended unremarkably. Only later would this otherwise forgettable game be recognized as a historic moment, as an unsatisfying period placed at the conclusion of an era.

"It was really sad," Lea said. "Bart clearly felt a sense of duty, and he had to put up with an imbecile coach who knew his arm was shot. It was a terrible ending for such a great player."

Planning to return in 1972, Starr dedicated himself to a rigorous reha-bilitation program with Domenic Gentile, but when training camp opened and he started trying to pass, his thirty-eight-year-old body over-ruled his heart. Convinced that he could not recover enough strength to approach his old self, Starr announced his retirement on July 21, 1972. The news blanketed Wisconsin in a sea of melancholy.

The arc of Starr's sixteen-year playing career had mirrored the Na-tional Football League's complicated journey from the shadows to the spotlight, from a struggling, cautious twelve-team league considered ir-relevant by much of the country to a dynamic twenty-six-team colossus occupying a central place in American culture.

No 17th-round draft choice had ever exerted so much influence on a franchise or a sport, but in the end, he was just another aging athlete with a battered body.

"I have exhausted every effort to recover from the pain I have experi-enced in my arm," Starr said at a hastily called news conference. "I want to thank the Green Bay Packer organization for the honor of representing it for so many years."

When Devine asked him to stay on as quarterbacks coach for the 1972 season, Starr agreed but made clear he was signing on for a one-year deal only. Even though he had been approached about taking over the strug-gling Florida State program in 1970—and later was courted by at least one NFL franchise—Starr insisted he was not interested in pursuing a coaching career.

Scott Hunter, suddenly elevated to starting quarterback, endeavored to soak up Starr's knowledge like a sponge. "It's like opening an encyclo-pedia," said Hunter, a former Alabama star. "Every day you turn a differ-ent page . . . and you never get to the end of it."

After helping the Packers take a major step forward, winning the

NFC Central Division title with a 10-4 record before losing to the Washington Redskins in the first round of the 1972 playoffs, Starr resigned his job with the Packers, planning to walk away from football for good.

"I'm excited with the challenge of doing something else," he told reporters when the news became official. "I know I'm going to miss football. But I'm very excited about our business ventures."

He thought he had heard the last of the cheers—and the last of the boos.

NINE

RISKING THE LEGEND

Some athletes have a difficult time leaving football behind, unable to adjust to life away from the spotlight, incapable of dealing with the nuanced world beyond the bold white lines. But after two years away from the field, Starr was proving quite definitively that he did not *need* the game.

In addition to his growing automotive empire in Birmingham, Starr owned a motel and dabbled in real estate, and he continued to be highly sought across the country for product endorsements and after-dinner speeches, headlining events for major corporations including American Express, 3M, DuPont, and Pepsi. As the Lombardi era faded into the history books, enhancing the late coach's already imposing stature, Starr regaled audiences with colorful anecdotes and life lessons learned under the master, bathing himself in the enduring glow of professional football's greatest dynasty. Soon after he left the Packers in early 1973—the year when the last American combat forces returned from Vietnam—Starr signed on as an NFL analyst with the CBS television network. He won high marks from critics while staying close to the action. "As a former quarterback—and a great one—he is very observant of things that don't normally get a comment, except from a quarterback of his magnitude and intelligence," said broadcast partner Pat Summerall.

Privately—and not so privately—Republican leaders persisted in their pursuit, urging him to put his high name recognition, All-American image, and conservative political views to work for the GOP. He repeatedly demurred. "I've tried several times to get him to run," said Congressman Jack Kemp of New York, who negotiated the leap to politics after playing quarterback for the AFL's San Diego Chargers and Buffalo Bills. In addition to his role as general chairman of Rawhide Ranch, Starr served on the Board of Governors of Green Bay's First United Methodist Church and the Board of Directors of Bellin Hospital, and chaired fund drives for the Cerebral Palsy Association, Easter Seals, and the YMCA.

During his two years away from football—amid the first oil shock, which sent gasoline prices soaring, and the Watergate scandal, which fostered a new level of distrust in government—the Packers stumbled to seasons of 5-7-2 and 6-8, causing confidence in Dan Devine to plummet. The division championship in 1972—when Starr called the plays from the sidelines—had looked like the curtain rising on another winning era in Green Bay, but by 1974, the franchise was reeling from a combination of bad personnel decisions and poor coaching. After Devine negotiated one of the greatest tactical retreats in the history of football—resigning, under pressure, from the Packers to replace Ara Parseghian at Notre Dame, where he would win a national championship in 1977—Green Bay went searching not just for a new coach, but for a unifying figure who could turn back the clock.

The short list began and ended with one name.

"The groundswell for Bart [to get the job] was tremendous," recalled Cliff Christl, who covered the Packers for the *Green Bay Press-Gazette*.

"There would've been hell to pay if they had hired anybody else," said Dale Hofmann of the *Milwaukee Sentinel*.

"It was almost like he was drafted," said longtime *Press-Gazette* sportswriter and team historian Lee Remmel. "The Packers reached out to Bart at a pretty desperate time and made it very difficult for him to say no."

More than ever, the struggling Packers needed a hero.

Among the vast majority of fans and shareholders, the enormous respect for No. 15's demonstrated leadership skills—for the *memory* of him, piloting one championship run after another—trumped the cold hard reality that, with no head coaching experience and only one year as an assistant, he would be forced to learn on the job while being handicapped by an organization severely lacking in talent and draft choices.

As he wrestled with the decision—and several close friends urged him, *begged* him, not to take the job—Starr confided in his eldest son, Bart Jr., then a junior in high school. "Dad knew he wasn't adequately prepared to be a head coach," he said. "He knew how bad the situation was . . . how far down the Packers were, how difficult it was going to be to win anytime soon."

Well aware that his father did not have a burning desire to be a head coach or need it as some sort of validation, the teenager asked him a simple but fundamental question: *Why would you do it?*

"I admired his answer," Bart Jr. recalled. "He said, 'Sometimes you do what's right for the organization. This is the organization that gave me a chance. They could have cut me but they didn't. I owe everything I have to them.'"

A powerful sense of obligation colored Starr's entire life, but this magnetic impulse was never more compelling than on Christmas Eve 1974, when, after two sleepless nights, he overlooked the various logical, practical reasons to rebuff his old team and accepted a three-year contract as head coach and general manager of the Green Bay Packers.

Because they believed in him then.

Because they needed him now.

In the context of his unlikely rise from obscurity to fame, framed by a very rigid sense of ethics, by a strong sense of right and wrong and an overriding desire to always step up, to always be responsible, it was as if a member of his family had called him in desperation. In a way few people could fully appreciate, the Green Bay Packers were a part of him, connected by sixteen years of blood, sweat, and tears, but mostly, by one life-altering act of faith.

"In the context of his character," remarked former teammate and longtime friend Bill Curry, "I don't think he had any choice but to take the job."

Reaction among fans and former and current Packers was universally gleeful, typified by the comments of onetime battery mate Max McGee: "I think Santa Claus came early in this state. They picked the best man available for the job. I'm extremely elated."

Standing before a packed news conference, in front of a sign commemorating the franchise's championship heritage, Starr exuded self-assurance.

"I'm absolutely ecstatic about this opportunity," he said, adding, "I'm not as qualified as I'd like to be, but I'm willing . . . I ask for your prayers and your patience. We will earn everything else . . ." Quoting Winston Churchill, the history buff radiated erudition: "To every man there comes in his lifetime, that special moment when he is figuratively tapped on the shoulder and offered the chance to do a very special thing . . ."

In the end, say those who know him best, Starr's judgment was clouded by loyalty.

Reflecting on the decision many years later, he said, "When you've had a love affair with an organization like the Green Bay Packers, it's tough to say no. Had I planned to coach, I would have prepared for it. But I didn't have the guts to say to myself: 'You're not prepared.' It was a mistake . . . a poor, emotional decision on my part."

Starr, the most revered and beloved figure in the state of Wisconsin, was remembered in a nostalgic mist, forever young, strong, resolute. No one could tarnish his legend. No one except Starr himself.

By returning to the Packers and assuming responsibility for the rise or fall of the franchise, by risking criticism and failure, Starr was stepping off the pedestal Green Bay fans had erected for him. In the cause of reviving his beloved Packers, he was mortgaging his glowing legend.

"It was love that made him do it," remarked former teammate Willie Davis. "Nothing but love."

In 1974, the year Richard Nixon resigned the presidency, battering the American psyche like few events in the nation's history, and the economy, buffeted by soaring unemployment and inflation, slipped into its deepest recession since World War II, a charismatic entrepreneur named Gary Davidson launched the World Football League. Davidson, the man behind the American Basketball Association, the World Hockey League, and World Team Tennis, brought his brand of professional football to football-starved American cities including Honolulu, Birmingham, Jacksonville, and Memphis, as well as longtime NFL hometowns such as Baltimore, Chicago, and Philadelphia. The poorly financed WFL was headed for a rocky two-year run before sinking into the crowded graveyard of professional leagues, but it managed to impact the sport in several significant ways while poaching a long list of prominent NFL players with significant salary increases—including Miami Dolphins stars Larry Csonka, Jim Kiick, and Paul Warfield—and driving up the price of talent across the entire league.

On the way to winning the first World Bowl championship, the Birmingham Americans played an exciting brand of football and attracted a significant following, often filling storied Legion Field. As part of the team's initial season ticket drive in the spring of 1974, the Americans ran a full-page advertisement in both local daily newspapers, *The Birmingham News* and *Birmingham Post-Herald*, touting the WFL's major league cities while poking fun at the NFL's smallest market:

WFL FOOTBALL
IF GREEN BAY HAD APPLIED
FOR A FRANCHISE, WE'D HAVE
TURNED THEM DOWN

"Green Bay was lucky," read the snarky ad copy. "They went major league back when the getting was good. But today, they'd have no place in the big leagues. Like the WFL."

Alerted to the ad, Bart Starr, fiercely loyal to the Packers and the NFL, and a prominent figure in the Birmingham business community through his automotive dealerships, was not amused.

"What a disappointment to read your spot in the paper," he wrote in a letter to Bill Putnam, president of the Americans. "It reflects shameful irresponsibility on your part, and I personally resent it . . . The great players through the years who have performed for Green Bay and the loyal fans of that area who have supported the Packers through good times and bad deserve better than the cheap shot which appears in your ad . . ."

Less than two years later, the WFL and the Americans would be no more than a memory and little Green Bay would still have a chip in the big game.

By 1975, five years after the merger with the AFL, the National Football League, under the astute leadership of Commissioner Pete Rozelle, was stronger and more popular than ever, aided by the symbiotic partnership with television as demand for tickets—and merchandise and apparel through NFL Properties—surged. *Monday Night Football*, once turned down by CBS and NBC in a moment of corporate shortsightedness, both unwilling to devote a night of lucrative prime time to such an unproven proposition, consistently ranked among the week's top 10 programs for surging underdog ABC, transforming Howard Cosell and "Dandy" Don Meredith into water-cooler icons while fundamentally altering the nation's leisure habits. The Super Bowl, already the most important event in sports, was well on its way to something much larger: the biggest and most anticipated shared experience in American culture. Perhaps the greatest testament to the league's ascendance was the amount of money aspiring owners were willing to throw around in order to join the elite fraternity. A quarter century after businessmen in Dallas and Baltimore closed shop in fiscal surrender rather than sustain continued losses, groups in Seattle and Tampa Bay paid $16 million each to become the NFL's twenty-seventh and twenty-eighth franchises in 1976. What a bargain these deals would turn out to be. The numbers kept growing to the sky. In 1989, oilman Jerry Jones paid a record $140 million for the then-struggling Dallas Cowboys. In 2002, the new owners of the Houston Texans paid a staggering $700 million for the privilege of joining the league . . . before they ever sold a ticket or earned a first down.

In the years after the Green Bay Packers faded, the balance of power in the NFL shifted as five franchises surged to the forefront: the Dallas Cowboys and Minnesota Vikings in the National Football Conference (NFC), and the Pittsburgh Steelers, Miami Dolphins, and Oakland Raiders in the American Football Conference (AFC). Don Shula's Dolphins became the first team since the Packers to capture consecutive Super Bowls—including the historic achievement of a perfect 17-0 season in 1972—but for the entire decades of the seventies, the Steelers and Cowboys battled for supremacy and dynastic recognition.

Much like Lombardi's Packers, Tom Landry's Cowboys, led by coolly efficient and unflappable quarterback Roger Staubach, methodically dominated opponents, advancing five times to the Super Bowl over a nine-year period while claiming the controversial, chest-thumping moniker of America's Team, simultaneously emerging as a standard of excellence and a big fat target emblazoned with a silver star. The Cowboys featured more sophisticated schemes, but in many ways, their machinelike consistency made them the natural heirs to Lombardi's Packers.

However, it was the long-suffering Steelers, storming out of the shadows of their futile history, who approached the achievements of the Green Bay dynasty. Led by Terry Bradshaw—a strong-armed quarterback from Louisiana who had grown up idolizing Bart Starr—Pittsburgh won four Super Bowls in six seasons between 1974 and 1979, setting a new high-water mark for the postmerger era but falling short of Green Bay's five titles in seven years and three consecutive league championships.

The memory of all those trophies in Titletown proved to be both a blessing and a curse for Starr, who was dealt a very poor hand.

Green Bay was a franchise in shambles.

The talent level was poor. The roster was aging fast. The scouting operation was antiquated. And Dan Devine had crippled his successor with one of the worst trades in NFL history.

Convinced he could not win with either Scott Hunter or Jerry Tagge at quarterback, Devine engineered a blockbuster trade with the Los Angeles Rams, acquiring veteran John Hadl, coming off an outstanding season when he was named NFC Player of the Year in 1973. But he was thirty-four years old and no one could say how many good years he might have left.

Unfortunately for the Packers, the answer was zero.

The price was enormous: To land a quarterback past his prime, the Packers surrendered their first- and second-round draft picks in 1975 as well as their first-, second-, and third-round selections in 1976.

Dave "Hawg" Hanner, Starr's former teammate who became the only member of Devine's staff retained by the new coach, memorably called it "the Lawrence Welk trade."

A one and a two, and a one, two, three . . .

Already saddled with a weak team, Starr found his ability to replenish his roster severely hampered even before he coached his first game. The Hadl trade was like a lead weight dangling from his neck.

"We have no illusions," he said prior to his first training camp, noting the deficiencies at various positions. "We have weaknesses to shore up and are thin in ranks. We have a lot of work to do."

Soon after taking the job, the new head, well aware that he needed to reverse the team's losing attitude, installed several signs featuring memorable Lombardi slogans in the tunnel leading from the home dressing room to the playing surface at Lambeau Field, including own of his personal favorites:

LEAVE

NO REGRETS

ON THE FIELD

When defensive star Ted Hendricks demanded a no-cut clause during negotiations on a new contract prior to the season, Starr refused, and Hendricks wound up signing with the Oakland Raiders. The resulting hole made a mediocre defense even more porous.

As Starr negotiated a steep learning curve in 1975, the year when the North Vietnamese communists captured Saigon, President Gerald Ford survived two assassination attempts, and *Jaws* invented the concept of the summer blockbuster, the Packers stumbled out of the gate, losing their first four games.

"We believe in what we're doing," Starr insisted. "It's a systematic procedure and I'm not that concerned with our bad start. Of course, I'm not enjoying the losses, but if we do the job the results will show eventually."

In the closing minutes against Dallas, after the Packers' punt team forced a fumble, John Hadl hit Rich McGeorge for a 26-yard touchdown, giving winless Green Bay a 19–17 upset win over the Super Bowl–bound Cowboys.

"We're elated. We're about three feet off the ground now," Starr said after his first head-coaching victory.

The celebration was short-lived. Green Bay proceeded to lose four straight on the way to a disastrous 4-10 season.

"It was a humbling and learning experience," Starr conceded.

As the magnitude of the rebuilding job began to sink in to all concerned, Cherry gave her husband a gift for his office wall: a portrait of a battered but defiant cowboy declaring, "There were a helluva lot of things they didn't tell me when I signed on with this outfit."

The print reflected Starr's ability to good-naturedly make light of his circumstances even as he took the task very seriously.

Still learning what it took to be a head coach as well as a general manager,

Starr continued to modernize the scouting operation, made the first of a long list of changes to his coaching staff, began upgrading the Packers' facilities—including the planning of a much-needed indoor practice facility—and seized every opportunity to pick the brain of his peers, from the Miami Dolphins' Don Shula to Ohio State's Woody Hayes.

"Nobody worked harder or wanted to win more than Coach Starr," said middle linebacker Rich Wingo.

During the season, Cherry rarely saw her husband. He left the house around 5 A.M., sometimes not returning until after 11 P.M., forever confident that he could overcome his lack of coaching experience by putting in long hours at his desk, in front of the projector, and with his players and assistants.

In time he would learn a very painful lesson: He could not will himself to become a successful coach; it was more complicated than that. Intellectually, he understood this. He had never been a coordinator, and his one year as an assistant coach was scant experience in a league where he would have to match wits with a long line of able and competitive coaches with impressive résumés, including Tom Landry of the Dallas Cowboys, Bud Grant of the Minnesota Vikings, and George Allen of the Washington Redskins. He had never hired an assistant coach or piloted a draft-day operation. It was all new to him.

But it was the way of his life, and he met the challenge with the same diligence that made him a legend on the field, blinded by his love for the organization.

"Bart walked into a very bad situation and tried to do too many jobs at once," Bill Curry said. "He just about worked himself to death trying to turn that franchise around."

Starr quickly concluded that Hadl—who had thrown a staggering 21 interceptions and just 6 touchdowns in 1975, ranking near the bottom of the league's passing stats—could not lead his team to the next level. Eighteen months after he was acquired, Hadl was dealt to the Houston Oilers for quarterback Lynn Dickey. To unload Devine's mistake for a promising young quarterback, Starr gave up defensive back Ken Ellis and two draft picks.

Within two years, Hadl was out of football. The Packers would be paying the price of his acquisition for years to come.

In the Bicentennial year of 1976, when former peanut farmer Jimmy

Carter was elected president of the United States and two guys named Steve—Jobs and Wozniak—invented the personal computer under the Apple label, Starr was inducted into the Alabama Sports Hall of Fame, joining a list of legends including Paul "Bear" Bryant, Joe Lewis, and Willie Mays. As he continued to lay a foundation in Green Bay, he desperately needed a game-breaker in the backfield, a big-play receiver, more earth-movers up front on offense, and greater speed and athleticism on defense, but without the draft choices squandered in the Hadl trade, he found it hard to adequately address all of his team's various weaknesses. He fought through the process, on various levels, of learning how to coach. As Lynn Dickey struggled in his first year as the quarterback and the defense surrendered 21 points per game, the Packers stumbled to a 5-9 finish, stuck in the NFC Central Division cellar for the second consecutive year.

When Bart Jr. and some underage buddies sneaked into a Green Bay strip club to see an especially gifted young woman, he was startled to see Packers guard Bruce Van Dyke sitting close to the stage. "I won't tell if you won't," Van Dyke insisted.

Negotiating his formative years as the Packers dominated professional football and his father was celebrated far and wide, Bart Jr. was proud to be Bart Starr's son and wore the distinction effortlessly. Thanks to the very grounded way Bart and Cherry raised their two boys, the elder son never displayed any sense of entitlement and never felt burdened to live up to his name. Like his father, he was studious, disciplined, driven, and athletic. He never gave his parents a moment of trouble. While attending the University of Alabama on a golf scholarship, he pursued a bachelor's degree in business before earning his law degree.

Seven years can be a long spread between siblings, especially when the younger son grows up hearing his father blamed for the continuing futility of everybody's favorite team.

Bret, who moved into adolescence early in his father's rebuilding project, was a shy, sensitive boy who lacked interest in school or sports, forced to deal with the burden of his father's very public struggle.

"I think he had a difficult time being Bart's son," Cherry said. "It must have been hard for him . . . going to school and facing his friends."

Smothering Bret with love, the Starrs indulged his interest in music. During his high school years, Bret, a talented guitarist, fronted a rock band and played dates at several venues in the Green Bay area. Stay-at-home mom Cherry, happy to see her son passionate about something, learned to tolerate the noise from his rehearsal room in the basement. "Oh, they were loud!"

When Bret surreptitiously ordered a subscription to *Playboy,* his mother learned about the purchase, observing with a sense of amusement as he came home from school day after day and checked the mailbox in hormone-raging anticipation. Finally, the first issue arrived and Cherry decided to have a little fun. When Bret raced to the mailbox and finally hit pay dirt, he rushed to his room, closed the door, tore open the plain brown wrapper, and discovered that Cherry had ripped out the centerfold of his dreams . . . replacing it with a large photo of a monkey, clipped out of the newspaper.

Crushed—and embarrassed—the boy didn't talk to his mother for several days.

In the spring of 1977, Starr telephoned Bill Moseley, his old high school coach, and asked for a favor: *Would you mind introducing me at the Pro Football Hall of Fame?*

"He was doing *me* a favor," Moseley insisted, "a great honor, in fact."

With Lombardi gone, the selection of the former Lanier coach made perfect sense. After all, he had been there at the very beginning, watching his pupil's rise from untested high school backup to professional superstar.

After two frustrating seasons at the Green Bay helm, Starr's enshrinement in Canton—in the same class with former teammate Forrest Gregg—represented the culminating achievement of his remarkable playing career.

"I can very well remember the skinny, freckle-faced kid," Moseley said as he looked out from the podium, glancing over to acknowledge the middle-aged man he had grown to admire. "Bart was not born a naturally great quarterback. Bart had to work to make himself into an outstanding field general . . ."

As the football world paused to honor the man who led the Packers to all those championships, Moseley listed some of Starr's relevant statistics, including his NFL records for career completion percentage (57.4), consecutive passes without an interception (294), and lowest percentage of passes intercepted in a season (1.2, in 1966).

Starr's unlikely journey to Canton seemed all the more amazing considering one rarely discussed fact: only thirteen players drafted after the tenth round had ever been inducted, and of those, only five had been selected later than Starr.

When it was time for Starr to take the podium, he humbly thanked a long list of people, including his wife, his parents, and his teammates. As usual, he stood ramrod straight, his voice full of authority, looking very much like some clean-cut ideal of American manhood: strong, confident, steadfast, betraying no hint of the war he was fighting to remain relevant in a game he loved. He quoted General Douglas MacArthur on the value of athletic competition in building character and acknowledged the enormous impact Vince Lombardi exerted on his career and his life.

"He taught us the meaning of teamwork and unselfishness, purpose, pride, excellence . . .

"That the team must always come first and that you must be willing to subjugate your own desires, egos and ambitions for the good of the team . . ."

For those who understood what the old quarterback was now up to in Green Bay, this line landed with a powerful thunderbolt of irony.

Far removed from those difficult years following Bubba's death, Ben Starr smiled big, enormously proud of his son. Yes, he was wrong, terribly wrong, but in the end, it had all worked out so very right, and Bart would always appreciate his old man's central role in motivating him to reach for the power inside himself. The Master Sergeant died in 1985, ten years before his wife.

Armed with his full complement of early draft choices for the first time in 1977, Starr had scored big by landing Kansas defensive end Mike Butler, a future All-Pro, as well as quarterback David Whitehurst. He was starting to perceive a certain amount of progress. But the 1977 season was a disaster, in more ways than one. Not only did the Packers finish a miserable 4-10, but in a November loss to the Los Angeles Rams, quarterback Lynn Dickey suffered a broken leg. His comeback trail would take nearly two years, dealing a devastating blow to Starr's rebuilding project.

Although he had initially signed a three-year contract, Starr had been rewarded with a two-year extension, giving him a measure of security amid all the losses. But he hated to lose. It tore him up inside.

"Had the Packers decided to release me after the 1977 season," he said, "I wouldn't have blamed them."

Like countless boys across Wisconsin and beyond in the 1960s, John Anderson gravitated to his family's television set to watch Lombardi's Packers each Sunday, rushing out during halftime, football in hand, to join his friends for a furious struggle of their own, without referees, without pads, across their own patch of frozen tundra.

"You had to be somebody and I was always Bart Starr," Anderson said.

After winning the right to contend in the Punt, Pass and Kick competition at Milwaukee's County Stadium prior to a Packers game, Anderson and his father stepped onto an elevator at the posh Phister Hotel, just ahead of his hero, who greeted them politely as they rode up together.

"I was in such awe, I couldn't talk," recalled Anderson, who grew up in the southern Wisconsin town of Waukesha. "To me, Bart Starr was bigger than life."

Nearly a decade later, after an outstanding career as a linebacker for Bo Schembechler's University of Michigan Wolverines, Anderson was selected by the Packers in the first round of the 1978 NFL Draft. He quickly became a mainstay of the Green Bay defense.

All grown up in the age of disco, Anderson watched as his boyhood idol, a novice head coach without a magic wand, struggled to find a winning formula.

He watched the giant from the elevator become human.

"Bart didn't have to be there, going through what amounted to on-the-job training," Anderson said. "But he was . . . trying to lead the Packers through this tough time . . . trying to lead us to a better place. What I remember most about Bart is the grace he exhibited under a tremendous amount of pressure. I gained a tremendous amount of respect for him, not just as a coach, but as a man."

Even as he pursued the various strategic objectives necessary to transform the Packers into a winning organization, Starr slowly evolved—through trial and error. Before he could seek the right answers he needed to learn which questions to ask. "When I got to Green Bay, I think Bart was still trying to find himself as a coach," said offensive tackle Greg Koch, selected in the third round out of Arkansas in 1977. "Sometimes it seemed like he was intent on punishing us if we didn't play well. That changed. He became much less of a micromanager. Gradually, he became a much better coach."

He was not Lombardi and never tried to be. "Sometimes I wished he'd had a little more fire in him," said defensive end Mike Butler.

As a coach, Starr could not escape who he was in real life: A man who approached everything in a very methodical way, forever controlled and without guile. "He was always very positive," said Paul Coffman, elevated to starting tight end after Starr released veteran Rich McGeorge. "He was going to believe in you until you showed him that you didn't deserve that sort of faith."

Beyond the reality that Green Bay was saddled with one of the weakest rosters in the league, a narrative began to take shape in some circles: Starr was too nice to be a successful coach. It was a familiar refrain, echoing how Lombardi once viewed his quarterback. When he told his players, "Don't confuse meekness with weakness," he was acknowledging the inherent tension between his mild-mannered persona and his burning desire to build a winning team. He proved very capable of making the difficult decisions, including altering his defensive scheme and firing various assistant coaches—most notably, defensive assistant Dave "Hawg" Hanner, his former teammate—and front office staff in the continuing struggle to pull the franchise out of the cellar.

Still, the comparisons to Lombardi were inevitable, even as he struck a different tone. "What Lombardi had going for him was respect and fear," said former *Milwaukee Journal* sports editor Bill Dwyer. "But people never feared Bart."

Even as he searched for a winning formula, Starr felt an enormous responsibility to accommodate his fans.

When Starr and offensive line coach Bill Curry were busy working in the living room of his house, a middle-aged man rang the front doorbell and asked Cherry if he could leave a photograph to be signed for his elderly father, who was a big fan of Starr and the Packers. He never expected what happened next.

Hearing the conversation in the distance, Starr stopped his business with Curry in midsentence and walked to the front of the house, pleasantly greeting the dumbfounded man.

"Where's your father?" Starr asked.

"Oh, well, it doesn't matter," the startled man responded, not wanting to take up any more of the famed quarterback's time. "If you could just sign this," he said, waving the photograph, "I'll get out of your way."

Starr was insistent. "I said: Where's your father?"

"Well, he's in the car . . ."

The man had left his father in his car parked at the curb, promising to be right back as soon as he dropped off a picture, for retrieval at some later date. Never in his wildest imagination did he expect to have a conversation with the Packers legend.

Starr walked out the front door and returned a few moments later with the father, then proceeded to show the man some of his trophies while chatting about the glory days. "You should have seen the look on the old man's face," Curry said. "I was afraid he was going to faint."

While the emergence of second-year man Mike Butler and rookie John Anderson lifted the mediocre Green Bay defense in 1978, the arrival of first-round draft pick James Lofton finally gave Starr a big-time receiver—someone with excellent speed, hands and moves. Unfortunately, with Lynn Dickey still mending, the Packers were not blessed with a big-time quarterback.

Green Bay jumped out to a 6-1 start, causing many to believe the franchise had turned a corner. But as second-year quarterback David Whitehurst struggled in the second half of the season, unable to put the ball in Lofton's hands often enough at a time when the Packers needed to outscore opponents to win, unable to grab the team by the jugular, Green Bay slumped to an 8-7-1 finish, tying for the NFC Central Division title but losing the tiebreaker—and the automatic playoff bid—to Minnesota.

"We were only an average team . . . not yet a mature ballclub," Starr surmised, unsatisfied with Green Bay's first winning season since 1972.

The newly expanded NFL playoffs included another wildcard for each conference, but on the last day of the season, the combination of Green Bay's loss to the Rams and Philadelphia's victory over the Giants put Dick Vermeil's resurgent Eagles in the postseason. In an indirect way, the most infamous play of Joe Pisarcik's life cost the Packers the bid: The previous meeting between the Giants and Eagles, a month earlier at the Meadowlands, had been won in unbelievable fashion by Philadelphia when Pisarcik, the Giants' quarterback, fumbled a risky handoff in the closing seconds instead of simply taking a knee.

His legend began to take shape on a miserably cold day against a dramatic backdrop.

Like millions of other football fans, Bart Starr watched Joe Montana—fighting off the effects of hypothermia and the flu—rally Notre Dame for a stunning 35–34 victory over the University of Houston in the 1979 Cotton Bowl. Afterward, the whole country was talking about the gutty performance in the snow. Suddenly, everyone knew Montana's name.

Still, despite his heroics in the so-called Chicken Soup Game, many NFL coaches and front office officials—sobered by the intricate calculus of the increasingly sophisticated scouting process—doubted Montana's arm strength and his ability to withstand the necessary punishment.

Reassured by an intense workout conducted by quarterbacks coach Zeke Bratkowski—convincing him that Montana's arm was good enough and that his lean frame could carry some additional weight—Starr decided to draft the former Notre Dame star, especially since he was expected to last until the third round.

As both head coach and general manager, the choice was his, and even as he pored over the empirical data pointing to Montana, he was especially attracted to the player's unmistakable leadership qualities. Montana was a winner with a burning desire, and as much as any coach in the NFL, Starr understood how such intangibles translated into victories and championships. All he needed to do was look in the mirror.

Approaching the fifth year of Starr's rebuilding project, the Packers remained a team with numerous glaring needs, especially on defense, so when the defensive coaches pushed him to bypass Montana in order to take former Maryland defensive tackle Charles Johnson, Starr reluctantly deferred to their superior experience. In later years, he would concede the decision was one of his worst blunders as the Green Bay coach. "I blew it," he said. "There's no question that I made a terrible mistake." While Johnson did little to help the struggling Packers defense—and exited the league after just three seasons—Montana, drafted in round three by San Francisco, emerged as the signature quarterback of the age, leading the 49ers to four Super Bowls.

The Packers desperately needed a quarterback who could grab them by the throat and lead them to the promised land.

They needed another Bart Starr.

While it is impossible to know how Montana's presence might have altered the trajectory of Starr's coaching career, the decision demonstrated a weakness that undermined his tenure in Green Bay: Too often, he failed to trust his gut. "My most serious mistakes inevitably occurred when I failed to follow my convictions and deferred to someone with more experience," he said.

Starr was trying too hard to compensate for his lack of coaching experience by overruling his own finely tuned knowledge of the game, effectively negating one of his greatest strengths as a coach—demonstrating how his humility, so often an asset, sometimes flipped to weakness.

Several weeks before training camp in 1979, Bart and Cherry flew off to the annual league meetings in Hawaii, planning to linger for a few extra days of vacation. Flexing his romantic muscles as their twenty-fifth anniversary loomed, Bart told his wife to pack a nice dress for one special evening but otherwise remained cagey about the details of their trip to paradise.

"It was all very mysterious," Cherry said. "I couldn't get him to tell me anything."

The first surprise was the presence of Gary and Emily Knafelc, two of their closest friends, who had flown out separately to spend the week vacationing with the Starrs.

"Bart had been planning this deal for months and Cherry didn't know a thing," Gary said.

After dinner one evening at their resort on the island of Kauai, the Starrs and the Knafelcs sailed up the river to the famed Fern Grotto, passing through the picturesque landscape while Hawaiian chanters serenaded the couples. After stepping off the boat in one of the most romantic settings on the planet, adorned by beautiful flowers, tiny candles, and a breathtaking view, Cherry learned the real surprise: Bart had arranged for a Hawaiian minister to help the Starrs renew their wedding vows while the chanters sang the "Hawaiian Wedding Song."

"I was just speechless," Cherry said. "Bart had gone to all this trouble. It was really incredible and so, so sweet."

At the heart of it all, beyond his starring role in the rise of the National Football League, Bart Starr was a man desperately in love with his wife. Still. "Cherry has been my foundation from the day I married her," Starr said years later. "Every time I hear Bette Midler's 'Wind Beneath My Wings,' I think of her, because she has been just that. I can't imagine my life without her. We've actually grown closer through the years. We're more in love than ever!"

All those years after the shy teenager somehow worked up his courage to ask for a date, the arc of his life unfolded in the context of their continuing love story.

"Cherry is such a strong person and I don't think there's any doubt, Bart has fed off her strength," said her friend M. E. Bratkowski. "They have one of those very special relationships. It's absolutely gotten stronger through the years. You can't imagine one without the other."

While Cherry's bubbly personality and lively sense of humor often kept Bart on his toes, the fine line between Starr's fame and his humility could be seen during the anniversary trip.

Time after time in Hawaii, strangers recognized Starr and often asked for an autograph. Accustomed to such interruptions, Bart, ever the gentleman, always greeted the person warmly before introducing his wife and their friends. In such situations through the years, he was always sensitive to the feelings of less well-known teammates, frequently going out of his way to deflect—or at least, share—the spotlight. Since tight ends tend to be much more anonymous than quarterbacks, no one ever recognized six-foot-four, 250-pound Gary Knafelc, who had played a significant role in Lombardi's first two championships.

Several days and countless fan interruptions into their trip, the mischievous Knaflec sneaked downstairs early one morning, seizing an opportunity to mock his buddy's glowing notoriety.

When the couples convened in the hotel restaurant for breakfast, a pretty young Hawaiian woman approached their table with an excited expression.

"Excuse me!" she said in perfect English, "Aren't you Gary Knaflec of the Green Bay Packers?"

She even pronounced Knafelc correctly, as if someone had helped her practice all those clanging consonants and vowels.

Smiling big, reveling for a few precious moments in his Polynesian fame, Gary said, "Well, yes I am!"

"Oh, I thought so! I've always been a big fan of yours! May I have your autograph?"

She had never heard of Knafelc or for that matter, Starr, but was convincing enough to earn a big tip. Everybody had a good laugh.

After narrowly missing the 1978 playoffs, the rising tide of optimism surging across the Dairy State heading toward the 1979 season could be seen in the ubiquitous bumper stickers proclaiming, "The Pack is back."

But the excitement was premature, because Starr's honeymoon period was ending.

In 1979, as Terry Bradshaw piloted the Pittsburgh Steelers to their fourth Super Bowl victory in six years, drawing inevitable comparisons to Lombardi's Packers, Starr's Packers regressed.

In time, the decision not to select Montana would haunt Starr—as well as the choice to bypass future Hall of Fame defensive back Ronnie Lott two years later—but the 1979 draft proved fruitful in other ways. Chief among the acquisitions: No. 1 pick Eddie Lee Ivery, a speedy tailback from Georgia Tech who quickly won a starting job during the preseason. Finally, it seemed Starr would have a powerful and potentially explosive running threat. But in an exhibition game against the Bears, Ivery suffered a severe knee injury and was lost for the entire season, a devastating blow for an offense still waiting for Lynn Dickey to fully recuperate. The injury-plagued defense struggled.

Despite upsetting New England 27–14, in the first *Monday Night Football* game played at Lambeau Field, Starr's most significant victory to date, the Packers stumbled to a 5-11 finish.

In a tied game against the Minnesota Vikings, Starr, playing the percentages, decided to run out the clock at the end of regulation rather than risk a turnover. After winning the toss, Minnesota quickly drove for a touchdown, handing the Packers a frustrating 27–21 overtime loss.

James Lofton, the 1978 NFC Offensive Rookie of the Year, stormed into the locker room breathing fire, throwing his shoulder pads to the floor during the postgame prayer.

"We weren't playing to win!" Lofton thundered. "We were just playing not to lose!"

Starr, irritated at the insult to his coaching and the intrusion on his postgame routine, quickly confronted Lofton.

"Knock it off! You play. I'll coach."

It was not 1962 anymore, and James Lofton was Exhibit A.

Between the white lines, the evolution of professional football from the sixties to the seventies was shaded in subtlety and nuance: increased sophistication in the passing game; greater speed, size, and strength; play-calling migrating from quarterbacks to coaches; the advent of a limited form of sudden death for regular-season games; the benefits and perils of artificial turf.

But the progression in the men who played the game was much more pronounced.

Influenced by a decade of cultural upheaval and a rapid escalation in salaries, fostering a new age of assertiveness and entitlement, many professional football players of the day saw the world differently than the dutiful Starr, shaped by a world congealed in absolutes, before Vietnam, Woodstock, and Watergate.

To a generation of Green Bay fans conditioned by the culture-affirming life force of Lombardi's Packers, James Lofton, one of the most talented receivers ever to wear the green and gold, became an unwitting symbol of the societal changes spilling over into professional football.

During a bitterly disappointing home loss to the Jets on November 4, Lofton fumbled and a loud chorus of boos erupted across Lambeau Field. Losing his cool, the former Stanford star climbed off the field, provoked by the sound of the crowd's frustration, and defiantly shot the fans the bird, causing them to boo even louder. Instead of apologizing for the vulgar act, Lofton aggravated the situation during a postgame interview with a local television station, launching into a profanity-laced tirade against the Green Bay fans.

Half a world away, while Packer backers seethed, Iranian militants seized the American Embassy in Tehran, sparking a 444-day hostage crisis, crippling Jimmy Carter's presidency, and demonstrating the limits of American power.

Each in their own way, the two isolated events assaulted the senses, causing many to long for a more civilized time, when sports heroes felt the responsibility to act like role models and American leaders could not be rendered impotent by a bunch of third-world thugs.

Trying to explain his middle-finger thrust several years later, Lofton said: "I came back [in 1979] expecting things to get better, and when they didn't, I became frustrated. I complained about the coaches and the offense, and I felt this rage inside. I thought the anger would make me play better, but of course it didn't."

After several clashes, Starr learned how to manage Lofton's surging intensity and Lofton, bound for the Hall of Fame, grew up.

While some players saw Starr growing into the job, some fans, media, and members of the Packers board began to lose faith as the losses mounted. The criticism grew more vocal in 1980, the year Ronald Reagan was elected president and John Lennon was gunned down outside his New York apartment. Despite Lynn Dickey's return to the starting lineup and James Lofton's 1,226 receiving yards, Green Bay struggled to a 5-10-1 finish. Desperately lacking a big-play noseguard after losing first-round draft pick Bruce Smith to the Canadian Football League—one of the biggest and most embarrassing blows of Starr's tenure—the Packers' new 3-4 defense proved to be one of the league's most porous.

After a newspaper columnist suggested that Starr was incapable of producing a winning team, the stone-faced coach, sensitive to the criticism, convened a meeting of his team and wheeled in a cart loaded with various trophies, rings, and plaques he had won during his playing career.

As his players leaned over one another gawking at the hardware, he said softly, "Does anybody doubt that I know what it takes to win?"

For a moment, the silence was deafening.

"Then everybody started whooping and hollering," recalled linebacker John Anderson. "[It was] a very inspirational moment . . . made us all remember who this guy was . . . made it very concrete for us."

Two days after Christmas, on the heels of a second straight losing season, the Packers board agreed to retain Starr through 1981 as head coach but stripped him of his general manager's title. Stunned by the news, he declined to address a specially called news conference until *Milwaukee Journal* reporter and frequent critic Dave Begel—whom he had stopped talking to—left the room.

Accustomed to a supportive media during his playing career, Starr was forced to deal with mounting criticism from some sportswriters empowered by an evolving media landscape. The days of fawning sports journalism were fading, and writers began to question many aspects of his administration, from the wisdom of specific personnel decisions to play-calling to his continued employment.

Some suggested he was in over his head.

Others never forgave him for not being Vince Lombardi.

"We had a pretty contentious relationship," said Dale Hofmann, who covered the Packers for the *Milwaukee Sentinel*. "In Bart's eyes, you were either with him or against him. But I had a job to do like all the guys on the beat and I don't think he understood our job at all."

After all those years of unparalleled success, Starr was dealing with a very public failure, televised each Sunday in living color, challenging his sense of self, and surely causing him private moments of doubt. "All that second-guessing affected him," said Zeke Bratkowski, who eventually left the Packers to become offensive coordinator of Robert Irsay's Baltimore Colts. "Made him even tougher. More determined."

He tried to shield his players from the pressure, but the strain of leadership and failure fell heavily at the top. "I think it wore on him, the burden all on his shoulders," said tight end Paul Coffman.

The criticism of Starr came with the territory of being a head coach in the NFL, but it landed especially hard on Cherry, who was so closely invested in every aspect of her husband's world. "It really was the most difficult time of our lives," she said. She lost weight and suffered with stomach problems, causing her friends, including M. E. Bratkowski, to worry about her health. "It was just so stressful on the both of us."

Each negative article was like a body blow to Cherry, nearly as painful as watching him sustain all those devastating hits during his playing career. After one particularly blistering column, she canceled the family's subscription to the *Milwaukee Journal*, an act of capitalist defiance that made all the area papers.

"I wish things had turned out differently," Cherry said. "But going through that experience, as tough as it was, made us even closer as a couple, and I wouldn't change that."

Even as he assumed a more distant posture with some members of the press, a measure of Starr's decency could be seen when journalist Dale Hofmann mentioned that his young daughter was traveling to a Packers road game in Minnesota and would be sitting alone in the stands. He offered to have her sit with Cherry. "I was really sort of shocked, under the circumstances, considering the difficult relationship we had at the time," Hofmann said. "It was a very nice thing for him to do."

Removing the general manager's title was awash in symbolism, since the Packers failed to hire a new GM, but with only one year left on his contract, Starr felt understandably undermined. Immediately, he began pushing the board for an extension on his coaching pact to "allow us to operate from a position of strength, not weakness."

"I know the record doesn't indicate they should do that," he conceded, "but that would be the most solid base to work from."

Eight weeks into the 1981 season, with Green Bay off to a 2-6 start, Starr looked like a goner. But with the offense finally hitting on all cylinders—especially after Starr engineered a trade for receiver John Jefferson—the Packers won 6 of their final 8 to finish a much-improved 8-8. The board rewarded the coach with a one-year contract extension.

After one of the late-season losses, a 37–3 road rout by the Tampa Bay Buccanners, Gary Waller stood outside a fence near the visiting team's dressing room with his three young children, who desperately wanted to meet Bart Starr. Soon their daddy spotted Cherry stepping onto the team bus.

"Cherry! Cherry!" he yelled at the top of his voice. "It's Gary Waller!"

Hearing the familiar name, the quarterback's wife stepped off the bus, acknowledged her old Lanier High School classmate in the distance, and brought the losing head coach over for a quick visit.

A few minutes later, as the bus began to pull out, a driver noticed several folding chairs in the way. Prompted by their father, eight-year-old Susan and six-year-old John raced over to move the chairs, and the bus soon plowed through the gate and out into the creeping November shadows.

Suddenly, they both felt like Packers.

Don Reese was destined for obscurity—until he became a symbol.

In the summer of 1982, *Sports Illustrated* published a blockbuster article in which Reese, a former defensive end for the Miami Dolphins and New Orleans Saints, spoke candidly about his cocaine addiction and alleged widespread illicit drug use across the National Football League.

Many NFL players insisted the story was overblown, but in time it would be clear that the sport suffered from a significant problem. The toxic cocktail of money, fame, and immaturity exacerbated the prevalence of drugs in professional sports, but by the time Reese forced the NFL to confront the situation, addiction was ravaging all segments of American culture.

Around this time, teenager Bret Starr began to experiment with marijuana and cocaine.

Somewhere along the way, Bret fell in with a bad crowd, negotiating the lonely road from experimentation to addiction. Like many loving and involved parents, the Starrs failed to see the signs. During Bret's freshman year at the University of Wisconsin, his erratic behavior provoked a surprise visit from his parents, who were shocked to discover their boy's secret.

"The son we adored so much was standing before us like a frightened, hunted animal," Bart said.

"We were just devastated to find him like that," Cherry said.

After pulling Bret out of school, the Starrs arranged for him to be admitted to the Hazelden drug rehabilitation clinic in Minneapolis. Although he was unable to complete the program, Bret moved back into his parents' home and agreed to seek treatment as an outpatient for his chemical addiction. Even as Bart fought to keep his job, he was involved in a daily struggle, far from the spotlight, to save his son's life.

The last act began with Dominic Olejniczak's exit.

After twenty-four years as president of the Green Bay Packers, the man known affectionately as Oley retired in May of 1982. He was the man who hired Lombardi all those years before, setting the franchise on the road to all those championships, and he was the man who turned to Bart Starr in a moment of desperation and continued to believe in him as the losses mounted. To succeed him, the executive board appointed Robert J. Parins, a former circuit court judge with no experience in professional football.

Starr was too focused on his job to spend much time thinking about his new boss. He believed 1982 could be their year.

Green Bay's increasingly potent offense was the talk of the league. After years of struggle, quarterback Lynn Dickey was playing like an All-Pro, his passing game significantly bolstered by the addition of John Jefferson, giving the Packers two of the league's best deep threats. Eddie Lee Ivery was finally healthy. The offensive line was maturing into a cohesive unit behind center Larry McCarren and tackle Greg Koch.

The defense was still ordinary, undermanned at several key positions, but after opening the season 2-0 for only the second time in Starr's tenure, the Packers looked like a playoff contender.

Then came the 1982 players strike, the first significant labor stoppage in league history.

"The strike came at a very critical time for us," Starr said. "We were right on the verge. None of us knew how long the strike would last or what sort of effect it would have on our team."

In the wake of another record television contract, as the rival United States Football League prepared to launch the following spring, the NFLPA demanded a bigger cut of the league's fast-growing revenue stream. When owners resisted and called their bluff, the players went on strike, no doubt emboldened by the 1981 baseball walkout. Unlike abbreviated work stoppages in the past, when the players' union lacked unity, the 1982 strike lasted for fifty-seven days, causing dozens of games to be canceled, costing both sides millions of dollars, and giving the league a black eye with increasingly cynical fans.

As many of the Packers endeavored to stay in shape while the negotiations continued, players, wives, and girlfriends convened for a Halloween costume party at a Green Bay bar. No one knew when they might be able to go back to work but everyone was getting restless. Bored, and looking to have a little fun, Cherry convinced Bart to crash the affair—wearing outfits that concealed their identities.

Bart dressed as a farmer, complete with pillows stuffed strategically to make him appear fat, and a pig mask covering his face. Soon after they arrived, one player's wife approached him, squeezed his arm, and, clearly unimpressed, said, "Must be a punter."

Cherry dressed as a hideous-looking witch—with two dominant features: enormous fake breasts adorned with blinking lights.

A short while after the Starrs arrived, Paul Coffman, Larry McCarren, and Greg Koch walked through the door, disguised as the Killer Bees from *Saturday Night Live*.

Coffman, who had a reputation as a ladies' man, gravitated to the well-endowed witch and asked her to dance. When the music stopped, he took a long look at her prodigious figure and said, loud enough for the entire bar to hear, "You have great-looking tits!"

When the Starrs took off their masks, the entire room erupted in laughter as Coffman turned three shades of red.

"In my defense," Coffman said with a laugh many years later, "I didn't know I was coming on to the coach's wife."

The masquerade moment reflected Starr's rarely seen lighthearted side but also his particular burden as a coach. He wanted to be approachable. He wanted the players to understand how much he cared about them. He wanted to touch their lives as other coaches, especially Lombardi, had touched his. But just as he could never be Lombardi, a volcanic force of nature towering over the landscape, he could never allow himself to become Scooter McLean, the short-lived Packers coach who boozed and shuffled his way out of a job. As a great admirer of General Douglas MacArthur, General George S. Patton, and other military giants, the Master Sergeant's son understood the need for the commanding officer to maintain a certain distance from his troops.

"Deep down, I think Bart wanted to be one of the guys," Coffman said. "But he walked this fine line."

Cherry was free to stumble over the line. When middle linebacker Rich Wingo was recuperating from back surgery, he woke up in his hospital bed to see the coach's wife standing in front of him, wearing an enormous Jimmy Durante–style nose, determined to make him laugh. "I thought I was seeing things, until I realized it was Cherry trying to cheer me up," Wingo said.

After the strike ended in a settlement, Green Bay won its way into the revamped playoffs with a 5-3-1 record. Even after clinching the bid by crushing the Atlanta Falcons 38–7 in the next-to-last week of the regular season, Starr, though clearly elated, endeavored to restrain his feelings. "In the emotion of the moment, you might overstate something," he said cautiously. Still, he conceded, "It was a tremendously big win for the players who have been here for some time and haven't been able to get in to the playoffs."

Hosting the franchise's first postseason game since the Ice Bowl, the Packers crushed St. Louis 41–16, as Dickey threw for three touchdowns, Ivery ran for two more, and the much-maligned defense mounted a memorable goal-line stand. It was an enormous breakthrough after years of struggle. A week later, heavily favored Dallas eliminated Green Bay 37–26, but the Packers showed plenty of fight and looked like a team of the future.

The defense remained suspect at several key positions. As the 1983 draft approached, Starr placed a priority on re-signing defensive end Mike Butler, a gifted athlete who had played out his option and was being courted by the USFL's Tampa Bay Bandits. Butler was a difference-maker and the Packers needed him to take the next step. Despite repeated assurances that he would re-sign Butler, Judge Parins let him slip away, refusing to meet the suddenly elevated price for his services. Privately, Starr seethed, feeling undermined by an incredibly shortsighted decision.

"Judge Parins, running the football team, was absolutely clueless," said offensive tackle Greg Koch. "Look at the Butler deal. No way he should have lost Butler. That one decision was huge. Huge."

The offense proved to be even more potent in 1983, but the loss of Butler and several key injuries decimated the defense.

In the season finale at Soldier Field, Green Bay led Chicago 21–20, late in the fourth quarter, needing a victory to make the playoffs for a second consecutive year. But the Bears drove downfield in the closing minutes and kicked a field goal to sink the Packers, 23–21. The painful loss dropped Green Bay to 8-8.

The next morning, six days before Christmas, Starr was in his office preparing for a staff meeting when his boss walked through the door.

"I want to talk to you, Bart," Judge Parins said.

"The coaches are waiting for me. Is it going to take long?"

"Not long at all. You don't have to worry about your meeting, because as of this moment, I am relieving you of your coaching position."

Stunned by the cold manner in which he was dismissed after twenty-six years with the organization, Starr closed the door to his office and began to cry.

As he struggled with feelings of rejection in the weeks and months after his firing—hurt by the way Judge Parins delivered the news, without so much as a thank-you for his many years of service—Starr understood the bottom line: He didn't win enough games. Nine years was a long time, and his 53-77-3 record included five losing seasons. Only Bart Starr could have survived so long with such poor numbers. He was not the sort of man to make excuses, but after negotiating a steep learning curve, he believed the Packers had finally turned a corner under his leadership.

He remained popular with his players, and many of them agreed with this assessment, including Greg Koch, who lashed out at the Packers board in the press. "I think [Starr] got shafted by people who listen too much to what the media put out and not enough to the realistic situation," he said, pointing to the failure to retain Mike Butler as a crippling blow to the defense.

Resisting the temptation to criticize Judge Parins or the board, Starr exited the scene with dignity, giving his former players yet another reason to respect him. But he could not help feeling estranged from his old team. Cherry saw it. Her husband was not just a failed coach. He was a man with a broken heart.

The wound was still tender when he was invited to join his old teammates early in the 1984 season to commemorate the first Super Bowl championship. Cherry wondered whether he should go, but Bart said he owed it his teammates and to the fans. "It was so difficult for him," she said.

When the public address announcer called his name, he walked onto the Lambeau Field playing surface, wearing his old number 15 jersey, not knowing how the crowd would react to a fired coach who had tarnished his legend by following his heart. But his anxiety quickly vanished as the stadium erupted in cheers, giving the old quarterback a long and loud ovation, providing one of the most emotional moments of his life.

This scene and countless others to follow demonstrated something profound about Starr's relationship with the Green Bay fans.

Instead of blaming him for his failed coaching tenure, allowing those nine years to alter the way they felt about him, many fans, perhaps unconsciously, compartmentalized their memories, choosing to remember him as the young warrior who led Lombardi's teams to all those championships. Their selective amnesia helped heal Starr's wound, turning back the clock and bringing him home for good.

TEN

FEARING THE SILENCE

As soon as he heard about Judge Parins's most famous verdict, John Colbrunn began scrambling for Bart Starr's telephone number.

It was early afternoon in frigid Green Bay by the time Colbrunn reached the suddenly unemployed Starr at home and began telling him about an effort he was overseeing to land a National Football League expansion franchise for fast-growing Phoenix. The call was brief, but Starr was immediately intrigued. Several days after Christmas in 1983, still stinging from his abrupt separation from the Packers, he flew to Colorado to meet with Thomas Stoen, chairman of the board of Pacific Energy and Minerals, Ltd., and the primary investor behind the bid.

"I was very impressed with Tom, who is a super gentleman, very down to earth, and a man of great character," Starr said. "I could tell he was very serious [about landing a franchise] and wanted to do it the right way. He would have made an outstanding owner."

After discussing the matter with Cherry and negotiating a tentative deal, Starr agreed to lend his name and his knowledge to the Arizona Firebirds, becoming head coach, general manager, minority partner, and public face of a team that did not yet exist.

Three years into Stoen's effort, as the NFL continued to vacillate on the issue of expansion, the acquisition of Starr gave the Firebirds instant credibility with the league and an edge on a competing Phoenix bidder. Acting like a coach who had just plucked an all-star player off the waiver wire, Colbrunn told reporters gathered for a news conference, "[Starr's unexpected availability] was the greatest Christmas present the Arizona Firebirds could have received. A season of miracles has come to Arizona. We have, as a group, said that if there was one man in the United States who we wanted to be the cornerstone of our franchise, it would be Bart Starr."

The thought of building a franchise from scratch proved very attractive to Starr, who was assured that he would have the complete authority that had eluded him in his final days with the Packers. "It's very, very exciting," Starr said. "I have always tried to take the posture that all things happen for the best. If this comes to pass, if this franchise comes into being, then perhaps that statement will be true."

As the Firebirds continued to surmount the various hurdles required to make the group and Phoenix attractive to the NFL—including the planning of a 65,000-seat stadium and hosting an exhibition game between the Packers and Broncos, which drew 67,500 fans to Arizona State University's Sun Devil Stadium in 1987—Bart and Cherry eventually packed up their lives and left Green Bay after thirty-one years, buying a house in suburban Scottsdale. No one at the NFL was making any promises, but the signs looked very good. Everyone involved with the Firebirds believed it was only a matter of time: Phoenix, growing into the nation's twelfth largest television market, was destined to be an NFL city, and the well-funded operation fronted by one of the leading figures in the sport's history was methodically negotiating the long road from concept to reality.

At least two existing NFL franchises approached Stoen about relocating to Phoenix, but like Starr, he resisted such a strategy. To them, it was a matter of principle. "We have always been opposed to a team moving from one city to another," Starr said. "A franchise is a public trust."

In 1982, while Starr was still coaching the Packers, Al Davis, the irascible majority owner of the Oakland Raiders, had defied the league's other owners by moving his team to Los Angeles. To Davis, who had been feuding with the NFL suits since the days of the AFL-NFL war, when their merger agreement threw him out of a job, football was a bottom-line business with no room for sentiment. After negotiating a more favorable deal with Los Angeles Memorial Coliseum, he believed it was his right to relocate the Raiders for economic reasons, regardless of the impact on the fans of Oakland who considered the Raiders part of the fabric of their city, regardless of the wishes of the league's other owners. Eventually prevailing after filing an antitrust lawsuit against the NFL, Davis set the precedent for a new era of franchise musical chairs.

Two years later, in the wee hours of March 28, 1984, a caravan of Mayflower moving vans negotiated the snowy, darkened streets of Baltimore, headed north by northwest. The news spread quickly, like a death in the family. The next day, Baltimore fans awoke to the shocking reports that Robert Irsay had sealed a deal to relocate their beloved Colts—Johnny U's Colts—to Indianapolis, sneaking off without any warning, like a thief in the night. "I did not believe the NFL would ever let that happen," recalled longtime fan Bob Weltner. "I wanted to blow the tires out on the Mayflower vans." All across the city, fists pounded tables in anger. During a television report, the mayor wept. "The grand old days of the NFL died . . . that night," remarked fan Eric C. Glenn.

Unwilling to steal another city's team, the Firebirds patiently stuck to their plan, waiting for the NFL owners to expand. Meanwhile, the league was preoccupied with outside competition and labor strife. After contesting three spring seasons, with mixed results, the owners of the USFL made the fateful decision to switch to a fall schedule in 1986, when they planned to butt heads directly with the NFL. But as an antitrust lawsuit against the NFL slogged slowly through the courts—eventually producing a pyrric victory for the rival circuit, victorious in judgment that awarded only three dollars in damages—the USFL faded into the history books. The competition for players between the two leagues drove player salaries soaring, but in 1987, with the USFL vanquished, a dispute over free agency led to a twenty-four-day player strike. Refusing to agree to the NFLPA's demands, the owners filled their rosters with replacement players—most of them NFL castoffs or wannabes—and staged three weeks of games as veterans, holding a firm line, walked picket lines. The replacement games bombed with increasingly skeptical fans but eventually succeeded in breaking the strike.

Sixteen days before Doug Williams led Joe Gibbs's Washington Redskins to a 42–10 victory over the Denver Broncos in Super Bowl XXII, Bill Bidwell, the longtime owner of the St. Louis Cardinals, announced his intention to relocate the franchise to Phoenix, which the NFL's owners subsequently approved, effective for the 1988 season.

"We were all very disappointed," Starr said. "So many people worked so long, so hard, especially Tom, who had the vision . . ."

Devastated but gracious in defeat, Starr welcomed the Cardinals to town and quietly shut down the Firebirds, reduced to a footnote in the history of the NFL, soon to be forgotten in the gathering frenzy of the Phoenix Cardinals, eventually rebranded as the Arizona Cardinals. "Starr's group did the groundwork and worked hard to promote Phoenix around the NFL," noted sportswriter Gary Van Sickle. "Maybe the group did its job too well."

Starr's principled determination to uphold the NFL's old order, even as it crumbled around him, had cost him a football team—and the chance at redemption. During the four years he invested in Phoenix, he had repeatedly declined to discuss other coaching opportunities, intent on taking the Firebirds all the way. Now he would never have a chance to prove Judge Parins wrong.

In his last significant act on the NFL stage, Starr had demonstrated something he had learned many times over from his father, his mother, and even Lombardi: Sometimes, winning isn't the only thing.

Bart knew something was wrong.

"I just had a gut feeling . . . a terrible gut feeling," the old quarterback recalled, eyes moistening as he descended back into the nightmare, the horror forever vivid.

Bret always phoned his parents every day or two from his home in Florida, just to check in, so when three days came and went over the Fourth of July weekend in 1988 without a call from their youngest son, concern quickly turned to fear.

"At that point in his life, it was out of character for him not to call. . . ."

After years of riding Bret's addiction roller coaster, the Starrs had learned to dread silence most of all.

Several months after Bart's dismissal from the Packers, believing Bret had conquered his problem, the Starrs had agreed to help finance him and a friend in launching an exotic animal importing business in Tampa. Gratified by their son's passion for animals, like his interest in music, they wanted to encourage and support him in trying to find some sort of purpose for his life, even though he lacked business experience.

Unfortunately, drugs quickly regained control over his life, causing the young man to distance himself from his family, sometimes even forgetting his parents' birthdays. For three years in a row, he refused to join his family for Christmas, repeatedly disappointing his parents, coloring their lives in a painful fog of deceptions and broken promises.

"We felt so powerless," said Bart, who frequently joined Cherry in praying for guidance.

Refusing to give up on their son, the Starrs helped him to seek treatment with a prominent Tampa addiction specialist, Dr. Ed Klein, but the counseling eventually ended after Bret faked a urinalysis test and missed several appointments.

Around this time, Bart's father passed away, which hit him hard, and his mother was suffering from a variety of physical ailments. Cherry, forever the loving daughter-in-law, spent much of her time traveling back and forth to Montgomery to take care of Lulu, who died in 1995.

One night in 1986, after experiencing an epiphany while flipping across a television program in which Dr. Klein discussed how drug abuse ultimately hurt those who loved the users, Bret phoned his parents. Sobbing, he said, "Mom, I want to get this shit out of my life."

Cherry's eyes welled up in tears because she knew her boy was struggling mightily to regain control over his life.

It was the most painful sentence for a mother to hear, reflecting both anguish and resolve.

"Bret was a good young man," Cherry said. "He was a kind person with so many wonderful qualities. He just got into something he couldn't handle."

In time, Bart and Cherry would look upon this moment as a turning point, because Bret later told them that he immediately stopped using drugs, apparently motivated not by thoughts of his own well-being, but by a desire to cease causing heartache for his parents. Determined to find a new outlet, he threw himself into bodybuilding, even as he looked beyond himself for strength, developing a new spirituality and a renewed closeness with his parents, who helped him seek treatment.

Bart and Cherry accompanied Bret to his first meeting with a new doctor, and the old quarterback would never forget how the doctor laid it on the line. "I want you and your parents to know: I will check you whenever I want to. Maybe in the middle of the night. Maybe three times a week. You'll never know when I'm going to check you. And if you turn up one time testing positive, we're done. You're on your second chance and there won't be any others."

Even as Nancy Reagan's often-mocked "Just Say No" campaign placed the prestige of the White House behind the effort to reduce drug abuse among American youth, the nation's sports establishment was still grappling with how to combat the problem. The issue of random drug testing became just another bargaining chip, pitting NFL management against the players' union.

In 1983, as he fought to save his job with the Packers, Starr was confronted with running back Eddie Lee Ivery's cocaine addiction. After being removed from the roster, Ivery sought treatment at Minnesota's Hazelden Center, eventually returning to the starting lineup in 1984.

In 1985, Midfield High School in suburban Birmingham became one of the first public schools in the nation to implement a random drug-testing program for athletes, but many others resisted the concept, citing civil liberties concerns and the argument that such a process unfairly targeted athletes.

Then came Len Bias.

In the wee hours of June 19, 1986, less than two days after being selected first overall in the NBA Draft by the Boson Celtics, the University of Maryland basketball star died from cardiac arrhythmia induced by his recreational use of cocaine. The resulting media firestorm focused attention as never before on the dangers of illicit drug use, leading directly to a new generation of tougher drug laws and contributing to a renewed sense of urgency among the nation's sports leagues to adopt more stringent policies featuring testing and the possibility of suspension for violators.

Around this time, Bart Jr. and his wife, Martha, moved to the Nashville area with their three young girls. After deciding to celebrate the family Christmas in Bart Jr.'s home in Franklin, Bart and Cherry sent Bret an airplane ticket. For three years in a row, he had failed to use a ticket purchased by his parents, no doubt ashamed of his circumstances, not wanting his family to see him in the grips of his addiction, and also suffering from a paranoia concerning travel and crowds. For three years in a row, his absence had cast a shadow of sadness over their holiday.

"We were getting used to his last-minute excuses," Bart said.

Gripped by fear, Bret stopped at a pay phone on the way to the Tampa airport and dialed his brother's number, planning to make up some excuse about why he could not make the trip. But he hung up before anyone answered, gathering strength from his ability to overcome one moment of weakness.

When Bret showed up in Nashville as planned, he looked healthy and seemed in very good spirits, laughing and joking, and openly shared the most intimidate details of his addiction for the first time with his older brother, who listened patiently, struck by his surprising candor. He hugged everyone like he had never hugged them before—like he didn't want to let go.

During the exchanging of gifts, Bret pulled his mother aside and handed her a card, which she immediately opened and read, silently at first, then aloud to her family as she fought back tears.

Dear Mom and Dad,

The patience and understanding you showed during my problems means more than you will ever know. Without your love and caring, I could never have gotten over it. You stood by me when most parents would have finally turned their backs. I love you so much for that and can finally understand that you are truly my two best friends.

Love,
Bret

It was one of the happiest moments of all their lives, embroidered with love, redemption and hope.

"I saw him turning the corner," Bart Jr. said. "We were all so optimistic. We thought he had put many of his troubles behind him."

Like all parents confronted with such a situation, the Starrs struggled for years with feelings of guilt, wondering if they had somehow been responsible for Bret's addiction.

"The burden of guilt was tremendous," Cherry said. "Was it something we had done? Something we had not done? I had this concept of people who had children on drugs of being neglectful or abusive, too involved in their own interests. That wasn't true in our case. I was a stay-at-home mom who was very involved. Bart was a very loving father. The boys adored him. But that didn't stop us from feeling the guilt. We felt that way for a long, long time."

A measure of solace arrived in the form of a letter, written by Bret as a Mother's Day present in 1988. In addition to thanking his parents for standing beside him and apologizing for all the grief he had caused, the son assured Bart and Cherry that in no way had they been responsible for his addiction, for which he took complete responsibility. "It was the sweetest thing for him to do," Cherry said. "And it gave me a little peace of mind."

Several weeks later, Bret returned to Green Bay for a visit, joining his dad at the annual Vince Lombardi Golf Classic, which raises funds for cancer research.

While in town, he visited with several friends from high school, including Connie Grunwaldt, who accompanied him on an outing to an amusement park and a dinner with his parents. "He was very excited to be back," Grunwaldt said. "Everything was coming together."

When he returned to Tampa, Bret continued his ritual of calling his parents every day or two, until the Fourth of July weekend, when once more, Bart and Cherry knew enough to fear the silence.

Unable to reach his son on the phone, Starr caught a flight to Tampa and drove to the house twenty-four-year-old Bret had rented in an affluent neighborhood in northwest Hillsborough County.

Standing at the front door, he began knocking forcefully. "Bret! Bret!" he yelled, loud enough for a neighbor to hear. "It's Dad!" As he pounded on the door, Bart could hear Bret's two Rottweiler dogs barking over the blare of a radio tuned to a rock music station. He smelled a foul odor.

Unable to find a way to enter the locked house, Starr drove to a nearby sheriff's station and returned to the home with a deputy. Peering in from a rear window, the two men could see a body sprawled on the floor of the dining room.

On the floor, within reach of the body, lay a greeting card Cherry had given her son the last time they saw each other, about three weeks earlier. It read, "Love means believing in someone."

When paramedics pronounced Bret dead, Bart picked up the telephone and called his friend and former teammate Gary Knafelc. The old tight end was playing golf in Atlanta and someone drove a cart out to find him and bring him back to the clubhouse. "He was calm, as Bart always is, but he was just devastated," Knafelc said. "You could hear it in his voice. I told him I would jump on the next plane [to Tampa] but he told me there was no need to do that. I've always regretted not going. I should have been there to help him."

When the painful truth began to soak in, Bart slid down by the side of the house and began to cry.

Several years later, when the Bratkowskis' son died in a horrible accident, giving the friends yet another point of connection, Bart advised M. E. against seeing her son's body—stressing that she should remember him the way he was. "I know that has haunted Bart all these years, seeing Bret like that," she said.

The circle of tragedy also engulfed the Knafelcs, who lost a son to suicide many years later.

Back in Scottsdale, nervously awaiting word from her husband, Cherry had reluctantly driven to the Mayo Clinic to keep a difficult-to-get doctor's appointment. An avid tennis player, she was in terrible pain, suffering from an injury to her Achilles tendon, and barely able to walk. For two hours, she sat in the waiting room. For another hour, she sat in a small examination room. Still no doctor. Finally, she hobbled out the door, telling the nurse, "I'm sorry but I have to leave."

Like the vast majority of the American population at the time, Cherry did not own a cell phone, so when she walked through the front door of her house, their housekeeper told her that Bart had been trying to reach her. When he broke the news on the telephone, "It seemed like a bad dream, like it couldn't possibly be true."

Leaning on a friend who owned a local travel agency and volunteered to drive her to the airport, Cherry caught the next flight to Tampa on United Airlines. "The people with the airline were so gracious and considerate," she said, "but that was the longest flight. I thought I would never get there."

By the time Cherry arrived, the coroner determined that Bret, who was fully clothed, had been dead for three to four days. His body was badly decomposed, which accounted for the foul smell emanating from the house.

"It was the most horrible thing I've ever experienced in my life," Bart said.

As the tragedy erupted into a national news story, the Starrs learned that their son, who had been clean for more than two years, apparently had started using drugs again. The Hillsborough County medical examiner determined that Bret had died from "cardiac arrhythmia due to an acute indulgence of cocaine," mirroring Len Bias's death. Only minute traces of cocaine were detected in his system, but the amount was enough to cause his heart to stop beating.

"Minute traces."

Twenty years later, the phrase still resonated with Bart as he dissected the details of his son's death.

Flashing back to the day he and Cherry met with the medical examiner, Starr said, "I was immediately struck by what he said about Bret having only minute traces in his system. This was an important point. He said, 'There's something I don't think that either one of you know, and I hope you will pass it along: You don't have to overdose to die. You can die from a very small amount, because we don't know why the body reacts in a certain way.'"

Less than a year before Bret's death, the family's confidence in his recovery was reflected in Bart's decision to mention his son's drug problem in his 1987 autobiography, written with Murray Olderman. Bret gave his blessing to the inclusion, on the hopes that his story might help someone struggling with addiction. Exactly how and why he relapsed—and whether the dose that killed him was his first since quitting cold turkey—remained a mystery that his family would never be able to solve.

"Those last six months, he seemed to be making such great progress," recalled his brother. "There was so much hope, a new level of optimism. Then he's gone. The hope we had made his death even worse to deal with."

After burying their son at a cemetery in Montgomery, the Starrs convened for a tearful memorial service at Green Bay's packed First United Methodist Church, where pastor Donald A. Ott's impassioned eulogy could be condensed to one powerful sentence: "You never expect to bury your own child."

More than forty years after Bubba's sudden death, Starr finally could understand the full measure of pain his parents had experienced. But Bart was not his father, and he dealt with his heartache in a dramatically different way.

Devastated, Bart and Cherry leaned on each other as they endeavored to deal with the tragedy.

"We were already so close, but sharing that awful experience . . . somehow, it made us even closer," Cherry said.

Unlike his father, who dealt with Bubba's death by erecting emotional walls, Bart found comfort in the love of his family and friends. Well aware of how Bubba's death had driven a wedge between his parents, he was determined to chart a different course.

"Through all that, Cherry was a source of tremendous strength for me," he said.

As the Cardinals completed their move to Phoenix, closing a chapter of his professional life, Starr was briefly mentioned as a candidate to replace the retiring Judge Parins as the Packers president. But when the position went to his longtime friend, Bob Harlan, and he began planning a new business venture in the medical industry, the couple decided to move to Birmingham. The choice was awash in symbolism. Bart Jr. and his family had recently moved to Alabama's largest city, and at a time when they could have lived anywhere, Bart and Cherry wanted to be near their son, daughter-in-law, and grandchildren.

Two decades after the Ice Bowl proved what Starr was capable of as an athlete in the most extreme conditions, the aftermath of his son's death, as he faced the most trying time of his life, revealed the content of his character, especially his enormous capacity for generosity.

Determined to assure that Bret had not died in vain, Bart and Cherry began taking their very personal antidrug message to groups of young people across the country, sharing their private pain in hopes of somehow saving someone else's child.

The first stop was down the road in Tuscaloosa.

Several days after Bret's death, Bill Curry, then the head coach at the University of Alabama, called to offer his condolences. During the conversation, Bart told him that when he was able, he wanted to address Curry's team on the subject of drugs.

Several months later, Starr called his old friend.

"We're ready," he said.

"We?"

"Yes. Cherry wants to come, too."

During what Curry recalled as "the most extraordinary team meeting

I have ever been a part of," Cherry stood before the entire Alabama football squad, consisting of boys only a few years younger than Bret, and started talking about her son.

"Bret was not a bad boy," she said, looking around the room. "He was a good kid, like all of you. He just fell in with a bad crowd. Something got hold of him that he couldn't control. . . ."

By this point in the evolution of American sports, college athletes were accustomed to being bombarded with antidrug messages. Some had heeded Nancy Reagan's advice. Some had not. Some competitive athletes who had once chased what they viewed as a little harmless buzz were scared straight by Len Bias; some were not. Drug experimentation was no more prevalent among athletes than in the general population, so it stood to reason that the vast majority of the young men in the room were probably clean. The dangers of illicit drugs were well known, but no matter what some well-intentioned coach said, the same impulse that pushed young men to do the things necessary to become high-achieving athletes sometimes promoted a certain recklessness. Like Bias and so many others, a certain percentage of the young men in the room felt bulletproof, which made them susceptible to the same forces that consumed the late Maryland star.

But every man in the room had a mother. Cherry Starr, grief written all over her face, immediately grabbed their attention.

"We couldn't believe this superstar and his wife were doing what they were doing," said offensive tackle Roger Schultz, who watched from near the front of the meeting room, captivated by the power of one mother's honesty. "I can't imagine how tough it was."

After speaking for a few minutes and begging the players not to get mixed up in drugs, her voice began to break. Tears ran down her cheeks. Seeing his wife falter, Bart rose up out of his seat, gently placed his arm around her shoulders, and started speaking about his experience in discovering his son's body. Fighting back tears, they held each other and shared their anguish with a roomful of perfect strangers. It was a day none of them would ever forget.

ELEVEN

SLIDING DOORS

One afternoon in the early 1990s, third-grader Shannon Starr raced through her front door in suburban Birmingham.

"Dad! Dad!" she yelled out, struggling to catch her breath. "I have some really exciting news!"

"What's that, sweetie?"

Bart Starr, Jr. could see his nine-year-old daughter was anxious to share her latest discovery.

"Did you know Granddaddy was a famous quarterback with the Green Bay Packers?" she said breathlessly. "My friends at school told me he won these things called Super Bowls and championships . . ."

She didn't know, because no one in the family had ever told her.

This innocent moment demonstrated something central about Starr's character. Approaching the fourth quarter of his life, he remained remarkably unaffected by his enduring celebrity, secure enough in himself to have somehow avoided the subject for all those years with his grandchildren, perfectly content to allow them to someday stumble upon it.

"The only thing important to him was that they thought of him as a good and loving grandfather, which they certainly do," Bart Jr. said. "I think that says a lot about what sort of person he is."

Long after the cheering stopped, Starr continued to use his name to earn a living. He proved to be a very astute businessman who zealously guarded his interests. After a dispute with partner Tom Acheson, who owned the majority stake in Bart Starr Lincoln-Mercury, he sued for breach of contract. A jury eventually awarded him $2.3 million in damages. Starr lent his image to a short list of major brands, including Ford Motor and UnitedHealthcare's Secure Horizons, and made speeches for a variety of corporate and civic audiences.

Financially comfortable after a lifetime of meticulous saving and investing, Starr could have retired after the disappointing end of the Phoenix project. But he was fifty-three, and still hungry. A couple of isolated real estate deals led to the founding of a company that built and managed facilities for hospitals. Catching the wave of the 1990s boom in health care, he and his partners opened buildings across the country before selling out for a handsome profit to a real estate investment trust.

In this, as well as so many other things, being Bart Starr, hero of the Ice Bowl, opened doors—especially in Wisconsin.

In the years after his firing, the Packers languished under the guidance of Forrest Gregg, his former teammate, and Lindy Infante. The years of frustration faded into the history books as head coach Mike Holmgren and record-setting quarterback Brett Favre brought the magic back to Titletown, leading the green and gold to two more Super Bowls and a string of playoff appearances.

In 2000, Starr's intense lobbying played a significant, perhaps decisive, role in the narrow passage of a special Brown County sales tax referendum required to partially fund the $295 million renovation of aging Lambeau Field. He made a series of speeches and television appearances promoting the cause, helping the franchise keep pace with big market teams in the facilities arms race.

Seventeen years after the Packers dumped him, humiliated him, broke his heart, Starr once more came to the franchise's rescue, placing his prestige on the line, giving Green Bay fans yet another reason to admire him.

Enshrined for the ages with a large ribbon emblazoned with his name dangling from the ceiling of the state-of-the-art Lambeau Field atrium (alongside Johnny Blood, Don Hutson, Tony Canadeo, Ray Nitschke, and Reggie White), Starr somehow survived—*transcended*—his failed coaching tenure to remain the most beloved Packer of all.

If anything, he grew larger still with the passage of time, unable to buy a cup of coffee in Green Bay without being mobbed.

One reason for Packer fans' continuing affection could be seen on a bitterly cold January morning in 2008, when Bart and Cherry slipped into a booth at a favorite Green Bay restaurant. In town to administer the coin toss prior to the NFC Championship Game—and mark the fortieth anniversary of the Ice Bowl—in the age of the Brett Favre, Bart managed to have a few bites of his breakfast before the first fan spotted him.

Through the years, Cherry learned to notice the stolen glances across a crowded room. "Most people are nervous, and reluctant to come up, because they don't want to interrupt someone's meal," she said. They appreciate the consideration but most don't understand the sense of obligation—and gratification—Bart feels in such instances. Still. After a lifetime of signing his name. In these instances, whenever some fan starts praising his greatness, he always changes the subject to the skill and dedication of his teammates and his coaches. Always. "If I see someone who's clearly wondering [about approaching us], I sort of give them a nod or a sign, to let them know it's okay," Cherry said. "I've seen some celebrities be really rude to people in that situation, which to me is just unforgivable. We really don't think like that. We're grateful for the fans."

After several minutes of soul searching, the young man, born too late to have seen Starr play, approached the table, apologized for interrupting, and asked his hero to sign his prized No. 15 jersey, which he happened to be wearing at the time.

Ever the gentleman, Starr smiled, stood up from the table, firmly shook the man's hand, and introduced his wife.

He was busted now, and as the young fan kneeled at his feet, Starr took a pen and carefully scribbled his name on the jersey, which completely blew his cover. So much for a quiet breakfast. Soon, fans of all ages descended on his table, many wearing green and gold 15s, all shocked by their good fortune, for this was a moment they would be talking about for the rest of their lives.

When one fan asked how he might obtain an autographed picture, Bart requested the young man to write his name and address on a sheet of paper, so he could have his office take care of the matter when he returned to Birmingham. By the time the Starrs paid the bill and walked out into the cold, the list had grown to thirty-two names. Within a few days, every single person on the list received a personally autographed picture in the mail.

Decades after he became a legend, the bond between Starr and the Packer fans remained incredibly strong because of moments such as this, when his unmistakable class touched them in a very personal way. They loved him because he played his guts out to help them win five championships. They also loved him because he loved them back.

But even Starr sometimes confronted the inevitable: All fame is fleeting.

While the couple waited for a flight at Detroit's Wayne County Airport, Cherry noticed a woman looking in their direction, whispering to her little boy and pointing. A few moments later, the boy, prodded by her mother, walked up to the legend and said, "Excuse me. Aren't you Bart Simpson?"

The boy didn't know who Bart Starr was, but the mother, who did, was mortified.

After they stopped laughing, Bart and Cherry took great pains to assuage the woman's embarrassment, because that's the sort of people they are.

Most of the time, Bart slips in and out of public places without being recognized, which is just fine with him because, while he is comfortable with his fame, he remains a very humble, unpretentious person who just wants to live a normal life.

Many times through the years, he has pulled off on the side of Birmingham's roads to help strangers change tires, without revealing his identity.

After close friends Zeke and M. E. Bratkowski retired to Florida's Emerald Coast, Bart and Cherry bought a condo nearby, so they could spend more time together, giving Bart and Zeke ample opportunity to continue their decades-old athletic competition on the area's golf courses. (After two hip replacements, M. E.'s serve-and-volley days came to a close, leaving Cherry to continue her passion for tennis with several longtime partners in Birmingham.) Once, on the way back to the Magic City from the beach, in the midst of a driving rainstorm, the Starrs encountered a young hitchhiker and his dog. Something made them stop. They just had to stop. After talking with the young man for a few minutes, and learning that he had no money and was desperately trying to get home, they drove him and his wet dog to the nearest airport and bought him a ticket.

The man didn't know that he had been rescued by the MVP of the first two Super Bowls. All he knew was that a very generous couple had gone way out of their way to help him find his way home.

It would be easy to start the clock with Charles Barkley, who famously proclaimed, "I am not a role model," prompting a provocative 1993 Nike advertising campaign and sparking a national debate. But long before the National Basketball Association star disavowed any claim to setting a good example for the nation's youth, America's professional athletes began to chafe under the responsibility. Somewhere along the way, fans stopped being shocked at the latest troubling headline, blanketing an entire age in disconnection and cynicism.

Starr dutifully accepted the responsibility, not out of some attempt to promote himself as some perfect person, but rather like so many aspects of his life, out of a sense of obligation. It was yet another example of the continuing influence of his father, the military man who infused him with a strong sense of right and wrong. It was yet another residual by-product of his time with Lombardi, when the mantle of leadership included setting a good example for his teammates.

"I firmly believe that we in the public eye have a tremendous ability to influence the way young people act, what sort of values they cling to," Starr said. "We mimic the people we see. Everything filters down. So we should take very seriously the responsibility to promote positive values."

Like Vince Lombardi and the Ice Bowl, the word "character" seems almost permanently attached to Bart Starr. Long before the country started complaining about the negative influence of troubled athletes, Starr's determination to promote traditional values colored his persona in an All-American glow. Even as he became a symbol of American manhood—strong, silent and virtuous in the mold of Gary Cooper—the people who know him best appreciated his unmistakable decency.

In even the smallest ways, Starr was determined to live a life of integrity, which could seen in the aftermath of a trip to see the Packers play the Baltimore Ravens two months after the 9/11 terrorist attacks of 2001. For some reason, Bart and Cherry stopped to pick up a young couple walking to the stadium from a distant parking spot. They looked like they needed a ride. Neither recognized Bart . . . until fans walking past began yelling out to him. Convinced that no one would ever believe they had ridden to the stadium with Bart Starr, they asked him to sign a photo with an appropriate message as proof. He agreed. No problem. Cherry took down their names and address, but she lost the scrap of paper. Instead of letting the matter drop, the dutiful wife of the dutiful quarterback penned a letter to the editor of the *Green Bay Press-Gazette*, explaining the situation and asking the two strangers to get in touch with her. "We feel really terrible that we may have disappointed them," she said.

More than forty-five years after John Gillespie's telephone call, Rawhide Ranch proved central to Starr's legacy. The facility continued to provide a lifeline for troubled boys who needed discipline, growing from a fragile dream, rescued and sustained by Starr's fame, to a robust institution spread across a sprawling campus. It included a school known as Starr Academy, which provided individualized education to meet the specialized needs of at-risk teens. On occasion, the man who owns the 1968 Corvette donated by Starr all those years ago pulled into the ranch to show it off, giving John Solberg, the current director, a chance to tell the story of how the raffle kept Rawhide afloat—offering yet another object lesson about what it means to be a responsible human being with a generous heart.

"This is a place of second chances," explained one young man who arrived in the distant woods and began to turn his life around. "This is a place of love."

In the aftermath of the Columbine High School shooting in 1999, which focused attention as never before on the inherent dangers of a new era in education and parenting, Wisconsin governor Tommy Thompson asked the man whose legacy was closely tied to Rawhide Ranch to headline a summit on community and youth. "We live in a society where we put 'I' or 'me' on top. That's where a lot of our problems come from," he told the conference attendees, calling for a renewed emphasis on basic values including personal responsibility. "Every successful person is disciplined. Discipline is a wonderful, positive word."

Teammates, rivals, and the men who played for Starr talk about him with admiration and respect, many peppering their comments with cherished memories that demonstrate his acts of kindness far beyond the football field. Rich Wingo, who played middle linebacker for the Packers, would always remember the day soon after Starr's firing that receiver Ron Cassidy's little boy died suddenly, swallowing the team in grief. Wingo turned around at the funeral and there was his old coach, still stinging from his dismissal—a man without a team, but determined to be there for one of his men.

"You're talking about one of the outstanding people I've ever known in my life," said Wingo, who once watched his old coach, as a favor to him, lead an early-morning Bible study at his Birmingham church.

In 2001, when his grown son died suddenly of kidney failure, former Packers linebacker Dave Robinson was incredibly distraught.

"I was in a deep depression," he said. "I mean, I was right on the edge."

Several former teammates phoned to offer condolences, but it was Starr's call that made the difference. "I can't tell you exactly what he said, but it was very powerful to me at that pretty desperate moment in my life, when I was in danger of getting a divorce or just going crazy from grief," he said. "See, we weren't talking like former teammates. We were two fathers who had lost their sons."

More than a decade after his own tragedy, Starr's enormous capacity for generosity continued to reverberate through the lives of his friends and one-time teammates.

"I want my kids to grow up to be just like him," said former Packers offensive tackle Greg Koch. "He's the classiest guy I've ever known."

This is a familiar thought, uttered over and over again by those who know him.

In an age hardened by the long line of athletes who abdicated their responsibilities in willful defiance or as misguided followers of Barkley's postmodern ethos, poisoning the well for the many good ones, the natural temptation is to confront Starr's pristine image with skepticism: Surely no one can be so good. Even his family and friends wrestle with this inevitable thought. They even joke about it. But the evidence to the contrary is absolutely overwhelming.

More compelling is the question of the onerous burden that the image has placed on Starr: Surely, he must feel the weight of all those great expectations. But this thought stands up to scrutiny only if his persona is indeed some sort of act, which it most assuredly is not. Starr is just being himself. He doesn't view being a role model as a lead weight dangling from around his neck. He sees it as a gift—a precious treasure awarded him by virtue of his achievements as an athlete, passed down as a sacred trust. It's no heavier than his two Super Bowl rings.

In twenty-first-century America, awash in vulgarity and entitlement, Starr struck all who knew him as strangely out of place, like a time traveler from a more civilized age.

When civic officials unveiled a seven-and-a-half-foot-tall statue of Starr in Green Bay—"a larger-than-life statue for a larger-than-life man," one of the organizers explained—a crowd of several hundred people showed up, including former teammate Paul Hornung and Gale Sayers, the outstanding Bears running back. Starr was touched by the gesture and a little embarrassed. (Lisle Blackbourn, the onetime Packers head coach, once said of his young quarterback, "When you praised him, he was inclined to back up a little on you." Even as his confidence grew and he was universally praised, he never completely lost this quality.) The master of ceremonies, onetime Packers center Larry McCarren, told the cheering mob, "He used to tell us, and hammer it in, that everything you do is a reflection of attitude . . . There is probably not a day in my life that that hasn't dawned on me."

Attitude.

Long after leaving the playing field for good, Starr always emphasized the power of the word that had proven so instrumental in his rise.

"Every single thing that we do, how we react to other people, is a reflection of our attitude," he said. "God gives us our talent but he also gives us the strength to control that word, which enhances your talent. I feel you have the opportunity to do some great things if your attitude is right."

Six decades after he followed his athletic talent out of Montgomery toward an uncertain future, learning along the way to tap something deeper in order to make his way in the world, Starr offered a powerful example that transcended the game. It was his positive and tenacious attitude that allowed him to prove his father wrong, fortified him in his struggle to meet Lombardi's exacting standards, filled him with hope when he returned to the Packers as head coach, and gave him peace when his tenure ended in failure. This same way of looking at the world colored his reaction to Bret's death. As devastated as he was, he did not withdraw or give in to the despair. The same mental toughness that drove him to become a legendary quarterback also allowed him to deal with this tragedy and somehow emerge from the heartbreak as the same happy and kind person.

"The way my dad can maintain such a positive outlook, no matter what, is really quite extraordinary," said Bart Jr. "There's no doubt that has been fundamental to his success. It's a source of enormous strength."

In 1988, the National Football League recognized the power of the old quarterback's example by creating the Bart Starr Award (BSA). At a time of mounting scandals, the NFL partnered with Athletes in Action, the sports ministry of the Campus Crusade for Christ, to honor an active NFL player who best exemplifies "outstanding character and leadership in the home, on the field and in the community."

"[Starr] will always be remembered as both an outstanding player and an equally outstanding person," said NFL Commissioner Roger Goodell. "His legacy will be forever preserved and honored."

One of the league's most coveted honors, the Bart Starr Award, determined by a vote of active players and presented at the annual Super Bowl Breakfast, evolved into a significant part of Starr's legacy to the game, reflecting not only his hard-earned reputation as a man of class and integrity, but also his desire to promote and recognize such standards among the current generation of players. Winners have included Tampa Bay Buccaneers running back Warrick Dunn, Seattle Seahawks receiver Steve Largent, Houston Oilers quarterback Warren Moon, and Chicago Bears middle linebacker Mike Singletary.

"You always hear about the negative stuff, but how often do you hear about the good?" Starr said. "The truth is, there are good guys all across the league having a positive impact, and I'm honored to be a part of shining a spotlight on some of those people."

Sometimes, the light has exposed the league's flaws.

Hours after receiving the BSA, prior to Super Bowl XXXIII in Miami in 1999, Atlanta Falcons safety Eugene Robinson was arrested for soliciting a prostitute, creating a public relations nightmare for the league. Robinson returned the award, and the NFL and Athletes in Action resolved to avoid such a blind-side hit in the future.

Decades after he became part of the vocabulary of a new era, as the league began counting in Roman numerals, the Bart Starr Award transformed Lombardi's quarterback into a permanent fixture at the Super Bowl. Like virtually every other facet of his life, it was an experience he shared with his devoted wife, which could be seen during the 2008 Super Bowl Breakfast at the Arizona Biltmore in Phoenix.

After joining her husband at the microphone and welcoming the packed house—including dozens of league dignitaries, most notably, former Colts head coach Tony Dungy, the keynote speaker—Cherry launched into a story about driving to their beach place in Florida, listening to Il Divo's version of "Unchained Melody."

"Bart was very moved by this song, which is so beautiful," she explained to the crowd. "At one point, he reached over and very sweetly took my hand and said, just as serious as he could be, 'Honey, please promise me: You'll have this played at my *wedding*.'"

The breakfast crowd erupted in laughter, right on cue, and Cherry turned to brush the arm of her smiling husband, who knew exactly where she was going.

"And I looked at him and said, 'Your *wedding*! I'm not even gone yet and you're planning for your next wedding?!'"

After explaining that her husband had meant to say "funeral," Cherry came in for her big finish.

"He said, 'Honey, please promise me you'll never tell anyone about this. . . .'"

Now it was a secret shared with five hundred of their closest friends, who blanketed the banquet room in laughter and applause.

While the scene showcased Cherry's playful side, central to their successful relationship, it also demonstrated Bart's self-deprecating wit.

Even in this setting, especially in this setting, Starr was not trying to pass himself off as some mythical figure. Rather, he was just another guy capable of botching a tender moment with his wife. At an affair where he was being held up as a example to the rest of the league, Starr was willing to mock himself, revealing his humanity in a very personal and easily accessible way. Unlike many famous athletes who zealously protect every aspect of their image, determined to project the illusion of perfection, Starr was very comfortable in his own skin, at ease with his own imperfections.

When Starr presented the award to 2008 honoree LaDainian Tomlinson, the San Diego Chargers running back fought back tears. Honored for his Tomlinson's Touching Lives Foundation, which provides a wide range of assistance to underprivileged families in San Diego and his native Texas, he choked up while explaining the way his mother inspired him as a young man.

"I'm honored to be mentioned in the same breath as Bart Starr," Tomlinson said.

"Bart! Jason can see you about 5:30!"

On a warm spring afternoon in 2008, Cherry was standing in her kitchen, cradling a phone with one hand while stirring a pot on the stove. While talking with the receptionist at Bart's physical therapist's office, she was making soup for her granddaughter, who was ill and unable to eat solid food.

Seated within earshot of his wife, on the couch in the adjoining living room of their large, modern home located on a cul-de-sac in a quiet suburban Birmingham neighborhood, Starr interrupted his conversation with a house guest and turned to answer. The old quarterback was in pretty good shape for an old quarterback, after all those years of traumatic collisions, but he was nursing an injury to his knee and needed some treatment.

After discussing the situation for a few minutes, he decided to make an appointment for the next morning. It was dinnertime and, while chatting about football and life, the three of them were trying to decide between P. F. Chang's and the dining room of a nearby country club.

"Did you see what Terrell Owens did in that game in the playoffs?"

"Scored a touchdown. Then walked right over to the first row of seats and handed the ball to a young fan."

Then the old legend smiled.

"Now, that's class."

More than thirty-five years after taking his final snap, Starr still closely followed the game of his life. He attended several Green Bay games each year—growing close to Brett Favre, who broke all of his old records before moving on to New York and Minnesota. As one of the league's leading elder statesmen, he often participated in official NFL events, such as a pregame ceremony prior to Super Bowl XL in 2006, when he walked onto the field in a procession of onetime MVPs. Mostly, he watched television like everyone else. Some of what he saw bothered him, especially the unmistakable rise of egocentric players and the various off-the-field problems that gave the institution of professional football a bad name. Outspoken in his belief that that teams and the league should hold players to a high standard of personal and professional conduct, he emerged as a strong supporter of Commissioner Roger Goodell's efforts to crack down on bad behavior with stiff fines and suspensions—for the good of the league and larger society.

"Society has a big problem and unfortunately, when youngsters see someone they look up to doing something they shouldn't be doing, and there is little or no consequence for their actions, it filters down," Starr said. "It's hard not to get drawn into that. Those people [in charge of] all sports should make sure that their personnel clean up their act or suffer the consequences."

He remained an NFL man, proud of his old league, wanting very much to feel a kinship with the current generation of players.

So when the old quarterback saw the often-controversial Terrell Owens make that fan's day, the gesture touched him deeply.

Starr remained in demand for endorsements and speaking engagements across the country. He maintained an office several miles away, where his secretary received a steady stream of requests for autographed pictures. His contract as a celebrity spokesman with UnitedHealthcare kept them on the go, all across the country, but like many wives of a certain age, Cherry kept pushing him to slow down, to start telling people no, so they could spend more time relaxing at their condo in Florida. But he hated to say no.

First stop on the way to supper in Bart's SUV was down the street at the home of some neighbors who were out of town. Cherry had promised to feed their cat.

"Hey there, sugar!" she said, reaching out to pet the kitty as Bart helped her with the food. "Bet you are getting hungry, aren't you?"

Well known for their work with the Birmingham Humane Society, the Starrs have provided a home to many furry creatures through the years, including the frightened stray dog they once stopped to pick up during a driving rainstorm in the dark of night. The pit bull was standing in the middle of the street, without a collar, as cars whizzed by. He looked lost.

After gently coaxing him into their backseat, they took the nervous pooch to their home, fed him, and carefully made a comfortable place for him to sleep in the laundry room, only to discover the next morning that he had broken into a nearby box of old clothes Cherry was sending to her friend and longtime housekeeper from the Green Bay days. Nothing was ruined but all those nice dresses and blouses were pulled out and scattered across the floor. "He was just frustrated because he didn't know where he was," Cherry said. Unable to locate his owner, the Starrs eventually took him to the shelter. Someone named him Bart.

Cherry's forbearance with the animal kingdom was long established. In the days of Ralph, Bret's pet rat, the Starrs began to miss things, including a single earring. A search of the house eventually uncovered a stash of items in the drawer of a stereo cabinet downstairs. "From then on, if you were missing something, you could open that drawer and there it would be," she said.

Marveling at his mother's passion for animals, further demonstrated by the Starrs' habit of stocking a feeder in the backyard every night, Bart Jr. often witnessed possums, foxes, raccoons, and other wild animals converging on the wooded area to feast on the bounty. "I keep waiting for a knock-down, drag-out fight among all those animals," said the son, who lives several miles away. "But I guess they've all learned to share."

Like many animal lovers, the Starrs were deeply disturbed by the Michael Vick saga. Bart was especially troubled since Vick was a member of an elite fraternity. Even as the Atlanta Falcons quarterback, implicated in a dog-fighting ring, became a glaring symbol of animal cruelty while mocking the concept of the athlete as role model—eventually sentenced to twenty-three months in federal prison and suspended indefinitely from the NFL, before mounting a comeback two years later with the Philadelphia Eagles—Starr, another quarterback from another age, privately provided a stark contrast: He made time to accompany his wife on a daily sweep of the area, feeding a long list of stray cats. The sight of the MVP of the first two Super Bowls driving a chuck wagon for four-legged critters probably would have made his old teammates laugh, but he takes the assignment very seriously, carefully navigating from one location to the next while his wife steps out of the car, feast in hand, and sweetly greets the kitties that have become like members of their family.

Moving through the buffet line at the country club, Cherry said, "Oh, Bart! I went by to feed Winfrey, and her bowl was completely empty! Some other animal has been eating her food!"

Winfrey, one of her favorites, lives in a parking garage at Riverchase Galleria, discovered after a trip to the mall and immediately adopted. They named her after the adjacent hotel.

As the dinner conversation meandered from Denzel Washington's *The Great Debaters*, to the latest Josh Groban CD, to the wisdom of Winston Churchill, to their shared admiration for George W. Bush, Cherry launched into a story about a memorable night at a Milwaukee hotel.

"We heard this knock on the door. Bart went to see who it was and it was this Secret Service agent . . ."

Somehow President Reagan, in town on a campaign swing, had found out that the Starrs were staying at the same hotel.

"The man asked if we would like to have breakfast the next morning with the president . . ."

Taking the verbal handoff while munching on a plate of chicken fingers, Bart, who had campaigned for Reagan, said, "We assumed we were being invited to some sort of breakfast gathering [the president] was putting together . . ."

But the next morning, when they walked in to the hotel restaurant, they discovered that the leader of the free world, who was then somewhat busy winning the cold war, had arranged to have breakfast alone with the celebrated quarterback and his wife. They talked about many things, including Reagan's admiration for Lombardi.

"It was just the three of us," said Cherry, adding, "What a charming man. Very nice. And a great president."

Sometimes it was tough and challenging and tedious to be a famous former athlete, shouldering the burden of all those memories.

But sometimes it was just plain cool.

Several weeks after dinner at the club, about five hundred people packed a crowded gymnasium at Athens Bible School, in the heart of Alabama's Tennessee Valley, to catch a glimpse of the legend and hear him talk about the glory days of the Green Bay Packers. He looked good: fit, trim, spry. He could have been mistaken for just another retiree with thinning hair and a weathered face. But when he stepped to the podium, he spoke with the ring of authority, sounding very much like a military man, punching his words carefully, owning the room.

While helping the Christian school raise funds for a building campaign, he regaled the rapt dinner audience with stories about Lombardi, the Ice Bowl, and the lessons he learned from the famed coach. He cued someone on the stage and then invited everyone to truly listen to the lyrics while Bette Midler's "The Rose" blared from the public address system. He talked about the power of attitude and perseverance. He talked about the power of love. After the program concluded, he took a seat at a table in the lobby and spent the next half hour signing his name across photographs, jerseys, helmets, and hastily gathered sheets of paper. He chatted and posed for pictures. After saying his good-byes, Starr walked out to his car and drove a hundred miles into the night, home to his beloved Cherry.

As a rockin' cut from The Beatles' "Hard Day's Night" faded slowly into the background, bumping the show back from a commercial break, Paul Finebaum leaned in to the mike inside his Birmingham radio studio. "Let's grab some phone calls for Bart Starr."

On a blistering August day, Starr was seated a few feet away, making one of his frequent guest appearances on Finebaum's popular syndicated sports talk program. He chatted about everything from his admiration for Lombardi, to his appreciation for what Nick Saban was doing for the Alabama program, to his role as cochairman of the Alabama Sports Hall of Fame's Youth Outreach Program, which promotes the importance of goal-setting, responsibility, and positive lifestyle choices across the state.

"Charley is in Montgomery, Alabama."

"Mr. Starr, thank you for taking my call. I want you to know I'm calling from Delray Court in Montgomery, right down the street from where Master Sergeant Ben Starr lived. And I wanted to tell you: He was an inspiration to you, but as a young sergeant, he was terribly inspirational to me."

"You're very kind to call. I can easily appreciate why you would feel that way, because I've always been indebted to my dad for what he meant to me growing up. He was a great, great leader and a wonderful dad, although he was very, very tough."

"Yeah. I can say that. He showed you the way. But it was the right way. And I'm very impressed with what you do for our society, all over Alabama and everywhere else, Mr. Starr. Thank you."

"Well, thank you for calling. I'll always be grateful for my father."

A steady stream of callers peppered him with questions about his Packers, the twenty-first-century Packers, the modern-day Crimson Tide, and the various negative headlines confronting the NFL. On a show that frequently includes interviews and call-in opportunities with some of the biggest names in contemporary American sports—and a steady diet of smack-talking, especially related to Alabama and Auburn football—the universal respect for Starr was impossible to miss. Some just called to say how much they admired him.

When one caller began a question by greeting him as "Mr. Starr," the hero of the Ice Bowl insisted, "Please call me Bart." The man on the other end of the line laughed nervously and reluctantly complied with the request, clearly uncomfortable with referring to the sports giant in such a casual way.

In a state forever mesmerized by the enduring legend of Paul "Bear" Bryant and the hearty men who met his demanding standards on way to one championship after another, Bart Starr's Alabama legacy is awash in complexity. Very few Bama fans know much about his years in Tuscaloosa, in those dark days before Bryant, or can comprehend how the most successful quarterback in the history of the NFL could have been so poorly utilized by such an inept coaching staff. Some younger fans are shocked to hear that Vince Lombardi's quarterback played for Bama at all.

But despite this handicap—despite the absence of personal memories and the emotional connection they can stir—Starr remains one of the most beloved and admired figures in Alabama football history.

Unable to revere him for his college career, Alabama fans nevertheless point with pride to his unparalleled accomplishments in Green Bay, remembering him for the Ice Bowl, the first two Super Bowls, and all those other moments of green and gold glory, which caused thousands of Alabamians to adopt the Packers as an extension of their football family.

They admire him for the sort of man he has proven himself to be, and how this ultimately reflects upon their little corner of the world.

The circumstances of Starr's inglorious end in Tuscaloosa could have embittered him for life toward his old school, but instead of distancing himself from the program, he embraced it, eventually taking his place among the immortal names in Alabama history. All those years after the Whitworth regime would not even provide him with a sack of footballs as he battled enormous odds trying to make the Green Bay roster, Starr often went out of his way to participate in reunions and commemorative events, such as the dedication of the newly expanded Bryant-Denny Stadium in 2010.

Alabama fans love to talk about the magic of Broadway Joe and Super Bowl III, but Starr stirs a different sort of pride, which can be heard during his appearances on the Finebaum show, when the phone lines invariably jam with callers anxious for a few precious moments of his time.

"When Bart is on, the reaction is always the same: breathtaking," Finebaum said. "It doesn't matter whether it's a nine-year-old kid or a ninety-year-old great-grandfather. He makes everyone feel important. Usually, the audience is talking about him for days."

Beyond the complexity of his Crimson Tide pedigree, Starr's appeal with the Alabama crowd is in reality quite simple: In the reflected glory of his legend, his unmistakable class makes them proud to *be* Bama fans.

The heresy started with Allen Barra. First in his 1987 book, *Football By the Numbers*, and again in 2004's *Big Play*, Barra dared to question the conventional wisdom concerning Bart Starr. Armed with a detailed statistical analysis, Barra, who has written for *The Wall Street Journal* and *The Village Voice*, made a strong case for Number 15's greatness, especially as a postseason master. Furthermore, he broke with the crowd and pronounced Starr the ultimate victor in his Space Race–era rivalry with Johnny Unitas.

"Bart Starr was, without question, the finest pro quarterback of the sixties and is thus worthy of comparison with any other quarterback in football history," he insisted. In the land that Robert Irsay forgot, this was a profane thought. But he was right.

Inspired by Barra, Kerry J. Byrne began crunching his own numbers.

Amid the crowded landscape of journalists who cover professional football in the Internet age, Byrne had carved out his own particular niche, editing the popular coldhardfootballfacts.com, a Web site devoted exclusively to examining the NFL, past and present, through the prism of unyielding numbers.

Byrne never saw Starr play, but as he pored through mountains of statistical data, both ancient and relatively new, with the meticulous eye of a forensic scientist, a mosaic of numbers began to emerge.

Challenging the traditional measures of quarterbacking greatness (especially total yards and touchdown passes) while drawing a correlation between certain other stats (including fewest interceptions and yards per attempt) and winning, Byrne was surprised when Starr's name kept popping up near the top.

Bart Starr? Really? Wasn't he the guy who just handed off to Hornung and Taylor?

"I don't know how that myth got started, but the closer I looked, the more I realized: It just wasn't true," Byrne said.

In his analysis of career-passing leaders in the so-called "dead-ball" era, which ended in 1978, when rule changes tilted the game in favor of offenses, Starr ranked third (passer rating of 80.47), trailing only Sonny Jurgensen (82.62) and Len Dawson (82.56). Behind him, in order: Johnny Unitas, Otto Graham, Frank Ryan, Norm Van Brocklin, Sid Luckman, Don Meredith, and Roman Gabriel.

After Byrne closely examined Starr's prolific postseason numbers, which leave a long line of modern-day Super Bowl heroes in the dust, and his historically low interception rate, particularly in the playoffs (a league record of 1.14), the case grew stronger still when he focused on the all-important career yards per attempt. Measured against other quarterbacks from both the live-ball and dead-ball eras, Starr ranked eighth (7.849). In his rearview mirror: A cast of all-stars, including Johnny Unitas, Peyton Manning, Roger Staubach, and Joe Montana. In fact, Starr reached the benchmark of 8.2 yards per attempt six times in the sixties—four times more than Manning accomplished in his first decade with the Indianapolis Colts.

Greatest passing teams of the Super Bowl era? The cold, hard calculations ranked the 1966 Packers (with league MVP Starr at the controls) 11th on this list, demonstrating a little-recognized fact: By the end of the

Lombardi dynasty, Starr was carrying the offense as the running game became much less productive.

Even before factoring in a truckload of intangibles, particularly play-calling mastery and overall leadership, personified by the climactic drive in one of the epic games in football history, the injustice of Starr's largely overlooked body of work began to gather momentum in Byrne's mind.

By 2008, the evidence had reached a tipping point, just as the world was slobbering all over Tom Brady, understandably enamored with the masterful way he had led the New England Patriots to three Super Bowl championships in four years.

Just as some others began suggesting that Brady might be the greatest quarterback ever, the writers at coldhardfootballfacts.com checked and rechecked the numbers, and then pulled a name out of the shadowy past.

The Definitive List: Top 10 NFL Quarterbacks
1. Bart Starr
2. Joe Montana
3. Sammy Baugh
4. Otto Graham
5. Tom Brady
6. Johnny Unitas
7. Roger Staubach
8. Steve Young
9. Peyton Manning
10. Brett Favre

In explaining the ranking, Byrne told his readers, "History has done a great disservice to the legacy of Starr," calling him "the most clutch and most cruelly efficient passing assassin of his or any other generation."

But ancient myths die hard.

More often, those fans and journalists who took the time to look back continued to underrate Starr, unable to fully appreciate, from the vantage point of an age when coaches call most of the plays from the sidelines, what he meant to Lombardi's Packers and, indeed, to the entire NFL, all those years ago.

Viewed through the proper lens, the statistical case for Starr is compelling. But his most important quality cannot be reduced to a mathematical equation: He was one of the greatest *leaders* in the history of American sports.

Thus, one digit in the Bart Starr story makes all others shrink to insignificance.

One digit defines him for the ages.

Beyond yards per attempt, interception percentage, passer rating, and all the other formulas devised to reflect the sort of achievement that translates to winning, the cumulative weight of those five championship rings ultimately trumps every argument.

Forty years after the cheering stopped, every quarterback in football is still chasing Bart Starr.

For nearly four decades, one of Starr's finest performances gathered dust in a Pennsylvania attic.

At a time when videotape remained expensive and many network shows were never saved, careless officials at CBS and NBC apparently failed to preserve the broadcast of Super Bowl I. Except for the highlight reel crafted by NFL Films, no official record survived of the first championship game of the modern age. In time, historians began actively searching for the lost telecast, leading *Sports Illustrated* to place a price tag of "more than $1 million" on such a tape, if indeed one somehow existed beyond the clutches of the league and the networks.

It would be another eight years before the 1975 introduction of consumer videotape recorders, which launched a new era in home viewing, presaging the liberating age of DVRs when the entirety of the television universe suddenly was available for capture in some distant haze of ones and zeros. For some reason, in 1967, the year of the Summer of Love and *The Graduate*, a Pennsylvania man gained access to a bulky and costly professional tape machine at his place of business . . . and, in a stroke of archival instinct, recorded the live broadcast carried by WDAU-TV, the CBS affiliate in Scranton/Wilkes-Barre.

Nobody knew the tape existed—until it was found nearly thirty-eight years later, somewhat grimy and incomplete but still in good working order. Sparked by the *Sports Illustrated* story on lost treasures, the man who found it, while zealously guarding his anonymity, arranged for the tape to be restored by the Paley Media Center in New York.

The secret lasted until *The Wall Street Journal* reported the discovery on February 5, 2011, the day before the Green Bay Packers played the Pittsburgh Steelers in Super Bowl XLV.

In NFL terms, the find proved as historic as stumbling across the original copy of the Declaration of Independence, if the founding document of American liberty had somehow been stuffed away in Thomas Jefferson's sock drawer.

Viewed from the vantage point of twenty-first-century abundance, when cable television, the Internet, and mobile devices place instantaneous NFL highlights and news at the fingertips of football fans around the globe, it's difficult for a new generation to understand how such an epic event— featuring Starr's 37-yard touchdown pass to Max McGee, the first score in Super Bowl history—could have been so carelessly discarded.

The search for the artifact that HBO executive Rick Bernstein called "the Holy Grail" of sports treasures was a powerful reminder of Starr's unique place in the history of professional football. But it was also a symbol of how dramatically the world had changed, for he was a creature from a different age, unspoiled by the ubiquity of YouTube videos, Twitter feeds, and TMZ stalkers, when it was still possible to be a superstar and also have a certain mystique.

Despite the large amount of video available from Starr's playing days, the sturdy endurance of his legend will never require manipulating a mouse and clicking PLAY.

For Green Bay fans of a certain age, it lives in a more powerful media device, draped in vivid hues of green and gold glory, forever young, strong, triumphant.

All they have to do is close their eyes . . . and remember.

The collective force of all those shared memories sometimes is manifested in unexpected ways. Several days before Super Bowl XLV at Cowboys Stadium in Arlington, Packers quarterback Aaron Rodgers, faced with a flurry of questions about his difficult relationship with predecessor Brett Favre, told reporters: "You're revered in Green Bay for not only how you play but how you carry yourself, and I think Bart Starr is a prime example of that. He's a great guy I've gotten to know and, obviously, someone I'd love to model my career after."

Rodgers, born twelve years after Starr played his final game, nevertheless lived in the shadow of his elder's lasting legacy.

Searching for historic context, forty-five years after the days of jet packs and empty seats, reporters pursued Starr all week, immersed in nostalgia, posing familiar questions about the good old days. In the glow of Green Bay's 31–25 victory, one image surpassed all others: During the postgame presentation of the Lombardi Trophy, as Packers fans everywhere rejoiced and confetti swirled in the palace that Jerry Jones built, the television broadcast cut to a shot of Bart and Cherry in a distant skybox, smiling broadly while soaking up the latest title for Titletown.

In this electric moment, Starr was a powerful symbol of all that the Green Bay Packers once were—and all they aspired to forever be.

The large metal door squeezed shut and the jam-packed elevator launched with a thud, pushing the still-earthbound crowd of impatient football fans a bit closer to the promised land of the cage.

In the distance, someone yelled Tod Smith's name, and the Florence stockbroker turned to find the voice.

Surrounded by the creeping shadows of Bryant-Denny Stadium on a steamy autumn day, Smith and his old friend shook hands and chatted for a moment or two. Then the voice moved on, disappearing back into the pulsating electricity of another game day in Tuscaloosa.

Holding a special pass that allowed him to ride to his upper-deck seat, Smith, a tall man with jet-black hair who wore glasses, turned back to face the front of the long elevator line, moving slowly but inevitably toward the fenced-off landing area, the on-deck circle for the lucky few.

Just then, another voice, this one unfamiliar, shot through the crowd.

"Hey, that's Bart Starr!"

Bart Starr?

The Bart Starr?

Stunned to see Starr and his wife standing less than ten feet away—smiling, chatting, shaking hands with the other fans lingering nearby—Smith soon found himself joining in the small-talk and glad-handing.

"I couldn't believe that this giant in football history was standing there in line with us ordinary folks," Smith said. "It was such a thrill to meet someone I'd heard about my whole life."

Too young to have seen him quarterback Vince Lombardi's Green

Bay Packers, Smith nevertheless grew up in a world where his name was uttered with a certain reverence—where Bart Starr was remembered as one of the iconic figures in professional football history.

Like an entire generation born after the advent of color television, Smith never saw Starr hit a streaking Boyd Dowler for six.

He never saw him confer with Lombardi on a frigid Green Bay sideline.

He never saw him sustain a devastating lick, climb off the turf, and hobble back to the huddle.

He never saw the Ice Bowl.

But on a Saturday four decades later in Tuscaloosa, far from the glare of the spotlight, far from the frozen tundra, Smith witnessed a moment he knew he would never forget.

Several minutes after Starr's anonymity was blown, the Smiths, the Starrs, and others nearby finally moved into the cage, placing them next in line for one of the two elevators. Their wait grew a bit longer when a small group led by Dr. Robert Witt, the University of Alabama's president, walked to the front of the line. No one said a word when the ushers running the orderly procession allowed them to take the next elevator. "We certainly understood that Dr. Witt probably had urgent business that he needed to attend to," said Smith, who knew the president through mutual friends.

As they stepped through the doors, one of Witt's associates, who had spotted Starr, whispered something in the president's ear. Witt stepped off the elevator, introduced himself to the old quarterback, and invited Bart and Cherry to join him in his waiting elevator.

But Starr politely declined passage on the VIP Express.

"No, thank you," he said with a smile, sending Witt back to the waiting elevator.

"No one would have thought any less of Mr. Starr if he had gotten on that elevator," Smith recalled. "After all, he's a big celebrity athlete and all. But to watch him turn it down . . . that was a real eye-opening moment for me and a lot of people who witnessed it. It really said something about the man."

Sometimes, the smallest gesture can reveal a great deal about a man's character.

By demonstrating an obligation to wait his turn, rather than an entitlement to trade on his celebrity, Starr touched a nerve with a group of fans who had been conditioned to expect less from their heroes.

As the elevator door closed and word quickly spread up and down the line, the fans began to clap, filling the air with a thunderous ovation.

BART STARR'S PASSING STATS

SEASON	GAMES	ATT	COMP	PCT.	YARDS	TD	INT
1956	9	44	24	54.5	325	2	3
1957	12	215	117	54.4	1,489	8	10
1958	12	157	78	49.7	875	3	12
1959	12	134	70	52.2	972	6	7
1960	12	172	98	57.0	1,358	4	8
1961	14	295	172	58.3	2,418	16	16
1962	14	285	178	62.5	2,438	12	9
1963	13	244	132	54.1	1,855	15	10
1964	14	272	163	59.9	2,144	15	4
1965	14	251	140	55.8	2,055	16	9
1966	14	251	156	62.2	2,257	14	3
1967	14	210	115	54.8	1,823	9	17
1968	12	171	109	63.7	1,617	15	8
1969	12	148	92	62.2	1,161	9	6
1970	14	255	140	54.9	1,645	8	13
1971	4	45	24	53.3	286	0	3
TOTALS	196	3,149	1,808	57.4	24,718	152	138

BART STARR'S POST-SEASON PASSING STATS

	A/C	YARDS	TD	INT
1960 NFL Championship Game (Eagles 17, Packers 13)	21–34	178	1	0
1961 NFL Championship Game (Packers 37, Giants 0)	10–17	164	3	0
1962 NFL Championship Game (Packers 16, Giants 7)	9–21	85	0	0
1965 Western Conference Championship Game (Packers 13, Colts 10)	1–1	10	0	0
1965 NFL Championship Game (Packers 23, Browns 12)	10–18	147	1	1
1966 NFL Championship Game (Packers 34, Cowboys 27)	19–28	304	4	0
Super Bowl I (Packers 35, Chiefs 10)	16–23	250	2	1
1967 Western Conference Championship Game (Packers 28, Rams 7)	17–23	222	1	1
1967 NFL Championship Game (Packers 21, Cowboys 17)	14–24	191	2	0
Super Bowl II (Packers 33, Raiders 14)	13–24	202	1	0
TOTALS	130–213	1,753	15	3

SOURCE NOTES

Unless otherwise indicated, all direct quotes were taken from interviews conducted by the author.

Page   **INTRODUCTION**
   3   "The greatest big-game": Salon.com, Dec. 5, 2001.

ONE: BUBBA'S GHOST
  15   "I felt guilty": Bart Starr with Murray Olderman, *Starr: My Life in Football* (New York: William Morrow, 1987).

  21   "Babe had extremely fast": Bart Starr, *Quarterbacking*, (New York: Prentice-Hall, 1967).

TWO: TIDE PRIDE
  26   "We are more interested": *Birmingham News*, Nov. 20, 1952.

  26   "In these days of modern football": *The Crimson White*, Nov. 25, 1952.

  36   "A person extremely close": *Birmingham News*, Sept. 13, 1953.

  44   "Lotta boys, they'd want": *Birmingham News*, Sept. 26, 1954.

44 "The best passer": *Birmingham News*, Sept. 28, 1954.

45 "The Alabama dressing room": *The Montgomery Advertiser*, Nov. 28, 1954.

45 "I knew there was no time": *Birmingham News*, Jan. 4, 1955.

45 "When the thing went in": *Birmingham News*, Jan. 4, 1955.

46 "How could there possibly be": *Birmingham News*, Jan. 4, 1955.

46 "These boys have got some fire": *The Atlanta Journal*, Sept. 9, 1955.

46 "You walk down that hallway": *The Atlanta Journal*, Sept. 9, 1955.

THREE: THE TENTH QUARTERBACK

61 "Professional football as played": *Green Bay Press-Gazette*, Aug. 3, 1956; "Give me something": Michael MacCambridge, *America's Game* (New York: Random House, 2004).

62 "The greatest player": *The New York Times*, Dec. 18, 2003; "I threw the ball": *The New York Times*, Dec. 18, 2003.

63 "Whether they know it or not": Paul Brown Biography, Paul E. Brown Museum.

69 "I can make more money": *Green Bay Press-Gazette*, Aug. 2, 1956.

70 "Starr's long suit": *Green Bay Press-Gazette*, Aug. 16, 1956.

70 "Way to go in there": *Green Bay Press-Gazette*, Aug. 19, 1956; "I was a little bit nervous": *Green Bay Press-Gazette*, Aug. 19, 1956.

72 "I feel sorry for rookies": *Dallas Times Herald*, Aug. 15, 1963.

76 "I lost confidence": Bart Starr with Murray Olderman, *Starr: My Life in Football* (New York: William Morrow, 1987).

78 "I don't have the authority": David Maraniss, *When Pride Still Mattered* (New York: Simon & Schuster, 1999).

78   "Who the hell": David Maraniss, *When Pride Still Mattered* (New York: Simon & Schuster, 1999).

FOUR: FOUR LITTLE WORDS

81   "Completed a cycle": David Maraniss, *When Pride Still Mattered* (New York: Simon & Schuster, 1999).

83   "The importance of Fordham": David Maraniss, *When Pride Still Mattered* (New York: Simon & Schuster, 1999).

86   "The first thing I need": *Sports Illustrated*, Oct. 12, 1966.

86   "A notably direct man": *Sports Illustrated*, Jan. 8, 1962.

90   "It was the first time": Bart Starr with Murray Olderman, *Starr: My Life in Football* (New York: William Morrow, 1987).

90   "The only thing I do remember": Bart Starr with Murray Olderman, *Starr: My Life in Football* (New York: William Morrow, 1987).

91   "The club doesn't really have": *Green Bay Press-Gazette*, Oct. 22, 1959.

94   "A damned Communist": Michael MacCambridge, *America's Game* (New York: Random House, 2004).

100   "Your quarterback has to be": Vince Lombardi with W. C. Heinz, *Run to Daylight* (New York: Prentice Hall, 1963).

100   "This does a lot for a person": *Philadelphia Daily News*, Oct. 24, 1967.

102   "I think the Packers are": Bart Starr with Murray Olderman, *Starr: My Life in Football* (New York: William Morrow, 1987).

102   "I think Bart Starr has": *Green Bay Press-Gazette*, Dec. 24, 1960.

103   "It definitely wasn't a gamble" *Green Bay Press-Gazette*, Dec. 27, 1960.

104   "Like an enraged beer truck": *The New York Times*, Dec. 27, 1960.

104   "We didn't cash in": *Green Bay Press-Gazette*, Dec. 27, 1960.

104   "There were a lot of little things": *Green Bay Press-Gazette*, Dec. 27, 1960.

104   "I'm very proud": *Green Bay Press-Gazette*, Dec. 27, 1960.

109   "Why does Rice play Texas?": James Shefter, *The Race*, (New York: Doubleday, 1999);

109   "This would be an ideal spot": *The New York Times*, Dec. 31, 1961.

109   "Look, they spelled": Bud Lea, *Magnificent Seven*, (Chicago: Triumph Books, 2002).

110   "Scarcely a minute passed": *The New York Times*, Jan. 1, 1962.

111   "It was like Cedar Rapids": *Sports Illustrated*, Jan. 8, 1962.

111   "Kramer's speed put him": Player's Archives, Pro Football Hall of Fame.

111   "Today you were the best": *Sports Illustrated*, Jan. 8, 1962; "Give all the credit": *Milwaukee Journal*, Jan. 1, 1962.

FIVE: CHASING PERFECTION

117   "[Professional athletes] have": *Packer Plus*, May 30-June 22, 1994.

119   "All he has to do": *Milwaukee Journal*, Jan. 4, 1968.

120   "Starr is definitely": *Dell*, September 1963.

120   "Bart Starr with that analytic mind": Vince Lombardi with W. C. Heinz, *Run to Daylight* (New York: Prentice Hall, 1963).

120   "[Lombardi] really gets you ready": *Dell*, September 1963.

120   "On your quick passes": Vince Lombardi with W. C. Heinz, *Run to Daylight* (New York: Prentice Hall, 1963).

121 "That's the way": Vince Lombardi with W. C. Heinz, *Run to Daylight* (New York: Prentice Hall, 1963).

123 "You don't have time": *Sport*, March 1967.

124 "When the coaches": Jerry Kramer, Lombardi: Winning is the only thing (New York: The World Publishing Co., 1970).

125 "[Starr] calls automatics": *Sport*, September 1963.

127 "Conscientious conservatism": Vince Lombardi with W. C. Heinz, *Run to Daylight* (New York: Prentice Hall, 1963).

127 "He doesn't throw": Vince Lombardi with W. C. Heinz, *Run to Daylight* (New York: Prentice Hall, 1963).

127 "If I could just get him": Vince Lombardi with W. C. Heinz, *Run to Daylight* (New York: Prentice Hall, 1963).

129 "My wife has said": Bart Starr, *Quarterbacking* (New York: Prentice Hall, 1967).

129 "You can tell from the way": *Dell*, September 1963.

130 "I thought it was the end": Vince Lombardi with W. C. Heinz, *Run to Daylight* (New York: Prentice Hall, 1963).

135 "We want zeros": *coldhardfootballfacts.com*, Jan. 8, 2009.

137 "Let's remember this": Vince Lombardi with W. C. Heinz, *Run to Daylight* (New York: Prentice Hall, 1963).

138 "You didn't think": David Maraniss, *When Pride Still Mattered* (New York: Simon & Schuster, 1999).

140 "If we win this game": Bud Lea, *Magnificent Seven* (Chicago: Triumph Books, 2002).

141 "Bumping into a cast-iron": Vince Lombardi with W. C. Heinz, *Run to Daylight* (New York: Prentice Hall, 1963).

142 "Did everything I could": Bud Lea, *Magnificent Seven* (Chicago: Triumph Books, 2002).

143 "I'm real satisfied": *Green Bay Press-Gazette*, Dec. 31, 1962.

145 "I remember something": *Pro Football's Longest Day*, Blair Motion Pictures, 1963.

146 "I made a terrible mistake": David Maraniss, *When Pride Still Mattered* (New York: Simon & Schuster, 1999).

147 "That's when I realized": *The Houston Post*, Oct. 22, 1963.

147 "I almost went crazy": *Milwaukee Journal*, March 3, 1964.

150 "Starr's the boy": *Milwaukee Sentinel*, Nov. 25, 1963.

150 "Bart did a magnificent job": *Milwaukee Sentinel*, Nov. 25, 1963.

151 "You're playing for third place": Michael MacCambridge, *America's Game* (New York: Random House, 2004).

151 "A hinky-dinky football game": David Maraniss, *When Pride Still Mattered* (New York: Simon and Schuster, 1999).

153 "I sort of shuddered": *Milwaukee Journal*, Nov. 23, 1964.

153 "The call was Bart's": *Milwaukee Journal*, Nov. 23, 1964.

153 "I've called it before": *Milwaukee Journal*, Nov. 23, 1964.

154 "If I can point to one": Bart Starr, *Quarterbacking* (New York: Prentice Hall, 1967).

SIX: RESPECT

158 "The only player I ever talk money": Tom Callaghan, *Johnny U* (New York: Crown, 2006).

158 "On a trip": Tom Callaghan, *Johnny U* (New York: Crown, 2006).

159 "For five years Bart Starr": *The Detroit News*, Oct. 18, 1965.

159 "Unitas may be able to burn you": *The Detroit News*, Oct. 18, 1965.

159 "You can't take any": *The New York Times*, Dec. 26, 1966.

160 "Bart is a fine quarterback": *Sports Illustrated*, Oct. 12, 1966.

160 "I really stunk up": *Green Bay Press-Gazette*, Nov. 22, 1965.

160 "Goddammit!": Donald T. Phillips, *Run to Win* (New York: St. Martin's Press, 2001).

162 "If I told you": Bud Lea, *Magnificent Seven* (Chicago: Triumph Books, 2002).

163 "I'm always aware": *Sports Illustrated*, Jan. 10, 1966

164 "Just a couple of old-timers": *St. Louis Post-Dispatch*, Jan. 3, 1966.

165 "We wanted to make": *Sports Illustrated*, Jan. 10, 1966.

165 "Their defense played": *Sports Illustrated*, Jan. 10, 1966.

165 "To pick anybody but Bart Starr": *Dallas Times Herald*, Jan. 6, 1967.

165 "It came so hard": *Sports Illustrated*, Jan. 10, 1966.

166 "This team": *Green Bay Press-Gazette*, Jan. 3, 1966.

168 "The forgotten man": *New York World Journal Tribune*, Jan. 17, 1967.

171 "I saw a guy who tips": Mark Kriegel, *Namath* (New York: Viking Penguin, 2004).

172 "If he's worth $400,000": Michael MacCambridge, *America's Game* (New York: Random House, 2004).

173 "Hi, I'm Bart Starr": SportsCentury documentary, ESPN, Jan. 12, 2004.

183   "I am proud and grateful": *Green Bay Press-Gazette*, Dec. 12, 1966.

184   "He's probably the best": *Milwaukee Sentinel*, Dec. 5, 1966.

184   "Bart Starr is not": *Sport*, March, 1967.

185   "I have no intention": Bud Lea, *Magnificent Seven* (Chicago: Triumph Books, 2002).

187   "We didn't have a very good": *Sports Illustrated*, Jan. 9, 1967.

188   "This game will prove": *Green Bay Press-Gazette*, Jan. 2, 1967.

188   "How sweet it is": *Dallas Times Herald*, Jan. 2, 1967.

188   "I've never seen you any better": *New York Post*, Jan. 5, 1967.

189   "I didn't go into the game": *Dallas Times Herald*, Jan. 2, 1967.

189   "Pour it on, boys": *Sports Illustrated*, Jan. 9, 1967.

189   "Good for Stram": *The New York Times*, Jan. 2, 1967.

189   "The greatest buildup": *The New Yorker*, Feb. 4, 1967.

190   "It was a good lesson": *Los Angeles Times*, Jan. 17, 1987.

191   "I knew if we went out": NFL Game Program, Dec. 28, 1980.

191   "A game played on a stage": *Sports Illustrated Special Edition*, Fall 1995.

191   "Lombardi, the mystique": *Sports Illustrated Special Edition*, Fall 1995.

192   "Everyone has waited": *Dallas Times Herald*, Jan. 15, 1967.

192   "I don't know if": David Maraniss, *When Pride Still Mattered* (New York: Simon & Schuster, 1999).

193   "Every owner in the league": *Sports Illustrated Special Edition*, Fall 1995.

194   "I guess Anderson": *The New York Times*, Jan. 16, 1967.

195   "The only difference": *Los Angles Herald-Examiner*, Jan. 16, 1967.

195   "I accept this on behalf": *Green Bay Press-Gazette*, Jan. 16, 1967.

195   "It reads hokey on paper": *New York World Journal Tribune*, Jan. 17, 1967.

195   "I don't know where": *Los Angeles Herald-Examiner*, Jan. 16, 1967.

196   "It took the Super Bowl": *New York World Journal Tribune*, Jan. 17, 1967.

197   "Coach, I'm not going": Bart Starr with Murray Olderman, *Starr: My Life in Football* (New York: William Morrow, 1987).

SEVEN: THE COLDEST WAR

199   "Nobody had to say anything": *Los Angeles Times*, Jan. 9, 1996.

200   "I classify Bart Starr": *Green Bay Press-Gazette*, April 25, 1967.

200   "I've told him this many times": *Green Bay Press-Gazette*, April 25, 1967.

201   "Bart Starr was voted": *Green Bay Press-Gazette*, April 25, 1967.

201   "I've probably worked harder": *Milwaukee Sentinel*, July 12, 1967.

205   "[Starr's] got so much character": Jerry Kramer and Dick Schapp, *Instant Replay* (New York: The New American Library, 1968).

206   "One man made us look": Jerry Kramer and Dick Schapp, *Instant Replay* (New York: The New American Library, 1968).

206   "He didn't seem to be throwing": *Chicago American*, Sept. 25, 1967.

206   "I'd rather not talk": *Chicago American*, Sept. 25, 1967.

207   "I don't want to be rude": *The Atlanta Constitution*, Oct. 2, 1967.

207   "He's in a slump": *Dallas Times Herald*, Oct. 8, 1967.

207   "The blow was right behind": *Green Bay Press-Gazette*, June 14, 1971.

207   "Tell Nobis to sign": Nobis Biography, TommyNobisCenter.org.

207   Moments after Tumbling; see Len Wagner Story, *Green Bay Press-Gazette*, Oct. 2, 1967.

208   "Really, he's been playing": Associated Press story, Oct. 5, 1967.

208   "I want to tell you this": Jerry Kramer and Dick Schapp, *Instant Replay* (New York: The New American Library, 1968).

208   "I am sure you are disturbed": David Maraniss, *When Pride Still Mattered* (New York: Simon and Schuster, 1999).

208   "Society today is so permissive": *Milwaukee Sentinel*, June 25, 1970.

209   "Coach Lombardi is probably": *Lombardi* documentary, NFL Films, 1968.

210   "Tells you that if you give": *Lombardi* documentary, NFL Films, 1968.

210   "He's still hurt": *Sports Illustrated*, Oct. 30, 1967.

210   "Bart is our man": *Sports Illustrated*, Oct. 30, 1967.

210   "This man is one great coach": Jerry Kramer and Dick Schapp, *Instant Replay* (New York: The New American Library, 1968).

210   "This may make your 38": *Lombardi* documentary, NFL Films, 1968.

212   "One of the best rushes": Bart Starr, *Quarterbacking*, (New York: Prentice Hall, 1967).

212   "Every quarterback we met": *PlanetRams.com*, 2007.

216 "When the temperature dropped": Bud Lea, *Magnificent Seven* (Chicago: Triumph Books, 2002).

216 "That bastard Lombardi!": Bud Lea, *Magnificent Seven* (Chicago: Triumph Books, 2002).

218 "I think I'll take another bite": David Maraniss, *When Pride Still Mattered* (New York: Simon & Schuster, 1999).

219 "I want that third championship": Jerry Kramer and Dick Schapp, *Instant Replay* (New York: The New American Library, 1968).

222 "I damn near froze": Bud Lea, *Magnificent Seven* (Chicago: Triumph Books, 2002).

223 "We really didn't know": *Cowboys Star* magazine, Aug. 9, 1980.

223 "After you forgot": Publicity Archive, Pro Football Hall of Fame.

223 "We had control of the game": *Green Bay Press-Gazette*, Jan. 1, 1968.

224 "It was like being": Associated Press story, Jan. 13, 1996.

224 "I don't think the Packers": *Dallas Times Herald*, Jan. 1, 1968.

230 "I understood my responsibility": Publicity Archive, Pro Football Hall of Fame.

231 "When I heard the cheer": Mike Shropshire, *The Ice Bowl* (New York: Donald I. Fine Books, 1997).

231 "We gambled": *Green Bay Press-Gazette*, Jan. 1, 1967.

232 "It was a dumb call": Bud Lea, *Magnificent Seven* (Chicago: Triumph Books, 2002).

234 "It's the last game": Jerry Kramer and Dick Schapp, *Instant Replay* (New York: The New American Library, 1968).

234 "All the glory": Jerry Kramer and Dick Schapp, *Instant Replay* (New York: The New American Library, 1968).

235 "I love it when": Associated Press story, Jan 15, 1968.

235 "It's the threat of the run": Associated Press story, Jan. 15, 1968.

235 "After three consecutive": Associated Press story, Jan. 15, 1968.

235 "What I think I will do": *Cleveland Press*, Jan. 15, 1968.

EIGHT: BLOOD AND GUTS

243 "I was never prouder": *Dallas Morning News*, Feb. 18, 1968.

244 "The very nature of the system": *Milwaukee Journal*, July 1, 1971.

244 "How can you call": *Dallas Morning News*, March 9, 1968.

245 "Although I'll miss": *Miami News*, April 16, 1968.

246 "Coach Lombardi called me": David Maraniss, *When Pride Still Mattered* (New York: Simon & Schuster, 1999).

246 "The thing about quarterbacks": *The Sporting News*, Nov. 23, 1968.

247 "Give me protection": *Milwaukee Sentinel*, July 22, 1969.

247 "Our greatest glory": *The* (Washington, D.C) *Evening Star*, July 8, 1969.

248 "At times I feel": *Quarterback* magazine, Nov. 28, 1969

249 "How do you feel?": *Pittsburgh Press*, Nov. 3, 1969.

249 "[The arm] has been bothering": *Pittsburgh Press*, Nov. 3, 1969.

249 "That's as well": *Pittsburgh Press*, Nov. 3, 1969.

251 "Johnny Unitas is a great, great": *The Washington Post*, Feb. 27, 1970.

254 "The first time I finish": *Milwaukee Journal*, Oct. 26, 1970.

254 "Domenic deserves": *Milwaukee Journal*, May 4, 1970.

254 "The muscles he should have": *Milwaukee Journal*, June 13, 1971.

255 "If there is one thing": *Milwaukee Journal*, Oct. 18, 1970.

255 "Today I feel like the luckiest": *Green Bay Press-Gazette*, Oct. 19, 1970.

255 "I really love the game": *Detroit Free Press*, Dec. 20, 1970.

255 "You ain't gonna quit": Jerry Kramer and Dick Schapp, *Instant Replay* (New York: The New American Library, 1968).

257 "I know you're going to be back": *Green Bay Press-Gazette* (quoting White House transcript), April 16, 2002.

257 "The arm was so weak": *Milwaukee Sentinel*, Nov. 23, 1971.

258 "I have exhausted every effort": *New York Post*, July 22, 1972.

258 "It's like opening": *Green Bay Press-Gazette*, July 22, 1972.

259 "I'm excited with the challenge": *Football Digest*, April 1973.

NINE: RISKING THE LEGEND

260 "As a former quarterback": *Miami Herald*, Jan. 4, 1974.

261 "I've tried several times": *Washington Star-News*, Feb. 20, 1974.

262 "I think Santa Claus came early": *Milwaukee Sentinel*, Dec. 25, 1974.

263 "I'm absolutely ecstatic": *Milwaukee Sentinel*, Dec. 25, 1974.

263 "To every man there comes": *Green Bay Press-Gazette*, Dec. 25, 1974.

264 "Green Bay was lucky": Correspondence Archive, Pro Football Hall of Fame.

264 "What a disappointment": Correspondence Archive, Pro Football Hall of Fame.

266 "We have no illusions": *New York Daily News*, Aug. 21, 1975.

267 "We believe in what": Publicity Archive, Pro Football Hall of Fame.

267 "We're elated": Publicity Archive, Pro Football Hall of Fame

267 "It was a humbling": *Football Digest*, May/June 1976.

270 "I can remember very well": Induction ceremony transcript, Pro Football Hall of Fame.

271 "He taught us": Induction ceremony transcript, Pro Football Hall of Fame.

272 "Had the Packers decided": Bart Starr with Murray Olderman, *Starr: My Life in Football* (New York: William Morrow, 1987).

273 "What Lombardi had": SportsCentury documentary, ESPN, Jan. 12, 2004.

274 "We were only": Bart Starr with Murray Olderman, *Starr: My Life in Football* (New York: William Morrow, 1987).

276 "My most serious": Bart Starr with Murray Olderman, *Starr: My Life in Football* (New York: William Morrow, 1987).

280 "I came back": *Sports Illustrated*, Dec. 6, 1982.

282 "Allow us to operate": *Cleveland Plain Dealer*, Dec. 30, 1980.

282 "I know the record doesn't": *Cleveland Plain Dealer*, Dec. 30, 1980.

283 "The son we adored so much": Bart Starr with Murray Olderman, *Starr: My Life in Football* (New York: William Morrow, 1987).

286 "In the emotion of the moment": *Green Bay Press-Gazette*, Dec. 27, 1982.

287 "I think [Starr] got shafted": *Green Bay Press-Gazette*, Dec. 19, 1983.

TEN: FEARING THE SILENCE

290 "The greatest Christmas present": *Milwaukee Journal*, Jan. 15, 1984.

290 "It's very, very exciting": *Milwaukee Journal*, Jan. 15, 1984.

290 "We have always been opposed": *Milwaukee Journal*, Jan. 17, 1988.

291 "I did not believe the NFL": *Baltimore Sun*, March 27, 2009.

291 "The grand old days": *Baltimore Sun*, March 27, 2009

292 "Starr's group did the groundwork": *Milwaukee Journal*, Jan. 17, 1988.

295 "Dear Mom and Dad": Bart Starr with Murray Olderman, *Starr: My Life in Football* (New York: William Morrow, 1987).

296 "He was very excited": *Milwaukee Journal*, July 10, 1988.

298 "You never expect to bury": *Milwaukee Sentinel*, July 12, 1988.

ELEVEN: SLIDING DOORS

306 "We feel really terrible": *Green Bay Press-Gazette*, Nov. 21, 2001.

306 "We live in a society": *Milwaukee Journal*, May 24, 1999.

308 "A larger-than-life statue": *Green Bay Press-Gazette*, Sept. 21, 2004.

308 "When you praised him": *Milwaukee Sentinel*, Dec. 25, 1974

308 "He used to tell us": *Green Bay Press-Gazette*, Sept. 21, 2004.

315 "Let's grab some": Audio transcript, Paul Finebaum Radio Network, Aug. 22, 2007.

316 "Please call me Bart": Audio transcript, Paul Finebaum Radio Network, Aug. 22, 2007.

317   "Bart Starr was": Allen Barra, *Big Play* (Washington, D.C.: Potomac Books, 2004).

319   "History has done a great": *coldhardfootballfacts.com*, Jan. 8, 2008.

321   "The Holy Grail": *The Wall Street Journal*, Feb. 5, 2011.

321   "You're revered in Green Bay": Madison.com, Feb. 3, 2011.

ACKNOWLEDGMENTS

I started the research for this book in 2005, not knowing whether Bart Starr would cooperate. He did, in a very meaningful way. Bart granted me a series of in-depth interviews and accommodated several follow-ups. Cherry and Bart Jr. also cooperated fully. Their participation in this project helped me to achieve a much greater understanding of their lives while providing a new level of anecdotal detail, giving the narrative a more intimate texture and allowing me to more effectively write an objective biography. I would like to take this opportunity to express my deep appreciation to Bart, Cherry, and Bart, Jr.

When you spend several years trying to accurately capture the arc of someone's life and place your subject in the proper historical context, the list of people who help in some significant way is invariably long. So it was with *America's Quarterback*. I owe a debt to many, many people who helped me bring the Bart Starr story to life.

The list begins with my longtime literary agent David Black, who believed in this book from the start and nurtured it throughout the process. Thanks for everything, David. I'm lucky to have you in my corner.

This is my third book with the Thomas Dunne imprint of St. Martin's Press, and I am fortunate to have had the opportunity to work once more with my good friend Pete Wolverton, one of the best editors in the business. Pete understood what this book should be and helped me drive toward the end zone, converting several possession downs along the way. After my father died, he graciously arranged to shift the publication schedule back and allow me additional time to get this book right, and for this, I am grateful.

Thanks to the entire crew of dedicated professionals at St. Martin's Press who were involved with this book, including the very able assistant editor Anne Bensson.

Beyond the involvement of the Starrs, the research for this book included dozens of interviews with former Green Bay, Alabama, and Lanier teammates, coaches, friends, and others. They all have my sincere gratitude.

Former Green Bay Packers who granted me interviews included Paul Hornung, Jim Taylor, Zeke Bratkowski, Fuzzy Thurston, Gary Knafelc, Dave "Hawg" Hanner, Max McGee, Dave Robinson, Tom Brown, Babe Parilli, Willie Davis, Forrest Gregg, Bill Curry, Carroll Dale, Bob Skoronski, Chuck Mercein, Gale Gillingham, John Martinkovic, Deral Teteak, Steve Wright, Ken Bowman, Rich Wingo, John Anderson, Mike Butler, Greg Koch, and Paul Coffman.

The interview list also included former University of Alabama players Harry Lee, Clell Hobson, Nick Germanos, Hootie Ingram, Bobby Barnes, Tommy Lewis, Bobby Luna, Albert Elmore, Wesley Thompson, and Baxter Booth; former Sidney Lanier High School head coach Bill Moseley; as well as Lanier alumni Sparky Allen, Larry Watkins, and Gary Waller.

Many others whose lives somehow connected with Starr's graciously made time for my questions, including M.E. Bratkowski, Ann Forrester, Jack Kubicsyn, Leon Marlaire, Steve Sabol, Tod Smith, John Gillespie, Jan Gillespie, Peter Zukas, John Solberg, Bud Lea, Dale Hoffman, Hugh Farmer, Jr., Herschel Norred, Bill McNabb, Bobby Lee, Charley Mansour, Ellis Mansour, Bill Headley, Edgar Welden, Billy Alford, Martha Gibbs, Joe Adams, Steve Crispigna, Gary Wetzel, Lee Remmel, Cliff Christl, Art Daley, Vern Biever, Paul Finebaum, Tony Verna, and Kerry J. Byrne.

Special thanks to NFL commissioner Roger Goodell and his staff, especially Greg Aiello.

Steve Sabol, the NFL Films guru, influenced this book in several important ways. His very personal story concerning the formative days of NFL Films, especially the 1962 championship game, proved very useful in demonstrating the league's awakening. He also provided me with rare copies of some of the earliest NFL Films productions, including the very first, focusing on the 1962 title game. Thanks for everything, Steve.

The Green Bay Packers organization helped me throughout the process, particularly in tracking down telephone numbers. Thanks especially to Aaron Popkey and Jeff Blumb.

Fortunately, the published record concerning the Green Bay Packers, Vince Lombardi, Bart Starr, and the National Football League is big enough to fill Lambeau Field, and my narrative owes a significant debt to a long list of authors and journalists who furthered my knowledge with their outstanding work.

No book influenced mine more profoundly than David Maraniss' landmark biography of Lombardi, *When Pride Still Mattered*. His masterful book is the gold standard concerning the legendary coach and the Packers of the 1960s. Among other things, it helped me understand Lombardi, strengthening my ability to accurately portray his critical relationship with Starr.

Like Maraniss and many others, I found *Run to Daylight*, written by W.C. Heinz in partnership with Lombardi, incredibly helpful. Time after time, I found myself referring to this book, enriched by the sensation that I was hearing Lombardi speaking in his own voice.

Many years ago, I read *Instant Replay*, so, long before embarking on this project, Jerry Kramer's diary-style account of the 1967 season, written with the great Dick Schaap, informed my knowledge of the Green Bay dynasty. What a wonderful book. Rereading it during this project gave me a real feel for the climactic days of the Lombardi dynasty.

But Lea's terrific *Magnificent Seven*, which focuses on the seven championship game victories of the Lombardi era, proved to be a great help as I began the process of examining the important games of Starr's career.

More than two decades ago, Starr collaborated with journalist Murray Olderman to write his autobiography, *Starr: My Life in Football*. Their narrative laid a solid foundation and pointed me in the right direction on several fronts.

Quarterbacking, the book Starr authored after his MVP season, brought the technical aspects of his game into sharp focus and increased my understanding of how he approached the position.

Through the years, I have read several books dealing with the history of the NFL, but none approaches the depth and storytelling of Michael MacCambridge's *America's Game*. It is a superb book that should be read by every serious fan of professional football. MacCambridge's book bolstered, and in some cases, challenged, my knowledge of the NFL's rise before, during, and after Starr.

Other good books that proved helpful include Mike Shropshire's *The Ice Bowl*; Tom Callahan's *Johnny U*; Mark Kriegel's *Namath*; Jerry Kramer's *Lombardi: Winning is the only thing*; Paul Hornung and Billy Reed's *Golden Boy*; Allen Barra's *Big Play*; David Harris' *The League: The Rise and Decline of the NFL*; Paul Hornung and Billy Reed's *Lombardi and Me*; Ed Gruver's *The Ice Bowl*; Donald T. Phillips's *Run to Win*; and John Eisenberg's *That First Season*.

Of the various sources who helped me learn about the unique heritage of the Green Bay Packers, I owe a particular debt to longtime team historian Lee Remmel, who spent many years as a sportswriter for the *Green Bay Press-Gazette* before joining the club's staff. Remmel graciously spent several hours answering my questions and regaling me with stories about the good old days.

For the sections concerning Rawhide Ranch, John and Jan Gillespie were incredibly helpful. They are very special people who have made a difference in this world, and I am grateful for their assistance, especially in locating Pete Zukas, whose surprising candor demonstrated the impact Rawhide has made in the lives of so many. Thanks to the staff of Rawhide, especially current director John Solberg, who gave me complete access to the facility on my visit to the little camp in the distant woods.

If you are looking for a good cause, Rawhide is a very worthy charity that can use your help. For information about how to donate, visit www.rawhide.org or call 800-729-4433.

In writing sports books, I stand on the shoulders of so many people, especially the long line of sports journalists who covered the day-to-day dramas on deadline. I am especially indebted to former Packers beat writers Bud Lea, Art Daley, Dale Hoffman, and Cliff Christl, who took the time to visit with me. The fine work of these men and several others (including the aforementioned Lee Remmel) in the *Green Bay Press-Gazette*, *The Milwaukee Journal*, and *Milwaukee Sentinel* informed this book in many ways. Individual quotes are noted in the Source Notes, but in a larger sense, the solid reporting and careful writing contained in those newspapers and others across the league, especially the *New York Times*, created a road map that made my football archeology much easier. *Sports Illustrated*'s excellent coverage of the big games also proved invaluable, particularly the expert analysis of longtime pro-football writer Tex Maule.

I would like to express my sincere appreciation to the good folks at the Pro Football Hall of Fame in Canton, Ohio, including Pete Fierle, for their significant assistance, especially in sharing their voluminous clip file and a mountain of statistics.

Thanks to the staffs of the Brown County Public Library, the Milwaukee Public Library, the New York Public Library, the University of Wisconsin-Madison Libraries, and Ingram Library at the University of West Georgia.

My friends at the Paul W. Bryant Museum on the campus of the University of Alabama provided significant assistance, especially Ken Gaddy and Taylor Watson, along with Tommy Ford, Brenda Burnette, and Kent Gidley in the University of Alabama athletic department.

Harry Lee, who played college football with Starr and has been an official of the A-club letterman's association for many years, probably knows more about Alabama football history than any man alive. He aided me in so many ways, especially in understanding the state of the Alabama program in the early fifties. I'm grateful for all your help, Harry.

Thanks to longtime friend Paul Finebaum and his staff—especially network director Pat Smith and technology guru Dave Sibley—for providing audio files of Starr's appearances on the Paul Finebaum Radio Network. And to Mark Mandell for locating a copy of ESPN's *SportsCentury* episode on Starr. Thanks also to Joe Lavine of HBO Sports for providing a DVD of that network's recent *Lombardi* documentary as this project neared the goal line.

I'm grateful to Kerry J. Byrne of coldhardfootballfacts.com for sharing his statistical analysis concerning Starr and other NFL quarterbacks.

Thanks to Bart Starr's executive assistant, Maggie Gallaher, for loads of help along the way, and the staff of Athletes in Action for their assistance at the Super Bowl Breakfast.

As usual my family, friends, and business associates contributed to this effort in various ways, large and small. Thanks to all, including Tom, Alice, Ron, Patti, Jim, and Tracy Dunnavant; Rosalyn and David Boyd; Alex McRae; Joe Beamon; Jonathan Hickman; and Casey, Melissa, Cile, and Chad Smith and the entire staff at the Redneck Gourmet. An extra special thank-you is due my niece Aimee and her husband, Jake, who hosted me on my trip to the Super Bowl in Phoenix in 2008.

When you spend several years writing a biography of a well-known person, the research inevitably includes a long list of dead ends, including many stories that might prove interesting but not terribly relevant to the larger narrative. You set out to learn all you possibly can about your subject, filling up your notebook, but ultimately, you build the biographical sketch around a tiny fraction of what you discover.

Sometimes, you hear a story and you just know.

Over lunch in Florence, Alabama, Alan Bush, one of my oldest friends, related a story concerning a stockbroker colleague. This is how I first heard about Tod Smith's powerful memory at the Bryant-Denny Stadium elevator, which supplied the dramatic ending to the book. Thanks, Alan, for a tip worthy of Blue Horseshoe.

Around the same time, during a brisk walk through predawn stillness in my suburban Atlanta neighborhood, friend and neighbor Bill Headley yelled in my direction, "Do you know about the time Bart Starr came to Newnan?" Headley, a local construction magnate, had not even lived in the town all those years before. But he had a connection, and a memory, nevertheless, and even before my morning coffee, I was interested enough to investigate. One phone call led to another. In time, it proved to be just the sort of anecdote I was looking for, reflecting something important about Starr and the world in which he lived. Thanks, Bill.

These two isolated encounters with two individuals who had no direct connection to Starr reinforced a basic rule of journalism that I hope I never forget: It pays to listen.

INDEX